ICTS 107 Early Childhood Education

Teacher Certification Exam

By: Sharon Wynne, M.S.
Southern Connecticut State University

"And, while there's no reason yet to panic, I think it's only prudent that we make preparations to panic."

XAMonline, INC.

Boston

To obtain permission(s) to use the material from this work for any purpose including workshops or seminars, please submit a written request to:

XAMonline, Inc.
21 Orient Ave.
Melrose, MA 02176
Toll Free 1-800-509-4128
Email: info@xamonline.com
Web www.xamonline.com
Fax: 1-781-662-9268

Library of Congress Cataloging-in-Publication Data

Wynne, Sharon A.
    Early Childhood Education 107: Teacher Certification / Sharon A. Wynne.   -2nd ed.
    ISBN 978-1-58197-599-4
    1. Early Childhood Education 107   2. Study Guides.   3. ICTS
    4. Teachers' Certification & Licensure.   5. Careers

Managing Editor	Dr. Harte Weiner	Senior Editor	Deborah Harbin
Assistant Editor	Anna Wong	Production Coordinator	David Aronson

Disclaimer:
The opinions expressed in this publication are the sole works of XAMonline and were created independently from the National Education Association, Educational Testing Service, or any State Department of Education, National Evaluation Systems or other testing affiliates.

Between the time of publication and printing, state specific standards as well as testing formats and website information may change that is not included in part or in whole within this product. Sample test questions are developed by XAMonline and reflect similar content as on real tests; however, they are not former tests. XAMonline assembles content that aligns with state standards but makes no claims nor guarantees teacher candidates a passing score. Numerical scores are determined by testing companies such as NES or ETS and then are compared with individual state standards. A passing score varies from state to state.

Printed in the United States of America
ICTS: Early Childhood Education 107
ISBN: 978-1-58197-599-4

Table of Contents

<u>SUBAREA I.</u>   <u>LANGUAGE AND LITERACY DEVELOPMENT</u>

SUBAREA III. DIVERSITY, COLLABORATION, AND PROFESSIONALISM IN THE EARLY CHILDHOOD PROGRAM

Great Study and Testing Tips!

What to study in order to prepare for the subject assessments is the focus of this study guide but equally important is *how* you study.

You can increase your chances of truly mastering the information by taking some simple, but effective steps.

Study Tips:

1. <u>Some foods aid the learning process</u>. Foods such as milk, nuts, seeds, rice, and oats help your study efforts by releasing natural memory enhancers called CCKs (*cholecystokinin*) composed of *tryptophan*, *choline*, and *phenylalanine*. All of these chemicals enhance the neurotransmitters associated with memory. Before studying, try a light, protein-rich meal of eggs, turkey, and fish. All of these foods release the memory enhancing chemicals. The better the connections, the more you comprehend.

Likewise, before you take a test, stick to a light snack of energy boosting and relaxing foods. A glass of milk, a piece of fruit, or some peanuts all release various memory-boosting chemicals and help you to relax and focus on the subject at hand.

2. <u>Learn to take great notes</u>. A by-product of our modern culture is that we have grown accustomed to getting our information in short doses (i.e. TV news sound bites or USA Today style newspaper articles.)

Consequently, we've subconsciously trained ourselves to assimilate information better in <u>neat little packages</u>. If your notes are scrawled all over the paper, it fragments the flow of the information. Strive for clarity. Newspapers use a standard format to achieve clarity. Your notes can be much clearer through use of proper formatting. A very effective format is called the *"Cornell Method."*

> Take a sheet of loose-leaf lined notebook paper and draw a line all the way down the paper about 1-2" from the left-hand edge.

> Draw another line across the width of the paper about 1-2" up from the bottom. Repeat this process on the reverse side of the page.

Look at the highly effective result. You have ample room for notes, a left hand margin for special emphasis items or inserting supplementary data from the textbook, a large area at the bottom for a brief summary, and a little rectangular space for just about anything you want.

3. <u>Get the concept then the details</u>. Too often we focus on the details and don't gather an understanding of the concept. However, if you simply memorize only dates, places, or names, you may well miss the whole point of the subject.

A key way to understand things is to put them in your own words. If you are working from a textbook, automatically summarize each paragraph in your mind. If you are outlining text, don't simply copy the author's words.

Rephrase them in your own words. You remember your own thoughts and words much better than someone else's, and subconsciously tend to associate the important details to the core concepts.

4. <u>Ask Why?</u> Pull apart written material paragraph by paragraph and don't forget the captions under the illustrations.

Example: If the heading is "Stream Erosion", flip it around to read "Why do streams erode?" Then answer the questions.

If you train your mind to think in a series of questions and answers, not only will you learn more, but it also helps to lessen the test anxiety because you are used to answering questions.

5. <u>Read for reinforcement and future needs</u>. Even if you only have 10 minutes, put your notes or a book in your hand. Your mind is similar to a computer; you have to input data in order to have it processed. *By reading, you are creating the neural connections for future retrieval.* The more times you read something, the more you reinforce the learning of ideas.

Even if you don't fully understand something on the first pass, *your mind stores much of the material for later recall.*

6. <u>Relax to learn so go into exile</u>. Our bodies respond to an inner clock called biorhythms. Burning the midnight oil works well for some people, but not everyone.

If possible, set aside a particular place to study that is free of distractions. Shut off the television, cell phone, and pager and exile your friends and family during your study period.

If you really are bothered by silence, try background music. Light classical music at a low volume has been shown to aid in concentration over other types. Music that evokes pleasant emotions without lyrics is highly suggested. Try just about anything by Mozart. It relaxes you.

7. <u>Use arrows not highlighters</u>. At best, it's difficult to read a page full of yellow, pink, blue, and green streaks. Try staring at a neon sign for a while and you'll soon see that the horde of colors obscure the message.

A quick note, a brief dash of color, an underline, and an arrow pointing to a particular passage is much clearer than a horde of highlighted words.

8. <u>Budget your study time</u>. Although you shouldn't ignore any of the material, *allocate your available study time in the same ratio that topics may appear on the test.*

Testing Tips:

1. Get smart, play dumb. **Don't read anything into the question.** Don't make an assumption that the test writer is looking for something else than what is asked. Stick to the question as written and don't read extra things into it.

2. Read the question and all the choices _twice_ before answering the question. You may miss something by not carefully reading, and then re-reading both the question and the answers.

If you really don't have a clue as to the right answer, leave it blank on the first time through. Go on to the other questions, as they may provide a clue as to how to answer the skipped questions.

If later on, you still can't answer the skipped ones . . . _Guess._ The only penalty for guessing is that you _might_ get it wrong. Only one thing is certain; if you don't put anything down, you will get it wrong!

3. Turn the question into a statement. Look at the way the questions are worded. The syntax of the question usually provides a clue. Does it seem more familiar as a statement rather than as a question? Does it sound strange?

By turning a question into a statement, you may be able to spot if an answer sounds right, and it may also trigger memories of material you have read.

4. Look for hidden clues. It's actually very difficult to compose multiple-foil (choice) questions without giving away part of the answer in the options presented.

In most multiple-choice questions you can often readily eliminate one or two of the potential answers. This leaves you with only two real possibilities and automatically your odds go to Fifty-Fifty for very little work.

5. Trust your instincts. For every fact that you have read, you subconsciously retain something of that knowledge. On questions that you aren't really certain about, go with your basic instincts. **Your first impression on how to answer a question is usually correct.**

6. Mark your answers directly on the test booklet. Don't bother trying to fill in the optical scan sheet on the first pass through the test.

Just be very careful not to miss-mark your answers when you eventually transcribe them to the scan sheet.

7. **<u>Watch the clock</u>!** You have a set amount of time to answer the questions. Don't get bogged down trying to answer a single question at the expense of 10 questions you can more readily answer.

Pre Test

Subarea I. Language and Literacy Development

1. **The complex linguistic deficiency marked by the inability to remember and recognize words by sounds and the inability to break words down into component units describes:**
(Average rigor) (Skill 1.1)

    A. Oral processing disorder

    B. Attention deficit disorder

    C. Dyslexia

    D. Autism

2. **Above what age does learning a language become increasingly difficult?**
(Average rigor) (Skill 1.1)

    A. 3

    B. 5

    C. 7

    D. 10

3. **Children typically develop oral language by listening to:**
(Easy) (Skill 1.1)

    A. Teachers

    B. Parents

    C. Peers

    D. All of the above

4. **Which of the following skills have a reciprocal relationship?**
(Average rigor) (Skill 1.4)

    A. Reading and phonics

    B. Writing and phonics

    C. Reading and writing

    D. Reading and comprehension

5. **Children having difficulties with spelling, reading accuracy, and reading comprehension skills are also likely to have difficulties with:**
(Rigorous) (Skill 1.6)

    A. Cognitive skills

    B. Development factors

    C. Math skills

    D. Speech and language skills

6. **Which of the following is a convention of print that children learn during reading activities?**
(Average rigor) (Skill 1.6)

    A. The meaning of words

    B. The left to right motion

    C. The purpose of print

    D. The identification of letters

7. **Which of the following concepts of print can be taught during a read aloud?**
(Average rigor) (Skill 1.6)

   A.   Front and back of book

   B.   Author

   C.   Title location

   D.   All of the above

8. **Mr. Phillips has called a meeting with Maria's parents. Maria is struggling to acquire the necessary comprehension skills to maintain grade level standards. Maria's parents speak Spanish and are eager to do anything to help Maria succeed in school. Which of the following strategies below will help Maria, while maintaining and fostering the importance of her native language?**
(Rigorous) (Skill 1.7)

   A.   Encouraging Maria's parents to enroll in an English language course

   B.   Making sure Maria speaks only English during classroom activities

   C.   Encouraging Maria's parents to read and discuss books written in Spanish

   D.   Ensuring that Maria's parents only speak English in the home

9. **Which of the following literary devices is most commonly found in kindergarten classrooms?**
(Easy) (Skill 1.7)

   A.   Metaphor

   B.   Repetition

   C.   Simile

   D.   Analogy

10. **John is having difficulty reading the word reach. In isolation, he pronounces each sound as /r/ /ee/ /sh/. Which of the following is a possible instructional technique which could help solve John's reading difficulty?**
(Rigorous) (Skill 2.1)

   A.   Additional phonemic awareness instruction

   B.   Additional phonics instruction

   C.   Additional skill and drill practice

   D.   Additional minimal pair practice

11. Mrs. Myers has discovered words that are repeatedly misspelled in Tina's writing. Tina seems to use these same words in a lot of her writing as well. What would Mrs. Myers be best to do? *(Average rigor) (Skill 2.1)*

    A.   Drill Tina on those words

    B.   Add those words to Tina's regular weekly spelling test

    C.   Work with Tina to make an individual spelling dictionary to help her learn these words

    D.   Have Tina look the words up in the dictionary and correct them

12. Research into students who are learning English as a second language has found that they have difficulty manipulating the sound system of English. This difficulty is in which area of reading development? *(Rigorous) (Skill 2.2)*

    A.   Comprehension

    B.   Fluency

    C.   Phonics

    D.   Phonemic Awareness

13. The smallest unit of sound is the: *(Easy) (Skill 2.2)*

    A.   Phoneme

    B.   Morpheme

    C.   Syllable

    D.   Letter

14. Which of the following early reading skills develops first? *(Average rigor) (Skill 2.2)*

    A.   Comprehension

    B.   Phonics

    C.   Phonemic awareness

    D.   Letter identification

15. The idea that students need to be able to take spoken words apart and blend different sounds together to make words describes: *(Average rigor) (Skill 2.4)*

    A.   The alphabet principle

    B.   Syntax

    C.   Phonics

    D.   Morphology

16. Which of the following is NOT an effective strategy to aid students with spelling instruction?
(Average rigor) (Skill 2.5)

A. Knowledge of patterns, sounds, and letter-sound association

B. Memorizing sight words

C. Writing words one or two times

D. Writing the words correctly in personal writing

17. Johnny loves to listen to stories and points to signs all around the room that have letters on them. This suggests that Johnny:
(Average rigor) (Skill 2.6)

A. Will be a good reader

B. Has good emergent literacy skills

C. Has good phonemic awareness skills

D. Understands grammar

18. Which of the following is the most commonly practiced strategy to encourage literacy growth?
(Average rigor) (Skill 2.6)

A. Storybook reading

B. Teaching phonics

C. Teaching fluency

D. Letter identification

19. Which of the following is an appropriate way for students to respond to literature?
(Easy) (Skill 2.6)

A. Art

B. Drama

C. Writing

D. All of the above

20. Which of the following is NOT true about phonological awareness?
(Average rigor) (Skill 3.1)

A. It may involve print.

B. It is a prerequisite for spelling and phonics.

C. Activities can be done by the children with their eyes closed.

D. It starts before letter recognition is taught.

21. Ms. Walker's lesson objective is to teach her first graders the concept of morphology in order to improve their reading skills. Which group of words would be most appropriate for her to use in this lesson?
(Rigorous) (Skill 3.2)

   A.   Far, farm, farmer

   B.   Far, feather, fever

   C.   Far, fear, fare

   D.   Far, fare, farce

22. A teacher writes the following words on the board: cot, cotton, and cottage. What is the teacher most likely teaching the students about?
(Rigorous) (Skill 3.2)

   A.   Morphology

   B.   Syntax

   C.   Semantics

   D.   Pragmatics

23. Children who are having difficulty understanding non-literal expressions are having difficulties with which of the following areas?
(Rigorous) (Skill 3.2)

   A.   Syntax

   B.   Morphology

   C.   Semantics

   D.   Phonics

24. When introducing new vocabulary to students, the number of new words being taught at one time should be:
(Rigorous) (Skill 3.4)

   A.   One to two

   B.   Two to three

   C.   Three to four

   D.   Four to five

25. Students are about to read a text that contains concepts that will be difficult for students to grasp. When should the vocabulary be introduced to students?
(Rigorous) (Skill 3.4)

   A.   Before reading

   B.   During reading

   C.   After reading

   D.   It should not be introduced.

26. **Repeated readings of the same text are beneficial to developing readers because:** *(Rigorous) (Skill 4.1)*

    A. Repeated reading helps students memorize the text

    B. Repeated reading helps in pairing students

    C. Repeated reading ensures students recognize the words readily and can read at an improved pace

    D. Repeated reading helps teachers determine students' level of reading

27. **Which of the following is NOT a common method of teaching comprehension?** *(Average rigor) (Skill 4.2)*

    A. Summarizing

    B. Question asking

    C. Graphic organizers

    D. Phonics drills

28. **Mr. Lotus wants the class to compare two characters from a book. Which of the following would be a good tool for Mr. Lotus to use?** *(Rigorous) (Skill 4.4)*

    A. Venn diagram

    B. KWL Chart

    C. Outline

    D. Literature circle discussion

29. **The stories about Paul Bunyan, John Henry, and Pecos Bill are all exaggerated accounts of individuals with superhuman strength. What type of literature are these works?**
(Easy) (Skill 4.6)

   A.   Fables

   B.   Fairytales

   C.   Tall tales

   D.   Myths

30. **Which of the following is NOT a characteristic of a fable?**
(Easy) (Skill 4.6)

   A.   Have animal characters that act like humans

   B.   Considered to be true

   C.   Teaches a moral

   D.   Reveals human foibles

31. **An adolescent has not yet mastered spelling. What would be the best way for a teacher to address this?**
(Rigorous) (Skill 5.2)

   A.   Provide the student with extra instruction on spelling rules

   B.   Ensure that the student fully understands all the exceptions to rules

   C.   Encourage the student to master the use of a dictionary and thesaurus

   D.   Focus on teaching spelling and grammar in isolation

32. **Which of the following approaches to student writing assignments is least likely to lead to students becoming disinterested?**
(Average rigor) (Skill 5.2)

   A.   Designing assignments where students write for a variety of audiences.

   B.   Designing assignments where the teacher is the audience.

   C.   Designing assignments where students write to friends and family.

   D.   Designing assignments where students write to real people such as mayors, the principal, or companies.

33. In the process of writing, the introduction should be written at what stage of the paper
(Rigorous) (Skill 5.2)

   A. Before the thesis development

   B. After the entire paper is written

   C. During the brainstorming session

   D. Before writing the body

34. Which of the following strategies encourages print awareness in classrooms?
(Average rigor) (Skill 5.3)

   A. Word walls

   B. Using big books to read to students

   C. Using highlighters to locate upper case letters

   D. All of the above

35. The students in Tina's classroom are working together in pairs. Each student is reading another student's paper and asking who, what, when, where, why, and who questions. What is this activity helping the students to do?
(Rigorous) (Skill 5.5)

   A. Draft their writing

   B. Paraphrase their writing

   C. Revise their writing

   D. Outline their writing

36. Ms. Michaels is teaching her students about revising. What would Ms. Michaels be best to tell her students about revising?
(Average rigor) (Skill 5.5)

   A. Revising is an important part of the writing process and all writing should be revised.

   B. You will only have to revise until you become a good enough writer to get it perfect the first time.

   C. Revising can be skipped sometimes if you think it might ruin your writing.

   D. You will only need to revise work you complete that is to be handed in for assessment.

Subarea II. Learning Across the Curriculum

37. **How is the following read? (Easy) (Skill 6.1)**

    $3 < 5$

    A. Three is less than five

    B. Five is greater than three

    C. Three is greater than five

    D. Five is less than three

38. **What is the foundation of math skills and topics? (Easy) (Skill 6.1)**

    A. Number sense

    B. Place value

    C. Addition

    D. Computation skills

39. **Which math principle indicates that a student should "carry" the one in the following addition problem? (Rigorous) (Skill 6.1)**

    ```
     54
    +29
     83
    ```

    A. Counting by tens

    B. Properties of a base ten number system

    C. Problem checking

    D. Adding numbers that are too big

40. **Third grade students are studying percents. When looking at a circle graph divided into three sections, they see that one section is worth 80% and one section is worth 5%. What will the remaining section be worth? (Rigorous) (Skill 6.1)**

    A. 100%

    B. 85%

    C. 75%

    D. 15%

41. A teacher is introducing the concept of multiplication to her third grade students. What is another way she might write 4 x 5?
(Average rigor) *(Skill 6.1)*

   A. 4 + 5

   B. 5 + 4

   C. 4 + 4 + 4 + 4 + 4

   D. 5 + 5 + 5 + 5 + 5

42 First grade students are arranging four small squares of identical size to form a larger square. Each small square represents what part of the larger square?
(Average rigor) *(Skill 6.1)*

   A. One half

   B. One whole

   C. One fourth

   D. One fifth

43. A class has 30 magnets for 6 tables of students. Students are asked to determine how many magnets each table of students should get so that each table of students has the same number of magnets. What math principle would students apply to solve this problem?
(Rigorous) *(Skill 6.1)*

   A. Division

   B. Multiplication

   C. Percent

   D. Subtraction

44. Which of the following letters does NOT have a line of symmetry?
(Rigorous) *(Skill 6.1)*

   A. O

   B. D

   C. M

   D. J

45. What is the main purpose of having kindergarten students count by twos?
(Rigorous) *(Skill 6.1)*

   A.   To hear a rhythm

   B.   To recognize patterns in numbers

   C.   To practice addition

   D.   To become familiar with equations

46. Which would be a way for early childhood students to learn about basic geometric concepts?
(Rigorous) *(Skill 6.1)*

   A.   Using a ruler

   B.   Rote counting

   C.   Working with tangrams

   D.   Create an A-B color pattern

47. In which problem would students need an understanding of basic algebraic concepts?
(Average rigor) *(Skill 6.1)*

   A. $5 + 6 + 5 =$

   B. $3 + 3 + 3 + 3 + 3 =$

   C. $10 \times 0 =$

   D. $3 + \square = 9$

48. Students completing an activity with tangrams are learning what math principle?
(Average rigor) *(Skill 6.1)*

   A.   Basic geometric concepts

   B.   Repeating patterns

   C.   Counting

   D.   Identity property

49. Kindergarten students are participating in a calendar time activity. One student adds a straw to the "ones can" to represent that day of school. What math principle is being reinforced?
(Rigorous) *(Skill 6.1)*

   A.   Properties of a base ten number system

   B.   Sorting

   C.   Counting by twos

   D.   Even and odd numbers

50. Kindergarten students are doing a butterfly art project. They fold paper in half. On one half, they paint a design. Then they fold the paper closed and reopen. The resulting picture is a butterfly with matching sides. What math principle does this demonstrate?
(Rigorous) (Skill 6.1)

A. Slide

B. Rotate

C. Symmetry

D. Transformation

51. What would be a good choice when graphing the percent of time that a student spends on various after school activities?
(Average rigor) (Skill 6.1)

A. Line graph

B. Pie chart

C. Histogram

D. Scatter plot

52. What number comes next in this pattern?
(Average rigor) (Skill 6.2)

3, 8, 13, 18, _____

A. 21

B. 26

C. 23

D. 5

53. **Ms. Smith considers the use of quality children's literature to be one of the most important qualities of an early childhood teacher. She is asked to justify her reasons behind this consideration to her principal. Which of the following is an appropriate justification?**
(*Rigorous*) (*Skill 6.4*)

   A.   There are many different types of children's literature, so there will be something to which every child can relate.

   B.   Children's literature in early childhood classrooms provides the students with the opportunity to learn to read and process language.

   C.   Children are like adults in many ways and need to be exposed to a variety of types of literature.

   D.   Children's literature helps children improve their mental, social, and psychological skills and aids in the development in all of these areas.

54. **What should an experiment have a minimum number of to produce accurate and easily correlated results?**
(*Easy*) (*Skill 7.1*)

   A.   Controls

   B.   Variables

   C.   Samples

   D.   Participants

55. **Each time an experiment is completed, different results are obtained. This indicates that the experiment is not:**
(*Rigorous*) (*Skill 7.1*)

   A.   Objective

   B.   Significant

   C.   Reproducible

   D.   Accurate

56. **What does a primary consumer most commonly refer to?**
(*Average rigor*) (*Skill 7.2*)

   A.   Herbivore

   B.   Autotroph

   C.   Carnivore

   D.   Decomposer

57. **Which of the following causes the Earth to have seasons?**
(Rigorous) (Skill 7.2)

    A.   The Earth's magnetic field

    B.   The Earth's tilt on its axis

    C.   The Earth's moon

    D.   The Earth's tectonic plates

58. **What question would it be most important for a teacher to ask when deciding if a book will be appropriate for classroom use?**
(Average rigor) (Skill 7.3)

    A.   Do the characters provide positive role models for children?

    B.   Is the setting of the book modern?

    C.   Will every student in the class be interested in the subject of the book?

    D.   Is the book short enough for students to read in one sitting?

59. **Science and technology are best described as:**
(Average rigor) (Skill 7.6)

    A.   Different names for the same thing

    B.   Competing against each other

    C.   Closely related and intertwined

    D.   Independent of each other

60. **Which part of a map shows the relationship between a unit of measurement on the map versus the real world measure on the Earth?**
(Easy) (Skill 7.6)

    A.   Scale

    B.   Title

    C.   Legend

    D.   Grid

61. **Which of the following describes how citizens are able to directly participate in their own government by voting for and running for office?**
(Average rigor) (Skill 8.1)

    A.   Popular sovereignty

    B.   Due process

    C.   Rule of law

    D.   Democracy

62. The rights of U.S. citizens also imply certain responsibilities to be exercised. Which of the following is NOT a responsibility of U.S. citizens?
(Rigorous) *(Skill 8.1)*

A. Paying taxes

B. Jury duty

C. Respecting others' right

D. Freedom of religion

63. Economics is the study of how a society allocates its scarce resources to satisfy:
(Average rigor) *(Skill 8.1)*

A. Unlimited and competing wants

B. Limited and competing wants

C. Unlimited and cooperative wants

D. Limited and cooperative wants

64. The two elements of a market economy are:
(Rigorous) *(Skill 8.1)*

A. Inflation and deflation

B. Supply and demand

C. Cost and price

D. Wants and needs

65. The rights of U.S. citizens also imply certain responsibilities to be exercised. Which of the following is NOT a responsibility of U.S. citizens?
(Rigorous) *(Skill 8.1)*

A. Paying taxes

B. Jury duty

C. Respecting others' right

D. Freedom of religion

66. The primary social unit in most societies is:
(Easy) *(Skill 8.1)*

A. Religion

B. Family

C. School

D. Local government

67. **Which hypothesis is valid?**
(Rigorous) (Skill 8.3)

A. An unknown factor causes tomato plants to produce no fruit sometimes.

B. A tomato plant will produce tasty fruit if it is watered.

C. A tomato plant will grow faster in full sunlight than partial sunlight.

D. A tomato plant given this fertilizer will produce better fruit than all others.

68. **A teacher observes that a student appears sad, shows little interest in people or activities, and is having eating problems. What disorder do these observations suggest?**
(Easy) (Skill 9.1)

A. Claustrophobia

B. Autism

C. Dyslexia

D. Depression

69. **A person's understanding of his or her own body parts is known as:**
(Easy) (Skill 9.2)

A. Body awareness

B. Strength

C. Flexibility

D. Spatial awareness

70. **Which of the following is a social skill gained from participation in physical activities?**
(Easy) (Skill 9.2)

A. Problem solving skills

B. Communication skills

C. Judgment skills

D. All of the above

71. **Which of the following is NOT a good example of fine motor practice for young students?**
(Easy) (Skill 9.2)

A. Throwing a ball

B. Manipulating clay

C. Cutting

D. Tearing

72. **Young children learning to write commonly grip the pencil:**
(Average rigor) (Skill 9.2)

   A. Too far from the point

   B. With the wrong hand

   C. With too many fingers

   D. Too tightly

73. **Which type of physical education activity is most likely to encourage appreciation of diversity?**
(Average rigor) (Skill 9.3)

   A. Solitary activities

   B. Teamwork activities

   C. Competitive activities

   D. Creative activities

74. **The teaching of sports psychology incorporates physical education with:**
(Average rigor) (Skill 9.3)

   A. Physical science

   B. Natural science

   C. Mathematics

   D. Social science

75. **Which subject would a color wheel most likely be used for?**
(Easy) (Skill 10.1)

   A. Visual arts

   B. Music

   C. Movement

   D. Drama

76. In which subject is it most important for students to work with costumes and props?
(Easy) (Skill 10.3)

   A. Visual arts

   B. Music

   C. Movement

   D. Drama

77. In which subject is it most important for students to be encouraged to use all five senses?
(Average rigor) (Skill 10.3)

   A. Visual arts

   B. Music

   C. Movement

   D. Drama

78. Which of the following best explains why students will often interpret works of art differently?
(Rigorous) (Skill 10.3)

   A. Works of art are usually complicated.

   B. Works of art reflect the time that they were created.

   C. Each student is influenced by their prior knowledge.

   D. Students tend to focus on different senses.

79. What venues offer suitable opportunities for allowing students to view live performances?
(Easy) (Skill 10.5)

   A. Symphonies

   B. Dance companies

   C. Art museums

   D. All of the above

80. What should the arts curriculum for early childhood avoid?
(Average rigor) (Skill 10.6)

   A. Judgment

   B. Open expression

   C. Experimentation

   D. Discovery

Subarea III. Diversity, Collaboration, and Professionalism in the Early Childhood Program

81. What is the most significant development emerging in children at age two?
(Rigorous) (Skill 11.1)

   A. Immune system development

   B. Language development

   C. Socialization development

   D. Perception development

82. **Which of the following is a true statement?**
(Average rigor) (Skill 11.1)

   A.   Physical development does not influence social development.

   B.   Social development does not influence physical development.

   C.   Cognitive development does not influence social development.

   D.   All domains of development are integrated and influence other domains.

83. **A teacher notices that a student is sullen, and has several bruises on his head, arms, and legs. When asked, the student responds that he hit his arm getting out of bed that morning. The teacher should:**
(Average rigor) (Skill 11.1)

   A.   Attempt to get more information from the student

   B.   Report the suspected abuse

   C.   Inform the parents

   D.   Wait and see if other signs of abuse become evident

84. **Playing team sports at young ages should be done for the following purpose:**
(Rigorous) (Skill 11.2)

   A.   To develop the child's motor skills

   B.   To prepare children for competition in high school

   C.   To develop the child's interests

   D.   Both A and C

85. **Maintaining body weight is best accomplished by:**
(Average rigor) (Skill 11.3)

   A.   Dieting

   B.   Aerobic exercise

   C.   Lifting weights

   D.   Equalizing caloric intake relative to output

86. **Which of the following is the main source of energy in the diet?**
(Easy) (Skill 11.3)

   A.   Vitamins

   B.   Minerals

   C.   Water

   D.   Carbohydrates

87. Which of the following would be likely to influence a student's learning and academic progress?
(Easy) (Skill 11.4)

A.   Relocation

B.   Emotional abuse

C.   Bullying

D.   All of the above

88. Which of the following is the most likely cause of a child becoming easily agitated in class?
(Rigorous) (Skill 11.4)

A.   Lack of sleep

B.   Autism

C.   Emotional abuse

D.   Language difficulties

89. A student does not respond to any signs of affection and responds to other children by repeating back what they have said. What condition is the student most likely to have?
(Average rigor) (Skill 11.4)

A.   Mental retardation

B.   Autism

C.   Giftedness

D.   Hyperactivity

90. A child with a disability is one who has:
(Easy) (Skill 11.4)

A.   Sensory impairments

B.   Emotional disturbance

C.   Mental retardation

D.   Any of the above

91. A teacher is planning to get all of her students involved in sports for the purpose of helping develop hand-eye coordination and teamwork skills. What would be the most appropriate approach when planning the sports activities?
(Rigorous) (Skill 11.4)

A.   Encourage competition among students so they become used to the pressure of competing.

B.   Ensure that students who dislike sports continue until they enjoy sports.

C.   Choose activities that are beyond the student's current abilities so students are prompted to improve.

D.   Maintain a relaxed atmosphere and remind students that the sport is designed to be fun.

92. **Which of the following has been shown to have the greatest impact on a student's academic performance?**
(Easy) (Skill 11.4)

   A. The teacher's expectations

   B. Strict discipline

   C. The student's social skills

   D. Measurable objectives

93. **When teaching in a diverse classroom, teachers should:**
(Rigorous) (Skill 11.4)

   A. Plan, devise, and present material in a multicultural manner

   B. Research all possible cultures and expose the children to those

   C. Focus on the curriculum and whatever multicultural opportunities are built into it already

   D. Utilize single format instruction to present material in a multicultural l manner

94. **What are the critical elements of instructional process?**
(Rigorous) (Skill 11.5)

   A. Content, goals, teacher needs

   B. Means of getting money to regulate instruction

   C. Content, materials, activities, goals, learner needs

   D. Materials, definitions, assignments

95. **What should a teacher do when students have not responded well to an instructional activity?**
(Average rigor) (Skill 11.5)

   A. Reevaluate learner needs

   B. Request administrative help

   C. Continue with the activity another day

   D. Assign homework on the concept

96. **Mr. Gorman has taught a concept to his class. All of the students have grasped the concept except for Sam. Mr. Gorman should:**
(Rigorous) (Skill 11.5)

   A. Reteach the concept to the whole class in exactly the same way

   B. Reteach the concept to Sam in exactly the same way

   C. Reteach the concept to Sam in a different way

   D. Reteach the concept to the whole class in a different way

97. **Which strategy for adapting the curriculum would be most useful for the purpose of reducing the effect of a student's learning disability on completing an assessment task?**
(Rigorous) (Skill 11.5)

   A. Differentiated instruction

   B. Alternative assessments

   C. Testing modifications

   D. Total Physical Response

98. **According to Piaget, during what stage do children learn to manipulate symbols and objects?**
(Average rigor) (Skill 12.1)

   A. Concrete operations

   B. Pre-operational

   C. Formal operations

   D. Conservative operational

99. **Which of the following best describes how different areas of development impact each other?**
(Average rigor) (Skill 12.1)

   A. Development in other areas cannot occur until cognitive development is complete.

   B. Areas of development are inter-related and impact each other.

   C. Development in each area is independent of development in other areas.

   D. Development in one area leads to a decline in other areas.

100. **According to Piaget's theory of human development, which stage would a child be in if they understood abstract terms such as honesty and justice?**
(Rigorous) (Skill 12.1)

   A.   Concrete operations

   B.   Pre-operational

   C.   Formal operations

   D.   Sensory-motor

101. **According to IDEA, who must be involved in developing a child's IEP?**
(Average rigor) (Skill 12.5)

   A.   A medical doctor

   B.   The school psychologist

   C.   The parents or guardians

   D.   The principal

102. **A student who is deaf has an Individual Family Service Plan (IFSP) in place. This legal document is a way of providing:**
(Average rigor) (Skill 12.5)

   A.   Early intervention

   B.   Help for the family and the child

   C.   Services to deal with the child's disability

   D.   All of the above

103. **IDEA sets policies that provide for inclusion of students with disabilities. What does inclusion mean?**
(Rigorous) (Skill 12.5)

   A.   Inclusion is the name of the curriculum that must be followed in special education classes.

   B.   Inclusion is the right of students with disabilities to be placed in the regular classroom.

   C.   Inclusion refers to the quality of instruction that is important for student's academic success.

   D.   Inclusion means that students with disabilities should always be placed in special classes.

104. **To determine if a child has a disability that may qualify the child for services under IDEA, which of the following pieces of information should the school collect?**
(Average rigor) (Skill 12.5)

   A.   The present levels of academic achievement

   B.   Vision and hearing screening information

   C.   A complete psychological evaluation

   D.   All of the above

105. What is a good strategy for teaching ethnically diverse students?
(Rigorous) (Skill 13.2)

A. Don't focus on the students' culture

B. Expect them to assimilate easily into your classroom

C. Imitate their speech patterns

D. Use instructional strategies of various formats

106. Which of the following is an example of content which has been differentiated to meet the needs of individual learners?
(Rigorous) (Skill 13.2)

A. Flexible group activities on various levels

B. Accepting different final projects from various students

C. Research projects based on student's interests

D. Individual tutoring by the teacher to address student weaknesses

107. A teacher has a class with several students from low income families in it. What would it be most important for a teacher to consider when planning homework assignments to ensure that all students have equal opportunity for academic success?
(Rigorous) (Skill 13.2)

A. Access to technology

B. Ethnicity

C. Language difficulties

D. Gender

108. Young children do not concentrate for long periods of time. Generally, young children should be changing academic activities every:
(Rigorous) (Skill 13.2)

A. 10-15 minutes

B. 15-20 minutes

C. 20-45 minutes

D. 45 minutes-1 hour

109. **Why is it most important for teachers to ensure that students from different economic backgrounds have access to the resources they need to acquire the academic skills being taught?**
(Rigorous) (Skill 13.2)

   A. All students must work together on set tasks.

   B. All students must achieve the same results in performance tasks.

   C. All students must have equal opportunity for academic success.

   D. All students must be fully included in classroom activities.

110. **What does the Multiple Intelligence Theory developed by Howard Gardner explain?**
(Average rigor) (Skill 14.1)

   A. How the intelligence of students depends on the environment

   B. How the intelligence of students constantly change

   C. How students have different levels of overall intelligence

   D. How students learn in at least seven different ways

111. **What is the most important factor in raising academic outcomes for all students as required in the NCLB law?**
(Rigorous) (Skill 14.1)

   A. The curriculum model used

   B. The quality of instruction in the classroom

   C. The location of the school

   D. The number of years of experience the teacher has

112. **Head Start Programs were created in what decade?**
(Rigorous) (Skill 14.1)

   A. 1970's

   B. 1990's

   C. 1980's

   D. 1960's

113. In the majority of classrooms, the largest amount of floor space is devoted to the organization of student desks. Which of the following is most important in the organization of student desks?
(Average rigor) (Skill 14.2)

A. Desks arranged for proper lighting

B. Desks arranged for adequate ventilation

C. Desks arranged for student comfort

D. Desks arranged for eye contact with each student

114. What environmental element can cause some students to become restless and hyperactive?
(Average rigor) (Skill 14.2)

A. Bright lights

B. The arrangement of student desks

C. The proximity of the classroom to the playground

D. Comfortable seating

115. Which of the following is a right of parents?
(Easy) (Skill 14.3)

A. To be informed of the teacher's concerns about their child

B. To require the teacher to use the teaching method that works for the child

C. To administer discipline to their child in the classroom

D. To attend all classes to support their child

116. When addressing issues of concern in a parent-teacher conference, what is it best to focus on?
(Easy) (Skill 14.3)

A. Likely explanations

B. Personal opinions

C. Statements from other students

D. Observable behaviors

117. When sending a follow-up note to parents following a conference, which of the following is it best to include?
(Average rigor) (Skill 14.3)

A. Further details on the student's strengths and weaknesses

B. A summary of the agreed plan of action

C. A description of how the student has progressed since the conference

D. Praise for the parents on becoming involved in their child's education

118. When communicating with parents for whom English is not the primary language you should:
(Average rigor) (Skill 14.3)

A. Provide materials whenever possible in their native language

B. Use an interpreter

C. Provide the same communication as you would to native English speaking parents

D. All of the above

119. How should a teacher respond to criticism about her teaching strategies from a parent?
(Rigorous) (Skill 14.3)

A. Explain to the parent that negative feedback is hurtful and mean-spirited

B. Dismiss the criticism as an attempt to undermine her performance

C. Think about the criticism objectively and consider that it might be true

D. Change her teaching strategies to eliminate the aspect being criticized

120. Teachers and parents should be:
(Easy) (Skill 14.3)

A. Enemies

B. Friends

C. Partners

D. Strangers

121. **Which of the following should NOT be a purpose of a parent-teacher conference?** *(Average rigor) (Skill 14.3)*

    A. To involve the parent in their child's education

    B. To establish a friendship with the child's parents

    C. To resolve a concern about the child's performance

    D. To inform parents of positive behaviors by the child

122. **Which statement would it be most appropriate to make when speaking to parents about an issue of concern?** *(Rigorous) (Skill 14.3)*

    A. Sandra is often distracted easily.

    B. Sandra irritates other students.

    C. Sandra is a frustrating student.

    D. While completing the exam, Sandra started conversations with other students.

123. **What does portfolio assessment typically provide?** *(Average rigor) (Skill 14.5)*

    A. Opportunities for teachers to assess student's progress

    B. Opportunities for students to reflect on their own progress

    C. Opportunities for students to consider their approaches to problem-solving

    D. All of the above

124. **Which of the following is portfolio assessment most likely to encourage?** *(Average rigor) (Skill 14.5)*

    A. Self-esteem

    B. Self-directed learning

    C. Conflict management skills

    D. Time management skills

125. Mrs. Peck wants to justify the use of personalized learning communities to her principal. Which of the following reasons would she be best to use?
(Rigorous) (Skill 14.5)

A. They are likely to engage students and maintain their interest.

B. They provide a supportive environment to address academic and emotional needs.

C. They encourage students to work independently.

D. They are proactive in their nature.

Pre Test: Answer Key

1.	C	43.	A	85.	D
2.	C	44.	D	86.	D
3.	D	45.	B	87.	D
4.	A	46.	C	88.	A
5.	D	47.	D	89.	B
6.	B	48.	A	90.	D
7.	D	49.	A	91.	D
8.	C	50.	C	92.	A
9.	B	51.	B	93.	A
10.	A	52.	C	94.	C
11.	C	53.	D	95.	A
12.	D	54.	B	96.	C
13.	A	55.	C	97.	C
14.	D	56.	A	98.	A
15.	A	57.	B	99.	B
16.	C	58.	A	100.	C
17.	B	59.	C	101.	C
18.	A	60.	A	102.	D
19.	D	61.	A	103.	B
20.	A	62.	D	104.	D
21.	A	63.	A	105.	D
22.	A	64.	B	106.	C
23.	C	65.	D	107.	A
24.	B	66.	B	108.	B
25.	A	67.	C	109.	C
26.	C	68.	D	110.	D
27.	D	69.	A	111.	B
28.	A	70.	D	112.	D
29.	C	71.	A	113.	D
30.	B	72.	D	114.	A
31.	C	73.	B	115.	A
32.	A	74.	D	116.	D
33.	B	75.	A	117.	B
34.	D	76.	D	118.	D
35.	C	77.	D	119.	C
36.	A	78.	C	120.	C
37.	A	79.	D	121.	B
38.	A	80.	A	122.	D
39.	B	81.	B	123.	D
40.	D	82.	D	124.	B
41.	C	83.	B	125.	B
42.	C	84.	D		

Pre Test: Rigor Table

	Easy 20%	Average Rigor 40%	Rigorous 40%
Question #	3, 9, 13, 19, 29, 30, 37, 38, 54, 60, 66, 68, 69, 70, 71, 75, 76, 79, 86, 87, 90, 92, 115, 116, 120	1, 2, 4, 6, 7, 11, 14, 15, 16, 17, 18, 20, 27, 32, 34, 36, 41, 42, 47, 48, 51, 52, 56, 58, 59, 60, 63, 72, 73, 74, 77, 80, 82, 83, 85, 89, 95, 98, 99, 101, 102, 104, 110, 113, 114, 117, 118, 121, 123, 124	5, 8, 10, 12, 21, 22, 23, 24, 25, 26, 28, 31, 33, 35, 39, 40, 43, 44, 45, 46, 49, 50, 53, 55, 57, 62, 64, 65, 67, 78, 81, 84, 88, 91, 93, 94, 96, 97, 100, 103, 105, 106, 107, 108, 109, 111, 112, 119, 122, 125

Pre Test: Rationales with Sample Questions

Subarea I. Language and Literacy Development

1. **The complex linguistic deficiency marked by the inability to remember and recognize words by sounds and the inability to break words down into component units describes:**
    (Average rigor) (Skill 1.1)

    A. Oral processing disorder
    B. Attention deficit disorder
    C. Dyslexia
    D. Autism

Answer C: Dyslexia

Dyslexia is a very common reading disorder. It is a complex linguistic deficiency that typically causes problems recalling or recognizing words, as well as the inability to decode words. Oral processing disorder concerns a student's ability to listen and process audible information, attention deficit disorder concerns a student's ability to focus and maintain attention, and autism is a disorder that influences social interaction.

2. **Above what age does learning a language become increasingly difficult?**
    (Average rigor) (Skill 1.1)

    A. 3
    B. 5
    C. 7
    D. 10

Answer C: 7

The most important concept to remember regarding the difference between learning a first language and a second one is that if the learner is approximately age seven or older, learning a second language will occur very differently in the learner's brain than it will had the learner been younger. The reason for this is that there is a language-learning function that exists in young children that appears to go away as they mature. Learning a language prior to age seven is almost guaranteed, with relatively little effort.

3. **Children typically develop oral language by listening to:**
    (Easy) (Skill 1.1)

    A. Teachers
    B. Parents
    C. Peers
    D. All of the above

Answer D: All of the above

Children develop oral language by listening to others. This includes listening to teachers, parents, and peers.

4. **Which of the following skills have a reciprocal relationship?**
    (Average rigor) (Skill 1.4)

    A. Reading and phonics
    B. Writing and phonics
    C. Reading and writing
    D. Reading and comprehension

Answer A: Reading and writing

Often teachers will see a reciprocal relationship between reading and writing skills. As students are able to read sounds, they will notice these same sounds showing up in students writing. It is important for teachers to continually show students how the two relate and are connected.

5. **Children having difficulties with spelling, reading accuracy, and reading comprehension skills are also likely to have difficulties with:**
    (Rigorous) (Skill 1.6)

    A. Cognitive skills
    B. Development factors
    C. Math skills
    D. Speech and language skills

Answer D: Speech and language skills

While students who have difficulties with speech and language skills often have difficulties with reading, the converse is also true. Students who are struggling with spelling, reading accuracy and comprehension may also have hidden difficulties with speech and language skills

6. **Which of the following is a convention of print that children learn during reading activities?**
    (Average rigor) (Skill 1.6)

    A. The meaning of words
    B. The left to right motion
    C. The purpose of print
    D. The identification of letters

Answer B: The left to right motion

During reading activities, children learn conventions of print. Children learn the way to hold a book, where to begin to read, the left to right motion, and how to continue from one line to another.

7. **Which of the following concepts of print can be taught during a read aloud?**
    (Average rigor) (Skill 1.6)

    A. Front and back of book
    B. Author
    C. Title location
    D. All of the above

Answer D: All of the above

All concepts of print can and should be modeled to students through reading aloud activities.

8. **Mr. Phillips has called a parent meeting with Maria's parents. Maria is struggling with acquiring the necessary comprehension skills to maintain grade level standards. Maria's parents speak Spanish in the home and are eager and willing to do anything to help Maria succeed in school. Which of the following strategies below will help Maria, while maintaining and fostering the importance of her native language?**
    (Rigorous) (Skill 1.7)

    A. Encouraging Maria's parents to enroll in an English language course
    B. Making sure Maria speaks only English during classroom activities
    C. Encouraging Maria's parents to read and discuss books written in Spanish
    D. Ensuring that Maria's parents only speak English in the home

Answer C: Encouraging Maria's parents to read and discuss books written in Spanish

The foundations upon which comprehension skills are learned are not unique to one language. If Maria is indeed struggling with comprehension, it does not matter which language she uses to practice her skills. By encouraging Maria's parents to utilize their skills in their native language, they can feel a more active member of Maria's educational process and continue to embrace their heritage and native language.

9. **Which of the following literary devices is most commonly found in kindergarten classrooms?** *(Easy) (Skill 1.7)*

    A. Metaphor
    B. Repetition
    C. Simile
    D. Analogy

Answer B: Repetition

Young children often have difficulties with the more complex literary devices (metaphors, symbolism, similes and analogies). Often you will find text repetition used in big books or other forms of literature for young children.

10. **John is having difficulty reading the word reach. In isolation, he pronounces each sound as /r/ /ee/ /sh/. Which of the following is a possible instructional technique which could help solve John's reading difficulty?**
   (Rigorous) (Skill 2.1)

   A. Additional phonemic awareness instruction
   B. Additional phonics instruction
   C. Additional skill and drill practice
   D. Additional minimal pair practice

Answer A: Additional phonemic awareness instruction

John is having difficulty with the sound symbol relationship between the /ch/ and /sh/. While it may appear at first that this is a phonics problem, in fact, it is important to begin with the earlier skill of phonemic awareness to ensure the student has a solid foundational understanding of the oral portions before moving totally into the sound symbol arena. If John is able to distinguish between the two sounds orally, it is obvious more phonics instruction is needed. However, proceeding directly to phonics instruction may be pointless and frustrating for John if he is unable to hear the distinctions.

11. **Mrs. Myers has discovered numerous words that are repeatedly spelled wrong in Tina's writing. These same words seem to be used by Tina in a lot of her writing as well. What would Mrs. Myers be best to do?**
   (Average rigor) (Skill 2.1)

   A. Drill Tina on those words
   B. Add those words to Tina's regular weekly spelling test
   C. Work with Tina to make an individual spelling dictionary to help her learn these words
   D. Have Tina look the words up in the dictionary and correct them

Answer C: Work with Tina to make an individual spelling dictionary to help her learn these words

While there are teachers who will do any of the choices listed, it is most effective to provide individual spelling dictionaries or spelling word wall file folders to help students to improve specific and individual words which may or may not be beneficial to other students.

12. Research into students who are learning English as a second language has found that they have difficulty manipulating the sound system of English. This difficulty is in which area of reading development?
     (Rigorous) (Skill 2.2)

     A. Comprehension
     B. Fluency
     C. Phonics
     D. Phonemic Awareness

Answer D: Phonemic Awareness

As is the case with many students who struggle with reading, it has also been found that students who are learning English as a second language often have difficulties with phonemic awareness skills.

13. The smallest unit of sound is the:
     (Easy) (Skill 2.2)

     A. Phoneme
     B. Morpheme
     C. Syllable
     D. Letter

Answer A: Phoneme

A phoneme is the smallest unit of sound that has a different meaning. A morpheme is a word or word part that cannot be divided into any smaller parts of meaning.

14. Which of the following early reading skills develops first?
     (Average rigor) (Skill 2.2)

     A. Comprehension
     B. Phonics
     C. Phonemic awareness
     D. Letter identification

Answer D: Phonemic awareness

In typically developing children, phonemic awareness skills should be developed before the other reading skills listed.

15. **The idea that students need to be able to take spoken words apart and blend different sounds together to make words describes:**
    (Average rigor) (Skill 2.4)

    A.   The alphabet principle
    B.   Syntax
    C.   Phonics
    D.   Morphology

Answer A: The alphabet principle

The alphabet principle consists of four basic features. The first feature is listed in the question above, while the other three are discussed here. These principles are:
  • Students need to apply letter sounds to all their reading
  • Teachers need to use a systematic, effective program in order to teach children to read

The teaching of the alphabetic principle usually begins in Kindergarten

16. **Which of the following is NOT an effective strategy to aid students with spelling instruction?**
    (Average rigor) (Skill 2.5)

    A.   Knowledge of patterns, sounds, and letter-sound association
    B.   Memorizing sight words
    C.   Writing words one or two times
    D.   Writing the words correctly in personal writing

Answer C: Writing words one or two times

Answers A, B, and D are all effective strategies listed that can be used to aid students with spelling instruction. Writing words multiple times, rather than just once or twice, is another effective strategy.

17. **Johnny loves to listen to stories and points to signs all around the room that have letters on them. This suggests that Johnny:**
(Average rigor) (Skill 2.6)

   A.   Will be a good reader
   B.   Has good emergent literacy skills
   C.   Has good phonemic awareness skills
   D.   Understands grammar

Answer B: Has good emergent literacy skills

Enjoying stories and being aware of environmental print are factors in emergent literacy skills, not necessarily directly attributed to phonemic awareness, phonics, or future reading abilities. However, those students with good emergent literacy skills are more likely to be more successful in all of those skills than students who have poor emergent literacy skills.

18. **Which of the following is the most commonly practiced strategy to encourage literacy growth?**
(Average rigor) (Skill 2.6)

   A.   Storybook reading
   B.   Teaching phonics
   C.   Teaching fluency
   D.   Letter identification

Answer A: Storybook reading

Reading stories and reading aloud to children is the most common literacy growth strategy implemented in classrooms across the country.

19. **Which of the following is an appropriate way for students to respond to literature?**
(Easy) (Skill 2.6)

   A.   Art
   B.   Drama
   C.   Writing
   D.   All of the above

Answer D: All of the above

Responding to literature through art, writing, and drama helps children to reflect on the books they have read and make them a part of their lives.

20. Which of the following is NOT true about phonological awareness? *(Average rigor) (Skill 3.1)*

    A. It may involve print.
    B. It is a prerequisite for spelling and phonics.
    C. Activities can be done by the children with their eyes closed.
    D. It starts before letter recognition is taught.

Answer A: It may involve print.

All of the options are correct aspects of phonological awareness except the first one, because phonological awareness does not involve print.

21. Ms. Walker's lesson objective is to teach her first graders the concept of morphology in order to improve their reading skills. Which group of words would be most appropriate for her to use in this lesson? *(Rigorous) (Skill 3.2)*

    A. Far, farm, farmer
    B. Far, feather, fever
    C. Far, fear, fare
    D. Far, fare, farce

Answer A: Far, farm, farmer

The concept of morphology is to understand how words relate to each other and can be built upon to increase reading skills. In the correct answer, the student can utilize the information they learned from learning to read far to help them decode the other words.

22. A teacher writes the following words on the board: cot, cotton, and cottage. What is the teacher most likely teaching the students about? *(Rigorous) (Skill 3.2)*

    A. Morphology
    B. Syntax
    C. Semantics
    D. Pragmatics

Answer A: Morphology

Morphology is the study of word structure. When readers develop morphemic skills, they are developing an understanding of patterns they see in words. For example, English speakers realize that cat, cats, and caterpillar share some similarities in structure. This understanding helps readers to recognize words at a faster and easier rate, since each word doesn't need individual decoding.

23. **Children who are having difficulty understanding non-literal expressions are having difficulties with which of the following areas?**
 (Rigorous) (Skill 3.2)

 A. Syntax
 B. Morphology
 C. Semantics
 D. Phonics

Answer C: Semantics

Listening and understanding the intentions of speakers (teacher/peers) involves semantics. A student that is having difficulty understanding non-literal expressions is having difficulty with semantics.

24. **When introducing new vocabulary to students, the number of new words being taught at one time should be:**
 (Rigorous) (Skill 3.4)

 A. One to two
 B. Two to three
 C. Three to four
 D. Four to five

Answer B: Two to three

The number of words that require explicit teaching should only be two or three. If the number is higher than that, the children need guided reading and the text needs to be broken down into smaller sections for teaching. When broken down into smaller sections, each text section should only have two to three words that need explicit teaching.

25. **Students are about to read a text that contains concepts that will be difficult for students to grasp. When should the vocabulary be introduced to students?**
 (Rigorous) (Skill 3.4)

 A. Before reading
 B. During reading
 C. After reading
 D. It should not be introduced.

Answer A: Before reading

If the text, itself, in the judgment of the teacher, contains difficult concepts for the children to grasp, the vocabulary should be introduced before reading.

26. **Repeated readings of the same text are beneficial to developing readers because:**
    (Rigorous) (Skill 4.1)

    A. Repeated reading helps students memorize the text
    B. Repeated reading helps in pairing students
    C. Repeated reading ensures students recognize the words readily and can read at an improved pace
    D. Repeated reading helps teachers determine students' level of reading

Answer C: Repeated reading ensures students recognize the words readily and can read at an improved pace

Repeated readings allow students to have repeated exposure to the same vocabulary, sentences, and punctuation. This repeated exposure allows students to learn the right way to read something the first time while then providing ample opportunities to internalize the elements of the text. Some argue that repeated reading helps students to simply memorize the text, however this can be checked by the teacher by having the student start at different points in the text.

27. **Which of the following is NOT a common method of teaching comprehension?**
    (Average rigor) (Skill 4.2)

    A. Summarizing
    B. Question asking
    C. Graphic organizers
    D. Phonics drills

Answer D: Phonics drills

Summarizing, question asking, and graphic organizers are just a few of the strategies for teaching comprehension. Others include studying text structure, question answering, monitoring comprehension, textual marking, and discussion. Phonics drills may help students to decode and identify words better, but they do not directly help students to comprehend what they are reading.

28. **Mr. Lotus wants the class to compare two characters from a book. Which of the following would be a good tool for Mr. Lotus to use?**
(Rigorous) (Skill 4.4)

   A.   Venn diagram
   B.   KWL Chart
   C.   Outline
   D.   Literature circle discussion

Answer A: Venn diagram

A Venn diagram is a tool that is commonly used to compare and contrast two characters, stories, or objects.

29. **The stories about Paul Bunyan, John Henry, and Pecos Bill are all exaggerated accounts of individuals with superhuman strength. What type of literature are these works?**
(Easy) (Skill 4.6)

   A.   Fables
   B.   Fairytales
   C.   Tall tales
   D.   Myths

Answer C: Tall tales

Tall tales are purposely exaggerated accounts of individuals with superhuman strength. The stories about Paul Bunyan, John Henry, and Pecos Bill are all examples of tall tales. Fables are usually stories about animals with human features that often teach a lesson. Fairytales usually focus on good versus evil, reward and punishment. Myths are stories about events from the earliest times.

30. **Which of the following is NOT a characteristic of a fable?**
(Easy) (Skill 4.6)

   A.   Have animal characters that act like humans
   B.   Considered to be true
   C.   Teaches a moral
   D.   Reveals human foibles

Answer B: Considered to be true

The common characteristics of fables are animals that act like humans, a focus on revealing human foibles, and teaching a moral or lesson. Fables are not considered to be true.

31. **An adolescent has not yet mastered spelling. What would be the best way for a teacher to address this?**
(Rigorous) (Skill 5.2)

   A. Provide the student with extra instruction on spelling rules
   B. Ensure that the student fully understands all the exceptions to rules
   C. Encourage the student to master the use of a dictionary and thesaurus
   D. Focus on teaching spelling and grammar in isolation

Answer C: Encourage the student to master the use of a dictionary and thesaurus

The multiplicity and complexity of spelling rules based on phonics, letter doubling, and exceptions to rules - not mastered by adulthood - should be replaced by a good dictionary. As spelling mastery is also difficult for adolescents, our recommendation is the same. Learning the use of a dictionary and thesaurus will be a more rewarding use of time.

32. **Which of the following approaches to student writing assignments is least likely to lead to students becoming disinterested?**
(Average rigor) (Skill 5.2)

   A. Designing assignments where students write for a variety of audiences.
   B. Designing assignments where the teacher is the audience.
   C. Designing assignments where students write to friends and family.
   D. Designing assignments where students write to real people such as mayors, the principal, or companies.

Answer A: Designing assignments where students write for a variety of audiences.

In the past, teachers have assigned reports, paragraphs and essays that focused on the teacher as the audience with the purpose of explaining information. However, for students to be meaningfully engaged in their writing, they must write for a variety of reasons. Writing for different audiences and aims allows students to be more involved in their writing. If they write for the same audience and purpose, they will continue to see writing as just another assignment.

33. **In the process of writing, the introduction should be written at what stage of the paper?**
(Rigorous) (Skill 5.2)

   A.   Before the thesis development
   B.   After the entire paper is written
   C.   During the brainstorming session
   D.   Before writing the body

Answer B: After the entire paper is written

It is important to remember that in the writing process, the introduction should be written last. This is necessary because, until the body of the paper has been determined, it's difficult to make strategic decisions regarding the introduction.

34. **Which of the following strategies encourages print awareness in classrooms?**
(Average rigor) (Skill 5.3)

   A.   Word walls
   B.   Using big books to read to students
   C.   Using highlighters to locate upper case letters
   D.   All of the above

Answer D: All of the above

Classrooms rich in print provide many opportunities to students to see, use, and experience text in various forms. Word walls, big books, and highlighting certain textual features are all ways to expose students to various forms of text.

35. **The students in Tina's classroom are working together in pairs. Each student is reading another student's paper and asking who, what, when, where, why, and who questions. What is this activity helping the students to do?**
(Rigorous) (Skill 5.5)

   A.   Draft their writing
   B.   Paraphrase their writing
   C.   Revise their writing
   D.   Outline their writing

Answer C: Revise their writing

Students need to be trained to become effective at proofreading, revising and editing strategies. One way to do this is to have the students read their partners' papers and ask at least three who, what, when, why, how questions. The students answer the questions and use them as a place to begin discussing the piece.

36. **Ms. Michaels is teaching her students about revising. What would Ms. Michaels be best to tell her students about revising?**
(Average rigor) (Skill 5.5)

   A.   Revising is an important part of the writing process and all writing should be revised.
   B.   You will only have to revise until you become a good enough writer to get it perfect the first time.
   C.   Revising can be skipped sometimes if you think it might ruin your writing.
   D.   You will only need to revise work you complete that is to be handed in for assessment.

Answer A: Revising is an important part of the writing process and all writing should be revised.

Revision is probably the most important step for the writer in the writing process. Here, students examine their work and make changes in wording, details and ideas. Students should be encouraged to develop, change, and enhance their writing as they go, as well as once they've completed a draft. Students should also be reminded that all writing must be revised to improve it.

Subarea II. Learning Across the Curriculum

37.   **How is the following read?**
      (Easy) (Skill 6.1)

      3 < 5

      A.   Three is less than five
      B.   Five is greater than three
      C.   Three is greater than five
      D.   Five is less than three

Answer A: Three is less than five

Reading left to right: *three is less than five.*

38.   **What is the foundation of math skills and topics?**
      (Easy) (Skill 6.1)

      A.   Number sense
      B.   Place value
      C.   Addition
      D.   Computation skills

Answer A: Number sense

As with the phonemic awareness skills in reading, number sense is the foundation upon which all future math topics will be built. Providing young children with the opportunity to interact with objects across multiple contexts will help children begin to develop these concepts of number sense.

39. **Which math principle indicates that a student should "carry" the one in the following addition problem?**
(Rigorous) (Skill 6.1)

```
  54
 +29
  83
```

    A.   Counting by tens
    B.   Properties of a base ten number system
    C.   Problem checking
    D.   Adding numbers that are too big

Answer B: Properties of a base ten number system

In a base ten number system, groups of ten ones are regrouped and carried into the tens column. In the addition problem shown, four ones plus nine ones is equal to 13 ones. The ten ones are regrouped and carried into the tens column.

40. **Third grade students are studying percents. When looking at a circle graph divided into three sections, they see that one section is worth 80% and one section is worth 5%. What will the remaining section be worth?**
(Rigorous) (Skill 6.1)

    A.   100%
    B.   85%
    C.   75%
    D.   15%

Answer D: 15%

Percentages use the base ten number system. Percentages of a total amount will always add up to 100%. Since the two sections add to 85%, the third section must be 15%.

41. **A teacher is introducing the concept of multiplication to her third grade students. What is another way she might write 4 x 5?**
(Average rigor) (Skill 6.1)

 A. 4 + 5
 B. 5 + 4
 C. 4 + 4 + 4 + 4 + 4
 D. 5 + 5 + 5 + 5 + 5

Answer C: 4 + 4 + 4 + 4 + 4

The multiplication concept can translate to an addition problem. 4 x 5 is the same as the number 4 added 5 times.

42. **First grade students are arranging four small squares of identical size to form a larger square. Each small square represents what part of the larger square?**
(Average rigor) (Skill 6.1)

 A. One half
 B. One whole
 C. One fourth
 D. One fifth

Answer C: One fourth

Four of the small squares make up the area of the large square. Each small square is one fourth of the larger square.

43. **A class has 30 magnets for 6 tables of students. Students are asked to determine how many magnets each table of students should get so that each table of students has the same number of magnets. What math principle would students apply to solve this problem?**
(Rigorous) (Skill 6.1)

 A. Division
 B. Multiplication
 C. Percent
 D. Subtraction

Answer A: Division

The magnets need to be divided equally between 6 tables of students. The division principle is applied to solve this problem (60 ÷ 6 = 5). Each table gets five magnets.

44. **Which of the following letters does NOT have a line of symmetry?**
    (Rigorous) (Skill 6.1)

    A. O
    B. D
    C. M
    D. J

Answer D: J

For an object to show symmetry, it must be able to be divided into identical halves. The letter O has an unlimited number of lines of symmetry. The letter D has a horizontal line of symmetry. The letter M has a vertical line of symmetry. The letter J does not have a line of symmetry.

45. **What is the main purpose of having kindergarten students count by twos?**
    (Rigorous) (Skill 6.1)

    A. To hear a rhythm
    B. To recognize patterns in numbers
    C. To practice addition
    D. To become familiar with equations

Answer B: To recognize patterns in numbers

Recognizing patterns in numbers is an early skill for multiplication. It will also help children recognize patterns in word families such as *bit, hit, fit.*

46. **Which would be a way for early childhood students to learn about basic geometric concepts?**
    (Rigorous) (Skill 6.1)

    A. Using a ruler
    B. Rote counting
    C. Working with tangrams
    D. Create an A-B color pattern

Answer C: Working with tangrams

Tangrams, or puzzle pieces, are excellent manipulatives for children to use to explore geometric shapes and relationships. They allow students to transform shapes through flips and rotations as well as to take them apart and put them together in different formations.

47. **In which problem would students need an understanding of basic algebraic concepts?**
(Average rigor) (Skill 6.1)

   A. $5 + 6 + 5 =$
   B. $3 + 3 + 3 + 3 + 3 =$
   C. $10 \times 0 =$
   D. $3 + \square = 9$

Answer D: $3 + \square = 9$

By rearranging the numbers in this equation to calculate for the missing value, students are demonstrating basic algebraic concepts. The other choices are simple computation problems.

48. **Students completing an activity with tangrams are learning what math principle?**
(Average rigor) (Skill 6.1)

   A.   Basic geometric concepts
   B.   Repeating patterns
   C.   Counting
   D.   Identity property

Answer A: Basic geometric concepts

The students are learning basic geometric concepts (number of sides and types of angles). The tangram picture may or may not be a repeating design. Counting and the identity property (a number plus zero always equals the original number) are not involved.

49. **Kindergarten students are participating in a calendar time activity. One student adds a straw to the "ones can" to represent that day of school. What math principle is being reinforced?**
(Rigorous) (Skill 6.1)

   A.   Properties of a base ten number system
   B.   Sorting
   C.   Counting by twos
   D.   Even and odd numbers

Answer A: Properties of a base ten number system

As the students group craft sticks into groups of tens to represent the days of school, they are learning the properties of our base ten number system.

50. Kindergarten students are doing a butterfly art project. They fold paper in half. On one half, they paint a design. Then they fold the paper closed and reopen. The resulting picture is a butterfly with matching sides. What math principle does this demonstrate? *(Rigorous) (Skill 6.1)*

    A.   Slide
    B.   Rotate
    C.   Symmetry
    D.   Transformation

Answer C: Symmetry

By folding the painted paper in half, the design is mirrored on the other side, creating symmetry and reflection. The butterfly design is symmetrical about the center.

51. What would be a good choice when graphing the percent of time that a student spends on various after school activities? *(Average rigor) (Skill 6.1)*

    A.   Line graph
    B.   Pie chart
    C.   Histogram
    D.   Scatter plot

Answer B: Pie chart

The type of graphic representation used to display observations depends on the data that is collected. A pie chart is useful when organizing data as part of a whole. A good use for a pie chart would be displaying the percent of time students spend on various after school activities.

52. **What number comes next in this pattern?**
(Average rigor) (Skill 6.2)

3, 8, 13, 18, _____

A. 21
B. 26
C. 23
D. 5

Answer C: 23

This pattern is made by adding five to the preceding number. The next number is found by adding 5 to 18, which gives the answer 23.

53. **Ms. Smith considers the use of quality children's literature to be one of the most important qualities of an early childhood teacher. She is asked to justify her reasons behind this consideration to her principal. Which of the following is an appropriate justification?**
(Rigorous) (Skill 6.4)

A. There are many different types of children's literature, so there will be something to which every child can relate.
B. Children's literature in early childhood classrooms provides the students with the opportunity to learn to read and process language.
C. Children are like adults in many ways and need to be exposed to a variety of types of literature.
D. Children's literature helps children improve their mental, social, and psychological skills and aids in the development in all of these areas.

Answer D: Children's literature helps children improve their mental, social, and psychological skills and aids in the development in all of these areas.

Modern educators acknowledge that introducing elementary students to a wide range of reading experiences plays an important role in their mental, social, and psychological development.

54. **What should an experiment have a minimum number of to produce accurate and easily correlated results?**
(Easy) (Skill 7.1)

   A.   Controls
   B.   Variables
   C.   Samples
   D.   Participants

Answer B: Variables

A variable is a factor or condition that can be changed in an experiment. A good experiment will try to manipulate as few variables as possible, so that the results of the experiment can be identified as occurring because of the change in the variable.

55. **Each time an experiment is completed, different results are obtained. This indicates that the experiment is not:**
(Rigorous) (Skill 7.1)

   A.   Objective
   B.   Significant
   C.   Reproducible
   D.   Accurate

Answer C: Reproducible

The question stage of scientific inquiry involves repetition. By repeating the experiment you can discover whether or not you have reproducibility. If results are reproducible, the hypothesis is valid. If the results are not reproducible, one has more questions to ask.

56. **What does a primary consumer most commonly refer to?**
     (Average rigor) (Skill 7.2)

     A. Herbivore
     B. Autotroph
     C. Carnivore
     D. Decomposer

Answer A: Herbivore

Autotrophs are the primary producers of the ecosystem. Producers mainly consist of plants. Primary consumers are the next trophic level. The primary consumers are the herbivores that eat plants or algae. Secondary consumers are the carnivores that eat the primary consumers. Tertiary consumers eat the secondary consumer. These trophic levels may go higher depending on the ecosystem.

57. **Which of the following causes the Earth to have seasons?**
     (Rigorous) (Skill 7.2)

     A. The Earth's magnetic field
     B. The Earth's tilt on its axis
     C. The Earth's moon
     D. The Earth's tectonic plates

Answer B: The Earth's tilt on its axis

Seasonal change on Earth is caused by the orbit and axial tilt of the planet in relation to the Sun's Ecliptic: the rotational path of the Sun. These factors combine to vary the degree of insolation (distribution of solar energy) at a particular location and thereby change the seasons.

58. **What question would it be most important for a teacher to ask when deciding if a book will be appropriate for classroom use?**
     (Average rigor) (Skill 7.3)

     A. Do the characters provide positive role models for children?
     B. Is the setting of the book modern?
     C. Will every student in the class be interested in the subject of the book?
     D. Is the book short enough for students to read in one sitting?

Answer A: Do the characters provide positive role models for children?

Children love to identify with the characters in books, so it is important to select books with characters that provide positive role models for children.

59. **Science and technology are best described as:**
    (Average rigor) (Skill 7.6)

    A. Different names for the same thing
    B. Competing against each other
    C. Closely related and intertwined
    D. Independent of each other

Answer C: Closely related and intertwined

Science and technology, while distinct concepts, are closely related. Science attempts to investigate and explain the natural world, while technology attempts to solve human adaptation problems. Technology often results from the application of scientific discoveries, and advances in technology can increase the impact of scientific discoveries.

60. **Which part of a map shows the relationship between a unit of measurement on the map versus the real world measure on the Earth?**
    (Easy) *(Skill 7.6)*

    A. Scale
    B. Title
    C. Legend
    D. Grid

Answer A: Scale

The scale of a map is used to show the relationship between a unit of measurement on the map versus the real world measure on the Earth

61. **Which of the following describes how citizens are able to directly participate in their own government by voting for and running for office?**
    (Average rigor) (Skill 8.1)

    A. Popular sovereignty
    B. Due process
    C. Rule of law
    D. Democracy

Answer A: Popular sovereignty

Popular sovereignty grants citizens the ability to directly participate in their own government by voting and running for public office. This ideal is based on a belief of equality that holds that all citizens have an equal right to engage in their own governance, and is established in the United States Constitution.

62. **The rights of U.S. citizens also imply certain responsibilities to be exercised. Which of the following is NOT a responsibility of U.S. citizens?**
(Rigorous) (Skill 8.1)

    A. Paying taxes
    B. Jury duty
    C. Respecting others' right
    D. Freedom of religion

Answer D: Freedom of religion

The responsibilities of U.S. citizens include respecting others' rights, obeying laws and rules, paying taxes, jury duty, and voting. Freedom of religion is a right of U.S. citizens, not a responsibility.

63. **Economics is the study of how a society allocates its scarce resources to satisfy:**
(Average rigor) (Skill 8.1)

    A. Unlimited and competing wants
    B. Limited and competing wants
    C. Unlimited and cooperative wants
    D. Limited and cooperative wants

Answer A: Unlimited and competing wants

Economics is the study of how a society allocates its scarce resources to satisfy what are basically unlimited and competing wants. A fundamental fact of economics is that resources are scarce and that wants are infinite.

64. **The two elements of a market economy are:**
    (Rigorous) (Skill 8.1)

    A. Inflation and deflation
    B. Supply and demand
    C. Cost and price
    D. Wants and needs

Answer B: Supply and demand

A market economy is based on supply and demand. Demand is based on consumer preferences and satisfaction and refers to the quantities of a good or service that buyers are willing and able to buy at different prices during a given period of time. Supply is based on costs of production and refers to the quantities that sellers are willing and able to sell at different prices during a given period of time.

65. **The rights of U.S. citizens also imply certain responsibilities to be exercised. Which of the following is NOT a responsibility of U.S. citizens?**
    (Rigorous) (Skill 8.1)

    A. Paying taxes
    B. Jury duty
    C. Respecting others' right
    D. Freedom of religion

Answer D: Freedom of religion

The responsibilities of U.S. citizens include respecting others' rights, obeying laws and rules, paying taxes, jury duty, and voting. Freedom of religion is a right of U.S. citizens, not a responsibility.

66. **The primary social unit in most societies is:**
(Easy) *(Skill 8.1)*

    A.   Religion
    B.   Family
    C.   School
    D.   Local government

Answer B: Family

Sociologists have identified five different types of institutions around which societies are structured: family, education, government, religion, and economy. These institutions provide a framework for members of a society to learn about and participate in a society, and allow for a society to perpetuate its beliefs and values to succeeding generations.

67. **Which hypothesis is valid?**
(Rigorous) *(Skill 8.3)*

    A.   An unknown factor causes tomato plants to produce no fruit sometimes.
    B.   A tomato plant will produce tasty fruit if it is watered.
    C.   A tomato plant will grow faster in full sunlight than partial sunlight.
    D.   A tomato plant given this fertilizer will produce better fruit than all others.

Answer C: A tomato plant will grow faster in full sunlight than partial sunlight.

A valid hypothesis must be able to be proven either right or wrong. "An unknown factor causes tomato plants to produce no fruit sometimes" cannot be proven definitely right or wrong since it is too vague. "A tomato plant will produce tasty fruit if it is watered" cannot be proven either right or wrong because the measurement "tasty" is subjective. "A tomato plant given this fertilizer will produce better fruit than all others" cannot be tested because it cannot be proven that the fruit is better than all others. "A tomato plant will grow faster in full sunlight than partial sunlight" is valid because it can be proven right or wrong.

68. **A teacher observes that a student appears sad, shows little interest in people or activities, and is having eating problems. What disorder do these observations suggest?**
(Easy) (Skill 9.1)

  A. Claustrophobia
  B. Autism
  C. Dyslexia
  D. Depression

Answer D: Depression

One of the most serious neurotic disorders is depression. Signs of depression include: seeming sad and depressed; crying; showing little or no interest in people or activities; having eating and sleeping problems; and sometimes talking about wanting to be dead. Teachers need to listen to what the child is saying and should take these verbal expressions very seriously.

69. **A person's understanding of his or her own body parts is known as:**
(Easy) (Skill 9.2)

  A. Body awareness
  B. Strength
  C. Flexibility
  D. Spatial awareness

Answer A: Body awareness

Body awareness refers to a person's understanding of his or her own body parts and their capability of movement. There are various ways to assess body awareness. These include: playing a game of "Simon Says"; having students make their bodies into various shapes; and having students use their body parts to clap their hands, stamp their feet, snap their fingers, or various other actions.

70. **Which of the following is a social skill gained from participation in physical activities?**
    (Easy) (Skill 9.2)

    A. Problem solving skills
    B. Communication skills
    C. Judgment skills
    D. All of the above

Answer D: All of the above

Participation in physical activities helps students develop a number of social skills. Problem solving skills and judgment skills are developed in both individual and team sports. Communication skills are especially developed in team sports.

71. **Which of the following is NOT a good example of fine motor practice for young students?**
    (Easy) (Skill 9.2)

    A. Throwing a ball
    B. Manipulating clay
    C. Cutting
    D. Tearing

Answer A: Throwing a ball

Manipulating clay, cutting, and tearing are all good examples of fine motor practice for young students. Throwing a ball is an activity that develops gross motor skills.

72. **Young children learning to write commonly grip the pencil:**
    (Average rigor) (Skill 9.2)

    A. Too far from the point
    B. With the wrong hand
    C. With too many fingers
    D. Too tightly

Answer D: Too tightly

A common problem for all young children learning to write is gripping the pencil too tightly, which makes writing tiresome. Usually the student learns to relax their grip as writing skill develops, but teachers can remind students to hold the instrument gently.

73. **Which type of physical education activity is most likely to encourage appreciation of diversity?**
(Average rigor) *(Skill 9.3)*

    A.   Solitary activities
    B.   Teamwork activities
    C.   Competitive activities
    D.   Creative activities

Answer B: Teamwork activities

One of the values that can be gained from physical education is appreciation of diversity. This is most likely to occur during teamwork activities, which often create opportunities for students to interact with other students they do not normally interact with. At the same time, students learn the value of the different skills that people have to offer.

74. **The teaching of sports psychology incorporates physical education with:**
(Average rigor) (Skill 9.3)

    A.   Physical science
    B.   Natural science
    C.   Mathematics
    D.   Social science

Answer D: Social science

Physical education can be incorporated with other learning areas, such as physical science, mathematics, natural science, and kinesiology. Teaching sports psychology is one example of incorporating physical education with social science.

75. **Which subject would a color wheel most likely be used for?**
(Easy) (Skill 10.1)

    A.   Visual arts
    B.   Music
    C.   Movement
    D.   Drama

Answer A: Visual arts

A color wheel is an important tool in teaching students visual arts. It is used to teach students about primary colors and secondary colors. It is also used to help students learn about mixing colors.

76. **In which subject is it most important for students to work with costumes and props?**
   (Easy) (Skill 10.3)

   A. Visual arts
   B. Music
   C. Movement
   D. Drama

Answer D: Drama

When studying drama, students should experience working with props and performing in costume. These can both help students act out experiences and tend to increase creativity.

77. **In which subject is it most important for students to be encouraged to use all five senses?**
   (Average rigor) (Skill 10.3)

   A. Visual arts
   B. Music
   C. Movement
   D. Drama

Answer D: Drama

In drama, students should be encouraged to use all five senses. All five senses should be used in observing the environment. Experiences should also be recreated and stories, myths, and fables told that incorporate the use of all five senses.

78. **Which of the following best explains why students will often interpret works of art differently?**
   (Rigorous) (Skill 10.3)

   A. Works of art are usually complicated.
   B. Works of art reflect the time that they were created.
   C. Each student is influenced by their prior knowledge.
   D. Students tend to focus on different senses.

Answer C: Each student is influenced by their prior knowledge.

Interpreting and responding to art is a subjective process. Each student is influenced by his or her prior knowledge and also by his or her personal experiences. This explains why students will usually interpret works of art differently.

79. **What venues offer suitable opportunities for allowing students to view live performances?**
(Easy) (Skill 10.5)

A. Symphonies
B. Dance companies
C. Art museums
D. All of the above

Answer D: All of the above

Live performances are an important part of learning arts and help to develop aesthetic appreciation of the arts. Local performing venues, art museums, symphonies, and dance companies can all provide opportunities for live performances.

80. **What should the arts curriculum for early childhood avoid?**
(Average rigor) (Skill 10.6)

A. Judgment
B. Open expression
C. Experimentation
D. Discovery

Answer A: Judgment

The arts curriculum for early childhood should focus on the experimental and discovery aspects of the arts. The emphasis should be on creative processes with little judgment and criticism should be minimal.

Subarea III. Diversity, Collaboration, and Professionalism in the Early Childhood Program

81. **What is the most significant development emerging in children at age two?**
(Rigorous) (Skill 11.1)

    A.   Immune system development
    B.   Language development
    C.   Socialization development
    D.   Perception development

Answer B: Language development

The most significant development emerging in children at age two is language development. General researchers have shown that children at 2 years old should have speech patterns that are about 70% intelligible.

82. **Which of the following is a true statement?**
(Average rigor) (Skill 11.1)

    A.   Physical development does not influence social development.
    B.   Social development does not influence physical development.
    C.   Cognitive development does not influence social development.
    D.   All domains of development are integrated and influence other domains.

Answer D: All domains of development are integrated and influence other domains.

Child development does not occur in a vacuum. Each element of development impacts other elements of development. For example, as children develop physically, they develop the dexterity to demonstrate cognitive development, such as writing something on a piece of paper.

83. **A teacher notices that a student is sullen, and has several bruises on his head, arms, and legs. When asked, the student responds that he hit his arm getting out of bed that morning. The teacher should:** *(Average rigor) (Skill 11.1)*

   A.   Attempt to get more information from the student
   B.   Report the suspected abuse
   C.   Inform the parents
   D.   Wait and see if other signs of abuse become evident

Answer B: Report the suspected abuse

The most important concern is for the safety and wellbeing of the student. Teachers should not promise students that they won't tell because they are required by law to report suspected abuse. Failure or delay in reporting suspected abuse may be a cause for further abuse to the student. In some cases, a teacher's decision to overlook suspected abuse may result in revoking the teacher's license. Teachers are not required to investigate abuse for themselves or verify their suspicions

84. **Playing team sports at young ages should be done for the following purpose:** *(Rigorous) (Skill 11.2)*

   A.   To develop the child's motor skills
   B.   To prepare children for competition in high school
   C.   To develop the child's interests
   D.   Both A and C

Answer D: Both A and C

Sports, for both boys and girls, can be very valuable. Parents and teachers, though, need to remember that sports at young ages should only be for the purpose of development of interests and motor skills—not competition. Many children will learn that they do not enjoy sports, and parents and teachers should be respectful of these decisions.

85. **Maintaining body weight is best accomplished by:**
(Average rigor) (Skill 11.3)

    A.   Dieting
    B.   Aerobic exercise
    C.   Lifting weights
    D.   Equalizing caloric intake relative to output

Answer D: Equalizing caloric intake relative to output

The best way to maintain a body weight is by balancing caloric intake and output. Extensive dieting (caloric restriction) is not a good option as this would result in weakness. Exercise is part of the output process that helps balance caloric input and output.

86. **Which of the following is the main source of energy in the diet?**
(Easy) (Skill 11.3)

    A.   Vitamins
    B.   Minerals
    C.   Water
    D.   Carbohydrates

Answer D: Carbohydrates

The components of nutrition are carbohydrates, proteins, fats, vitamins, minerals, and water. Carbohydrates are the main source of energy (glucose) in the human diet. Common sources of carbohydrates are fruits, vegetables, grains, dairy products, and legumes.

87. **Which of the following would be likely to influence a student's learning and academic progress?**
(Easy) (Skill 11.4)

    A.   Relocation
    B.   Emotional abuse
    C.   Bullying
    D.   All of the above

Answer D: All of the above

Children can be influenced by social and emotional factors. Relocation, emotional, abuse, and bullying can all have a negative impact on a student's learning and academic progress.

88. **Which of the following is the most likely cause of a child becoming easily agitated in class?**
   (Rigorous) (Skill 11.4)

   A. Lack of sleep
   B. Autism
   C. Emotional abuse
   D. Language difficulties

Answer A: Lack of sleep

Symptoms of a lack of nutrition and sleep most notably include a lack of concentration, particularly in the classroom. Furthermore, children who lack sufficient sleep or nutrition may become agitated more easily than other children.

89. **A student does not respond to any signs of affection and responds to other children by repeating back what they have said. What condition is the student most likely to have?**
   (Average rigor) (Skill 11.4)

   A. Mental retardation
   B. Autism
   C. Giftedness
   D. Hyperactivity

Answer B: Autism

There are six common features of autism. They are: apparent sensory deficit; severe affect isolation; self-stimulation; tantrums and self-injurious behavior (SIB); echolalia; and severe deficits in behavior and self-care skills.

90. **A child with a disability is one who has:**
    (Easy) (Skill 11.4)

    A. Sensory impairments
    B. Emotional disturbance
    C. Mental retardation
    D. Any of the above

Answer D: Any of the above

Special education teachers should be aware that although students across disabilities may demonstrate difficulty in similar ways, the causes may be very different. For example, some disabilities are due to specific sensory impairments (hearing or vision), some due to cognitive ability (mental retardation), and some due to neurological impairment (autism or some learning disabilities). The reason for the difficulty should be a consideration when planning the program of special education intervention.

91. **A teacher is planning to get all of her students involved in sports for the purpose of helping develop hand-eye coordination and teamwork skills. What would be the most appropriate approach when planning the sports activities?**
    (Rigorous) (Skill 11.4)

    A. Encourage competition among students so they become used to the pressure of competing.
    B. Ensure that students who dislike sports continue until they enjoy sports.
    C. Choose activities that are beyond the student's current abilities so students are prompted to improve.
    D. Maintain a relaxed atmosphere and remind students that the sport is designed to be fun.

Answer D: Maintain a relaxed atmosphere and remind students that the sport is designed to be fun.

Sports can be valuable in child development. They can develop motor skills, social skills, and help students develop personal interests. It is important that sporting activities for young children focus on the positive benefits such as the development of motor skills and personal interests, rather than focusing on competition.

92. **Which of the following has been shown to have the greatest impact on a student's academic performance?**
(Easy) (Skill 11.4)

   A.   The teacher's expectations
   B.   Strict discipline
   C.   The student's social skills
   D.   Measurable objectives

Answer A: The teacher's expectations

Considerable research has been done, over several decades, regarding student performance. Time and again, a direct correlation has been demonstrated between the teacher's expectations for a particular student and that student's academic performance. This may be unintended and subtle but the effects are manifest and measurable.

93. **When teaching in a diverse classroom, teachers should:**
(Rigorous) (Skill 11.4)

   A.   Plan, devise, and present material in a multicultural manner
   B.   Research all possible cultures and expose the children to those
   C.   Focus on the curriculum and whatever multicultural opportunities are built into it already
   D.   Utilize single format instruction to present material in a multicultural manner

Answer A: Plan, devise, and present material in a multicultural manner

Curriculum objectives and instructional strategies may be inappropriate and unsuccessful when presented in a single format which relies on the student's understanding and acceptance of the values and common attributes of a specific culture which is not his or her own. Planning, devising and presenting material from a multicultural perspective can enable the teacher in a culturally diverse classroom to ensure that all the students achieve the stated, academic objective.

94. **What are the critical elements of instructional process?**
    (Rigorous) (Skill 11.5)

    A. Content, goals, teacher needs
    B. Means of getting money to regulate instruction
    C. Content, materials, activities, goals, learner needs
    D. Materials, definitions, assignments

Answer C: Content, materials, activities, goals, learner needs.

Goal-setting is a vital component of the instructional process. The setting of goals should take into account the individual learner's needs, background, and stage of development. Making an educational program child-centered involves building on the natural curiosity children bring to school, and asking children what they want to learn. Student-centered classrooms contain not only textbooks, workbooks, and literature but also rely heavily on a variety of audiovisual equipment and computers. There are tape recorders, language masters, filmstrip projectors, and laser disc players to help meet the learning styles of the students. Planning for instructional activities entails identification or selection of the activities the teacher and students will engage in during a period of instruction.

95. **What should a teacher do when students have not responded well to an instructional activity?**
    (Average rigor) (Skill 11.5)

    A. Reevaluate learner needs
    B. Request administrative help
    C. Continue with the activity another day
    D. Assign homework on the concept

Answer A: Reevaluate learner needs

The value of teacher observations cannot be underestimated. It is through the use of observations that the teacher is able to informally assess the needs of the students during instruction. These observations will drive the lesson and determine the direction that the lesson will take based on student activity and behavior.

96. **Mr. Gorman has taught a concept to his class. All of the students have grasped the concept except for Sam. Mr. Gorman should:**
    (Rigorous) (Skill 11.5)

    A. Reteach the concept to the whole class in exactly the same way
    B. Reteach the concept to Sam in exactly the same way
    C. Reteach the concept to Sam in a different way
    D. Reteach the concept to the whole class in a different way

Answer C: Reteach the concept to Sam in a different way

There is always more than one way to approach a problem, an example, a process, fact or event, or any learning situation. Varying approaches for instruction helps to maintain the students' interest in the material and enables the teacher to address the diverse needs of individuals to comprehend the material.

97. **Which strategy for adapting the curriculum would be most useful for the purpose of reducing the effect of a student's learning disability on completing an assessment task?**
    (Rigorous) (Skill 11.5)

    A. Differentiated instruction
    B. Alternative assessments
    C. Testing modifications
    D. Total Physical Response

Answer C: Testing modifications

Testing modifications are changes made to assessments that allow students with disabilities equal opportunity to demonstrate their knowledge and ability on the task.

98. **According to Piaget, during what stage do children learn to manipulate symbols and objects?**
    (Average rigor) (Skill 12.1)

    A. Concrete operations
    B. Pre-operational
    C. Formal operations
    D. Conservative operational

Answer A: Concrete operations

In the pre-operational stage, children begin to understand symbols. In the concrete operations stage, children go one step beyond this and begin to learn to manipulate symbols, objects and other elements.

99. **Which of the following best describes how different areas of development impact each other?**
(Average rigor) *(Skill 12.1)*

    A.   Development in other areas cannot occur until cognitive development is complete.
    B.   Areas of development are inter-related and impact each other.
    C.   Development in each area is independent of development in other areas.
    D.   Development in one area leads to a decline in other areas.

Answer B: Areas of development are inter-related and impact each other.

Child development does not occur in a vacuum. Each element of development impacts other elements of development. For example, as cognitive development progresses, social development often follows. The reason for this is that all areas of development are fairly inter-related.

100. **According to Piaget's theory of human development, which stage would a child be in if they understood abstract terms such as honesty and justice?**
(Rigorous) (Skill 12.1)

    A.   Concrete operations
    B.   Pre-operational
    C.   Formal operations
    D.   Sensory-motor

Answer C: Formal operations

Jean Piaget's theory describes how human minds develop through four stages. The first stage is the sensory-motor stage. This occurs up to age 2 and involves understanding the world via the senses. The second stage is the pre-operational stage. It occurs from ages 2 to 7 and involves understanding symbols. The concrete operations stage occurs from ages 7 to 11 and is where children begin to develop reason. The final stage is the formal operations stage. It involves the development of logical and abstract thinking.

101. According to IDEA, who must be involved in developing a child's IEP? (Average rigor) (Skill 12.5)

    A.   A medical doctor
    B.   The school psychologist
    C.   The parents or guardians
    D.   The principal

Answer C: The parents or guardians

Under the IDEA, parent/guardian involvement in the development of the student's IEP is required and absolutely essential for the advocacy of the disabled student's educational needs. IEPs must be tailored to meet the student's needs, and no one knows those needs better than the parent/guardian and other significant family members.

102. A student who is deaf has an Individual Family Service Plan (IFSP) in place. This legal document is a way of providing: (Average rigor) (Skill 12.5)

    A.   Early intervention
    B.   Help for the family and the child
    C.   Services to deal with the child's disability
    D.   All of the above

Answer D: All of the above

An IFSP is an Individual Family Service Plan and is a legal document. This plan is put in place for young children who have disabilities, such as deafness or other special needs. The focus of the plan is to help the family and the child by providing services, such as family based programs and the services of professionals to deal with the child's disability. The IFSP is a way of providing early intervention under IDEA (Individuals with Disabilities Education Act). It is not only designed to enhance the child's education but it is also designed to help the family facilitate the child's development.

103. **IDEA sets policies that provide for inclusion of students with disabilities. What does inclusion mean?**
(Rigorous) (Skill 12.5)

   A.   Inclusion is the name of the curriculum that must be followed in special education classes.
   B.   Inclusion is the right of students with disabilities to be placed in the regular classroom.
   C.   Inclusion refers to the quality of instruction that is important for student's academic success.
   D.   Inclusion means that students with disabilities should always be placed in special classes.

Answer B: Inclusion is the right of students with disabilities to be placed in the regular classroom.

Inclusion, mainstreaming and least restrictive environment are interrelated policies under the IDEA, with varying degrees of statutory imperatives. Inclusion is defined as the right of students with disabilities to be placed in the regular classroom. Least restrictive environment is the mandate that children be educated to the maximum extent appropriate with their non-disabled peers. Mainstreaming is a policy where disabled students can be placed in the regular classroom, as long as such placement does not interfere with the student's educational plan.

104. **To determine if a child has a disability that may qualify the child for services under IDEA, which of the following pieces of information should the school collect?**
(Average rigor) (Skill 12.5)

   A.   The present levels of academic achievement
   B.   Vision and hearing screening information
   C.   A complete psychological evaluation
   D.   All of the above

Answer D: All of the above

To begin the process of determining if a child has a disability, the teacher will take information about the child's present levels of academic achievement to the appropriate school committee for discussion and consideration. The committee will recommend the next step to be taken. Often subsequent steps may include a complete psychological evaluation along with certain physical examinations such as vision and hearing screening and a complete medical examination by a doctor.

105. What is a good strategy for teaching ethnically diverse students? *(Rigorous) (Skill 13.2)*

    A.   Don't focus on the students' culture
    B.   Expect them to assimilate easily into your classroom
    C.   Imitate their speech patterns
    D.   Use instructional strategies of various formats

Answer D: Use instructional strategies of various formats

When teaching students from multicultural backgrounds, instructional strategies may be inappropriate and unsuccessful when presented in a single format which relies on the student's understanding and acceptance of the values and common attributes of a specific culture which is not his or her own. A good approach for teaching ethnically diverse students is to use instructional strategies of various formats.

106. Which of the following is an example of content which has been differentiated to meet the needs of individual learners? *(Rigorous) (Skill 13.2)*

    A.   Flexible group activities on various levels
    B.   Accepting different final projects from various students
    C.   Research projects based on student's interests
    D.   Individual tutoring by the teacher to address student weaknesses

Answer C: Research projects based on student's interests

Differentiated instruction encompasses several areas: content, process, and product. Differentiating content means that students will have access to content that piques their interest about a topic, with a complexity that provides an appropriate challenge to their intellectual development.

107. **A teacher has a class with several students from low income families in it. What would it be most important for a teacher to consider when planning homework assignments to ensure that all students have equal opportunity for academic success?**
(Rigorous) (Skill 13.2)

   A.   Access to technology
   B.   Ethnicity
   C.   Language difficulties
   D.   Gender

Answer A: Access to technology

Families with higher incomes are able to provide increased opportunities for students. Students from lower income families will need to depend on the resources available from the school system and the community. To ensure that all students have equal opportunity for academic success, teachers should plan assessments so that not having access to technology does not disadvantage students from low income families.

108. **Young children do not concentrate for long periods of time. Generally, young children should be changing academic activities every:**
(Rigorous) (Skill 13.2)

   A.   10-15 minutes
   B.   15-20 minutes
   C.   20-45 minutes
   D.   45 minutes-1 hour

Answer B: 15-20 minutes

Students do not sit still and can not focus on one thing for long periods of time. Good teachers know how to capitalize on the need of children to move and change topics. Generally, young children should be changing academic activities every 15-20 minutes. This means that if a teacher wants to fill a block of two hours for literacy learning in the morning, the teacher should have about 6-8 activities planned.

109. Why is it most important for teachers to ensure that students from different economic backgrounds have access to the resources they need to acquire the academic skills being taught?
(Rigorous) (Skill 13.2)

    A.   All students must work together on set tasks.
    B.   All students must achieve the same results in performance tasks.
    C.   All students must have equal opportunity for academic success.
    D.   All students must be fully included in classroom activities.

Answer C: All students must have equal opportunity for academic success.

The economic backgrounds of students can impact the resources they have. Regardless of the positive or negative impacts on the students' education from outside sources, it is the teacher's responsibility to ensure that all students in the classroom have an equal opportunity for academic success. This includes ensuring that all students have equal access to the resources needed to acquire the skills being taught.

110. What does the Multiple Intelligence Theory developed by Howard Gardner explain?
(Average rigor) (Skill 14.1)

    A.   How the intelligence of students depends on the environment
    B.   How the intelligence of students constantly change
    C.   How students have different levels of overall intelligence
    D.   How students learn in at least seven different ways

Answer D: How students learn in at least seven different ways

Gardner's Multiple Intelligence Theory suggests that students learn in (at least) seven different ways. These include visually/spatially, musically, verbally, logically/mathematically, interpersonally, intrapersonally, and bodily/kinesthetically

111. **What is the most important factor in raising academic outcomes for all students as required in the NCLB law?**
(Rigorous) (Skill 14.1)

    A.   The curriculum model used
    B.   The quality of instruction in the classroom
    C.   The location of the school
    D.   The number of years of experience the teacher has

Answer B: The quality of instruction in the classroom

The NCLB (No Child Left Behind) Act requires states to develop curriculum models demonstrating excellent academic outcomes for all children. The goal of any curriculum model is to provide consistency in instruction and create evaluation criteria for uniformity in programming. Researchers continue to show that most curriculum models produce effective academic outcomes when implemented as designed. However, there are limitations to how effectively the curriculum model is implemented in each classroom. Therefore, the quality of instruction for students by experienced educators will ultimately be what improves the academic outcomes for all students.

112. **Head Start Programs were created in what decade?**
(Rigorous) (Skill 14.1)

    A.   1970's
    B.   1990's
    C.   1980's
    D.   1960's

Answer D: 1960's

Head Start Programs were created in the early 1960's to provide a comprehensive curriculum model for preparation of low-income students for success in school communities.

113. **In the majority of classrooms, the largest amount of floor space is devoted to the organization of student desks. Which of the following is most important in the organization of student desks?**
(Average rigor) (Skill 14.2)

    A.   Desks arranged for proper lighting
    B.   Desks arranged for adequate ventilation
    C.   Desks arranged for student comfort
    D.   Desks arranged for eye contact with each student

Answer D: Desks arranged for eye contact with each student

In the majority of classrooms, the largest amount of floor space is devoted to the organization of student desks. Some teachers like to arrange desks in groups of four, while others utilize a U-shaped arrangement, allowing every student to have a front row seat. The most important thing is that desks are arranged so that eye contact can be made with every student.

114. **What environmental element can cause some students to become restless and hyperactive?**
(Average rigor) (Skill 14.2)

    A.   Bright lights
    B.   The arrangement of student desks
    C.   The proximity of the classroom to the playground
    D.   Comfortable seating

Answer A: Bright lights

Environmental preferences such as lighting, noise level, and room temperature are factors that can affect students in various ways and are often directly related to individual learning styles. A number of students learn best in bright light, but others learn considerably better in low-lighted areas. Bright light can actually cause some students to become restless and hyperactive.

115. Which of the following is a right of parents?
(Easy) (Skill 14.3)

    A.   To be informed of the teacher's concerns about their child
    B.   To require the teacher to use the teaching method that works for the child
    C.   To administer discipline to their child in the classroom
    D.   To attend all classes to support their child

Answer A: To be informed of the teacher's concerns about their child.

It is a parent's right to be involved in their child's education and to be informed of the teacher's reports on his/her progress as well as the teacher's concerns about their child's learning or behavior. Since parents are entrusting the child to the teacher's professional care, they are entitled to know what concerns the teacher about their child during their absence.

116. When addressing issues of concern in a parent-teacher conference, what is it best to focus on?
(Easy) (Skill 14.3)

    A.   Likely explanations
    B.   Personal opinions
    C.   Statements from other students
    D.   Observable behaviors

Answer D: Observable behaviors

When addressing issues of concern in a parent-teacher conference, teachers should focus on observable behaviors and on providing concrete examples.

117. When sending a follow-up note to parents following a conference, which of the following is it best to include?
(Average rigor) (Skill 14.3)

    A.   Further details on the student's strengths and weaknesses
    B.   A summary of the agreed plan of action
    C.   A description of how the student has progressed since the conference
    D.   Praise for the parents on becoming involved in their child's education

Answer B: A summary of the agreed plan of action

A follow-up note to parents should follow around two days after the conference. It should briefly summarize the plan, while ensuring that the note is professional and not chatty.

118. When communicating with parents for whom English is not the primary language you should:
(Average rigor) (Skill 14.3)

    A.   Provide materials whenever possible in their native language
    B.   Use an interpreter
    C.   Provide the same communication as you would to native English speaking parents
    D.   All of the above

Answer D: All of the above.

When communicating with non-English speaking parents, it is important to treat them as you would any other parent and utilize any means necessary to ensure they have the ability to participate in their child's educational process.

119. How should a teacher respond to criticism about her teaching strategies from a parent?
(Rigorous) (Skill 14.3)

    A.   Explain to the parent that negative feedback is hurtful and mean-spirited
    B.   Dismiss the criticism as an attempt to undermine her performance
    C.   Think about the criticism objectively and consider that it might be true
    D.   Change her teaching strategies to eliminate the aspect being criticized

Answer C: Think about the criticism objectively and consider that it might be true.

Any time a teacher receives negative feedback, her reaction should be to think about its validity. This approach would benefit the teacher's skills of self-assessment and awareness of her teaching, as well as being the appropriate professional response to negative feedback. Negative feedback and experiences should always be viewed as opportunities to better one's performance.

120. Teachers and parents should be:
(Easy) (Skill 14.3)

    A.   Enemies
    B.   Friends
    C.   Partners
    D.   Strangers

Answer C: Partners

It is very important that teachers act like they are partners in the children's education and development. Parents know their children best, and it is important to get feedback, information, and advice from them.

121. Which of the following should NOT be a purpose of a parent-teacher conference?
(Average rigor) (Skill 14.3)

    A.   To involve the parent in their child's education
    B.   To establish a friendship with the child's parents
    C.   To resolve a concern about the child's performance
    D.   To inform parents of positive behaviors by the child

Answer B: To establish a friendship with the child's parents.

The purpose of a parent teacher conference is to involve parents in their child's education, address concerns about the child's performance and share positive aspects of the student's learning with the parents. It would be unprofessional to allow the conference to degenerate into a social visit to establish friendships.

122. **Which statement would it be most appropriate to make when speaking to parents about an issue of concern?**
(Rigorous) (Skill 14.3)

   A. Sandra is often distracted easily.
   B. Sandra irritates other students.
   C. Sandra is a frustrating student.
   D. While completing the exam, Sandra started conversations with other students.

Answer D: While completing the exam, Sandra started conversations with other students.

When addressing issues of concern in a parent-teacher conference, teachers should focus on providing concrete examples, while avoiding making judgments. "While completing the exam, Sandra started conversations with other students" is the most appropriate statement to make because it provides concrete information and avoids judging Sandra.

123. **What does portfolio assessment typically provide?**
(Average rigor) (Skill 14.5)

   A. Opportunities for teachers to assess student's progress
   B. Opportunities for students to reflect on their own progress
   C. Opportunities for students to consider their approaches to problem-solving
   D. All of the above

Answer D: All of the above

Portfolio assessment has a number of useful purposes. It provides opportunities for teachers to assess student's progress, opportunities for students to reflect on their own progress, and opportunities for students to consider their approaches to problem-solving.

124. Which of the following is portfolio assessment most likely to encourage?
(Average rigor) (Skill 14.5)

    A.   Self-esteem
    B.   Self-directed learning
    C.   Conflict management skills
    D.   Time management skills

Answer B: Self-directed learning

One of the main advantages of portfolio assessment for students is that it provides them with the opportunity to assess and reflect on their own work. This encourages self-directed learning.

125. Mrs. Peck wants to justify the use of personalized learning communities to her principal. Which of the following reasons would she be best to use?
(Rigorous) (Skill 14.5)

    A.   They are likely to engage students and maintain their interest.
    B.   They provide a supportive environment to address academic and emotional needs.
    C.   They encourage students to work independently.
    D.   They are proactive in their nature.

Answer B: They provide a supportive environment to address academic and emotional needs.

Personalized learning communities provide supportive learning environments that address the academic and emotional needs of students. In personalized learning communities, relationships and connections between students, staff, parents and community members promote lifelong learning for all students. School communities that promote an inclusion of diversity in the classroom, community, curriculum and connections enable students to maximize their academic capabilities and educational opportunities.

SUBAREA I. **LANGUAGE AND LITERACY DEVELOPMENT**

COMPETENCY 1.0 **UNDERSTAND YOUNG CHILDREN'S ORAL LANGUAGE DEVELOPMENT AND HOW TO PROVIDE LEARNING EXPERIENCES THAT SUPPORT AND ENHANCE YOUNG CHILDREN'S LISTENING AND SPEAKING SKILLS**

Skill 1.1 **Recognize characteristics of young children's oral language, factors that influence young children's development of speaking and listening skills, indicators that a young child may be experiencing difficulties in oral language development, and strategies for addressing oral language needs**

Teachers can support the development of listening and speaking skills in several ways:

- **By modeling how language is used to communicate.** Children understand the meanings conveyed through facial expressions, body gestures, and voice tones. They can then learn how to pronounce specific words; make sense of standard rules of grammar; and enlarge their vocabularies.
- **By talking with children.** Children should be encouraged to express their needs, feelings, ideas, stories, and imaginations. Children learn how to be conversation partners by taking turns, staying on the topic, and waiting until the speaker is finished.
- **By reading to children.** This allows children to enjoy spending time with a favorite adult and associate reading with these positive feelings. Children also can begin to make discoveries about the connections between spoken and written words.

In everyday language, we attach affective meanings to words unconsciously; we exercise more conscious control of informative connotations. In the process of language development, the student must come not only to grasp the definitions of words but also to become more conscious of the affective connotations and how his listeners process these connotations. Gaining this conscious control over language makes it possible to use language appropriately in various situations and to evaluate its uses in literature and other forms of communication.

SEE Skill 3.2 for the basic components of language including phonics, phonological awareness, syntax, semantics, morphology and pragmatics.

Factors that Affect Oral Language Development

The development of speaking and listening skills requires an intensive attention to make sure that children acquire a good stock of words, learn to listen attentively, and speak clearly and confidently. In many instances however, students with speech and listening disabilities will experience speaking and listening difficulties.

Some of the most common factors that affect oral language development are:

- *Blindness:* Learners who are blind will not be able to see who is speaking, nor will they be able to see facial expression and body language as an additional means of interpreting what other people are saying.

- *Hearing Impairments/Deafness:* A young child's inability to hear properly can affect his or her ability to learn and develop language. Before they even reach school, children undergo hearing tests, and these tests can help determine a child's ability to hear. Hearing can be impaired for many reasons. They could have been born with a hearing deficiency, have been exposed to dangerously high decibel noise, or have hearing loss resulting from recurring ear infections. Deaf learners who use sign language will only be able to follow discussion by looking at their sign language interpreter. This will inevitably slow down the speed with which they can receive inputs, and also mean that they cannot always focus on the facial expressions of the speaker.

- *Autistic Disorders:* Some learners with autistic disorders may find it very hard to communicate directly with other people. Their disability makes aspects of social communication, for example eye contact, particularly difficult.

Delays in Oral Communication

Speech or language delays in children can be cause for concern or intervention. Understanding the development of language in young children can provide information on delays or differences. The efficiency of language for children develops in a pragmatic manner from the caregivers and social environment that they are exposed to during this crucial time of language acquisition. The focus during this period of development should not be on perceived problems such as a child's ability to pronounce certain vowels or consonants (for example a child's pronunciation of /r/ that sounds like /w/ making the word "right" sound like "white.")

Parents and teachers must understand the difference between developmental speech, word development and language delays/differences that may present potential oral language acquisition. The ability to differentiate between the natural ability of children's language patterns and the delayed development of those patterns should be the educated focus for the adult caregivers that provide environmental stimulus and language experience for children.

The mimic pattern of children developing patterns of language is learned from the vocal experiences of word and sentence usage that they hear on a daily basis. The constant exposure to language provides a virtual Webster's Dictionary of repetitive terms and word meanings that children will acquire and use as their word usage increases exponentially through the developmental years.

Speech intelligibility guidelines provide a tracking of a child's oral speech development. General researchers have shown that the following guidelines are recognizable age/language acquisition:

- Children at 2 years old should have speech patterns that are about 70% intelligible.
- Children at 3 years old should have an increased 10% speech pattern that is about 80% intelligible.
- Children at 4 years old should have a 20% speech pattern that is about 90% intelligible.
- Children at 5 years old should have a speech pattern that is 100% intelligible.
- Children >5 years old will develop speech patterns that continue at 100% intelligibility with increased vocabulary databases.

Given the speech intelligibility guidelines, parents, adult caregivers and teachers are able to track what is normal development versus language developmental delays or differences. If a child is not developing intelligible and recognizable speech patterns at age appropriate development levels, intervention and additional in depth evaluations will provide the proper tools to address and correct language delays that could have long range impacts on a child's final development of speech pattern intelligibility of language.

Teachers and parents who have concerns about a child's language development should be proactive in addressing language delays. Contacting speech pathologists, auditory specialists to test for hearing disorders, pediatricians to test for motor functioning delays, and utilizing other assessment resources for evaluation are effective steps for those concerned about a child's language delays or differences. Early intervention is the key to addressing children's language delays or differences.

Strategies for Addressing Oral Language Needs

Oral language involves both expressive (speaking) and receptive (hearing) language skills. Some students with language impairments will request to have directions repeated, while others may not be self-monitoring enough to recognize their own lack of comprehension. Students with severe oral language disabilities will require extensive support services. However the following strategies may also be utilized:

- Demonstrate or model what you want the student to do, talking through the task while performing it.
- Provide plenty of time for verbal responses to questions
- Have the student sit close to the teacher or in front of the classroom.
- Have the student orally describe visual materials, such as a picture or poster.
- Increase oral fluency by having the student say as many words in a category as he or she can think of within a minute time period.
- Use the student's interests and nonacademic and academic strengths as conversational topics.

Skill 1.2   Demonstrate knowledge of developmentally appropriate strategies for promoting young children's oral communication skills and enhancing their ability to apply these skills in various contexts

Teachers should remain focused on oral language skills throughout the day, even while teaching other subjects. The following activities encourage students to develop oral language skills in the early stages of oral language development.

Activities
Encourage meaningful conversation
Let students "read" a favorite book to you. Ask them why it is their favorite book. Ask questions prompting a purposeful discussion that allows the student to develop and demonstrate their speaking skills.

Allow dramatic playtime
Make sure children have time for "pretend play" to develop. Provide props that associate play to favorite books.

Let children share personal stories
Support their efforts to communicate complex thoughts by waiting patiently, suggesting words as needed, and encouraging their efforts to vocalize new words, while they compare their own experiences with other students.

Sing alphabet songs
Sing the alphabet song in order to teach students to enjoy and identify the different musical sounds of the alphabet.

Teach the art of questioning
Read a book to the students. Allow them to ask curiosity questions (who, what, why, when and where). This encourages the students to develop higher cognitive skills through questions.

Read rhyming books
By listening to a favorite book of rhymes, students can identify the rhyming words and sound them out.

Play listening games
Let students pretend they are talking on the phone to each other. Have them repeat the conversation. This encourages students to hear the words and then repeat them.

Encourage sharing of information
By encouraging each student to share information about an idea, the student is able to vocalize words and thoughts in a logical sequence

In order to stimulate the development of their oral language skills, children should be exposed to a challenging environment that is rich in opportunities.

Skill 1.3 **Demonstrate understanding of strategies for promoting young children's ability to listen and speak for various purposes (e.g., participating in discussions, conveying ideas and information, asking and responding to questions, interacting positively with others)**

Listening is not a skill that is talked about much, except when someone clearly does not listen. The truth is, though, that listening is a very specific skill for very specific circumstances. There are two aspects about listening that warrant attention. The first is comprehension. This is simply understanding what someone says, the purposes behind the message, and the contexts in which it is said. The second is purpose. While someone may completely understand a message, what is the listener supposed to do with it? Just nod and smile? Go out and take action? While listening comprehension is indeed a significant skill in itself that deserves a lot of focus in the classroom (much in the same way that reading comprehension does), we will focus on purpose here. Often, when we understand the purpose of listening in various contexts, comprehension will be much easier. Furthermore, when we know the purpose of listening, we can better adjust our comprehension strategies.

First, when complex or new information is provided to us orally, we must analyze and interpret that information. What is the author's most important point? How do the figures of speech impact meaning? How are conclusions arrived at? Often, making sense of this information can be tough when presented orally—first, because we have no place to go back and review material already stated; second, because oral language is so much less predictable and even than written language. However, when we focus on extracting the meaning, message, and speaker's purpose, rather than just "listen" and wait for things to make sense for us—in other words, when we are more "active" in our listening—we have greater success in interpreting speech.

Second, listening is often done for the purpose of enjoyment. We like to listen to stories; we enjoy poetry; we like radio dramas and theater. Listening to literature can also be a great pleasure. The problem today is that students have not learned to extract great pleasure on a wide-spread scale from listening to literature, poetry, or language read aloud. Perhaps that is because we have not done a good enough job of showing students how listening to literature, for example, can indeed be more interesting than television or video games. In the classrooms of exceptional teachers, we will often find that students are captivated by the reading-aloud of good literature. It is refreshing and enjoyable to just sit and soak in the language, story, and poetry of literature being read aloud. Therefore, we must teach students *how* to listen and enjoy such work. We do this by making it fun and giving many possibilities and alternatives to capture the wide array of interests in each classroom.

Finally, we will discuss listening in large and small group conversation. The difference here is that conversation requires more than just listening. It involves feedback and active involvement. This can be particularly challenging, as in our culture, we are trained to move conversations along, to discourage silence in a conversation, and to always get the last word in. This poses significant problems for the art of listening. In a discussion, for example, when we are instead preparing our next response—rather than listening to what others are saying— we do a large disservice to the entire discussion. Students need to learn how listening carefully to others in discussions actually promotes better responses on the part of subsequent speakers. One way teachers can encourage this in both large and small group discussions is to expect students to respond *directly* to the previous student's comments before moving ahead with their new comments. This will encourage them to pose their new comments in light of the comments that came just before them.

Strategies for Active Listening

Oral speech can be very difficult to follow. First, we have no written record in which to "re-read" things we didn't hear or understand. Second, oral speech can be much less structured and even than written language. Yet, aside from re-reading, many of the skills and strategies that help us in reading comprehension can help us in listening comprehension. For example, as soon as we start listening to something new, we should tap into our prior knowledge in order to attach new information to what we already know. This will not only help us understand the new information more quickly, it will also assist us in remembering the material.

We can also look for transitions between ideas. Sometimes, in oral speech, this is pretty simple when voice tone or body language changes. Of course, we don't have the luxury of looking at paragraphs in oral language, but we do have the animation that comes along with live speech. Human beings have to try very hard to be completely non-expressive in their speech. Listeners should take advantage of this and notice how the speaker changes character and voice in order to signal a transition of ideas.

Speaking of animation of voice and body language, listeners can also better comprehend the underlying intents of authors when they notice nonverbal cues. Simply looking to see expression on the face of a speaker can do more to signal irony, for example, than trying to extract irony from actual words. And often in oral speech, unlike written text, elements like irony are not indicated by the actual words, but rather by the tone and nonverbal cues.

One good way to follow oral speech is to take notes and outline major points. Because oral speech can be more circular (as opposed to linear) than written text, it can be of great assistance to keep track of an author's message. Students can learn this strategy in many ways in the classroom: by taking notes of the teacher's oral messages, as well as other students' presentations and speeches. Other classroom methods can help students learn good listening skills. For example, teachers can have students practice following complex directions. They can also have students orally retell stories—or retell (in writing or in oral speech) oral presentations of stories or other materials. These activities give students direct practice in the very important skills of listening. They provide students with outlets in which they can slowly improve their abilities to comprehend oral language and take decisive action based on oral speech.

Effective Listening

Teachers should relate to students the specific purpose of their reading assignment. This will help them to:

- ASSOCIATE: Relate ideas to each other.
- VISUALIZE: Try to see pictures in your mind as you read.
- CONCENTRATE: Have a specific purpose for reading.
- REPEAT: Keep telling yourself important points and associate details to these points.

Oral language (listening and speaking) involves receiving and understanding messages sent by other people and also to express our own feelings and ideas. Students must learn that listening is a communication process and in order to be successful must be an active process. In other words, they must be an active participant in this communication process. In active listening, meaning and evaluation of a message must take place before a student can respond to the teacher.

Speaking for Various Purposes

Teachers can encourage the development of a child's oral language skills by providing classroom environments filled with language development opportunities. Teachers should understand that each child's language or dialect is worthy of respect as a valid system for communication. It reflects the identities, values, and experiences of the child's family and community. By allowing children to lead to discuss their culture show them that their culture is respected. Teachers should also encourage positive interaction among children within their classroom. Peer learning is an important part of language development, especially in mixed-age groups. Activities involving a wide range of materials should promote talk, such as dramatic play, block-building, book-sharing, or carpentry.

One of the most important things in helping children learn to speak is to have frequent, friendly conversations with them. Treat children as if they are conversationalists. Children learn at a very early age about how conversations work, for example: taking turns, asking questions, looking attentively, using facial expressions, etc. The following strategies can provide students with techniques on how to improve their speaking skills with one another.

Strategies

- Look directly at a person when talking to them.
- Say something once and then wait for the other person to speak.
- If someone doesn't understand you, try to say it in a different way.
- Ask questions to show you are interested in what the other person has to say.
- Be sure you do not do all the talking.
- Say one thing then let the other person take a turn talking..

Young children also should be taught what not to do in a conversation, such as: don't interrupt the other person; don't ramble; don't change the topic abruptly; and don't fail to clarify when you are not understood.

Skill 1.4 Relate oral language development to the development of skills in written language and reading

SEE Skill 2.1 for information on reading development

SEE Skill 5.2 for information on writing development

Almost all children learn the rules of their language at an early age through use, and over time, without formal instruction. The development of oral language is obviously genetic because humans beings are born to speak; and they have an innate gift for figuring out the rules of the language used in their environment. Children seem born not just to speak, but also to interact socially and are equipped with higher order cognitive abilities such as the ability to read and write. As with reading and writing development, language acquisition is not predictable. One child may say her first word at 10 months, another at 20 months. One child may use complex sentences at 5 1/2 years, another at 3 years.

Oral language is the complex system that relates sounds to meanings, and is made up of three components: the phonological, semantic, and syntactic. The **phonological component** involves the rules for combining sounds. Speakers of English, for example, know that an English word can end, but not begin, with an /ng/ sound. We are not aware of our knowledge of these rules, but our ability to understand and pronounce English words demonstrates that we do know a vast number of rules.

The **semantic component** is made up of morphemes, the smallest units of meaning that may be combined with each other to make up words (for example, paper + s are the two morphemes that make up papers). A dictionary contains the semantic component of a language, but also what words (and meanings) are important to the speakers of the language.

The **syntactic component** consists of the rules that enable us to combine morphemes into sentences. As soon as a child uses two morphemes together, as in "more cracker," she is using a syntactic rule about how morphemes are combined to convey meaning. Like the rules making up the other components, syntactic rules become increasingly complex as the child develops.

Young children should have ready access to writing tools with which to express themselves in order to further develop their oral language skills. Books, papers, writing tools, and functional signs should be visible everywhere in the classroom so that children can see and use literacy for reading, writing and oral development.

Some children may need direct instruction in order to master a reading, writing or speech task, and teachers must try to achieve a balance between meaningful activities and developmental practices. If a child fails to make expected progress in a certain oral language skill or if his or her literacy skills are advanced, teachers also need to prepare more individualized instructional strategies to meet the child's needs.

Skill 1.5   Evaluate strategies and activities for promoting young children's oral language competence

Communication is more than words going from one person's mouth to the another person's ear. In addition to the words, messages are transferred by eye contact, physical closeness, the tone of voice, visual cues, and overall body language. Language employs symbols— gestures, visual clues, or spoken sounds—to represent communication between the teacher and the student. Children first learn to respond to messages by listening to and understanding what they hear (supported by overall body language); next, they experiment with expressing themselves through speaking.

As children become proficient in language, they expect straight messages from the teacher. A straight message is one in which words, vocal expression, and body movements are all congruent. Students need to feel secure and safe. If the message is not straight; if the words say one thing but the tone and facial expression say another, the child is confused. When students are confused, they often feel threatened in the school environment.

Evaluating Messages

Analyzing the speech of others is a very good technique for helping students improve their own public speaking abilities. Because in most circumstances, students cannot view themselves as they give speeches and presentations, when they get the opportunity to critique, question, and analyze others' speeches, they begin to learn what works and what doesn't work in effective public speaking. However, a very important word of warning: DO NOT have students critique each others' public speaking skills. It could be very damaging to a student to have his or her peers point out what did not work in a speech. Instead, video is a great tool teachers can use. Any appropriate source of public speaking can be used in the classroom for students to analyze and critique.

Some of the things students can pay attention to include the following:

- Volume: A speaker should use an appropriate volume—not too loud to be annoying, but not too soft to be inaudible.
- Pace: The rate at which words are spoken should be appropriate—not too fast to make the speech non-understandable, but not too slow so as to put listeners to sleep.
- Pronunciation: A speaker should make sure words are spoken clearly. Listeners do not have a text to go back and re-read things they didn't catch.
- Body language: While animated body language can help a speech, too much of it can be distracting. Body language should help convey the message, not detract from it.
- Word choice: The words speakers choose should be consistent with their intended purpose and the audience.
- Visual aids: Visual aids, like body language, should enhance a message. Many visual aids can be distracting, and that detracts from the message.

Overall, instead of telling students to keep these above factors in mind when presenting information orally, having them view speakers who do these things well and poorly will help them know and remember the next time they give a speech.

Activities for promoting oral language

The most basic activity is to let the children practice their oral language skills. So, it's ok if your classroom is noisy at times. There are many activities that encourage the development of oral language. Activities can include the following:

- Using finger puppets for retellings of stories
- Utilizing computer games for stimulating language development
- Writing new verses to existing poems and then reading them aloud
- Singing songs and chants that are fun to say
- Engaging in "word play" activities in which children change beginning, middle, or ending letters of related words, thus changing the words they decode and spell.
- Having discussions that focus on a variety of topics, including problem solving
- Practicing rhyming word families

Skill 1.6　Demonstrate understanding of strategies for integrating young children's instruction in oral language with the other language arts and other content areas

In the past the content of the curriculum has often been divided into separate subjects for science, social studies, art, music, reading, spelling, handwriting, etc., however, this often promotes the fragmentation of knowledge. These various subject matter areas can often be combined into themes or units, with instruction in oral language as a major factor.

Students can have discussions and debates about a subject in the current news that correlates with a Social Studies theme. Students can orally present their reactions to observations about a Science experiment. Teachers may even have students orally explain how they found the answers to certain Math problems. Giving speeches and sharing about personal experiences can also be related to themes and units.

It is important for teachers to evaluate each student's oral language development in the level in which they are at. Often, oral language impediments may show up and will this will allow the teacher to further assist the students with often hidden speaking difficulties.

Read Alouds

Read alouds promote language acquisition and correlates with literacy development, achieving better reading comprehension and overall success in school. Read alouds are a planned oral reading of a print excerpt, or a book, which is usually related to a theme or topic of study. The read alouds can be used to teach the student listener while developing background knowledge, increasing comprehension skills, and fostering critical thinking. Reading aloud to students increases their listening and comprehension skills through discussion before and after the reading.

Planning the read aloud
- Create a positive read aloud atmosphere
- Allow time for students to settle as you make yourself comfortable. Whether you are sitting in a low chair or on the floor, be sure that each child can see the book
- As you read, move the book around so that each student can see the illustrations
- Allow time for the student listeners to think about what they are hearing
- Develop open-ended questions to stimulate your student's imaginations
- Plan related activities to precede or follow the read aloud

Reading aloud effectively
- Set a purpose for listening by sharing the reason you selected the book
- Discuss the title, author and illustrator
- Read with expression; create a mood
- Modulate your voice to reflect emotions and emphasize key points
- Ask the students to imagine what he or she might do in a similar situation

Discuss the story

Through discussion, students can synthesize and extend their understanding of the reading. They can connect their prior knowledge to the new information presented in the reading. After reading the story, ask children to draw pictures of the setting, the main characters, or their favorite parts of the story.

Reading Activities

- *Reading campout:* Set up a tent in the classroom. Students can bring in their pillows and read by flashlight.
- *Pajama party:* Students can wear their slippers. They can bring in a blanket and favorite stuffed animal.
- *Hats off to a "reading" party:* Students create fun hats to wear or wear their favorite hats.

Skill 1.7 **Demonstrate understanding of how having a home language other than standard English influences oral language development and instruction and how to use young children's linguistic and cultural backgrounds to assess and promote listening and speaking skills**

Teachers and caregivers of children developing oral language proficiency can provide effective instructional cultural, linguistic and language development tools that enhance and increase language acquisition. Teachers and parents must remember that language development in children develops in an efficient manner, so the focus should be on allowing the child to create his/her own language scenarios in constructing language repertoires.

Children develop a diversity of language patterns and speech intelligible clarity as they produce foundational basis for language simulation. The act of simulating the sounds and words in their environment provides the child with language enhancement and acquisition. The promotion of language development should include repetition and language engagement. Children can be presented with a question that helps them process object and meaning association such as when pointing to the color blue in the sky "What color is that?" or to the sky, "What is that?"

The concentration for selecting instructional strategies for enhancing children's language development should including the following methodologies:

- Sustenance of the child's natural language development by providing cultural, linguistic and home environments that nurture and support oral language development opportunities.
- Incorporating a diversity of language enrichment activities, technological inclusion, community resources, and individualized engagement.

Additional strategies could include child-centered learning activities that provide different learning opportunities and stimuli for constructive learning. Engaging a child's interest is crucial during the language acquisition years.

Children's toys, games and books can be used to further language development. Providing language simulation activities that model for children how to ask questions or put words into sentences are effective instructional strategies that can provide children with proper guidance through the maze of language acquisition and oral communication.

Providing children with instructional language cues can facilitate learning and language development. Using strategic tools such as rephrasing sentences into questions such as "dada goed" into "Is daddy going?" can provide children with sentence formats and other ways of looking at oral meaning. When children are given labels for objects, they can use word association in developing language acquisition. Personalizing interactions with children during the formative years of oral and language development can become effective tools and strategies to create life long learners.

COMPETENCY 2.0 UNDERSTAND THE FOUNDATIONS OF LITERACY DEVELOPMENT AND HOW TO USE EFFECTIVE, DEVELOPMENTALLY APPROPRIATE STRATEGIES TO PROMOTE YOUNG CHILDREN'S LITERACY DEVELOPMENT

Skill 2.1 Demonstrate knowledge of young children's literacy development, factors that influence young children's development of reading skills, indicators that a young child may be experiencing difficulties in reading, and strategies for addressing reading needs

Learning to Read

In 2000, the National Reading Panel released its now well-known report on teaching children to read. In a way, this report slightly put to rest the debate between phonics and whole-language. It argued, essentially, that word-letter recognition was important, as well as understanding what the text means. The report's "big 5" critical areas of reading instruction are as follows:

- Phonemic Awareness: The acknowledgement of sounds and words. For example, a child's realization that some words rhyme. Onset and rhyme, for example, are skills that might help students learn that the sound of the first letter "b" in the word "bad" can be changed with the sound "d" to make it "dad." The key in phonemic awareness is that when you teach it to children, it can be taught with the students' eyes closed. In other words, it's all about sounds, not about ascribing written letters to sounds.

- Phonics: As opposed to phonemic awareness, the study of phonics must be done with the eyes open. It's the connection between the sounds and letters on a page. In other words, students learning phonics might see the word "bad" and sound each letter out slowly until they recognize that they just said the word.

- Comprehension: Comprehension simply means that the reader can ascribe meaning to text. Even though students may be good with phonics and even know what many words on a page mean, some of them are not good with comprehension because they do not know the strategies that would help them to comprehend. For example, students should know that stories often have structures (beginning, middle, and end). They should also know that when they are reading something and it does not make sense, they will need to employ "fix-up" strategies where they go back into the text they just read and look for clues. Teachers can use many strategies to teach comprehension, including questioning, asking students to paraphrase or summarize, utilizing graphic organizers, and focusing on mental images.

- Content area vocabulary is the specific vocabulary related to the particular concepts of various academic disciplines (social science, science, math, art, etc.). While teachers tend to think of content area vocabulary as something that should just be focused on at the secondary level (middle and high school), even elementary school-aged students studying various subjects will understand concepts better when the vocabulary used to describe them is explicitly explained. But it is true that in the secondary level, where students go to teachers for the various subjects, content area vocabulary becomes more important. Often, educators believe that vocabulary should just be taught in the Language Arts class, not realizing that (a) there is not enough time for students to learn the enormous vocabulary in order to be successful with a standards-based education, and (b) that the teaching of vocabulary, related to a particular subject, is a very good way to help students understand the subject better.

Delays in Reading Development

While we can anticipate that certain skills CAN BE mastered by certain ages, all children are different. But when development is too far off the general target, then intervention may be necessary. By their first year, babies can identify words and notice the social and directive impacts of language. By their second year, children have decent vocabularies, make-believe that they are reading books (especially if their role models read), and they can follow simple oral stories. By their third year, children have more advanced skills in listening and speaking. Within the next few years, children are capable of using longer sentences, retelling parts of stories, counting, and "scribbling" messages. They are capable of learning the basics of phonemic awareness. (See *http://www.learningpt.org/pdfs/literacy/readingbirthtofive.pdf* for more detailed information.)

At about five years old, children are really ready to start in on phonics. Many teachers mistake phonics as being just a step in the process toward comprehension, when in fact, children are fully capable of learning how to comprehend and make meaning at the same age. Phonics, though, ideally will be mastered by second to third grade.

As young students enter and work through the emergent stage of literacy, some common difficulties may be noticed by the teacher. Some of these common problems include:

- Difficulty maintaining concentration
- Finding the appropriate text level
- Frustration with not being able to understand the text
- Limited vocabulary hindering comprehension

Research on reading development has yielded information on the behaviors and habits of good readers vs. poor readers. Some of the characteristics of good readers are:

- They think about the information that they will read in the text, formulate questions that they predict will be answered in the text, and confirm those predictions from the information in the text.

- When faced with unfamiliar words, they attempt to pronounce them using analogies to familiar words.

- Before reading, good readers establish a purpose for reading, select possible text structure, choose a reading strategy, and make predictions about what will be in the reading.

- As they read, good readers continually test and confirm their predictions, go back when something does not make sense, and make new predictions.

Strategies for Assisting with Reading Delays

For students experiencing problems with concentration, make sure their desks are away from distractions and that their overall learning environment is comfortable and well lit. Try to encourage the student to work for set amounts of time, and then as the student's concentration improves, increase the amounts of time.

To help students select appropriate reading material, it is often helpful to organize your classroom library by level. For example, simpler texts may be labeled with a yellow dot, grade-level texts may be labeled with a red dot, and challenging texts may be labeled with a green dot. This helps students see which books may best suit their comfortable reading needs.

When students become frustrated and feel they do not understand the text, encourage students to break down the text into chunks. Then, after each chunk, encourage students to ask themselves questions about what they have read to improve understanding.

Limited vocabulary can often get in the way of a student's comprehension of a text. Have the students focus on the structure of words to help decode unfamiliar words. A helpful tip is for students to record new words in a notebook to create a personal glossary for each student. This way, students can refer to a dictionary with their list of words when necessary to help build their vocabulary.

Additional Strategies

Reading aloud to children helps them acquire information and skills such as the meaning of words, how a book works, a variety of writing styles, information about their world, differences between conversations and written language, and the knowledge of printed letters and words along with the relationship between sound and print. Using different types of books assures that each child will find at least a few books that meet his or her interests and preferences.

Children's storybooks are traditional favorites for many young students. Some children prefer to see books that have informational text such as those about animals, nature, transportation, careers, or travel. Alphabet books, picture dictionaries, and books with diagrams and overlays (such as those about the human body) catch the interest of children as well. Some children particularly enjoy books containing poetry, children's songs and verses, or folktales. Offering different types of books also gives flexibility in choosing one or two languages in which to read a story.

Illustrations for young children should support the meaning of the text and language patterns and predictable text structures should make these texts appealing to young readers. Illustrations can be key supports for emergent and early readers. Teachers should not only use wordless stories (books which tell their narratives through pictures alone), but can also make targeted use of Big Books for read-alouds, so that young children become habituated in the use of illustrations as an important component for constructing meaning. The teacher should model for the child, how to reference an illustration for help in identifying a word in the text the child does not recognize.

The content of the story should relate to the children's interests and experiences as the teacher knows them. Finally, children, particularly the emergent and beginning early readers, benefit from reading books with partners. The partners sit side by side and each one takes turns reading the entire text. Only after all these considerations have been addressed, can the teacher select "just right" books from an already leveled bin or list.

Children with Special Needs

Introducing language and literacy experiences through concrete, multi-sensory approaches will provide many children with disabilities with the supports they need to build the foundation for decoding words and understanding meaning. Having access to early literacy activities as part of the curriculum is key to the educational success of all children, including children with mild to severe disabilities. Each child's unique learning needs should be considered in a comprehensive approach to early literacy.

Skill 2.2 Demonstrate knowledge of the role of phonemic awareness in early reading development; ways to assess phonemic awareness; and effective instructional strategies, activities, and materials for promoting young children's phonemic awareness

Role of Phonemic Awareness

Phonemic awareness is the ability to break down and hear separate and/or different sounds and distinguish between the sounds one hears. These terms are different, yet interdependent. Phonemic awareness is required to begin studying phonics, where students will require the ability to break down words into the smalls units of sound, or phonemes, to later identify syllables, blends, and patterns.

A _phoneme_ is the smallest contrastive unit in a language system, and the representation of a sound. The phoneme has been described as the smallest meaningful psychological unit of sound. The phoneme is said to have mental, physiological, and physical substance: our brains process the sounds; the sounds are produced by the human speech organs; and the sounds are physical entities that can be recorded and measured. Consider the English words "pat" and "sat," which appear to differ only in their initial consonants. This difference, known as contrastiveness or opposition, is adequate to distinguish these words, and therefore the /p/ and /s/ sounds are said to be different phonemes in English. A pair of words, identical except for such a sound, is known as a minimal pair, and the two sounds are separate phonemes.

Assessing Phonemic Awareness

Children who have problems with phonics generally have not acquired or been exposed to phonemic awareness activities usually fostered at home and in preschool-2nd grade. This includes extensive songs, rhymes and read alouds.

Phonemic awareness is the acknowledgement of sounds and words, for example, a child's realization that some words rhyme. Onset and rhyme, for example, are skills that might help students learn that the sound of the first letter "b" in the word "bad" can be changed with the sound "d" to make it "dad." The key in phonemic awareness is that when you teach it to children, it can be taught with the students' eyes closed. In other words, it's all about sounds, not about ascribing written letters to sounds.

To be phonemically aware means that the reader and listener can recognize and manipulate specific sounds in spoken words. Phonemic awareness deals with sounds in words that are spoken. The majority of phonemic awareness tasks, activities, and exercises are ORAL.

Marilyn Jager Adams, who researches early reading, has outlined five basic types of phonemic awareness tasks.

Task 1- Ability to hear rhymes and alliteration.
For example, the children would listen to a poem, rhyming picture book or song and identify the rhyming words heard which the teacher might then record or list on an experiential chart.

Task 2- Ability to do oddity tasks (recognize the member of a set that is different {odd} among the group)
For example, the children would look at the pictures of a blade of grass, a garden and a rose—which starts with a different sound?

Task 3 –The ability to orally blend words and split syllables.
For example, the children can say the first sound of a word and then the rest of the word and put it together as a single word.

Task 4 –The ability to orally segment words.
For example, the ability to count sounds. The children would be asked as a group to count the sounds in "hamburger."

Task 5- The ability to do phonics manipulation tasks.
For example, replace the "r" sound in rose with a "p" sound.

Instructional Strategies

Since the ability to distinguish between individual sounds, or phonemes, within words is a prerequisite to association of sounds with letters and manipulating sounds to blend words (a fancy way of saying "reading"), the teaching of phonemic awareness is crucial to emergent literacy. Children need a strong background in phonemic awareness in order for phonics instruction to be effective. Methods that may be effective for teaching phonemic awareness can include:
- Clapping syllables in words
- Distinguishing between a word and a sound
- Using visual cues and movements to help children understand when the speaker goes from one sound to another
- Incorporating oral segmentation activities which focus on easily distinguished syllables rather than sounds
- Singing familiar songs (e.g. Happy Birthday, Knick Knack Paddy Whack) and replacing key words in it with words with a different ending or middle sound (oral segmentation)
- Dealing children a deck of picture cards and having them sound out the words for the pictures on their cards or calling for a picture by asking for its first and second sound.

Language games that encourage phonological and phonemic awareness will help students understand that language is a series of sounds that form words, and ultimately, sentences.

- *Listening games* will sharpen a student's ability to hear selective sounds.
- *Counting syllables* games help students discover that many words are made of smaller chunks
- *Rhyming games* will draw a student's attention to the sound structure of words
- *Word and sentence building games* help students to understand that language consists of words connect to form sentences.

Structured computer programs can also help teach or reinforce these skills. Daily reading sessions with the students (one-on-one or group) help develop their understanding of print concepts.

Skill 2.3 Demonstrate knowledge of concepts about print (e.g., letter, word, and sentence representation; directionality; tracking of print; understanding that print carries meaning); ways to assess young children's understanding of concepts about print; and effective instructional strategies, activities, and materials for promoting young children's understanding in this area

In order for students to understand concepts of print, they must be able to recognize text and understand the various mechanics that text contains. This includes:

- All text contains a message.
- The English language has a specific structure.
- In order to decode words and read text, students must be able to understand that structure.

The structure of the English language consists of rules of grammar, capitalization and punctuation. For younger children, this means being able to recognize letters and form words. For older children, it means being able to recognize different types of text, such as lists, stories and signs, and knowing the purpose of each one.

Understanding that print carries meaning is demonstrated every day in the elementary classroom as the teacher holds up a selected book to read it aloud to the class. The teachers explicitly and deliberately think aloud about how to hold the book, how to focus the class on looking at its cover, where to start reading, and in what direction to begin. Even in writing the morning message on the board, the teacher targets the children on the placement of the message and its proper place at the top of the board to be followed by additional activities and a schedule for the rest of the day.

When the teacher challenges children to make letter posters of a single letter and the items in the classroom, their home, or their knowledge base which start with that letter, the children are making concrete the understanding that print carries meaning.

Teachers need to look for five basic behaviors in students:

- Do students know how to hold the book?
- Can students match speech to print?
- Do students know the difference between letters and words?
- Do students know that print conveys meaning?
- Can students track print from left to right?

When reading to children teachers point to words as they read them. Illustrations and pictures also contribute to being able to understand the meaning of the text. Therefore, teachers should also discuss illustrations related to the text.

When reading to students, teachers also discuss the common characteristics of books (author, title page, table of contents, etc.) Asking students to predict what the story might be about is a good strategy to help teach students about the cover and its importance to the story. Pocket charts, big books and song charts provide ample opportunity for teachers to point to words as they read.

Instructional Strategies:

1. Using big books in the classroom.

Gather the children around you in a group with the big book placed on a stand. This allows all children to see the words and pictures. As you read point to each word. It is best to use a pointer so that you are not covering any other words or part of the page. When students read from the big book on their own, have them also use the pointer for each word.

When students begin reading from smaller books, have them transfer what they have learned about pointing to the words by using their finger to track the reading. Observation is a key point in assessing students' ability to track words and speech.

2. A classroom rich in print

Having words from a familiar rhyme or poem in a pocket chart lends itself to an activity where the students arrange the words in the correct order and then read the rhyme. This is an instructional strategy that reinforces directionality of print. It also reinforces punctuation, capitalization and matching print to speech.

Using highlighters or sticky tabs to locate upper and lower case letters or specific words can help students isolate words and learn about the structure of language they need to have for reading.

There should be plenty of books in the classroom for children to read on their own or in small groups. As you observe each of these groups, take note of how the child holds the book in addition to how he/she tracks and reads the words.

3. Word Wall

The use of a word wall is a great teaching tool for words in isolation and with writing. Each of the letters of the alphabet is displayed with words under each one that begin with that letter. Students are able to find the letter on the wall and read the words under each one.

4. Sounds of the letters

In addition to teaching the letter names, students should learn the corresponding sound of each letter. This is a key feature of decoding when beginning to read. The use of rhyming words is an effective way to teach letter sounds so that children have a solid background.

Students should be exposed to daily opportunities for viewing and reading texts. Teachers can do this by engaging the students in discussions about books during shared, guided and independent reading times. The teacher should draw the students' attention to the conventions of print and discuss with them the reasons for choosing different books. For example, teachers should let the students know that it is perfectly acceptable to return a book and select another if they think it is too hard for them.

Predictable books help engage the students in reading. Once the students realize what words are repeated in the text, they will eagerly chime in to repeat the words at the appropriate time during the reading. Rereading of texts helps the students learn the words and helps them to read these lines fluently.

Some things for teachers to observe during reading:

- Students' responses during reading conferences, such as pointing to letters or words.
- Ask students where they should begin reading and how they know to stop or pause depending on the punctuation.
- Student behavior when holding a book (e.g., holding the book right side up or upside down, reading from left to right, stopping to look at the pictures to confirm meaning)

Skill 2.4   **Demonstrate knowledge of the alphabetic principle; ways to assess young children's understanding of the alphabetic principle; and instructional strategies, activities, and materials for promoting young children's skills in this area**

The Alphabetic Principle is sometimes called graphophonemic awareness. This multi-syllabic technical reading foundation term details the understanding that written words are composed of patterns of letters which represent the sounds of spoken words.

There are basically two parts to the alphabetic principle:
- An understanding that words are made up of letters and that each of these letters has a specific sound
- The correspondence between sounds and letters leads to phonological reading. This consists of reading regular and irregular words and doing advanced analysis of words.

Since the English language is dependent on the alphabet, being able to recognize and sound out letters is the first step for beginning readers. Relying simply on memorization for recognition of words is just not feasible as a way for children to learn to recognize words. Therefore decoding is essential. The most important goal of beginning reading teachers is to teach students to decode text so that they can read fluently and with understanding.

There are four basic features of the alphabetic principle:
1. Students need to be able to take spoken words apart and blend different sounds together to make new words.
2. Students need to apply letter sounds to all their reading.
3. Teachers need to use a systematic effective program in order to teach children to read.
4. The teaching of the alphabetic principle usually begins in Kindergarten.

It is important to keep in mind that some children already know the letters and sounds before they come to school. Others may catch on to this quite quickly and still others need to have one-on-one instruction in order to learn to read.

Critical skills that students need to learn are:
- Letter sound correspondence
- How to sound out words
- How to decode text to make meaning

Skill 2.5   Demonstrate knowledge of spelling development and its significance for reading; stages of spelling development; ways to assess young children's spelling skills; and effective instructional strategies, activities, and materials for promoting young children's spelling skills

Spelling is of utmost importance in the writing process. At first young children will use invented spelling in which they write the words according to letter sounds. There are several factors that influence the development of spelling, such as:

- Surrounding students with an environment rich in print
- Understanding the developmental stages of spelling
- Understanding that learning to spell is problem solving
- Teaching the rules of spelling
- Promoting an awareness about spelling

Spelling should be taught within the context of meaningful language experiences. Giving a child a list of words to learn to spell and then testing the child on the words every Friday will not aid in the development of spelling. The child must be able to use the words in context and they must have some meaning for the child. The assessment of how well a child can spell or where there are problems also has to be done within a meaningful environment.
The main reasons for assessing spelling are:

- To find out what the child knows about spelling patterns and strategies
- To determine what the teacher needs to teach
- To develop spelling growth over a period of time

In order for spelling assessment to be authentic, it must have meaning for the child. Taking a list of words that a child misspells from a piece of writing is one example of a spelling list that the teacher can use. If the teacher keeps a list of words the children ask to spell, this can also be the basis for a word list.

Since spelling is something that does happen over time, teachers may notice that the child keeps spelling the same words incorrectly again and again. Through explicit teaching of strategies and even tricks to help spell the words, eventually they will see success in spelling. Assessment is something that has to happen over the course of a grade. Correct spelling is not something that children learn and retain automatically.

When assessing spelling, there are behaviors that teachers should look for:

- Knowledge of sounds and symbols
- Development of visual memory
- Development of morphemic knowledge
- Mastery of high frequency words at specific grade levels
- Location and knowledge of how to use spelling resources
- Attempts at spelling unknown words
- Risk taking attempts in using invented spelling

The process of learning to spell

There are five developmental stages in learning to spell:

1) **Pre-phonemic spelling**–Children know that letters stand for a message, but they do not know the relationship between spelling and pronunciation.

2) **Early phonemic spelling**–Children are beginning to understand spelling. They usually write the beginning letter correctly, with the rest consonants or long vowels.

3) **Letter-name spelling**–Some words are consistently spelled correctly. The student is developing a sight vocabulary and a stable understanding of letters as representing sounds. Long vowels are usually used accurately, but silent vowels are omitted. The child spells unknown words by attempting to match the name of the letter to the sound.

4) **Transitional spelling**—This phase is typically entered in late elementary school. Short vowel sounds are mastered and some spelling rules known. The students are developing a sense of which spellings are correct and which are not.

5) **Derivational spelling**—This is usually reached from high school to adulthood. This is the stage at which spelling rules are mastered.

Effective spelling strategies should emphasize these principles:
- knowledge of patterns, sounds, letter-sound association, syllables
- memorizing sight words
- writing those words correctly many times
- writing the words in personal writing

Spelling development, from invented to conventional spelling

There are basically four approaches for teaching spelling. These are the traditional spelling instruction, whole language, developmental, and the structured language approaches.

The **traditional approach** adheres strictly to a phonics based approach to spelling. The student uses invented spelling, using known sounds and skipping others. The teacher sequentially teaches phonics rules and their application to spelling, including those words that don't adhere to the rules. In the traditional approach, the student learns to spell by phonemes and word families. Spelling instruction is direct, systematic, and intensive and is believed to be the best way to insure student success. This approach utilizes the traditional basal speller, rote drill, repeated copying (especially of missed words), and weekly spelling tests.

The **whole language approach** for teaching spelling supports the idea that the student learns to spell by remembering what the word looks like, not by remembering how it sounds. Rebecca Sitton, who has developed a whole spelling series, spearheads this group. Proponents of this group believe student success lies in learning to spell words as they are needed for their personal writing. Students are directed in word wall study, both seeing, chanting, writing, and then using the words in their own personal writing. They are then taught to analyze the structure of words and learn what the base word, prefix, and suffixes look like and mean. Classrooms are print-rich, exposing the student to the sight of many utilitarian words. It is believed that the student best learns spelling by use in their own reading/writing tasks. Though a few words and word structures are taught, children mainly learn as they use the word.

The **developmental approach** suggests several stages of development that students go through in their development from invented spelling to conventional spelling. This approach holds that students should be allowed to just develop without overt instruction, as they will eventually develop to traditional spelling. Different studies have suggested different numbers of stages, but benchmark stages through the continuum are:
- Precommunicative – Random letters – may match beginning sound
- Semiphonetic - One or more letters representing sounds heard, usually without medial vowels
- Phonetic – More letters are included, as are more vowels. They are usually spelled exactly as the child perceives the sounds, i.e. the letter /u might be represented as 'you'
- Transitional- Letters are included for all sounds, words contain the correct number of syllables although some vowels may be misrepresented, i.e. '-er' might be represented as '-ur'
- Conventional- Mostly correct spelling with only errors in difficult spelling patterns

The **structured language approach**, which is considered to have been developed by Samual Orton, involves an in-depth focus on letter/sound relationships and progresses through letters, phonemes, blended syllables, to whole words. There are only 40-plus phonemes used to represent every speech sound made and these are spelled with only 26 letters, so variations have to be learned (as secondary sounds). Orton also identified spelling difficulties with reading difficulties and reasoned that a focus on spelling the 40-plus phonemes would also improve the reading ability of the student.

Each method of teaching spelling has shown documented success. It appears that the key to success is to actively address spelling issues, either in a structured format or based on words needed by individual students.

Some of the techniques teachers use to determine the words students need to spell include:

- Lists of misspelled words from student writing
- Lists of theme words
- Lists of words from the content areas
- Word banks

It is important for beginning writers to know that spelling is an important part of the writing process. However, insisting on correct spelling right from the beginning may actually hamper the efforts of beginning writers. In early spelling development, children should be allowed to experiment with words and use invented spelling. Spelling development is something that occurs over time as a developmental process. It does develop in clearly defined stages, which the teacher should take into consideration when planning lessons. Teachers should assess students' spelling knowledge and then plan mini-lessons to whole class and small groups as they are necessary.

Along with direct teaching of spelling, teachers should model the process at all times. By talking about spelling and having students assist in class writing, they will help students develop the awareness that spelling is important. Some activities where teachers can use this approach include:

- Experience charts
- Writing notes to parents
- Writing class poems and stories
- Editing writing with students
- Writing lists
- Writing daily news in the classroom
- Writing letters
- Writing invitations

Developing visual methods of recognizing correct spelling is also an aid to helping students learn to spell when they can trace around the shape of a word. This helps them develop a visual memory as to whether or not the word looks as if it is spelled correctly. Memory aids (mnemonics) also aid in spelling development, such as in the word PAINT – Pat Added Ink Not Tar.

Students also need to be encouraged to take risks with spelling. Rather than have students constantly asking how words are spelled, the teacher can use "Have a Go" Sheets. These sheets consist of three columns in which the student writes the word as he/she thinks it is spelled. Then the student asks the teacher or another student if it spelled correctly. If it is incorrect, the student will tell the student which letters are in the correct place and the student will try again. After the third try, the teacher can either tell the student how to spell the word and add it to the list of words the student has to learn, or work on the necessary spelling strategy

Other Spelling Activities

Spelling Bee
Have students practice their spelling words before having the actual test.

Newspaper Spelling
Have students find their spelling word in an article in the newspaper. Circle the spelling and then make a list.

Weekly Spelling Story
Post a picture or illustration on the board. Have the students to write a short paragraph or several sentences (depending on the level of ability) to narrate the picture.

Spelling Poems
Have students write a short poem that includes their weekly spelling words

Skill 2.6   **Relate reading development to the development of skills in oral and written language**

Emergent literacy is the concept that young children are emerging into reading and writing with no real ending or beginning point. The approach for many emergent readers focuses on the idea that children develop their ability to construct meaning by sharing books they care about with responsive peers and adults. Some characteristics of emerging readers include 1) the emergent reader can attend to left to right directionality and features of print, 2) an emergent reader can identify some initial sounds and ending sounds in words, 3) the reader can recognize some high frequency words, names, and simple words in context, and 4) pictures can be used to predict meaning. Emergent readers begin to understand that print contains a consistent message.

Methods used to teach these skills are often featured in a "balanced literacy" curriculum that focuses on the use of skills in various instructional contexts. For example, with independent reading, students independently choose books that are at their reading levels; with guided reading, teachers work with small groups of students to help them with their particular reading problems; with whole group reading, the entire class will read the same text, and the teacher will incorporate activities to help students learn phonics, comprehension, fluency, and vocabulary. In addition to these components of balanced literacy, teachers incorporate writing so that students can learn the structures of communicating through text.

The typical variation in literacy backgrounds that children bring to reading can make teaching more difficult. Often a teacher has to choose between focusing on the learning needs of a few students at the expense of the group and focusing on the group at the risk of leaving some students behind academically. This situation is particularly critical for children with gaps in their literacy knowledge.

Research on Reading Development

1. **Experiences with print (through reading and writing) help preschool children develop an understanding of the conventions, purpose, and functions of print.** Children learn about print from a variety of sources and in the process come to realize that print carries the story. They also learn how text is structured visually (i.e., text begins at the top of the page, moves from left to right, and carries over to the next page when it is turned). While knowledge about the conventions of print enables children to understand the physical structure of language, the conceptual knowledge that printed words convey a message also helps children bridge the gap between oral and written language.

2. **Phonological awareness and letter recognition** contribute to initial reading acquisition by helping children develop efficient word recognition strategies (e.g., detecting pronunciations and storing associations in memory.) Phonological awareness and knowledge of print-speech relations play an important role in facilitating reading acquisition. Therefore, phonological awareness instruction should be an integral component of early reading programs. Within the emergent literacy research, viewpoints diverged on whether acquisition of phonological awareness and letter recognition are preconditions of literacy acquisition or whether they develop interdependently with literacy activities such as story reading and writing.

3. **Storybook reading affects children's knowledge about, strategies for, and attitudes towards reading.** Of all the strategies intended to promote growth in literacy acquisition, none is as commonly practiced, nor as strongly supported across the emergent literacy literature as storybook reading. Children in different social and cultural groups have differing degrees of access to storybook reading. For example, it is not unusual for a teacher to have students who have experienced thousands of hours of story reading time, along with other students who have had little or no such exposure.

Design Principles in Emergent Literacy

Conspicuous Strategies
As an instructional priority, conspicuous strategies are a sequence of teaching events and teacher actions used to help students learn new literacy information and relate it to their existing knowledge. Conspicuous strategies can be incorporated in beginning reading instruction to ensure that all learners have basic literacy concepts. For example, during storybook reading teachers can show students how to recognize the fronts and backs of books, locate titles, or look at pictures and predict the story, rather than assume children will learn this through incidental exposure. Similarly, teachers can teach students a strategy for holding a pencil appropriately or checking the form of their letters against an alphabet sheet on their desks or the classroom wall.

Mediated Scaffolding
Mediated scaffolding can be accomplished in a number of ways to meet the needs of students with diverse literacy experiences. To link oral and written language, for example, teachers may use texts that simulate speech by incorporating oral language patterns or children's writing. Or teachers can use daily storybook reading to discuss book-handling skills and directionality-concepts that are particularly important for children who are unfamiliar with printed texts.

Teachers can also use repeated readings to give students multiple exposures to unfamiliar words or extended opportunities to look at books with predictable patterns, as well as provide support by modeling the behaviors associated with reading. Teachers can act as scaffolds during these storybook reading activities by adjusting their demands (e.g., asking increasingly complex questions or encouraging children to take on portions of the reading) or by reading more complex text as students gain knowledge of beginning literacy components.

Strategic Integration

Many children with diverse literacy experiences have difficulty making connections between old and new information. Strategic integration can be applied to help link old and new learning. For example, in the classroom, strategic integration can be accomplished by providing access to literacy materials in classroom writing centers and libraries. Students should also have opportunities to integrate and extend their literacy knowledge by reading aloud, listening to other students read aloud, and listening to tape recordings and videotapes in reading corners.

Primed Background Knowledge

All children bring some level of background knowledge (e.g., how to hold a book, awareness of directionality of print) to beginning reading. Teachers can utilize children's background knowledge to help children link their personal literacy experiences to beginning reading instruction, while also closing the gap between students with rich and students with impoverished literacy experiences. Activities that draw upon background knowledge include incorporating oral language activities (which discriminate between printed letters and words) into daily read-alouds, as well as frequent opportunities to retell stories, look at books with predictable patterns, write messages with invented spellings, and respond to literature through drawing.

Emergent Literacy

Emergent literacy research examines early literacy knowledge and the contexts and conditions that foster that knowledge. Despite differing viewpoints on the relation between emerging literacy skills and reading acquisition, strong support was found in the literature for the important contribution that early childhood exposure to oral and written language makes to the facility with which children learn to read.

Strategies for Promoting Awareness of the Relationship between Spoken and Written Language

- The teacher writes down what the children are saying on a chart.
- Highlight and celebrate the meanings, uses, and print products found in the classroom. These products include: posters, labels, yellow sticky pad notes, labels on shelves and lockers, calendars, rule signs, and directions.
- The intentional reading of big-print and oversized books to teach print conventions such as directionality.
- Practice exercises in reading to others (for K-2) where young children practice how to handle a book, how to turn pages, how to find tops and bottoms of pages, and how to tell the difference between the front and back covers of a book.
- Search and discuss adventures in word awareness and close observation where children are challenged to identify and talk about the length, appearance and boundaries of specific words and the letters which comprise them.
- Have children match oral words to printed words by forming an echo chorus as the teacher reads the story aloud-They echo the reading. Often this works best with poetry or rhymes.
- Have the children combine, manipulate, switch and move letters to change words and spelling patterns.
- Work with letter cards to create messages and respond to the messages that they create.

Methods used to teach these skills are often featured in a "balanced literacy" curriculum that focuses on the use of skills in various instructional contexts. For example, with independent reading, students independently choose and books that are at their reading levels; with guided reading, teachers work with small groups of students to help them with their particular reading problems; with whole group reading, the entire class will read the same text, and the teacher will incorporate activities to help students learn phonics, comprehension, fluency, and vocabulary. In addition to these components of balanced literacy, teachers incorporate writing so that students can learn the structures of communicating through text.

COMPETENCY 3.0 **UNDERSTAND WORD IDENTIFICATION STRATEGIES AND VOCABULARY DEVELOPMENT AND HOW TO USE EFFECTIVE, DEVELOPMENTALLY APPROPRIATE STRATEGIES TO PROMOTE YOUNG CHILDREN'S WORD IDENTIFICATION AND VOCABULARY SKILLS**

Skill 3.1 **Demonstrate knowledge of phonics and its role in decoding; ways to assess young children's phonics skills; and effective instructional strategies, activities, and materials for promoting young children's phonics skills**

Children develop the ability to decode and recognize words automatically. They then can extend their ability to decode to multi-syllabic words. For information on phonemic awareness, **SEE** Skills 2.2 and 3.2

Phonics & Phonological Awareness

Phonics is a widely used method for teaching students to read. This method includes studying the rules and patterns found in language. By age 5 or 6, children can typically begin to use phonics to begin to understand the connections between letters, their patterns, vowel sounds (i.e., short vowels, long vowels) and the collective sounds they all make.

Phonological awareness means the ability of the reader to recognize the sound of spoken language. This recognition includes how these sounds can be blended together, segmented (divided up), and manipulated (switched around). This awareness then leads to phonics, a method for teaching children to read. It helps them "sound out words."

Development of phonological skills may begin during pre-K years. Indeed by the age of 5, a child who has been exposed to rhyme can recognize a rhyme. Such a child can demonstrate phonological awareness by filling in the missing rhyming word in a familiar rhyme or rhymed picture book.

You teach children phonological awareness when you teach them the sounds made by the letters, the sounds made by various combinations of letters and to recognize individual sounds in words.

Phonological awareness skills include:
1. Rhyming and syllabification
2. Blending sounds into words—such as pic-tur-bo-k
3. Identifying the beginning or starting sounds of words and the ending or closing sounds of words
4. Breaking words down into sounds-also called "segmenting" words
5. Recognizing other smaller words in the big word, by removing starting sounds, "hear" to ear

Word analysis (a.k.a. phonics or decoding) is the process readers use to figure out unfamiliar words based on written patterns. Word recognition is the process of automatically determining the pronunciation and some degree of the meaning of an unknown word. In other words, fluent readers recognize most written words easily and correctly, without consciously decoding or breaking them down. These elements of literacy below are skills readers need for word recognition.

Decoding

Decoding refers to students' abilities to sound out a word by translating different letters or groups of letters (graphemes) into sounds (phonemes). If students do not have the ability to hear, identify, and manipulate individual sounds in spoken words and do not understand that spoken words and syllables are made up of sequences of speech sounds, they will have difficulty connecting sounds with letters or groups of letters.

To decode means to change communication signals into messages. Reading comprehension requires that the reader learn the code within which a message is written and be able to decode it to get the message. Encoding involves changing a message into symbols: for example, to encode oral language into writing (spelling) or to encode an idea into words or to encode a mathematical or physical idea into appropriate mathematical symbols.

Although effective reading comprehension requires identifying words automatically (Adams, 1990, Perfetti, 1985), children do not have to be able to identify every single word or know the exact meaning of the every word in a text to understand it. Indeed, Nagy (1988) says that, children can read a book with a high level of comprehension even if they do not fully know as many as 15 percent of the words within a given text.

Decoding text is age appropriate for children who have existing knowledge of the reading material. When children decode words they are able to read single words and understand meaning of single words as singular entities in a textual context. There is a foundational pattern to language acquisition that children must first develop before the complexity of decoding text can begin. Children must be able to learn individual alphabet sounds and understand that each letter has a sound. As students progress from alphabet sound, they can learn about how letters are put together to form words that produce different sounds and meanings.

Tasks for assessing word-analysis and decoding skills can be grouped into three categories:
- comparing sounds
- blending phonemes into words
- segmenting words into phonemes

Procedures for assessing how students compare sounds are the easiest to use. Teachers can ask the student which words begin with the same sound or ask them to find words that rhyme. Teachers need to assess the students' general level of phonemic awareness in order to adjust the instructional time and effort in accordance withy students' prior knowledge and needs.

Teachers can use a list of words and ask the students to read the words. When students have difficulty, the teacher should ask them to try to sound out the word and make note of the strategies used. Another informal assessment is to use cards with letters on them. Ask the students to make the sound of the letter. They can also use cards with nonsense words on them that contain various combinations of consonants and vowels. A checklist of various phonemes is also helpful in recording students needs. These would include such items as:

- identify individual phonemes
- identify patterns of phonemes
- categorize phonemes
- blends
- segmenting words into phonemes
- adding phonemes
- substituting phonemes

The best way to assess students' reading needs is to use decodable texts for informal reading tests. Decodable texts help students develop decoding abilities. Beginning readers are encouraged to sound out words and rely on phonetic cues. Once the strategies are in place, these readers can read short texts easily and quickly.

Teachers should assess for learning early in the school year. They can then make note of which strategies students use and which ones they need to be taught. The teacher can then plan the instruction based on these needs and assess on regular intervals.

Teachers can provides a multitude of opportunities for children to progress from sounding out words orally to decoding words silently. When a child decodes a text that is age appropriate, he or she is able to look at the spelling and pronunciation of specific words that are familiar. _The Cat in the Hat_ book series provides children with story scenarios that are rhythmic and patterned. Crucial to decoding is the child's knowledge of word meaning from prior knowledge and current word usage.

Classroom and social interactions that create child-centered opportunities to question, respond and decode the world around them can create bridges of understanding in decoding simple and complex words and language into smaller understandable chunks of relevant information. Providing children with lessons and activities that require decoding to understand a context of meaning will provide practice for decoding mechanics. For example children who are engaged in a dramatic play must understand the simple phrases that constitute meaning for the parts they portray. Having that incentive to use decoding skills will promote the acquisition of language development.

Skill 3.2 **Demonstrate knowledge of other word identification strategies, including syllabication, morphology (e.g., use of affixes and roots), and context cues (semantic and syntactic); ways to assess young children's use of word identification strategies; and effective instructional strategies, activities, and materials for promoting young children's use of word identification strategies**

Morphology

Morphology is the study of word structure. When readers develop morphemic skills, they are developing an understanding of patterns they see in words. For example, English speakers realize that cat, cats, and caterpillar share some similarities in structure. This understanding helps readers to recognize words at a faster and easier rate, since each word doesn't need individual decoding.

Knowledge of how words are build can help students with basic and more advanced decoding. A *root word* is the primary base of a word. A *prefix* is the affix (a morpheme that attaches to a base word) that is placed at the start of a root word, but can't make a word on its own. Examples of prefixes include re-, pre-, and un-. A *suffix* follows the root word to which it attaches and appears at the end of the word. Examples of suffixes include –s, -es, -ed, -ly, and –tion. In the word unlikely, "un" is a prefix, "like" is the root work, and "ly" is a suffix.

Root words: A root word is a word from which another word is developed. The second word can be said to have its "root" in the first. This structural component nicely lends itself to a tree with roots illustration which can concretize the meaning for students. Students may also want to literally construct root words using cardboard trees and/or actual roots from plants to create word family models. This is a lovely way to help students own their root words.

Base words: A stand-alone linguistic unit which can not be deconstructed or broken down into smaller words. For example, in the word "re-tell," the base word is "tell."

Contractions: These are shortened forms of two words in which a letter or letters have been deleted. These deleted letters have been replaced by an apostrophe.

Prefixes: These are beginning units of meaning which can be added (the vocabulary word for this type of structural adding is "affixed") to a base word or root word. They can not stand alone. They are also sometimes known as "bound morphemes," meaning that they can not stand alone as a base word.

Suffixes: These are ending units of meaning which can be "affixed" or added on to the ends of root or base words. Suffixes transform the original meanings of base and root words. Like prefixes, they are also known as "bound morphemes," because they can not stand alone as words.

Compound words occur when two or more base words are connected to form a new word. The meaning of the new word is in some way connected with that of the base word.

Inflectional endings are types of suffixes that impart a new meaning to the base or root word. These endings change the gender, number, tense, or form of the base or root words. Just like other suffixes, these are also termed "bound morphemes."

Syntax and Semantics

Syntax refers to the rules or patterned relationships that correctly create phrases and sentences from words. When readers develop an understanding of syntax, they begin to understand the structure of how sentences are built, and eventually the beginning of grammar.

Example:
"I am going to the movies"

This statement is syntactically and grammatically correct

Example:
"They am going to the movies"

This statement is syntactically correct since all the words are in their correct place, but it is grammatically incorrect with the use of the word "They" rather than "I."

Semantics refers to the meaning expressed when words are arranged in a specific way. This is where connotation and denotation of words eventually will have a role with readers.

All of these skill sets are important to developing effective word recognition skills, which help emerging readers develop fluency.

Pragmatics

Pragmatics is concerned with the difference between the writer's meaning and the sentence meaning (the literal meaning of the sentence) based on social context. When someone is competent in pragmatics, he or she is able to understand the writer's intended meaning or what the writer is trying to convey. In a simpler sense, pragmatics can be considered the social rules of language.

For example, a child sitting beside her mother at a fancy restaurant after her great-grandmother's funeral looks over to the table next to them. She sees a very elderly woman eating her dessert. "Mom?" she asks, patiently waiting for response. When her mother addresses her, she states loudly, "That woman is old like Grandma. Is she going to die soon too?" Of course embarrassed, the mother hushes her child. However, this is a simple example of immature pragmatics. The child has the vocabulary, the patience to wait her turn, and some knowledge of conversational rules; however, she is not aware that certain topics are socially inappropriate and therefore adapt her language to the situation.

Skill 3.3   Demonstrate knowledge of the role of sight words in reading; ways to assess young children's mastery of common, irregular sight words; and effective instructional strategies, activities, and materials for promoting young children's sight word recognition

Word acquisition for children is directly correlated with environmental stimuli, adult engagement in learning and normal speech and language development. When children at 18-23 months are able to understand functional words that occur in their daily lives such as "eat, sleep, talk, ear nose, mouth," they have begun the ability to associate words with activities or body parts. As children learn how to pronounce words that contain vowels and begin with soft consonants such as n, m, h, speech development occurs.

The clarity of speech during the younger years is more like sound mimics as children review simple words such as "milk or moo." Children who are between the ages of 3-4 have on average 50 words that can be simulated in book reading to differentiate regular word usage from the introduction of irregular words in their vocabulary. During this age range children can be introduced to a diversity of high frequency irregular words that are used intermittently in books and reading resources.

By the age of five years old, children have acquired a database of about 2,000 words and a multitude of expression formations that include the ability to learn irregular words and understand their contextual cues and applications in story formations. Providing children with constant review of new words can create a constant stream of language acquisition for young minds that act as sponges soaking up the presents of words, experiences, and opportunities of speech and language application.

When high frequency irregular words are isolated from the contextual resources and presented to children as activities that require definition, pronunciation, application, and synthesis, children are able to master and internalize the words more thoroughly. Classroom and learning opportunities to have exposure to irregular words are beneficial for children seeking to increase reading, vocabulary and communication skills.

Language and oral development are contingent upon children being provided with a diversity of word applications for use in language development and oral communication. As more irregular words are constantly being added to the dictionary, a child's vocabulary list is becoming inclusive of irregular words that are now becoming today's regular words in communication and written application.

Finally, students need plenty of exposure to the new words. They need to be able to hear and use the new words in many naturally-produced sentences.

A child's ability to recognize high-frequency irregular words through a selection process of choosing words in regular children's books and reviewing difficult words frequently can provide a comprehensive vocabulary listing. When children learn the decoding of regular words in children's books, the foundational learning of decoding strategies can help children recognize and provide phonetic pronunciation to new words.

Skill 3.4 **Demonstrate knowledge of the role of vocabulary development in reading; ways to assess young children's vocabulary development; and effective instructional strategies, activities, and materials for promoting young children's vocabulary development**

Students will be better at comprehension if they have a stronger working vocabulary. Research has shown that students learn more vocabulary when it is presented in context, rather than in vocabulary lists, for example. Furthermore, the more those students get to use particular words in context, the more they will (a) remember each word, and (b) utilize it in the comprehension of sentences that contain the words.

The explicit teaching of word analysis requires that the teacher pre-select words from a given text for vocabulary learning. These words should be chosen based on the storyline and main ideas of the text. The educator may even want to create a story map for a narrative text or develop a graphic organizer for an expository text. Once the story mapping and/or graphic organizing have been done, the educator can compile a list of words which relate to the storyline and/or main ideas. Next, the educator should decide which key words are already well defined in the text. Obviously, these will not need explicit class review.

Identify the words that the child can determine through use of prefixes, suffixes or base words. Again these words will not require direct teaching. Then reflect on the words in relation to the children's background, prior knowledge base and language experiences (including native language/dialect words). Based on the above steps, decide which words need to be taught.

The number of words that require explicit teaching should only be two or three. If the number is higher than that, the children need guided reading and the text needs to be broken down into smaller sections for teaching. When broken down into smaller sections, each text section should only have two to three words which need explicit teaching. Some researchers, including Tierney and Cunningham, believe that a few words should be taught as a means of improving comprehension. It is up to the educator whether the vocabulary selected for teaching needs review before reading, during reading, or after reading.

Introduce vocabulary BEFORE READING if. . .

- Children are having difficulty constructing meaning on their own. Children themselves have previewed the text and indicated words they want to know.
- The teacher has seen that there are words within the text which are definitely keys necessary for reading comprehension
- The text, itself, in the judgment of the teacher, contains difficult concepts for the children to grasp.

Introduce vocabulary DURING READING if . . .

- Children are already doing guided reading.
- The text has words which are crucial to its comprehension and the children will have trouble comprehending it, if they are not helped with the text.

Introduce vocabulary AFTER READING if. . .

- The children themselves have shared words which they found difficult or interesting
- The children need to expand their vocabulary
- The text itself is one that is particularly suited for vocabulary building.

Strategies, which can be used to support word analysis, and as a vehicle for enhancing and enriching reading comprehension, include:

- Use of a graphic organizer such as a word map
- Semantic mapping
- Semantic feature analysis
- Hierarchical and linear arrays
- Preview in context
- Contextual redefinition
- Vocabulary self-collection

The National Reading Panel has put forth the following conclusions about vocabulary instruction.

1. There is a need for direct instruction of vocabulary items required for a specific text.
2. Repetition and multiple exposures to vocabulary items are important. Students should be given items that will be likely to appear in many contexts.
3. Learning in rich contexts is valuable for vocabulary learning. Vocabulary words should be those that the learner will find useful in many contexts. When vocabulary items are derived from content learning materials, the learner will be better equipped to deal with specific reading matter in content areas.
4. Vocabulary tasks should be restructured as necessary. It is important to be certain that students fully understand what is asked of them in the context of reading rather than focusing only on the words to be learned.
5. Vocabulary learning is effective when it entails active engagement in learning tasks.
6. Computer technology can be used effectively to help teach vocabulary.
7. Vocabulary can be acquired through incidental learning. Much of a student's vocabulary will have to be learned in the course of doing things other than explicit vocabulary learning. Repetition, richness of context, and motivation may also add to the efficacy of incidental learning of vocabulary.
8. Dependence on a single vocabulary instruction method will not result in optimal learning. A variety of methods was used effectively with emphasis on multimedia aspects of learning, richness of context in which words are to be learned, and the number of exposures to words that learners receive.

The Panel found that a critical feature of effective classrooms is the instruction of specific words that includes lessons and activities where students apply their vocabulary knowledge and strategies to reading and writing. Included in the activities were discussions where teachers and students talked about words, their features, and strategies for understanding unfamiliar words. There are many methods for directly and explicitly teaching words. In fact, the Panel found twenty-one methods that have been found effective in research projects. Many emphasize the underlying concept of a word and its connections to other words such as semantic mapping and diagrams that use graphics. The keyword method uses words and illustrations that highlight salient features of meaning. Visualizing or drawing a picture either by the student or by the teacher was found to be effective. Many words cannot be learned in this way, of course, so it should be used as only one method among others. Effective classrooms provide multiple ways for students to learn and interact with words. The Panel also found that computer-assisted activities can have a very positive role in the development of vocabulary.

COMPETENCY 4.0 **UNDERSTAND READING COMPREHENSION AND HOW TO USE EFFECTIVE, DEVELOPMENTALLY APPROPRIATE STRATEGIES TO PROMOTE YOUNG CHILDREN'S APPLICATION OF READING COMPREHENSION SKILLS AND ENCOURAGE THEIR INDEPENDENT READING**

Skill 4.1 **Demonstrate understanding of factors affecting reading comprehension (e.g., reading rate and fluency, word recognition, prior knowledge and experiences)**

Accuracy

One way to evaluate reading fluency is to look at student accuracy, and one way to do this is to record running records of students during oral reading. Calculating the reading level lets you know if the book is at the level from which the child can read it independently or comfortably with guidance or if the book is at a level where reading it frustrates the child.

As part of the informal assessment of primary grade reading, it is important to record the child's word insertions, omissions, requests for help, and attempts to get the word. In informal assessment the rate of accuracy can be estimated from the ratio of errors to total words read.

Results of Running Record Informal Assessment can be used for teaching based on Text Accuracy. If a child reads from 95%-100% correct, the child is ready for independent reading. If the child reads from 92% to 97% right, the child is ready for guided reading. Below 92% the child needs a read-aloud or shared reading activity.

Automaticity

Fluency in reading is dependent on automatic word identification, which assists the student in achieving comprehension of the material. Even slight difficulties in word identification can significantly increase the time it takes a student to read material, may require rereading parts or passages of the material and reduces the level of comprehension expected. If the student experiences reading as a constant struggle or an arduous chore then he or she will avoid reading whenever possible and consider it a negative experience when necessary. Obviously, the ability to read for comprehension, and learning in general, will suffer if all aspects of reading fluency are not presented to the student as acquirable skills which will be readily accomplished with the appropriate effort.

Automatic reading involves the development of strong orthographic representations, which allows fast and accurate identification of whole words made up of specific letter patterns. Most young students move easily from the use of alphabetic strategies to the use of orthographic representations which can be accessed automatically. Initially word identification is based on the application of phonic word-accessibility strategies (letter-sound associations). These strategies are in turn based on the development of phonemic awareness, which is necessary to learn how to relate speech to print.

One of the most useful devices for developing automaticity in young students is through the visual pattern provided in the six syllable types.

EXAMPLES OF THE SIX SYLLABLE TYPES

1. **NOT** (CLOSED)
   <u>Closed</u> in by a consonant—vowel makes its **short** sound
2. **NO** (OPEN)
   <u>Ends</u> in a vowel—vowel makes its **long** sound
3. **NOTE** (SILENT "E")
   <u>Ends</u> in vowel consonant "e"--vowel makes its **long** sound
4. **NAIL** (VOWEL COMBINATION)
   <u>Two vowels together</u> make the sound
5. **BIRD** ("R" CONTROLLED)
   <u>Contains</u> a vowel plus 4—vowel sound is changed
6. **TABLE** (CONSONANT "L"-"E")
   <u>Applied</u> at the end of a word

These orthographic (letter) patterns signal vowel pronunciation to the reader. Students must become able to apply their knowledge of these patterns to recognize the syllable types and to see these patterns automatically, and ultimately, to read words as wholes. The move from decoding letter symbols to identify recognizable terms, to automatic word recognition is a substantial move toward fluency. A significant aid for helping students move through this phase was developed by Anna Gillingham when she incorporated the Phonetic Word Cards activity into the Orton-Gillingham lesson plan (Gillingham and Stillman, 1997). This activity involves having the students practice reading words (and some non words) on cards as wholes, beginning with simple syllables and moving systematically through the syllable types to complex syllables and two-syllable words. The words are divided into groups that correspond to the specific sequence of skills being taught.

The student's development of the elements necessary to automaticity continually moves through stages. Another important stage involves the automatic recognition of single graphemes as a critical first step to the development of the letter patterns that make up words or word parts. English orthography is made up of four basic word types:

1. Regular, for reading and spelling (e.g., cat, print
2. Regular, for reading but not for spelling (e.g. float, brain - could be spelled "flote" or "brane," respectively)
3. Rule based (e.g., canning - doubling rule, faking - drop e rule)
4. Irregular (e.g., beauty).

Students must be taught to recognize all four types of words automatically in order to be effective readers. Repeated practice in pattern recognition is often necessary. Practice techniques for student development can include speed drills in which they read lists of isolated words with contrasting vowel sounds that are signaled by the syllable type. For example, several closed syllable and vowel-consonant-"e" words containing the vowel a are arranged randomly on pages containing about 12 lines and read for one minute. Individual goals are established and charts are kept of the number of words read correctly in successive sessions. The same word lists are repeated in sessions until the goal has been achieved for several succeeding sessions. When selecting words for these lists, the use of high-frequency words within a syllable category increases the likelihood of generalization to text reading.

True automaticity should be linked with prosody and anticipation to acquire full fluency. Such things as which syllable is accented and how word structure can be predictive are necessary to true automaticity and essential to complete fluency.

A student, whose reading rate is slow, or halting and inconsistent, is exhibiting a lack of reading fluency. According to an article by Mastropieri, Leinart, & Scruggs (1999), some students have developed accurate word pronunciation skills but read at a slow rate. They have not moved to the phase where decoding is automatic, and their limited fluency may affect performance in the following ways:

1. They read less text than peers and have less time to remember, review, or comprehend the text
2. They expend more cognitive energy than peers trying to identify individual words
3. They may be less able to retain text in their memories and less likely to integrate those segments with other parts of the text

The simplest means of determining a student's reading rate is to have the student read aloud from a prescribed passage which is at the appropriate reading level for age and grade and contains a specified number of words. The passage should not be too familiar for the student (some will try to memorize or "work out" difficult bits ahead of time), and should not contain more words than can be read comfortably and accurately by a normal reader in one or two minutes. Count only the words <u>correctly</u> pronounced on first reading, and divide this word count into elapsed time to determine the student's reading rate. To determine the student's standing and progress, compare this rate with the norm for the class and the average for all students who read fluently at that specific age/grade level.

The following general guidelines can be applied for reading lists of words with a speed drill and a 1-minute timing: 30 correct wpm for first- and second-grade children; 40 correct wpm for third- grade children; 60 correct wpm for mid-third-grade; and 80 wpm for students in fourth grade and higher.

Various techniques are useful with students who have acquired some proficiency in decoding skill but whose levels of skill are lower than their oral language abilities. Such techniques have certain, common features:

1. Students listen to text as they follow along with the book
2. Students follow the print using their fingers as guides
3. Reading materials are used that students would be unable to read independently.

Experts recommend that a beginning reading program should incorporate partner reading, practice reading difficult words prior to reading the text, timings for accuracy and rate, opportunities to hear books read, and opportunities to read to others.

Prosody concerns versification of text and involves such matters as which syllable of a word is accented. It is that aspect which translates reading into the same experience as listening, within the reader's mind. It involves intonation and rhythm through such devices as syllable accent and punctuation.

In their article for *Perspectives* (Winter, 2002), Pamela Hook and Sandra Jones proposed that teachers can begin to develop awareness of the prosodic features of language by introducing a short three-word sentence with each of the three different words underlined for stress (e.g., *He is sick. He is sick. He is sick.*) The teacher can then model the three sentences while discussing the possible meaning for each variation. The students can practice reading them with different stress until they are fluent. These simple three-word sentences can be modified and expanded to include various verbs, pronouns, and tenses. (e.g., *You are sick. I am sick. They are sick.*) This strategy can also be used while increasing the length of phrases and emphasizing the different meanings (e.g., *Get out of bed. Get out of bed. Get out of bed now.*) Teachers can also practice fluency with common phrases that frequently occur in text. Prepositional phrases are good syntactic structures for this type of work (e.g., *on the _____, in the _____, over the _____,etc.*) Teachers can pair these printed phrases to oral intonation patterns that include variations of rate, intensity, and pitch. Students can infer the intended meaning as the teacher presents different prosodic variations of a sentence. For example, when speakers want to stress a concept they often slow their rate of speech and may speak in a louder voice (e.g., *Joshua, get-out-of-bed-NOW!*). Often, the only text marker for this sentence will be the exclamation point (!) but the speaker's intent will affect the manner in which it is delivered.

Practicing oral variations and then mapping the prosodic features onto the text will assist students in making the connection when reading. This strategy can also be used to alert students to the prosodic features present in punctuation marks. In the early stages using the alphabet helps to focus a student on the punctuation marks without having to deal with meaning. The teacher models for the students and then has them practice the combinations using the correct intonation patterns to fit the punctuation mark (e.g., "ABC." "DE?" "FGH!" "IJKL?" or "ABCD!" "EFGHI?" "KL.") Teachers can then move to simple two-word or three-word sentences. The sentences are punctuated with a period, question mark and exclamation point and the differences in meaning that occur with each different punctuation mark (e.g., *Chris hops. Chris hops? Chris hops!*) is discussed. It may help students to point out that the printed words convey the fact that someone named Chris is engaged in the physical activity of hopping, but the intonation patterns get their cue from the punctuation mark. The meaning extracted from an encounter with a punctuation mark is dependent upon a reader's prior experiences or background knowledge in order to project an appropriate intonation pattern onto the printed text. Keeping the text static while changing the punctuation marks helps students to attend to prosodic patterns.

Students who read word-for-word may benefit initially from practicing phrasing with the alphabet rather than words since letters do not tax the meaning system. The letters are grouped, an arc is drawn underneath, and students recite the alphabet in chunks (e.g., ABC DE FGH IJK LM NOP QRS TU VW XYZ). Once students understand the concept of phrasing, it is recommended that teachers help students chunk text into syntactic (noun phrases, verb phrases, prepositional phrases) or meaning units until they are proficient themselves. There are no hard and fast rules for chunking but syntactic units are most commonly used.

For better readers, teachers can mark the phrasal boundaries with slashes for short passages. Eventually, the slashes are used only at the beginning of long passages and then students are asked to continue "phrase reading" even after the marks end. Marking phrases can be done together with students or those on an independent level may divide passages into phrases themselves. Comparisons can be made to clarify reasons for differences in phrasing. Another way to encourage students to focus on phrase meaning and prosody in addition to word identification is to provide tasks that require them to identify or supply a paraphrase of an original statement.

Rate

It is important for students to have a level of high-frequency words that they recognize easily. The ability to recognize many words automatically is an essential element of fluency and the rate at which students read. When students have to spend time trying to decode words, this affects the fluency and the comprehension of the text. When students read slowly, they do not read as much and do not develop a love of reading.

At the emergent and early reading levels, the sentences and texts are short so that word-by-word reading does not interfere with comprehension. As the texts become more complex, students that are not fluent readers will encounter difficulties.

In order to promote fluency and a reading rate similar to the speed at which students speak, teachers should ensure that the reading materials are at the students' instructional level. For students that need help in fluency, teachers can give them home reading texts that they have read in class. The majority of words in the text should be familiar to the student.

Students need to be taught cueing strategies so that they are not reliant on having to sound out every word. One thing that is often difficult for teachers to do is to try not to intervene too often. When teachers automatically tell students what the word is the students can become reliant on receiving help in reading. Most of all fluent reading has to be modeled through read alouds and shared reading.

Teachers can use to help students develop fluency by modeling fluent reading and explaining to students what fluent reading sounds like as opposed to reading word by word.

Strategies that teachers can use to teach students sound-to-letter correspondence include:
- recognizing and producing rhyming words
- modeling the correct pronunciation of words
- orally breaking the words into syllables
- identifying where a sound occurs in a word
- identifying the number of phonemes in a word
- deleting initial, middle and final phonemes from a word
- substituting phonemes in a word

Once students know these strategies teachers can ensure success in reading by making sure that students choose texts at their instructional level for use in independent reading. The Guided Reading model of Fountas and Pinnell has texts leveled according to difficulty. Teachers can assess students' reading abilities and assign a leveled text for students.

Repeated readings of the same text ensure that students recognize the words readily and can read at a normal pace. Some might argue that the students have memorized the text, but this can be easily checked by choosing pages at random for the student to read to you.

Paired reading means that a good reader is paired with a struggling reader to read together. One student can read a page and then the other student can read a page. The struggling reader will then be able to see what fluent reading looks and sounds like.

There should be periods in the Language Arts class where student engage in silent reading. During this time, the teacher can select students and ask them to read aloud quietly from where they are. This will give the teacher information on whether or not the student is reading texts at his/her appropriate level. The silent reading period should start off for short periods of time and lengthen gradually throughout the year. Thus, if students are not reading at home, time is provided for them to do so in school.

Prior Knowledge and Experience

Another factor that can affect a child's reading comprehension is the prior knowledge that they possess and also their reading experiences. Prior knowledge can be explained as a combination of the learner's pre-existing experiences and knowledge:

Knowledge
- Beliefs about themselves as learners/readers
- Knowledge of their individual interests and strengths
- Motivation and their desire to read

Experiences
- Everyday activities that relate to reading
- Events in their lives that provide background understanding
- Family and community experiences that they bring to school with them

SEE also Skill 4.2

Skill 4.2 **Demonstrate understanding of strategies for facilitating comprehension for young children who are at different stages of reading development (e.g., before they learn to read, as they learn to read, as they increase reading proficiency) and for facilitating young children's comprehension before, during, and after reading (e.g., developing background knowledge, prompting young children to make predictions, leading discussions)**

Reading is often thought of as a hierarchy of skills, from processing of individual letters and their associated sounds to word recognition to text-processing competencies. Children learn to read in various stages but the following sequence should be implemented as students are in their various stages of reading comprehension development.

- learn decoding skills
- learn new vocabulary words
- increase word knowledge
- participate in comprehension strategies
- monitor their comprehension

Decoding
Before children can read the words, they have to be aware of the letters and the sounds are represented by letters so that sounding out and blending of sounds can occur to pronounce words. Explicit instruction in sounding out words has been well validated in helping many children in recognizing words easier.

Vocabulary

It is well established that students with good comprehension tend to have good vocabularies. However, this does not mean that teaching vocabulary words will increase a student's overall comprehension skills. It does allow students to have a broader base in which to understand the text while they are reading a story.

Comprehension

Good readers are aware of why they are reading a text, gain an overview of the text before reading, make predictions about the upcoming text, read selectively based on their overview, and can associate ideas in text to what they already know.

Prior Knowledge

Prior knowledge can be defined as all of an individual's prior experiences, learning, and development which precede his/her entering a specific learning situation or attempting to comprehend a specific text. Sometimes prior knowledge can be erroneous or incomplete. Obviously, if there are misconceptions in a child's prior knowledge, these must be corrected so that the child's overall comprehension skills can continue to progress. Prior knowledge, of even kindergarteners includes their accumulated positive and negative experiences both in and out of school.

Experiences might range from wonderful family travels, watching television, visiting museums and libraries, to visiting hospitals, prisons and surviving poverty. Whatever prior knowledge the child brings to the school setting, the independent reading and writing the child does in school immeasurably expands his/her prior knowledge and hence broadens his/her reading comprehension capabilities. Literary response skills are dependent on prior knowledge, schemata and background. Schemata (the plural of schema) are those structures which represent generic concepts stored in our memory. Effective comprehenders of text, whether they are adults or children, use both their schemata and prior knowledge PLUS the ideas from the printed text for reading comprehension, and graphic organizers help organize this information.

Strategies that help children improve their reading comprehension:

- Identifying key elements in a story and summarizing
- Predicting
- Questioning
- Making connections while reading
- Using pictures to help figure out the text
- Reading at the right level
- Writing or journaling

Skill 4.3 **Demonstrate knowledge of the levels of reading comprehension (i.e., literal, inferential, and evaluative); ways to assess young children's ability to comprehend at different levels; effective instructional strategies, activities, and materials for promoting young children's skills in this area**

Inferential Comprehension

In order to draw **inferences** and make **conclusions**, a reader must use prior knowledge and apply it to the current situation. A conclusion or inference is never stated. You must rely on your common sense.

Read the following passage.

> The Smith family waited patiently around carousel number 7 for their luggage to arrive. They were exhausted after their 5-hour trip and were anxious to get to their hotel. After about an hour, they realized that they no longer recognized any of the other passengers' faces. Mrs. Smith asked the person who appeared to be in charge if they were at the right carousel. The man replied, "Yes, this is it, but we finished unloading that baggage almost half an hour ago."

From the man's response we can infer that:
- (A) The Smiths were ready to go to their hotel.
- (B) The Smith's luggage was lost.
- (C) The man had their luggage.
- (D) They were at the wrong carousel.

Since the Smiths were still waiting for their luggage, we know that they were not yet ready to go to their hotel. From the man's response, we know that they were not at the wrong carousel and that he did not have their luggage. Therefore, though not directly stated, it appears that their luggage was lost. Choice (B) is the correct answer.

Conclusions are drawn as a result of a line of reasoning. Inductive reasoning begins with particulars and reasons to a generality. For example: "When I was a child, I bit into a green apple from my grandfather's orchard, and it was sour" (specific fact #1). "I once bought green apples from a roadside vendor, and when I bit into one, it was sour" (specific fact #2). "My grocery store had a sale on green Granny Smith apples last week, and I bought several only to find that they were sour when I bit into one" (specific fact #3). Conclusion: All green apples are sour. While this is an example of inductive reasoning, it is also an example of the weakness of such reasoning. The speaker has not tasted all the green apples in the world, and there very well may be some apples that are green that are not sour.

Deductive reasoning begins with the generalization: "Green apples are sour" and supports that generalization with the specifics.

An inference is drawn from an inductive line of reasoning. The most famous one is "all men are mortal," which is drawn from the observation that everyone a person knows has died or will die and that everyone else concurs in that judgment. It is assumed to be true and for that reason can be used as proof of another conclusion: "Socrates is a man; therefore, he will die."

Sometimes the inference is assumed to be proven when it is not reliably true in all cases, such as "aging brings physical and mental infirmity." Reasoning from that *inference*, many companies will not hire anyone above a certain age. Actually, being old does not necessarily imply physical and/or mental impairment. There are many instances where elderly people have made important contributions that require exceptional ability.

Literal Comprehension:

Main Idea
A **topic** of a paragraph or story is what the paragraph or story is about.

The **main idea** of a paragraph or story states the important idea(s) that the author wants the reader to know about a topic.

The topic and main idea of a paragraph or story are sometimes directly stated.

There are times; however, that the topic and main idea are not directly stated, but simply implied.

Look at this paragraph.

> Henry Ford was an inventor who developed the first affordable automobile. The cars that were being built before Mr. Ford created his Model-T were very expensive. Only rich people could afford to have cars.

The topic of this paragraph is Henry Ford. The main idea is that Henry Ford built the first affordable automobile.

The **topic sentence** indicates what the passage is about. It is the subject of that portion of the narrative. The ability to identify the topic sentence in a passage will enable the student to focus on the concept being discussed and better comprehend the information provided.

You can find the main ideas by looking at the way in which paragraphs are written. A paragraph is a group of sentences about one main idea. Paragraphs usually have two types of sentences: a topic sentence, which contains the main idea, and two or more detail sentences which support, prove, provide more information, explain, or give examples.

You can only tell if you have a detail or topic sentence by comparing the sentences with each other.

Look at this sample paragraph:

> Fall is the best of the four seasons. The leaves change colors to create a beautiful display of golds, reds, and oranges. The air turns crisp and windy. The scent of pumpkin muffins and apple pies fill the air. Finally, Halloween marks the start of the holiday season. Fall is my favorite time of year!

Breakdown of sentences:
Fall is the best of the four seasons. (TOPIC SENTENCE)
The leaves change colors to create a beautiful display of golds, reds, and oranges. (DETAIL)
The air turns crisp and windy. (DETAIL)
The scent of pumpkin muffins and apple pies fill the air. (DETAIL)
Finally, Halloween marks the start of the holiday season. (DETAIL)
Fall is my favorite time of year! (CLOSING SENTENCE – Often a restatement of the topic sentence)

The first sentence introduces the main idea and the other sentences support and give the many uses for the product.

Tips for Finding the Topic Sentence
The topic sentence is usually first, but could be in any position in the paragraph

- A topic is usually more "general" than the other sentences, that is, it talks about many things and looks at the big picture. Sometimes it refers to more that one thing. Plurals and the words "many", "numerous", or "several" often signal a topic sentence

- Detail sentences are usually more "specific" than the topic, that is, they usually talk about one single or small part or side of an idea. Also, the words "for example", "i.e.", "that is", "first", "second", "third", etc., and "finally" often signal a detail
- Most of the detail sentences support, give examples, prove, talk about, or point toward the topic in some way.

How can you be sure that you have a topic sentence? Try this trick: Switch the sentence you think is the topic sentence into a question. If the other sentences seem to "answer" the question, then you've got it.

For example:
Reword the topic sentence "Fall is the best of the four seasons" in one of the following ways:

"Why is fall the best of the four season?"
"Which season is the best season?"
"Is fall the best season of the year?"

Then, as you read the remaining sentences (the ones you didn't pick), you will find that they answer (support) your question.

If you attempt this with a sentence other than the topic sentence, it won't work.

For example:
Suppose you select "Halloween marks the start of the holiday season," and you reword it in the following way:

"Which holiday is the start of the holiday season?"

You will find that the other sentences fail to help you answer (support) your question.

Supporting Details

The **supporting details** are sentences that give more information about the topic and the main idea.

The supporting details in the aforementioned paragraph about Henry Ford would be that he was an inventor and that before he created his Model-T, only rich people could afford cars because they were too expensive.

Interpretive and evaluative comprehension:
In both fiction and non-fiction, authors portray ideas in very subtle ways through their skillful use of language. Style, tone, and point of view are the most basic of ways in which authors do this.

Style is the artful adaptation of language to meet various purposes. For example, authors can modify their word choice, sentence structure, and organization in order to convey certain ideas. For example, an author may write on a topic (the environment, for example) in many different styles. In an academic style, the author would use long, complex sentences, advanced vocabulary, and very structured paragraphing. However, in an informal explanation in a popular magazine, the author may use a conversational tone where simple words and simple sentence structures are utilized.

Assessing Reading Comprehension

There are a variety of methods in which teachers can assess reading comprehension skills. Reading comprehension tests can vary however, these three response formats are especially common: cloze, question-answering, and retellings.

1.) *Cloze* format tests present sentences or passages with blanks in them (e.g., "The fish were swimming in the _____"); the child is expected to read the text and provide an appropriate word to go in the blank

2.) Question-answering format, the child reads passages and answers questions about them; the questions may involve multiple-choice or open-ended items.

3.) Retellings require a child to read a text and then orally tell an examiner about what was just read, usually with some sort of coding system for scoring the quality of the retelling.

Children with comprehension difficulties often performed poorly on tests with questions requiring prior knowledge-based and elaborative answers. However, they are able to answer questions that pertained to specific and literal information.

If possible, teachers should use more than one test to assess reading comprehension performance. An average of scores across two or three tests may give a more accurate indicator of current reading comprehension. But most importantly; teachers should take everyday classroom performance into account. Observations of everyday classroom performance may provide valuable insights into comprehension strengths and weaknesses.

Instructional Strategies for Reading Comprehension

SEE Skill 4.4

Skill 4.4 **Demonstrate knowledge of various comprehension strategies (e.g., previewing, self monitoring, rereading); ways to assess young children's use of comprehension strategies; and effective instructional strategies, activities, and materials for promoting young children's skills in this area**

The point of comprehension instruction is not necessarily to focus just on the text(s) students are using at the very moment of instruction, but rather to help them learn the strategies that they can use independently with any other text. Some of the most common strategies for teaching comprehension are:

- Summarization: This is where, either in writing or verbally, students go over the main point of the text, along with strategically chosen details that highlight the main point. This is not the same as paraphrasing, which is saying the same thing in different words. Teaching students how to summarize is very important as it will help them look for the most critical areas in a text. For example, it will help them distinguish between main arguments and examples. In fiction, it helps students to learn how to focus on the main characters and events and distinguish those from the lesser characters and events.

- Question answering: While this tends to be over-used in many classrooms, it is still a valid method of teaching students to comprehend. As the name implies, students answer questions regarding a text, either out loud, in small groups, or individually on paper. The best questions are those that cause students to have to think about the text (rather than just find an answer within the text).

- Question generating: This is the opposite of question answering, although students can then be asked to answer their own questions or the questions of peer students. In general, we want students to constantly question texts as they read. This is important because it causes students to become more critical readers. To teach students to generate questions helps them to learn the types of questions they can ask, and it gets them thinking about how best to be critical of texts.

- Graphic organizers: Graphic organizers are graphical representations of content within a text. For example, Venn Diagrams can be used to highlight the difference between two characters in a novel or two similar political concepts in a Social Studies textbook. Or, a teacher can use flow-charts with students to talk about the steps in a process (for example, the steps of setting up a science experiment or the chronological events of a story). Semantic organizers are similar in that they graphically display information. The difference, usually, is that semantic organizers focus on words or concepts. For example, a word web can help students make sense of a word by mapping from the central word all the similar and related concepts to that word.

- Text structure: Often in non-fiction, particularly in textbooks, and sometimes in fiction, text structures will give important clues to readers about what to look for. Often, students do not know how to make sense of all the types of headings in a textbook and do not realize that, for example, the side-bar story about a character in history is not the main text on a particular page in the history textbook. Teaching students how to interpret text structures gives them tools in which to tackle other similar texts.

- Monitoring comprehension: Students need to be aware of their comprehension, or lack of it, in particular texts. So, it is important to teach students what to do when suddenly text stops making sense. For example, students can go back and re-read the description of a character. Or, they can go back to the table of contents or the first paragraph of a chapter to see where they are headed.

- Textual marking: This is where students interact with the text as they read. For example, armed with Post-it Notes, students can insert questions or comments regarding specific sentences or paragraphs within the text. This helps students to focus on the importance of the small things, particularly when they are reading larger works (such as novels in high school). It also gives students a reference point on which to go back into the text when they need to review something.

- Discussion: Small group or whole-class discussion stimulates thoughts about texts and gives students a larger picture of the impact of those texts. For example, teachers can strategically encourage students to discuss related concepts to the text. This helps students learn to consider texts within larger societal and social concepts, or teachers can encourage students to provide personal opinions in discussion. By listening to various students' opinions, this will help all students in a class to see the wide range of possible interpretations and thoughts regarding one text.

- Making Predictions: One theory or approach to the teaching of reading that gained currency in the late sixties and the early seventies was the importance of asking inferential and critical thinking questions of the reader which would challenge and engage the children in the text. This approach to reading went beyond the literal level of what was stated in the text to an inferential level of using text clues to make predictions and to a critical level of involving the child in evaluating the text. While asking engaging and thought-provoking questions is still viewed as part of the teaching of reading, it is only viewed currently as a component of the teaching of reading.

Many people mistakenly believe that the terms "research-based" or "research-validated" or "evidence-based" relate mainly to specific programs, such as early reading textbook programs. While research does validate that some of these programs are effective, much research has been conducted regarding the effectiveness of particular instructional strategies. In reading, many of these strategies have been documented in the report from the National Reading Panel (2000). However, just because a strategy has not been validated as effective by research does not necessarily mean that it is not effective with certain students in certain situations. The number of strategies far outweighs researchers' ability to test their effectiveness. Some of the strategies listed above have been validated by rigorous research, while others have been shown consistently to help improve students' reading abilities in localized situations.

More on Graphic Organizers

Graphic organizers solidify in a chart format a visual relationship among various reading and writing ideas including: sequence, timelines, character traits, fact and opinion, main idea and details, differences and likenesses (generally done using a VENN DIAGRAM of interlocking circles, KWL Chart, etc). These charts and formats are essential for providing scaffolding for instruction through activating pertinent prior knowledge.

KWL charts are exceptionally useful for reading comprehension by outlining what they KNOW, what they WANT to know, and what they've LEARNED after reading. Students are asked to activate prior knowledge about a topic and further develop their knowledge about a topic using this organizer. Teachers often opt to display and maintain KWL charts throughout a text to continually record pertinent information about students' reading.

When the teacher first introduces the K-W-L strategy, the children should be allowed sufficient time to brainstorm in response to the first question, what all of them in the class or small group actually know about the topic. The children should have a three-columned K-W-L worksheet template for their journals and there should be a chart to record the responses from class or group discussion. The children can write under each column in their own journal, and should also help the teacher with notations on the chart. This strategy involves the children actually gaining experience in note taking and having a concrete record of new data and information they have gleaned from the passage about the topic.

Depending on the grade level of the participating children, the teacher may also want to channel them into considering categories of information they hope to find out from the expository passage. For instance, they may be reading a book on animals to find out more about the animal's habitats during the winter or about the animal's mating habits.

When children are working on the middle (What I want to know) section of their K-W-L strategy sheet, the teacher may want to give them a chance to share what they would like to learn further about the topic and help them to express it in question format.

K-W-L is useful and can even be introduced as early as grade 2 with extensive teacher discussion support. It not only serves to support the child's comprehension of a particular expository text, but also models for children a format for note taking. Beyond note taking, when the teacher wants to introduce report writing, the K-W-L format provides excellent outlines and question introductions for at least three paragraphs of a report.

Cooper (2004) recommends this strategy for use with thematic units and with reading chapters in required science, social studies, or health text books. In addition to its usefulness with thematic unit study, K-W-L is wonderful for providing the teacher with a concrete format to assess how well children have absorbed pertinent new knowledge within the passage (by looking at the third L section). Ultimately it is hoped that students will learn to use this strategy, not only under explicit teacher direction with templates of K-W-L sheets, but also on their own by informally writing questions they want to find out about in their journals and then going back to their own questions and answering them after the reading.

Connecting Texts
The concept of readiness is generally regarded as a developmentally based phenomenon. Various abilities, whether cognitive, affective, or psychomotor, are perceived to be dependent on the mastery or development of certain prerequisite skills or abilities. Readiness, then, implies that the necessary prior knowledge, experience, and readiness prerequisites should not engage in the new task until first acquiring the necessary readiness foundation.

Readiness for subject area learning is dependent not only on prior knowledge, but also on affective factors such as interest, motivation, and attitude. These factors are often more influential on student learning than the pre-existing cognitive base.

When texts relate to a student's life or other reading materials or areas of study, they become more meaningful and relevant to students' learning. Students enjoy seeing reading material connect to their life, other subject areas and other reading material.

Discussing the Text

Discussion is an activity in which the children (and this activity works well from grades 3-6 and beyond) conclude a particular text. Among the prompts, the teacher-coach might suggest that the children focus on words of interest they encountered in the text. These can also be words that they heard if the text was read aloud. Children can be asked to share something funny or upsetting or unusual about the words they have read. Through this focus on children's response to words as the center of the discussion circle, peers become more interested in word study.

Furthermore, in the current teaching of literacy; reading, writing, thinking, listening, viewing, and discussing, are not viewed as separate activities or components of instruction, but rather as developing and being nurtured simultaneously and interactively.

Students need to be aware of their comprehension, or lack of it, in particular texts. So, it is important to teach students what to do when suddenly text stops making sense. For example, students can go back and re-read the description of a character. Or, they can go back to the table of contents or the first paragraph of a chapter to see where they are headed

Comprehension simply means that the reader can ascribe meaning to text. Even though students may be good with phonics and even know what many words on a page mean, some of them are not good with comprehension because they do not know the strategies that would help them to comprehend. For example, students should know that stories often have structures (beginning, middle, and end). They should also know that when they are reading something and it does not make sense, they will need to employ "fix-up" strategies where they go back into the text they just read and look for clues. Teachers can use many strategies to teach comprehension, including questioning, asking students to paraphrase or summarize, utilizing graphic organizers, and focusing on mental images.

Assessing Use of Comprehension Strategies

Comprehension is the act of placing meaning to the printed words on a page. There are several questions in which teachers can ask to assess student's use of comprehension skills that are being taught.

1.) *Summarization*
Are students able to choose the important idea of the text and give information about the major characters of the story?
2.) *Question and Answer*
Are students able to answer questions regarding a text, either out loud, or on paper?
3.) *Graphic Organizers*
Can students successfully draw a Venn diagram that can be used to highlight the difference between two characters in a novel? Do they understand the use of a KWL chart?
4.) *Discussion*
Are the students able to participate in a meaningful conversation about the storyline, action, and characters in a book?

Teachers should encourage students to become aware of their own comprehension levels in order to gain a better understanding of what comprehensions strategy will benefit them the most.

Skill 4.5   Demonstrate understanding of strategies for promoting young children's ability to locate, organize, and use information from various sources to answer questions, solve problems, and communicate ideas

In writing a report or preparing any written information to address specific topics, the use of reference resources to locate information is crucial for supplying factual data to support a given topic. Information can be obtained from a variety of locations within the media, reference, and technological resources that serve as databases of organized facts and files. In reference books, the table of contents and the glossary contain content chapters that are organized according to specific topic areas. Readers are able to locate specific factual information with page numbers to guide them quickly to the content areas that will provide data to support or refute their topic areas.

The index areas of resources contain more specified factual information that provides a more detailed arena of content support for research. Information that is necessary for research topics must contain a diversity of supported facts and visual support sources to provide the reader with alternative sources to learn about a specific topic. The intermixing of written text and graphic visuals in a report provide means of processing masses of information that is sometimes not as accessible within pages of written text.

The first resource that is commonly used for research is hardcopy and located in public or private libraries, bookstores, internet bookstores in the form of encyclopedias, reference books, or resources books. Libraries carry a diversity of catalog databases that provide an organized system of locating information from apples to zebras. Whether that information in the form of books is available for checkouts can provide a potential problem of accessibility of information resources. The databases located on the Internet are readily accessible for the researcher, since information can be downloaded from the source.

The ability to access technological sources in locating information can provide either major access or major roadblocks in research. Computers are located in libraries, classrooms and computer labs throughout educational communities providing a means of resource for people needing an Internet connection. With any resource, the researcher must be specific in what information is being requested in order to isolate the core from the myriad of kernels that could waste precious research time.

Determining the scope of the research by outlining the topic and subtopics will provide the words and subject matter to research using a diversity of resources. Whether the Internet is used to provide avenues to the topic area or the encyclopedia is accessed to look up that topic, the major resource must provide information quickly and thoroughly. It is easier to read through ten pages of research feedback then it is to look through 200 pages of information that when completed barely provides a page of relevant information. Your resources must be as specific as the information that you are researching.

Evaluating reference sources
In analyzing and assessing a writer's credibility and objectivity when reading a printed text, there are a few straightforward methods, as well as some subtle methods.

First, the straightforward methods include investigating the background of the author, looking for the level of details provided, and examining the extent to which various sides of an issue are presented. Investigating the background of an author is fairly simple when such details are available. If so, students should determine whether or not the writer is an expert in the subject. They might also look to see the types of activities the author has done in order to establish him or herself as an expert.

Looking for the level of details provided is another method to establish the writer's credibility, whether or not a biography is provided. If an author, for example, states a proposition and does not follow it up with significant evidence, perhaps this is a text to avoid. Anyone can offer opinions, but experts are better capable of providing plentiful details as support.

It is likewise important to see that, even if an author is arguing one side of an issue, both sides of an argument are presented. If an author does not provide the other side to his or her argument, it is either possible that he/she does not know the other side (and therefore has not fully thought-out the issue) or he/she does not want the reader to know about the other side, for fear that it will make his/her argument less appealing.

Some more subtle ways of determining whether or not an author has the expertise or is being fair enough to both sides including the analysis of the author's references and investigating the source of the text. If an author has either no references or only a few references, possibly that are very old, the author may not have kept up-to-date on the topic or there is a significant advancement in the field that the author would rather have readers ignore. Finally, investigating the source of the text is crucial. Even though it is acceptable—and even encouraged—to use websites, students need to remember that anyone can post a website. Furthermore, popularized magazines may be less credible than trade or professional journals. While sources from such locations should still be considered, students must realize that their credibility is lessened slightly when published in these forms.

Finally, it is important to emphasize that just because a source argues for one side of an issue does not mean it should not be used. Students simply need to realize what the author is arguing (hence, what the author wants the reader to know about the topic)—and then to use this information as simply one source of many sources on the topic.

Note Taking

Older children take notes in their reading journals, while younger children and those more in need of explicit teacher support contribute their ideas and responses as part of the discussion in class. Their responses are recorded on the experiential chart.

Skill 4.6 Demonstrate knowledge of developmentally appropriate literature for young children, including various authors and genres of young children's literature, and effective instructional strategies and activities for promoting young children's literary response and analysis

Children's literature is a genre of its own and emerged as a distinct and independent form in the second half of the 18th century. *The Visible World in Pictures* by John Amos Comenius, a Czech educator, was one of the first printed works and the first picture book. For the first time, educators acknowledged that children are different from adults in many respects. Modern educators acknowledge that introducing elementary students to a wide range of reading experiences plays an important role in their mental/social/psychological development. Some of the most common forms of literature specifically for children follow:

Traditional Literature: Traditional literature opens up a world where right wins out over wrong, where hard work and perseverance are rewarded, and where helpless victims find vindication—all worthwhile values that children identify with even as early as kindergarten. In traditional literature, children will be introduced to fanciful beings, humans with exaggerated powers, talking animals, and heroes that will inspire them. For younger elementary children, these stories in Big Book format are ideal for providing predictable and repetitive elements that can be grasped by these children.

Folktales/Fairy Tales: Some examples: *The Three Bears, Little Red Riding Hood, Snow White, Sleeping Beauty, Puss-in-Boots, Rapunzel* and *Rumpelstiltskin*. Adventures of animals or humans and the supernatural characterize these stories. The hero is usually on a quest and is aided by other-worldly helpers. More often than not, the story focuses on good and evil and reward and punishment.

Fables: Animals that act like humans are featured in these stories and usually reveal human foibles or sometimes teach a lesson. Example: Aesop's Fables.

Myths: These stories about events from the earliest times, such as the origin of the world, are considered true in their own societies.

Legends: These are similar to myths except that they tend to deal with events that happened more recently. Example: Arthurian legends.

Poem: The only requirement is rhythm. Sub-genres include fixed types of literature such as the sonnet, elegy, ode, pastoral, and villanelle. Unfixed types of literature include blank verse and dramatic monologue.

Tall tales: Examples: Paul Bunyan, John Henry, and Pecos Bill. These are purposely exaggerated accounts of individuals with superhuman strength.

Modern Fantasy: Many of the themes found in these stories are similar to those in traditional literature. The stories start out based in reality, which makes it easier for the reader to suspend disbelief and enter worlds of unreality. Little people live in the walls in *The Borrowers* and time travel is possible in The *Trolley to Yesterday*. Including some fantasy tales in the curriculum helps elementary-grade children develop their senses of imagination. These often appeal to ideals of justice and issues having to do with good and evil; and because children tend to identify with the characters, the message is more likely to be retained.

Science Fiction: Robots, spacecraft, mystery, and civilizations from other ages often appear in these stories. Most presume advances in science on other planets or in a future time. Most children like these stories because of their interest in space and the "what if" aspect of the stories. Examples: *Outer Space and All That Junk* and *A Wrinkle in Time*.

Modern Realistic Fiction: These stories are about real problems that real children face. By finding that their hopes and fears are shared by others, young children can find insight into their own problems. Young readers also tend to experience a broadening of interests as the result of this kind of reading. It's good for them to know that a child can be brave and intelligent and can solve difficult problems.

Historical Fiction: *Rifles for Watie* is an example of this kind of story. Presented in a historically-accurate setting, it's about a young boy (16 years) who serves in the Union army. He experiences great hardship but discovers that his enemy is an admirable human being. It provides a good opportunity to introduce younger children to history in a beneficial way.

Biography: Reading about inventors, explorers, scientists, political and religious leaders, social reformers, artists, sports figures, doctors, teachers, writers, and war heroes help children to see that one person can make a difference. They also open new vistas for children to think about when they choose an occupation to fantasize about.

Informational Books: These are ways to learn more about something you are interested in or something that you know nothing about. Encyclopedias are good resources, of course, but a book like *Polar Wildlife* by Kamini Khanduri shows pictures and facts that will capture the imaginations of young children.

Skill 4.7   Demonstrate knowledge of the importance of independent reading and effective approaches for guiding young children to select independent reading materials and for motivating young children to read independently

Books can be classified at three levels for a student: easy, just right, or challenging. Students should be encouraged to read mostly books that are a "just right" fit for them. Matching young children with "just right" books fosters their reading independently, no matter how young they are. The teacher needs to have an extensive classroom library of books. Books that emergent readers and early readers can be matched with should have fairly large print, appropriate spacing, so that the reader can easily see where word begins and ends, and few words on each page so that the young reader can focus on all important concerns of top-to bottom, left-to-right, directionality, and the one-to-one match of oral to print.

Students should be permitted to read easy books once in a while, but should also receive help in reading challenging books from time to time. In a reading log or journal, have students record titles of books they've read and the level. This way, teachers can monitor that a student is meeting their individual reading needs.

COMPETENCY 5.0   **UNDERSTAND WRITING PROCESSES AND DEVELOPMENTALLY APPROPRIATE STRATEGIES FOR PROMOTING YOUNG CHILDREN'S WRITING COMPETENCE**

Skill 5.1   **Recognize characteristics of young children's writing development, factors that influence young children's development of writing skills (e.g., phonemic awareness, fine-motor skills), indicators that a young child may be experiencing difficulties in written language development, and strategies for addressing written language needs**

For information on phonemic awareness, **SEE** Skill 2.2

Children develop writing skills through a series of steps. The steps and their characteristics are:

- Role Play Writing

In this stage, the child writes in scribbles and assigns a message to the symbols. Even though an adult would not be able to read the writing, the child can read what is written although it may not be the same each time the child reads it. He/She will be able to read back the writing because of prior knowledge that print carries a meaning. The child will also dictate to adults who can write a message or story.

- Experimental Writing

In this stage the child writes in simple forms of language. They usually write with letters according to the way they sound, such as the word "are" may be written as "r". However, the child does display a sense of sentence formation and writes in groups of words with a period at the end. He/She is aware of a correspondence between written words and oral language.

- Early Writing

Children start to use a small range of familiar text forms and sight words in their writing. The topics they choose for writing are ones that have some importance for them, such as their family, friends or pets. Because they are used to hearing stories, they do have a sense of how a story sounds and begin to write simple narratives. They learn that they do have to correct their writing so that others can easily read it.

- <u>Conventional Writing</u>

By the time students reach this stage of writing, they have a sense of audience and purpose for writing. They are able to proofread their writing and edit it for mistakes. They have gained the ability to transfer between reading and writing so that they can get ideas for writing from what they read. By this time students also have a sense of what correct spelling and grammar look like and they can change the order of events in the writing so that it makes sense for the reader.

- <u>Proficient Writing</u>

This is the final stage of writing in which the students have developed through the stages of the writing process and can easily work through the drafting, revising and editing stages. They are able to look for precise words to express meaning and use a variety of sentence structures. They are able to adopt different points of view and are able to fully develop a topic.

However all children do not progress through these steps at the same pace. Some are able to progress faster than others, which is why there is always a discrepancy in the level of writing competence in any one class. Some students need more instruction than others and may even need one-on-one intervention to help them make very little progress.

It is generally accepted that early writers are found in the primary grades with some students progressing to the conventional writing stage. However, it is quite possible to find students in late elementary still in the conventional stage as proficient writing is usually found in high school. No matter how much instruction a teacher provides in any one year, it seems that the teacher will have to go over the stages of the writing process at the beginning of every year and keep re-teaching it throughout the school year.

Detecting Difficulties in Learning to Write

Writing problems rarely occur in isolation, and are often are connected with the development of other non-writing-specific skills. Therefore, a problem with the development in one of these areas is likely to interfere with a child's progress as a writer. Listed below are some of the more common reasons why young students may experience difficulty with their writing skills.

Spatial Ordering Problem

Children who struggle with spatial ordering have decreased awareness regarding the spatial arrangement of letters, words, or sentences on a page. A spatial ordering problem may manifest itself in a child's writing as:

- poor use of lines on the paper
- organizational problems
- uneven spacing between letters

Language Problem

Good writing relies on a child's language abilities improving steadily over time. A language problem may manifest itself in a child's writing as:

- poor vocabulary
- difficulty with sentence structure and word order
- difficulty with word sounds, spelling, and meanings

Graphomotor Problem

Children with graphomotor problems struggle to coordinate the small muscles of the fingers in order to maneuver a pen or pencil, especially as assignment length increases. A child with a graphomotor problem might:

- write only very short passages
- write exceptionally slowly and with great effort
- use an awkward pencil grip

How to Work with Students with Writing Difficulties

When a teacher suspects a writing problem, a parent-teacher meeting should be scheduled to share information about the child. The following strategies may be implemented:

I.) Share observations of the child's writing profile and discuss where the difficulty is occurring.
Does the child have difficulty with a writing sub skill, such as letter formation, mechanics, or generating ideas? Do difficulties in graphomotor ability, language, or spatial ordering seem to affect the child's writing?

2.) Identify and discuss the child's strengths and interests.
What can be done to enhance his or her writing skills and motivation to complete written assignments?

3.) Talk with the children about their strengths and weaknesses.
Help children find their strengths, by emphasizing optimism. Help children realize that they can improve -- they can work on their weaknesses and make their strengths stronger.

Teachers need to create a safe environment for writing. They should evaluate content and mechanics separately. Teachers should encourage a variety of writing activities and also provide extra time for revision and proofreading.

Skill 5.2   Identify strategies for helping young children develop and apply skills for communicating through writing (e.g., writing in various formats and for various purposes, applying conventions of standard English, using effective writing processes)

There is no one specific method for teaching the writing process. Beginning teachers need to understand that this is a process that takes students a long time to master and that they need to continually model the steps in the writing process for the students. The prewriting stage is one that students prefer to skip and therefore is one that teachers need to constantly remind the students about. At first this part of the process will be teacher guided using such methodologies as helping the students discover what they want to say about a specific topic. Some of the ways students can become used to using this step before they start their actual draft include:

- Brainstorming
- Discussing
- Webbing
- Interviewing
- Surveying
- Listening
- Reading
- Writing jot notes
- Charting
- Mapping
- Outlining

Free writing is another way students can get their ideas down on paper before they start to refine their thoughts.

The Writing Process

Prewriting strategies assist students in a variety of ways. Listed below are the most common prewriting strategies students can use to explore, plan and write on a topic. It is important to remember when teaching these strategies that not all prewriting must eventually produce a finished piece of writing. In fact, in the initial lesson of teaching prewriting strategies, it might be more effective to have students practice prewriting strategies without the pressure of having to write a finished product. Here are some suggested prewriting strategies:

- Keep an idea book so that they can jot down ideas that come to mind.
- Write in a daily journal.
- Write down whatever comes to mind; this is called "free writing." Students do not stop to make corrections or interrupt the flow of ideas.

A variation of this technique is focused free writing - writing on a specific topic - to prepare for an essay.

- Make a list of all ideas connected with their topic; this is called brainstorming
- Make sure students know that this technique works best when they let their mind work freely. After completing the list, students should analyze the list to see if a pattern or way to group the ideas emerges.
- Ask the questions Who? What? When? Where? When? and How? Help the writer approach a topic from several perspectives.
- Create a visual map on paper to gather ideas. Cluster circles and lines to show connections between ideas. Students should try to identify the relationship that exists between their ideas. If they cannot see the relationships, have them pair up, exchange papers and have their partners look for some related ideas.
- Observe details of sight, hearing, taste, touch, and taste.
- Visualize by making mental images of something and write down the details in a list.

After they have practiced with each of these prewriting strategies, ask them to pick out the ones they prefer and ask them to discuss how they might use the techniques to help them with future writing assignments. It is important to remember that they can use more than one prewriting strategy at a time. Also they may find that different writing situations may suggest certain techniques.

When teaching the drafting process, teachers should encourage the students to skip lines. This allows them space for revising and editing when they get to this stage. Quite often students will ask how to spell words when they are writing their first draft. In this process, since spelling is not as important as it is in later stages, teachers often tell them to write the words the way they think they are spelled. There will be plenty of time to make corrections later.

Revising and editing are the hardest stages of the writing process to teach. Exemplars provide the students with examples of what good and poor writing looks like. When students have a chance to study the exemplars and discuss the merits of each they have an idea of the improvements they need to make in their writing. In revising, students should read the writing out loud, either to themselves or to another student to pick up on what parts make sense and what parts need additions or deletions. Author's chair is a way of encouraging students to provide comments on writing, but they do need to be encouraged not to make disparaging remarks and to only provide constructive criticism.

Editing is a time consuming task and it would be unreasonable to expect students to pick up on all the mistakes in a piece of writing. Therefore, teachers should ask students to edit for specific purposes at one time, such as correct spelling, capitalization or punctuation. The easiest way to pick up on incorrect spelling is to read the writing backwards. This way the students are focusing on each word rather than the meaning of the piece. The use of a word processor helps students in finding words that are not spelled correctly.

Publication means getting the writing ready for others to read. For many students it means illustrating the work, creating an attractive cover or even using a word processor to produce the final draft.

Common English Conventions

Sentence completeness
Avoid fragments and run-on sentences

Subject-verb agreement
A verb agrees in number with its subject. Making them agree relies on the ability to properly identify the subject.

> One of the boys *was playing* too rough.

> <u>No one</u> in the class, not the teacher nor the students, <u>was listening</u> to the message from the intercom.

> The <u>candidates,</u> including a grandmother and a teenager, <u>are debating</u> some controversial issues.

If two singular subjects are connected by *and* the verb must be plural.

> A *man* and his *dog* were jogging on the beach.

If two singular subjects are connected by *or* or *nor,* a singular verb is required.

> Neither Dot nor <u>Joyce</u> has missed a day of school
> this year.

If one singular subject and one plural subject are connected by *or* or *nor,* the verb agrees with the subject nearest to the verb.

> Neither the coach nor the <u>players</u> were able to sleep on the bus.

If the subject is a collective noun, its sense of number in the sentence determines the verb: singular if the noun represents a group or unit and plural if the noun represents individuals.

> The <u>House of Representatives</u> <u>has adjourned</u> for the holidays.

> The <u>House of Representatives</u> <u>have failed</u> to reach agreement on the subject of adjournment.

Students should proofread the draft for punctuation and mechanical errors. There are a few key points to remember when helping students learn to edit and proofread their work.

- It is crucial that students are not taught grammar in isolation, but in context of the writing process.
- Ask students to read their writing and check for specific errors like using a subordinate clause as a sentence.
- Provide students with a proofreading checklist to guide them as they edit their work.

Spelling
Concentration in this section will be on spelling plurals and possessives. The multiplicity and complexity of spelling rules based on phonics, letter doubling, and exceptions to rules - not mastered by adulthood - should be replaced by a good dictionary. As spelling mastery is also difficult for adolescents, our recommendation is the same. Learning the use of a dictionary and thesaurus will be a more rewarding use of time.

Most plurals of nouns that end in hard consonants or hard consonant sounds followed by a silent e are made by adding s. Some words ending in vowels only add s.

> fingers, numerals, banks, bugs, riots, homes, gates, radios, bananas

Nouns that end in soft consonant sounds s, j, x, z, ch, and sh, add es. Some nouns ending in o add es.

dresses, waxes, churches, brushes, tomatoes, potatoes

Nouns ending in y preceded by a vowel just add s.

boys, alleys

Nouns ending in y preceded by a consonant change the y to i and add es.

babies, corollaries, frugalities, poppies

Some nouns plurals are formed irregularly or remain the same.

sheep, deer, children, leaves, oxen

Capitalization

Capitalize all proper names of persons (including specific organizations or agencies of government); places (countries, states, cities, parks, and specific geographical areas); and things (political parties, structures, historical and cultural terms, and calendar and time designations); and religious terms (any deity, revered person or group, sacred writings).

Percy Bysshe Shelley, Argentina, Mount Rainier National Park, Grand Canyon, League of Nations, the Sears Tower, Birmingham, Lyric Theater, Americans, Midwesterners, Democrats, Renaissance, Boy Scouts of America, Easter, God, Bible, Dead Sea Scrolls, Koran

Capitalize proper adjectives and titles used with proper names.

California gold rush, President John Adams, French fries, Homeric epic, Romanesque architecture, Senator John Glenn

Note: Some words that represent titles and offices are not capitalized unless used with a proper name.

Capitalized	Not Capitalized
Congressman McKay	the congressman from Florida
Commander Alger	commander of the Pacific Fleet
Queen Elizabeth	the queen of England

Capitalize all main words in titles of works of literature, art, and music. The candidate should be cognizant of proper rules and conventions of punctuation, capitalization, and spelling. Competency exams will generally test the ability to apply the more advanced skills; thus, a limited number of more frustrating rules is presented here. Rules should be applied according to the American style of English, i.e. spelling theater instead of theatre and placing terminal marks of punctuation almost exclusively within other marks of punctuation.

Writing for Various Purposes

Persuasion is a piece of writing, a poem, a play, a speech whose purpose is to change the minds of the audience members or to get them to do something. This is achieved in many ways: (1) The credibility of the writer/speaker might lead the listeners/readers to a change of mind or a recommended action. (2) Reasoning is important in persuasive discourse. No one wants to believe that he accepts a new viewpoint or goes out and takes action just because he likes and trusts the person who recommended it. Logic comes into play in reasoning that is persuasive. (3) The third and most powerful force that leads to acceptance or action is emotional appeal. Even if a person has been persuaded logically, reasonably, that he should believe in a different way, he is unlikely to act on it unless he is moved emotionally. A man with resources might be convinced that people suffered in New Orleans after Katrina, but he will not be likely to do anything about it until he is moved emotionally, until he can see elderly people stranded on houses. Sermons are good examples of persuasive discourse.

Exposition is discourse whose only purpose is to inform. Expository writing is not interested in changing anyone's mind or getting anyone to take a certain action. It exists to give information. Some examples are driving directions to a particular place or the directions for putting together a toy that arrives unassembled. The writer doesn't care whether you do or don't follow the directions. She only wants to be sure you have the information in case you do decide to use them.

Narration is discourse that is arranged chronologically—something happened, and then something else happened, and then something else happened. It is also called a story. News reports are often narrative in nature as are records of trips, etc.

Description is discourse whose purpose is to make an experience available through one of the five senses—seeing, smelling, hearing, feeling (as with the fingers), and tasting. Descriptive words are used to make it possible for the reader to "see" with her own mind's eye, hear through her own mind's ear, smell through her own mind's nose, taste with her mind's tongue, and feel with her mind's fingers. This is how language moves people. Only by experiencing an event can the emotions become involved. Poets are experts in descriptive language.

In the past, teachers have assigned reports, paragraphs and essays that focused on the teacher as the audience with the purpose of explaining information. However, for students to be meaningfully engaged in their writing, they must write for a variety of reasons. Writing for different audiences and aims allows students to be more involved in their writing. If they write for the same audience and purpose, they will continue to see writing as just another assignment. Listed below are suggestions that give students an opportunity to write in more creative and critical ways.

- Write letters to the editor, to a college, to a friend, to another student that would be sent to the intended audience.
- Write stories that would be read aloud to a group (the class, another group of students, to a group of elementary school students) or published in a literary magazine or class anthology.
- Write plays that would be performed.
- Discuss the parallels between the different speech styles we use and writing styles for different readers or audiences.
- Write a particular piece for different audiences.
- Expose students to writing that is on the same topic but with a different audience and have them identify the variations in sentence structure and style.
- As part of the prewriting have students identify the audience. Make sure students consider the following when analyzing the needs of their audience.
    1. Why is the audience reading my writing? Do they expect to be informed, amused or persuaded?
    2. What does my audience already know about my topic?
    3. What does the audience want or need to know? What will interest them?
    4. What type of language suits my readers?

Remind your students that it is not necessary to identify all the specifics of the audience in the initial stage of the writing process but that at some point they must make some determinations about audience.

Skill 5.3 **Demonstrate understanding of strategies for integrating young children's instruction in writing with the other language arts and other content areas**

A student's developmental writing skills parallel their reading development stages of reading. Print awareness develops in young children as a result of listening to a story read to them by adults, and recognizing that words on a page symbolize meaning. Print awareness is the realization that writing is created with instruments such as pens, pencils, crayons and markers. Children began to imitate the shapes, and letters they see in a book or in text. Children soon learn that the power of writing is expressing one's own ideas in print form and can be understood by others.

Due to the social nature of children's learning, early instruction must provide rich demonstrations, interactions, and models of literacy. Children learn about the relation between oral and written language and the relation between letters, sounds, and words. Classrooms should include a wide variety of print and writing activities, that involve talking, reading, writing, playing, and listening to one another, Books, papers, writing tools, and functional signs should be visible everywhere in the classroom so that children can see and use literacy for multiple purposes.

Sitting down with a child and discussing their ideas helps them to organize their thoughts. This also gives students the opportunity to state their ideas before writing them out on paper. Allow students who have difficulty with writing to respond by art (drawing their favorite part or character) or drama (rehearsing the story). This extra time allows writers to rehearse their ideas before putting them on paper.

Most importantly, respect a student's writing. All students need to feel that their work is valued.

Writing in other Content areas

Too often the content of the curriculum has been divided into separate subjects for science, social studies, art, music, reading, spelling, handwriting, etc., however, this often promotes the fragmentation of knowledge. These various subject matter areas can often be combined into themes or units, with writing as a major factor.

Students can write letters to the local newspapers about a subject in the current news that correlates with a Social Studies theme. Students can write their reactions to observations about a Science experiment. Teachers may even have the students write out why and how they found the answers to certain Math problems. Writing about personal experiences can also be related to themes and units.

It is important for teachers to evaluate each student's writing in the context in which it is written. Often, writing irregularities may show up and will allow the teacher to further assist the students with often hidden writing difficulties.

Skill 5.4   Relate written language development to the development of skills in oral language and reading

Strategies for Promoting Awareness of the Relationship between Spoken and Written Language

- The teacher writes down what the children are saying on a chart.
- Highlight and celebrate the meanings, uses, and print products found in the classroom. These products include: posters, labels, yellow sticky pad notes, labels on shelves and lockers, calendars, rule signs, and directions.
- The intentional reading of big-print and oversized books to teach print conventions such as directionality.
- Practice exercises in reading to others-(for K-1/2) where young children practice how to handle a book, --how to turn pages, how to find tops and bottoms of pages, and how to tell the difference between the front and back covers of a book.
- Search and discuss adventures in word awareness and close observation where children are challenged to identify and talk about the length, appearance and boundaries of specific words and the letters which comprise them.
- Have children match oral words to printed words by forming an echo chorus as the teacher reads the story aloud-They echo the reading. Often this works best with poetry or rhymes.
- Have the children combine, manipulate, switch and move letters to change words and spelling patterns.
- Work with letter cards to create messages and respond to the messages that they create.

Methods used to teach these skills are often featured in a "balanced literacy" curriculum that focuses on the use of skills in various instructional contexts. For example, with independent reading, students independently choose and books that are at their reading levels; with guided reading, teachers work with small groups of students to help them with their particular reading problems; with whole group reading, the entire class will read the same text, and the teacher will incorporate activities to help students learn phonics, comprehension, fluency, and vocabulary. In addition to these components of balanced literacy, teachers incorporate writing so that students can learn the structures of communicating through text.

Skill 5.5   Evaluate strategies and activities for promoting young children's writing competence

When teaching writing, teachers must provide many opportunities for the children to write. In fact, writing should be a daily activity in the classroom, just as reading is. As the children are writing, teachers need to engage in ongoing assessment to determine the strengths and needs of the students. For some strategies, the teacher might need to teach or re-teach specific skills to a small group of students. At other times, there may be a need for whole class instruction.

Motivating students to write means helping them find topics that are of interest to them. By having students complete an interest survey, teachers will get an idea of what they like to read and write about. Before beginning any writing program, the teacher could ask the student to brainstorm a list of topics they could write about during the year and keep this list in their writing folders. As teachers work with the students through the stages of the writing process, teacher-student conferences provide the best information on the students' progress. Instead of letting students work all the way through a piece of writing and then grading the final copy, teachers should conference with each student through every stage. This way, the teacher will learn where the students need intervention and which students would make the best peer editors for other students.

Students who struggle with editing and revising need constant praise to keep them motivated. They often become overwhelmed with having to edit a large piece of text, especially if there are a lot of mistakes. Teachers could ask the student to edit for capitalization only, which will make it easier for the students. Teachers can also assess while the students are writing by reading over the drafts, make notes as to what corrections should be made and giving the students a second chance to improve the writing before they receive a final grade.

Monitoring Writing Development
Teachers need to continually monitor students' writing development throughout the school year. Aside from formal state and classroom assessments, teachers can gather information about students' writing progress in informal ways, too.

Some of these ways include:
- Writer's workshop portfolios
- Running records
- Portfolio assessment
- Journal writing
- Assignments scored with rubrics
- Application of writing to other subject areas and projects

Together with formal assessments, these methods can help teachers and parents watch students' writing develop throughout the year.

Skill 5.6 **Demonstrate knowledge of how having a home language other than standard English affects writing development and instruction and how to use young children's linguistic and cultural backgrounds to promote writing competence**

SEE Skill 1.7

SUBAREA II.   **LEARNING ACROSS THE CURRICULUM**

COMPETENCY 6.0   UNDERSTAND MATHEMATICAL SKILLS, CONCEPTS, AND PROCEDURES AND HOW TO PROMOTE YOUNG CHILDREN'S DEVELOPMENT OF MATHEMATICAL UNDERSTANDINGS AND THEIR ABILITY TO APPLY MATHEMATICAL SKILLS IN VARIED CONTEXTS.

Skill 6.1   Demonstrate understanding of key concepts, skills, procedures, and reasoning processes associated with different areas of mathematics, including number systems, number sense, geometry and spatial relationships, measurement, statistics, probability, and algebra.

NUMBER SYSTEMS AND NUMBER SENSE

PLACE VALUE

Place value is the basis of our entire number system. A place value system is one in which the position of a digit in a number determines its value. In the standard system, called base ten, each place represents ten times the value of the place to its right. You can think of this as making groups of ten of the smaller unit and combining them to make a new unit.

Ten ones make up one of the next larger unit, tens. Ten of those units make up one of the next larger unit, hundreds. This pattern continues for greater values (ten hundreds = one thousand, ten thousands = one ten thousand, etc.), and lesser, decimal values (ten *tenths* = one *one*, ten *hundredths* = one tenth, etc.).

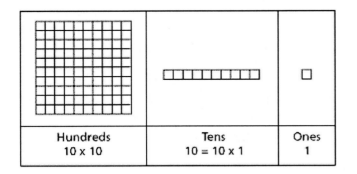

Hundreds 10 x 10	Tens 10 = 10 x 1	Ones 1

A popular activity that illustrates the base ten number system in many elementary classrooms is to count the days towards the 100th day of school. Students use straws (or small sticks) to represent each day. The students add a straw to their collection each day, and when they have ten, they bundle them with a rubber band. By the time they reach the 100th day, they have 9 bundles of 10, and when they add the last straw, they will have 10 bundles of 10. The students then bundle the 10 bundles of 10 into 1 bundle of 100.

Unifix Cubes are another excellent manipulative for teaching the base ten number system. They can be easily used as base ten blocks for exploring ones and tens. Each color can act as a group of ten when connected.

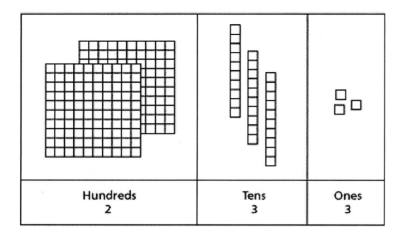

In standard form, the number modeled above is 233.

A place-value chart is a way to make sure digits are in the correct places. The value of each digit depends on its position or "place." A great way to see the place-value relationships in a number is to model the number with actual objects (place-value blocks, bundles of craft sticks, etc.), write the digits in the chart, and then write the number in the usual, or standard form.

Place value is vitally important to all later mathematics. Without it, keeping track of greater numbers rapidly becomes impossible. (Can you imagine trying to write 999 with only ones?) A thorough mastery of place value is essential to learning the operations with greater numbers. It is the foundation for regrouping ("borrowing" and "carrying") in addition, subtraction, multiplication, and division.

NUMBER SYSTEMS:

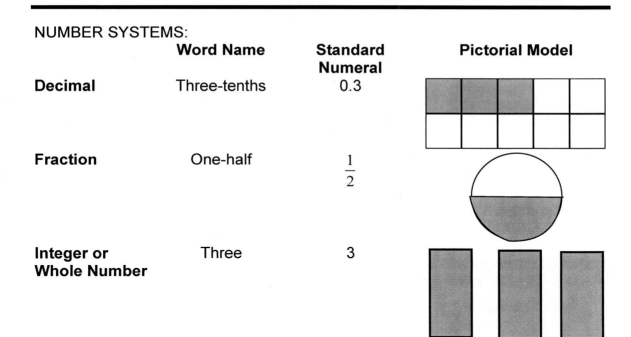

	Word Name	Standard Numeral	Pictorial Model
Decimal	Three-tenths	0.3	
Fraction	One-half	$\frac{1}{2}$	
Integer or Whole Number	Three	3	

The real number system includes all rational and irrational numbers.

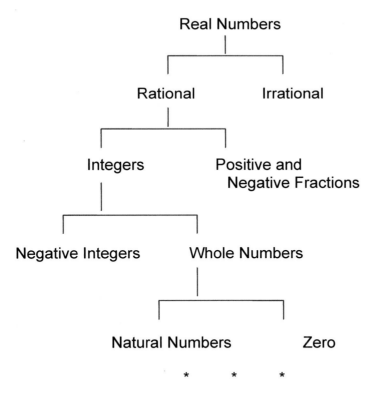

Real Numbers

Rational   Irrational

Integers   Positive and Negative Fractions

Negative Integers   Whole Numbers

Natural Numbers   Zero

*   *   *

Rational numbers can be expressed as the ratio of two integers, $\frac{a}{b}$ where b ≠ 0, for example $\frac{2}{3}$, $-\frac{4}{5}$, 5 = $\frac{5}{1}$.

The rational numbers include integers, fractions and mixed numbers, terminating and repeating decimals. Every rational number can be expressed as a repeating or terminating decimal and can be shown on a number line.

Integers are positive and negative whole numbers and zero.
...-6, -5, -4, -3, -2, -1, 0, 1, 2, 3, 4, 5, 6, ...

Whole numbers are natural numbers and zero.
0, 1, 2, 3, 4, 5, 6...

Natural numbers are the counting numbers.
1, 2, 3, 4, 5, 6...

Irrational numbers are real numbers that cannot be written as the ratio of two integers. These are infinite non-repeating decimals.
Examples: $\sqrt{5}$ = 2.2360..,   pi =$\prod$ = 3.1415927...

A **fraction** is an expression of numbers in the form of x/y, where x is the numerator and y is the denominator, which cannot be zero.

Example: $\dfrac{3}{7}$ 3 is the numerator; 7 is the denominator

If the fraction has common factors for the numerator and denominator, divide both by the common factor to reduce the fraction to its lowest form.

Example:

$$\dfrac{13}{39} = \dfrac{1 \times 13}{3 \times 13} = \dfrac{1}{3}$$ Divide by the common factor 13

A **mixed** number has an integer part and a fractional part.

Example: $2\dfrac{1}{4}$, $^{-}5\dfrac{1}{6}$, $7\dfrac{1}{3}$

Pre-K and primary students first learn about fractions with puzzles or other manipulatives that represent a pie. Paper plates can be cut into pieces or colored and folded to illustrate fractions to pre-K students. Even citrus fruits with segments, such as oranges, tangerines, or grapefruit, can be used to demonstrate fractions. Primary students also compare pictures of a bar divided into halves and then another of the same size divided into fourths. Virtual manipulatives can also be found on the Internet to help teach fractions to students.

Percent = per 100 (written with the symbol %). Thus $10\% = \dfrac{10}{100} = \dfrac{1}{10}$.

Decimals = deci = part of ten. To find the decimal equivalent of a fraction, use the denominator to divide the numerator as shown in the following example.

Example: Find the decimal equivalent of $\dfrac{7}{10}$.

Since 10 cannot divide into 7 evenly

Recognition and understanding of the relationships between concepts and topics is of great value in mathematical problem solving and the explanation of more complex processes.
For instance, multiplication is simply repeated addition. This relationship explains the concept of variable addition. We can show that the expression
4x + 3x = 7x is true by rewriting 4 times x and 3 times x as repeated addition, yielding the expression (x + x + x + x) + (x + x + x). Thus, because of the relationship between multiplication and addition, variable addition is accomplished by coefficient addition.

Properties are rules that apply for addition, subtraction, multiplication, or division of real numbers. These properties are:

Commutative: You can change the order of the terms or factors as follows.

For addition: $a + b = b + a$
For multiplication: $ab = ba$

Since addition is the inverse operation of subtraction and multiplication is the inverse operation of division, no separate laws are needed for subtraction and division.

Example: 5 + 8 = 8 + 5 = 13

Example: 2 × 6 = 6 × 2 = 12

Associative: You can regroup the terms as you like.

For addition: $a + (b + c) = (a + b) + c$
For multiplication: $a(bc) = (ab)c$

This rule does not apply for division and subtraction.

Example: $(2 + 7) + 5 = 2 + (7 + 5)$
          $9 + 5 = 2 + 12 = 14$

Example: $(3 \times 7) \times 5 = 3 \times (7 \times 5)$
          $21 \times 5 = 3 \times 35 = 105$

Identity: Finding a number so that when added to a term results in that number (additive identity); finding a number such that when multiplied by a term results in that number (multiplicative identity).

For addition: $a + 0 = a$ (zero is additive identity)
For multiplication: $a \cdot 1 = a$ (one is multiplicative)

Example: $17 + 0 = 17$

Example: $34 \times 1 = 34$
The product of any number and one is that number.

Inverse: Finding a number such that when added to the number it results in zero; or when multiplied by the number results in 1.

For addition: $a - a = 0$
For multiplication: $a \cdot (1/a) = 1$

($-a$) is the additive inverse of a; ($1/a$), also called the reciprocal, is the multiplicative inverse of a.

Example: $25 - 25 = 0$

Example: $5 \times \frac{1}{5} = 1$
The product of any number and its reciprocal is one.

Distributive: This technique allows us to operate on terms within parentheses without first performing operations within the parentheses. This is especially helpful when terms within the parentheses cannot be combined.

$$a\,(b + c) = ab + ac$$

Example: $6 \times (4 + 9) = (6 \times 4) + (6 \times 9)$
$6 \times 13 = 24 + 54 = 78$

To multiply a sum by a number, multiply each addend by the number, then add the products.

Addition of whole numbers

Example: At the end of a day of shopping, a shopper had $24 remaining in his wallet. He spent $45 on various goods. How much money did the shopper have at the beginning of the day?

The total amount of money the shopper started with is the sum of the amount spent and the amount remaining at the end of the day.

$24
+ 45
$69   The original total was $69.

Example: A race took the winner 1 hr. 58 min. 12 sec. on the first half of the race and 2 hr. 9 min. 57 sec. on the second half of the race. How much time did the entire race take?

1 hr. 58 min. 12 sec.
+ 2 hr. 9 min. 57 sec.   Add these numbers
3 hr. 67 min. 69 sec.
      + 1 min -60 sec.   Change 60 seconds to 1 min.
3 hr. 68 min. 9 sec.
+ 1 hr.-60 min.   Change 60 minutes to 1 hr.
4 hr. 8 min. 9 sec.   ← final answer

Subtraction of Whole Numbers

Example: At the end of his shift, a cashier has $96 in the cash register. At the beginning of his shift, he had $15. How much money did the cashier collect during his shift?

The total collected is the difference of the ending amount and the starting amount.

$$\begin{array}{r} \$96 \\ -\ \ 15 \\ \hline \$81 \end{array}$$ The total collected was $81.

I.   Multiplication of whole numbers

Multiplication is one of the four basic number operations. In simple terms, multiplication is the addition of a number to itself a certain number of times. For example, 4 multiplied by 3 is the equal to 4 + 4 + 4 or 3 + 3 + 3 +3. Another way of conceptualizing multiplication is to think in terms of groups. For example, if we have 4 groups of 3 students, the total number of students is 4 multiplied by 3. We call the solution to a multiplication problem the product.

The basic algorithm for whole number multiplication begins with aligning the numbers by place value with the number containing more places on top.

$$\begin{array}{r} 172 \\ \times\ \ 43 \end{array} \longrightarrow$$ Note that we placed 122 on top because it has more places than 43 does.

Next, we multiply the ones' place of the second number by each place value of the top number sequentially.

$$\begin{array}{r} (2) \\ 172 \\ \times\ \ 43 \\ \hline 516 \end{array} \longrightarrow \{3 \times 2 = 6,\ 3 \times 7 = 21,\ 3 \times 1 = 3\}$$

Note that we had to carry a 2 to the hundreds' column because 3 x 7 = 21. Note also that we add, not multiply, carried numbers to the product.

Next, we multiply the number in the tens' place of the second number by each place value of the top number sequentially. Because we are multiplying by a number in the tens' place, we place a zero at the end of this product.

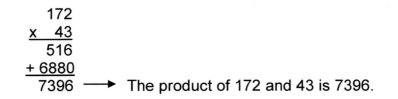

$$\begin{array}{r} (2) \\ 172 \\ \times\ \ 43 \\ \hline 516 \\ 6880 \end{array}$$ →   {4 x 2 = 8, 4 x 7 = 28, 4 x 1 = 4}

Finally, to determine the final product we add the two partial products.

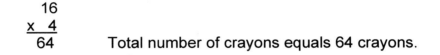

$$\begin{array}{r} 172 \\ \times\ \ 43 \\ \hline 516 \\ +\ 6880 \\ \hline 7396 \end{array}$$ →   The product of 172 and 43 is 7396.

Example: A student buys 4 boxes of crayons. Each box contains 16 crayons. How many total crayons does the student have?

The total number of crayons is 16 x 4.

$$\begin{array}{r} 16 \\ \times\ \ 4 \\ \hline 64 \end{array}$$ Total number of crayons equals 64 crayons.

Division of whole numbers

Division, the inverse of multiplication, is another of the four basic number operations. When we divide one number by another, we determine how many times we can multiply the divisor (number divided by) before we exceed the number we are dividing (dividend). For example, 8 divided by 2 equals 4 because we can multiply 2 four times to reach 8 (2 x 4 = 8 or 2 + 2 + 2 + 2 = 8). Using the grouping conceptualization we used with multiplication, we can divide 8 into 4 groups of 2 or 2 groups of 4. We call the answer to a division problem the quotient.

If the divisor does not divide evenly into the dividend, we express the leftover amount either as a remainder or as a fraction with the divisor as the denominator. For example, 9 divided by 2 equals 4 with a remainder of 1 or 4 ½.

The basic algorithm for division is long division. We start by representing the quotient as follows.

$14\overline{)293}$ ⟶ 14 is the divisor and 293 is the dividend.

This represents 293 ÷ 14.

Next, we divide the divisor into the dividend starting from the left.

$\begin{array}{r} 2 \\ 14\overline{)293} \end{array}$ ⟶ 14 divides into 29 two times with a remainder.

Next, we multiply the partial quotient by the divisor, subtract this value from the first digits of the dividend, and bring down the remaining dividend digits to complete the number.

$\begin{array}{r} 2 \\ 14\overline{)293} \\ -28\downarrow \\ \hline 13 \end{array}$ ⟶ 2 x 14 = 28, 29 – 28 = 1, and bringing down the 3 yields 13.

Finally, we divide again (the divisor into the remaining value) and repeat the preceding process. The number left after the subtraction represents the remainder.

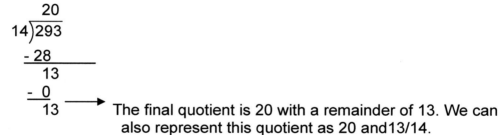

The final quotient is 20 with a remainder of 13. We can also represent this quotient as 20 and 13/14.

Example: Each box of apples contains 24 apples. How many boxes must a grocer purchase to supply a group of 252 people with one apple each?

The grocer needs 252 apples. Because he must buy apples in groups of 24, we divide 252 by 24 to determine how many boxes he needs to buy.

$$
\begin{array}{r}
10 \\
24\overline{)252} \\
-24 \\
\hline
12 \\
-\ 0 \\
\hline
12
\end{array}
$$

→ The quotient is 10 with a remainder of 12.

Thus, the grocer needs 10 boxes plus 12 more apples. Therefore, the minimum number of boxes the grocer can purchase is 11 boxes.

Example: At his job, John gets paid $20 for every hour he works. If John made $940 in a week, how many hours did he work?

This is a division problem. To determine the number of hours John worked, we divide the total amount made ($940) by the hourly rate of pay ($20). Thus, the number of hours worked equals 940 divided by 20.

$$
\begin{array}{r}
47 \\
20\overline{)940} \\
-80 \\
\hline
140 \\
-140 \\
\hline
0
\end{array}
$$

20 divides into 940, 47 times with no remainder.

John worked 47 hours.

Addition and Subtraction of Decimals

When adding and subtracting decimals, we align the numbers by place value as we do with whole numbers. After adding or subtracting each column, we bring the decimal down, placing it in the same location as in the numbers added or subtracted.

Example: Find the sum of 152.3 and 36.342.

$$
\begin{array}{r}
152.300 \\
+\quad 36.342 \\
\hline
188.642
\end{array}
$$

Note that we placed two zeroes after the final place value in 152.3 to clarify the column addition.

Example: Find the difference of 152.3 and 36.342.

$$
\begin{array}{cc}
2\ 9\ 10 & (4)11(12) \\
152.300 & 152.300 \\
-\quad 36.342 & -\ 36.342 \\
\hline
58 & 115.958
\end{array}
$$

Note how we borrowed to subtract from the zeroes in the hundredths' and thousandths' place of 152.300.

GEOMETRY AND SPATIAL RELATIONSHIPS

As students develop their knowledge about shapes, they will need to increase their critical thinking skills to include the development of mathematical arguments about the relationships between shapes. After the beginning levels of being able to identify, name, and create basic two- and three- dimensional shapes, students need to begin to compare and sort shapes.

During this comparison students will need to examine the various attributes of shapes to help them make predictions. Students should explore and make predictions about how shapes can be combined to for new shapes, what would happen if parts were taken off of shapes, and other extrapolations about the shapes. This exploration provides students the basis for later more complex understanding of geometric relationships.

Tangrams, or puzzle pieces, are excellent manipulatives for children to use to explore geometric shapes and relationships. They allow students to transform shapes through flips and rotations as well as to take them apart and put them together in different formations. Tangrams can be tangible pieces that students manipulate with their hands or they can be virtual pieces on the computer that students manipulate to visualize geometric shape changes.

A **triangle** is a polygon with three sides.

Triangles can be classified by the types of angles or the lengths of their sides.

Classifying by angles:

An **acute** triangle has exactly three *acute* angles.
A **right** triangle has one *right* angle.
An **obtuse** triangle has one *obtuse* angle.

            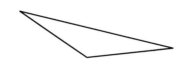

    acute   right   obtuse

Classifying by sides:

All *three* sides of an **equilateral** triangle are the same length.
Two sides of an **isosceles** triangle are the same length.
None of the sides of a **scalene** triangle are the same length.

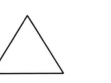   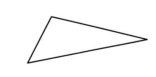

equilateral   **isosceles**   **scalene**

A **polygon** is a simple closed figure composed of line segments. In a **regular polygon** all sides are the same length and all angles are the same measure.

The union of all points on a simple closed surface and all points in its interior form a space figure called a **solid**. The five regular solids, or **polyhedra**, are the cube, tetrahedron, octahedron, icosahedron, and dodecahedron. A **net** is a two-dimensional figure that can be cut out and folded up to make a three-dimensional solid. Below are models of the five regular solids with their corresponding face polygons and nets.

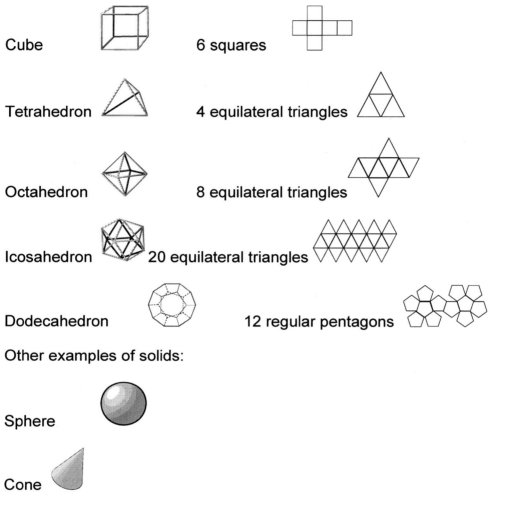

Cube   6 squares

Tetrahedron   4 equilateral triangles

Octahedron   8 equilateral triangles

Icosahedron   20 equilateral triangles

Dodecahedron   12 regular pentagons

Other examples of solids:

Sphere

Cone

TESSELLATIONS, ROTATIONS, REFLECTIONS, AND SLIDES

A **Tessellation** is an arrangement of closed shapes that completely covers the plane without overlapping or leaving gaps. Unlike **tilings**, tessellations do not require the use of regular polygons. In art the term is used to refer to pictures or tiles mostly in the form of animals and other life forms, which cover the surface of a plane in a symmetrical way without overlapping or leaving gaps. M. C. Escher is known as the "father" of modern tessellations. Tessellations are used for tiling, mosaics, quilts, and art.

If you look at a completed tessellation, you will see the original motif repeats in a pattern. There are 17 possible ways that a pattern can be used to tile a flat surface, or "wallpaper."

There are four basic transformational symmetries that can be used in tessellations: **translation, rotation, reflection,** and **glide reflection**. The transformation of an object is called its image. If the original object was labeled with letters, such as $ABCD$, the image may be labeled with the same letters followed by a prime symbol, $A'B'C'D'$.

The tessellation below is a combination of the four types of transformational symmetry we have discussed:

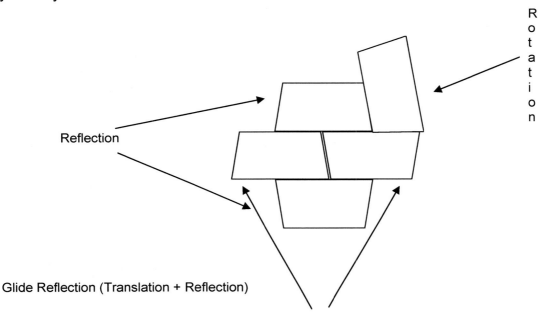

A **transformation** is a change in the position, shape, or size of a geometric figure. **Transformational geometry** is the study of manipulating objects by flipping, twisting, turning and scaling. **Symmetry** is exact similarity between two parts or halves, as if one were a mirror image of the other.

A **translation** is a transformation that "slides" an object a fixed distance in a given direction. The original object and its translation have the same shape and size, and they face in the same direction.

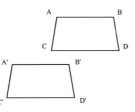

An example of a translation in architecture would be stadium seating. The seats are the same size and the same shape and face in the same direction.

A **rotation** is a transformation that turns a figure about a fixed point called the center of rotation. An object and its rotation are the same shape and size, but the figures may be turned in different directions. Rotations can occur in either a clockwise or a counterclockwise direction.

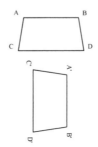

Rotations can be seen in wallpaper and art, and a Ferris wheel is an example of rotation.

An object and its **reflection** have the same shape and size, but the figures face in opposite directions.

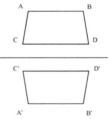

The line (where a mirror may be placed) is called the **line of reflection**. The distance from a point to the line of reflection is the same as the distance from the point's image to the line of reflection.

MEASUREMENT

People like to reduce everything in the real world to numbers, and the only way to do this with some things is to measure them. The most common things we measure are time, temperature, distance, weight and angles. Children have been exposed to some or all of these concepts before they start school.

One of the most important things that must be emphasized when beginning measurement activities is that now we are entering the world of approximations. No measurement can ever be exact, and teachers should refrain from using the word "exact" in connection with measurements. Many adults are confused about this concept, so we should try to set the children straight from the outset.

The stages of measuring something are: (1) determine what to measure, (2) decide on an appropriate tool, (3) select a reasonable unit of measure, (4) estimate how much or how long the measurement will be, (5) measure and finally (6) check the reasonableness of the results.

Start with **time**. Most people measure time with clocks or watches. What are the units? Most children are familiar with hours and minutes. Practice this with them. With older children, you can talk about timed athletic events like running, swimming, horse races, etc. At this point, they would probably see the need for a smaller unit, so we could talk about seconds and even tenths of seconds. Constantly point out that 10.3 seconds only means that the time in question is closer to 10.3 than it is to 10.2 or 10.4.

Next could be **temperature**. Most children are aware of temperature as it is given on TV, in Fahrenheit degrees in the United States. Introduce them to the thermometer with an actual thermometer and then with a large reproduction on paper showing the degree marks. Talk about how air temperature is physically measured. For example, would we want to put the thermometer in direct sunlight? What would be a comfortable temperature? What would be very hot? Very cold? Have them estimate air temperature each day and then measure it with the thermometer. Again point out that to say the temperature is 75 degrees only means that it is closer to 75 than to 74 or 76. Point this out on the paper diagram of a thermometer scale. With older students, here is a good chance to introduce the idea of negative numbers briefly. Also work with the Celsius (or centigrade) scale.

Next could be **length**. A great deal of time needs to be spent here. First, the students need to be convinced that we need a standard unit. Does foot mean the length of just anybody's foot? Get some objects for them to measure that are very close to 3 feet or 5 feet, etc. Then introduce something smaller so that they will see the need for a smaller unit.

Prior to introducing measurement with standard tools such as a ruler, it is appropriate to teach children how to measure with non-standard units such as paper clips. Students are taught to use the paper clip as a unit and by laying the paper clips end to end, they measure an object longer than the paper clip (repetition of a single unit to measure something larger than the unit).

Practice measuring objects to the nearest inch. After they have been measuring for a few weeks, introduce the millimeter as a still smaller unit. Most rulers nowadays have metric on one side and standard English units on the other.

As soon as possible, get them used to the **metric system**, sticking with millimeter and centimeter. Use these interchangeably with inches and feet. Older children can then proceed to yards and meters. Still older ones can work on paper (or the computer) with miles and kilometers. Many, many activities must be constantly presented to get children familiar with all these units.

Some work can be done occasionally with **weights**. Pounds would be the obvious starting unit, then ounces for a smaller unit and tons for a larger one. Early on in this work, introduce the kilogram and the gram. Guess the weights of objects before actually weighing them.

Another thing we measure is **liquids**. Introduce the idea of gallons and quarts, but fairly soon also work with liters and milliliters. Bring in soda bottles and notice that both metric and English units are given. Briefly talk about pints and cups, as used in recipes.

The concept of area is a difficult one for them. Try to get some hint that they are ready to tackle that one. Somewhere about the end of grade 2 or beginning of grade 3 would be an appropriate time to introduce this idea. Work with squares and rectangles first, then right triangles.

Finally, the concept of an angle can be approached, particularly a right angle because it can be associated with turns. There are many exercises available, both paper-and-pencil and computer software, for working with angles. It is probably not appropriate to introduce the protractor until about grade 3.

For all of these measurement activities, bring examples from newspapers and TV to class and discuss them. Have the children be on the lookout for such examples. What would they like to measure? What would be easy to measure? Hard to measure? Keep harping on the idea that no measurement is ever exact.

After you have decided that there is some object you want to measure, the first question to be answered is what attribute can be measured on this object. Most physical objects would have a length, although even here there are choices to be made. Since the world is three-dimensional, you have to choose which dimension will be the length, which the width, and which the height. We use those words to distinguish the three dimensions from each other, but of course, all three would be measured in length units. Other measurable attributes of common physical objects are their weight, surface area, volume, and temperature.

In Pre K-3, **volume** is not an appropriate topic, except as it might enter into a discussion of liquid measure. In addition, the time spent on area concepts will probably be short. Measurement of temperature will normally be confined to air temperature for this age group.

When it comes to choosing between standard and nonstandard units of measurement, it depends on what country you are in. In the United States English units are still considered standard, while metric are nonstandard. It would be nice if the world could agree on a single system. If we ever did, the most natural and easiest to use would have to be metric. Children should be introduced to metric units right along with English units. The only way the change will ever be made in this country is if young children grow up knowing the metric system. By using it and seeing how easy it converts from one unit to another because it goes in powers of 10, they should be convinced that it is the better way to go.

With the advent of good and inexpensive digital cameras, math teachers have some wonderful opportunities to show students how pervasive mathematics and measuring are in their lives. The teacher can go around the immediate area of the school taking pictures of physical objects that illustrate various things they are studying. For example, if you are working on length measures and also geometric figures, before having them measure the length and width of a bunch of rectangles on paper, show them pictures (a PowerPoint demonstration would be ideal here) of different rectangles around the neighborhood. For example, walls of the classroom, tiles on the floor or ceiling, sidewalks, exteriors of buildings, etc.

Do the same for other geometric figures. Bridges are good to get triangles. Church windows are often circular. Children are usually quite familiar with circles, but circles introduce some very real problems. With younger students the perimeter can be approximated (remember that all measurements are approximate anyway). Using a piece of string and fitting it around a circle on a piece of paper, then measuring the length of the string that seems to fit, makes a nice little exercise.

Every math classroom should be equipped with various measuring devices-- a set of rulers, a few meter sticks, some thermometers, a few different scales for weighing objects, clocks and perhaps a stopwatch and protractors. Hands-on exercises are definitely the way to go when measuring. When showing pictures of objects we want to measure in the immediate environment, ask the students how we could measure these objects and what would be an appropriate instrument to use. What units would be best to express the measurement? Have them guess the result of measuring the object. Where could they go to find out if their guess was a good approximation to the reported measurement of this object?

Angles are difficult to teach to young children. They can be introduced by having them stand up, face front, then turn to face sideways right. What if we turned only part way to the right? How could we measure this? Do not be too fast to tell them how we adults talk about and measure angles for this. You might have some interesting ideas presented for solving this problem. Eventually, you will tell them about angles and how they are measured. Draw some angles and talk about what exactly is being measured here. Point out that the angle is no bigger if you extend the sides indefinitely. Actual measuring with protractors could be introduced if you feel the children are ready, but getting the idea of what we mean by the concept of angle is more important at first.

Students should be able to determine what unit of measurement is appropriate for a particular problem, as indicated by the following table:

Problem Type	Unit (Customary System)	Unit (Metric System)
Length	Inch	Millimeter
	Foot	Centimeter
	Yard	Meter
Distance	Mile	Kilometer
Area	Square inches	Square millimeters
	Square feet	Square centimeters
	Square yards	Square meters
	Square miles	Square kilometers
Volume	Cubic inches	Cubic millimeters
	Cubic feet	Cubic centimeters
	Cubic yards	Cubic meters
Liquid volume	Fluid ounces	Milliliters
	Cups	Liters
	Pints	
	Quarts	
	Gallons	
Mass		Milligrams
		Centigrams
		Grams
		Kilograms
Weight	Ounces	Milligrams
	Pounds	Centigrams
	Tons	Grams
		Kilograms
Temperature	Degrees Fahrenheit	Degrees Celsius or Kelvin

The units of **length** in the customary system are inches, feet, yards and miles.

12 inches (in.) = 1 foot (ft.)
36 in. = 1 yard (yd.)
3 ft. = 1 yd.
5280 ft. = 1 mile (mi.)
760 yd. = 1 mi.

To change from a **larger unit to a smaller unit, multiply**.
To change from a **smaller unit to a larger unit, divide**.

Example:

$$4 \text{ mi.} = \underline{\hspace{1cm}} \text{ yd.}$$

Since 1760 yd. = 1 mile, multiply $4 \times 1760 = 7040$ yd.

Example:

$$21 \text{ in.} = \underline{\hspace{1cm}} \text{ ft.}$$

$$21 \div 12 = 1\tfrac{3}{4} \text{ ft.}$$

The units of **weight** are ounces, pounds and tons.

16 ounces (oz.) = 1 pound (lb.) 2,000 lb. = 1 ton (T.)

Example: $2\tfrac{3}{4}$ T. = $\underline{\hspace{1cm}}$ lb.

$$2\tfrac{3}{4} \times 2,000 = 5,500 \text{ lb.}$$

The units of **capacity** are fluid ounces, cups, pints, quarts, and gallons.

8 fluid ounces (fl. oz.) = 1 cup (c.) 2 c. = 1 pint (pt.) 4 c. = 1 quart (qt.) 2 pt. = 1 qt. 4 qt. = 1 gallon (gal.)

Example1: 3 gal. = $\underline{\hspace{1cm}}$ qt.

$$3 \times 4 = 12 \text{ qt.}$$

Example: $1\tfrac{1}{4}$ cups = $\underline{\hspace{1cm}}$ oz.

$$1\tfrac{1}{4} \times 8 = 10 \text{ oz.}$$

Example: 7 c. = $\underline{\hspace{1cm}}$ pt.

$$7 \div 2 = 3\tfrac{1}{2} \text{ pt.}$$

Square units can be derived with knowledge of basic units of length by squaring the equivalent measurements.

1 square foot (sq. ft.) = 144 sq. in.
1 sq. yd. = 9 sq. ft.
1 sq. yd. = 1296 sq. in.

<u>Example:</u> 14 sq. yd. = _____ sq. ft.

14 × 9 = 126 sq. ft.

METRIC UNITS

The metric system is based on multiples of <u>ten</u>. Conversions are made by simply moving the decimal point to the left or right.

kilo-	1000	thousands
hecto-	100	hundreds
deca-	10	tens
nit		
deci-	.1	tenths
centi-	.01	hundredths
milli-	.001	thousandths

The basic unit for **length** is the meter. One meter is approximately one yard.

The basic unit for **weight** or mass is the gram. A paper clip weighs about one gram.

The basic unit for **volume** is the liter. One liter is approximately a quart.

These are the most commonly used units.

1 m = 100 cm	1000 mL= 1 L	1000 mg = 1 g
1 m = 1000 mm	1 kL = 1000 L	1 kg = 1000 g
1 cm = 10 mm		
1000 m = 1 km		

The prefixes are commonly listed from left to right for ease in conversion.

K H D U D C M

Example: 63 km = _____m

Since there are 3 steps from <u>Ki</u>lo to <u>U</u>nit, move the decimal point 3 places to the right.

63 km = 63,000 m

Example: 14 mL = _____L

Since there are 3 steps from <u>Mi</u>lli to <u>U</u>nit, move the decimal point 3 places to the left.

14 mL = 0.014 L

Example: 56.4 cm = _____ mm
56.4 cm = 564 mm

Example: 9.1 m = _____ km
9.1 m = 0.0091 km

Example 5: 75 kg = _____m
75 kg = 75,000,000 m

STATISTICS AND PROBABILITY

Working hand in hand with statistical analysis of data is the concept of probability. As students learn to examine data sets they should be able to:

- Describe what the data set shows
- Describe parts of the data set
- Compare sets of data or parts of the data set
- Represent data in a visual manner (chart/graph/table)
- Sort parts of the data sent
- Organize the data
- Answer and ask questions about data

In terms of probability, students should be able to understand the basic concepts. At the early childhood level, probability concepts include:

- Determine whether an event is possible, impossible, or certain to occur
- Compare simple events in terms of their likelihood to happen
- Predict the outcome of an event

In these primary grades, students usually explore the concepts of probability through the use of dice and spinners. A spinner which is divided and has the numbers one through six on it may be used to discuss probability by asking if it is possible or impossible to spin a ten. The same idea could be used with a die.

Discussing with students ideas and the vocabulary of possible, impossible and certain to occur is critical to the examination of probability. In a broader sense, it can be helpful to expose children to examples in real- life where probability is used on a daily basis. Weather forecasting is a real-life example students will be able to relate to with little difficulty.

Overall, at the early childhood level, the concept of probability is a brief introduction laying the foundation for future more complex learning. It is important students become familiar with the vocabulary terms and the ideas behind it during this time to lay the premise for future learning and activities.

BAR, LINE, PICTO-, AND CIRCLE GRAPHS

	Test 1	Test 2	Test 3	Test 4	Test 5
Evans, Tim	75	66	80	85	97
Miller, Julie	94	93	88	97	98
Thomas, Randy	81	86	88	87	90

Bar graphs are used to compare various quantities.

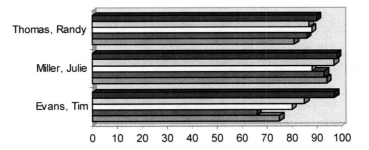

Line graphs are used to show trends, often over a period of time.

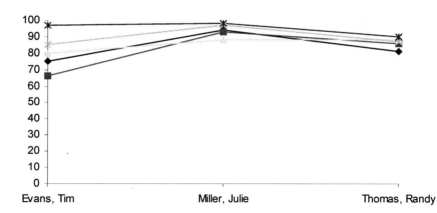

A **pictograph** shows comparison of quantities using symbols. Each symbol represents a number of items.

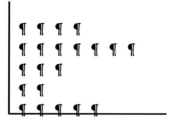

ALGEBRA

In the very primary grades, the concept of algebra is significantly different than what an adult remembers as algebra class. As adults, we typically recall the letters being used to hold the place of a number and solving various equations to find the answer for a variable. However, for young children the basis for this concept is developed through learning about patterns, the attributes of objects and how to describe objects in detail. These ideas help students to develop the fundamental thinking and concepts behind algebraic reasoning. These patterns may begin through concrete objects, but will be further developed into counting patterns and other recognition of the patterns of numbers.

Beginning with the basic understanding of the symbols used throughout math (numerical representations) students can investigate things around them. They can gather this information and begin to report it in a way that means something to others who look at it. These facts related to their own thinking can be expanded. As students look at a variety of situations and manipulate the objects to draw new conclusions, their problem solving skills are advanced. These skills will allow students to begin to solve missing number problems or solve for unknown pieces to a situation. This can be done with the youngest students as well. An example of a preschool missing object problem might be:

Red   yellow   red   _____   red   yellow   red   yellow   red

In this case, the students would be shown real objects of two colors set in a pattern and need to determine which one is missing from the center of the pattern. This type of thinking is more complex than "what comes next" types of questions.

As children begin to compare, sort, order and demonstrate seriating of objects using various characteristics their thinking changes. These changes are the beginning of algebraic thought. As they add on to patterns, make changes to patterns, build their own patterns, or convert patterns into new formats, they are thinking in more complex ways. Connecting this new thinking with the understanding of the number system is the beginning of using variables to define the relationships between mathematical concepts. This method of problem solving is then defined further into the expression of these relationships in a more traditional mathematical manner. Primary students may solve problems for the number that goes in the box. For example:

$3 + \boxed{} = 5$

Pre-K children should be able to recognize and extend simple repeating patterns using objects and pictures. By patterns, we mean a sequence of symbols, sounds, movements, or objects that follow a simple rule, such as ABBABBABB. Students should be presented with a simple pattern that they try to understand. Once they have an understanding of the pattern, they should copy and extend it. Students at this age are capable of assigning letters to their patterns to verbalize how the pattern repeats. These are the very early fundamental stages of algebra.

Skill 6.2 **Recognize approaches for exploring and solving mathematical problems (e.g., estimation, mental math, manipulative modeling, pattern recognition, technology-based approaches) and how to provide young children with learning experiences that promote their ability to use these approaches in varied contexts.**

It is important to realize that not all students learn the same way and, therefore, alternative instructional strategies may be appropriate. These strategies should provide alternatives to conventional basic skills instruction by emphasizing meaning and understanding, teaching discrete skills in context, and making real-world connections. Alternative methodologies include the use of:

- simulations
- group, cooperative, collaborative learning
- strategy and role-playing games
- peer tutoring
- toolkits
- learning by design
- multimedia
- storytelling structures
- coaching and scaffolding
- case studies

In addition, the following may be incorporated into instruction:

- use open-ended questions
- have students record, represent, or analyze data
- have students explain their reasoning when giving an answer
- have students work on longer mathematics investigations (a week or more in duration)
- encourage mathematical communication
- have students engage in hands-on mathematics activities
- encourage students to explore alternative methods for solutions
- have students share ideas or solve problems in small groups
- help students see connections between mathematics and other disciplines.

The use of supplementary materials in the classroom can greatly enhance the learning experience by stimulating student interest and satisfying different learning styles. Manipulatives, models, and technology are examples of tools available to teachers.

Manipulatives are materials that students can physically handle and move. Manipulatives allow students to understand mathematic concepts by allowing them to see concrete examples of abstract processes. Manipulatives are attractive to students because they appeal to the students' visual and tactile senses. Available for all levels of math, manipulatives are useful tools for reinforcing operations and concepts. They are not, however, a substitute for the development of sound computational skills. '

<u>Example</u>:
Using tiles to demonstrate both geometric ideas and number theory.
Give each group of students 12 tiles and instruct them to build rectangles.
Students draw their rectangles on paper.

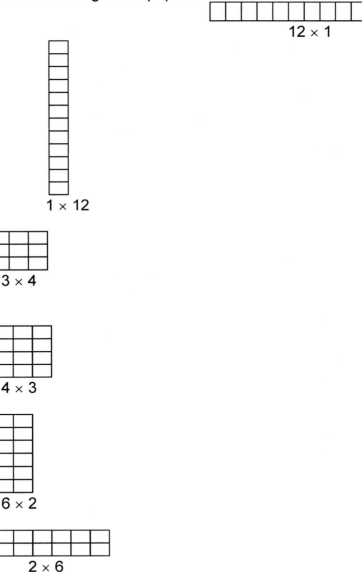

Encourage students to describe their reactions. Extend to 16 tiles. Ask students to form additional problems.

Models are another means of representing mathematical concepts by relating the concepts to real-world situations. Teachers must choose wisely when devising and selecting models because, to be effective, models must be applied properly. For example, a building with floors above and below ground is a good model for introducing the concept of negative numbers. It would be difficult, however, to use the building model in teaching subtraction of negative numbers.

Concepts of numeracy as well as other math concepts should be presented to children across situations, using a variety of materials and until levels of proficiency are reached. As concepts of math build upon another, it is imperative the appropriate foundation is in place for future learning to progress. Presenting concepts and ideas early will allow students the opportunity to experience and construct their own competencies.

Visual aids such as math fact posters and number lines can be beneficial in helping primary age students learn basic math concepts. A number line may be introduced to help students understand addition and subtraction. Suppose we want to show 6 + 3 on a number line.

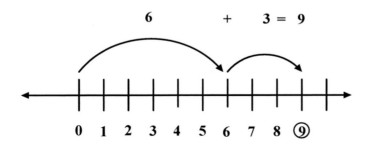

Addition can be thought of as starting from zero and counting 6 units to the right on the line (in the positive direction) and then counting 3 more units to the right. The number line shows that this is the same as counting 9 units to the right.

In the same way, a number line may be used to represent subtraction. Suppose we have 6 − 3 or rather 6 + (−3).

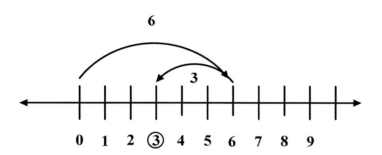

If 3 is shown by counting 3 positions to the right, then –3 can be shown as 3 positions to the left. We start from zero and count 6 positions to the right and then count 3 positions to the left. This illustrates how 6 + (–3) = 3.

Finally, there are many forms of **technology** available to math teachers. For example, students can test their understanding of math concepts by working on skill specific computer programs and websites. Math games on the computer or the smart board can supplement and reinforce the learning from the teacher. Graphing calculators can help students visualize the graphs of functions. Teachers can also enhance their lectures and classroom presentations by creating multimedia presentations.

Calculators are an important tool. They should be encouraged in the classroom and at home. They do not replace basic knowledge but they can relieve the tedium of mathematical computations, allowing students to explore more challenging mathematical directions. Even so, at times, it may be appropriate to have students complete the calculations themselves and then check it with a calculator. Some special needs students rely on calculators to complete computation, and all students are allowed to use calculators on certain standardized tests. An important thing to remember is that students will be able to use calculators more intelligently if they are taught how.

Students need to always check their work by estimating. **Estimation** and testing for **reasonableness** are related skills students should employ prior to and after solving a problem. These skills are particularly important when students use calculators to find answers.

Example:
Find the sum of 4387 + 7226 + 5893.

4300 + 7200 + 5800 = 17300   Estimation.
4387 + 7226 + 5893 = 17506   Actual sum.

By comparing the estimate to the actual sum, students can determine that their answer is reasonable.

The goal of mathematics is to prepare the child to survive in the real world. Technology is a reality in today's society

Teachers of mathematics should be aware of alternative positive assessment techniques that are performance-based and focus on conceptual understanding. These techniques include:

1) open-ended questions – allow students to express answers in their own words along with diagrams and/or pictures and express how they can apply their knowledge
2) mathematical investigations and projects – provide evidence of communication in mathematics
3) writing activities in mathematics – logbooks, journals, expository writing, creative writing to demonstrate writing ability and communication in mathematics
4) observations and interviews – checklists used over time to measure a student's attitude and aptitude
5) enhanced multiple-choice questions – require not only knowledge of basic facts, but also the ability to apply higher-order thinking skills to make sense of those facts
6) portfolio assessments – collections of students' work, showing progress over time, allowing students to demonstrate their ability to do major pieces of work as opposed to short exercises

Teaching young children mathematics requires a progression from the tangible to the abstract. As new concepts are introduced it is important for the teacher to utilize concrete objects. This allows students to manipulate, touch and explore the learning in a real way. This exploration provides the students the opportunity to be actively engaged in the learning. In this way, students can construct their own foundations, questions, and concepts related to numbers.

Providing the students with concrete and meaningful learning experiences is more involved than simply passing out blocks or beans to help introduce a concept. It involves utilizing and developing the language of subject. Inquiry based learning provides the students the opportunity to not only explore the materials and concepts, but to begin to organize the information in order to be able to communicate their ideas of mathematics.

Without this concrete level of exploration, students may be able to memorize rote processes for solving problems (algorithms), but they may lack the foundational understanding necessary to make mathematical connections to everyday situations and experiences. Some students will be unable to see the broader generalizations found throughout math unless they have the time and exposure to the concepts through concrete learning experiences.

Mathematics has its own language which requires practice and development. Often students who are struggling with the concepts presented, lack the appropriate vocabulary and exposure to mathematical language to be successful. It is important to promote the development of this vocabulary as you would do with reading vocabulary or in other subjects.

Successful math teachers introduce their students to multiple problem-solving strategies and create a classroom environment where free thought and experimentation are encouraged. Teachers can promote problem solving by allowing multiple attempts at problems, giving credit for reworking test or homework problems, and encouraging the sharing of ideas through class discussion. Once the students are successful at completing problem solving activities at the concrete level, students should be exposed to the semi concrete (use of pictures and symbols) level and finally to the abstract level (use of symbols or letters to represent numbers or concepts). There are several specific problem-solving skills with which teachers should be familiar.

The **guess-and-check** strategy calls for students to make an initial guess at the solution, check the answer, and use the outcome to guide the next guess. With each successive guess, the student should get closer to the correct answer. Constructing a table from the guesses can help organize the data.

Example: There are 100 coins in a jar, and 10 are dimes. The rest are pennies and nickels. There are twice as many pennies as nickels. How many pennies and nickels are in the jar?

There are 90 total nickels and pennies in the jar (100 coins – 10 dimes).

There are twice as many pennies as nickels. Make guesses that fulfill the criteria and adjust based on the answer found. Continue until you find the correct answer: 60 pennies and 30 nickels.

Number of Pennies	Number of Nickels	Total Number of Pennies and Nickels
40	20	60
80	40	120
70	35	105
60	30	90

When solving a problem where the final result and the steps to reach the result are given, students must **work backwards** to determine what the starting point must have been.

<u>Example</u>:
John subtracted 7 from his age, and divided the result by 3. The final result was 4. What is John's age?

Work backward by reversing the operations:
$4 \times 3 = 12$
$12 + 7 = 19$
John is 19 years old.

Throughout the process, students should be encouraged to develop methods for recording their information through the use of pictures, symbols, numbers or other more appropriate ideas. Venn diagrams are excellent for comparing mathematical concepts. Learning to use pictures and numbers together to represent an idea provide students with a means to communicate to each other the concepts they are learning. Teachers can build the vocabulary and thinking skills of their students by using these pictures or student created models and providing the students with the correct mathematical name or label for the idea. Together these student created and teacher labeled representations can provide students with not only a communication tool, but a concrete method for explaining conjectures to each other.

Skill 6.3   Demonstrate knowledge of methods for helping young children learn and apply concepts and skills in different areas of mathematics, including number systems, number sense, computation, numeration, measurement (e.g., length, weight, volume, temperature), geometry, spatial relationships, data collection and analysis, chance, and patterns and relationships.

Each paragraph below illustrates one method of teaching mathematics. All of these methods should be used, but depending on the age and mathematical skill of the child, they will be used in differing amounts.

The first method is "hands on." This is the first method to be used, particularly in Pre-K. Ideally you could have one teacher or one helper working with each child. By judicious discussion try to identify what the child already knows about numbers. Then work little by little to broaden this knowledge, based on the environment the child comes from and what experiences he is likely to encounter.

At this level, it is also important to provide children with centers/opportunities to explore math on their own. These types of centers/opportunities might include weighing themselves or other items on scales, covering the area of a shape with tiles, filling a shape with solids or liquids, comparing the size of objects, putting objects in order by size, sorting shapes, duplicating simple patterns with colored beads, and looking at books about numbers.

As the child moves into kindergarten and first grade continue to use this method whenever introducing new skills. Working one-on-one will probably not be possible here, so set up stations around the room where two or three children can work to answer specific questions using physical objects. The teacher would circulate around to each station checking on the work and perhaps making suggestions. Be careful about not making your suggestions too specific. Let the children work things out for themselves as much as possible, unless they appear to be hopelessly stuck.

Hopefully computers will be available in your classroom. There are tremendous amounts of very good software available for all age groups. Your job will be to familiarize yourself with these programs so that you can choose the best ones for your situation. Let the students work in pairs on the computer, as young children like to work together.

From first grade on, begin to introduce the class discussion as an introduction to a new topic. Then have some kind of hands-on work that each student can do individually or in pairs. Finally have some individual paper-and-pencil work. This would normally be a drill activity to solidify the concepts being learned.

Partner-quizzes are a good way to introduce testing in a non-frightening way. Students work in pairs and turn in a single paper as their joint quiz work, where they have agreed after discussion as to what the correct answers are.

Standardized tests are a fact of life in our classrooms now, but instead of spending any time specifically preparing students just before the test is to take place (cramming!), a better way is to build in constant review as you go along. Mathematics textbooks are notoriously bad in this regard. They seem to expect students to remember on page 100 something that they haven't mentioned since page 10.

A good way to prepare students for testing is to make a list of all the possible skills that they will be tested over during the year. Then introduce these skills early on, say one each week. During the second week as you introduce the second new topic, review the first one each day also. During the third week as you introduce the third new topic, review the second one each day, and the first one every other day. Continue in this manner, eventually reviewing every old topic at least once a week, and the newer ones more often. This frequent review will help children to remember what they have learned.

Skill 6.4 Identify developmentally appropriate strategies and activities for providing young children with opportunities to use mathematical problem solving in everyday situations.

Problem solving needs to be incorporated in a real way for students to understand, appreciate and value the process. Using daily activities or problems can help make problem solving a regular part of a child's day. As situations arise, in any subject area, it is important for the teacher to incorporate problem solving activities. Having the students help with lunch count, attendance, counting the number of days left in the school year, calculating the time left until recess, or other daily types of activities are examples of ways to include realistic problem solving in the classroom.

Bringing real situations into the classroom can also be an important strategy for incorporating everyday situations into the classroom. Examples might include:

- Bringing in three boxes of ice cream sandwiches for a treat and having the students decide how many sandwiches will be left over after everyone has one.
- Looking at the weather, finding the temperature and deciding whether or not they need to wear a coat outside based on the temperature.
- Keeping a calendar of important events for the students to share with their parents and having the students count down days until a special event

Additionally, problem solving activities should be incorporated into all subject areas. In science, children can graph the daily temperatures and make predictions for the future temperatures. In social studies, they can gather, tabulate and calculate the data related to the topic presented (how many classmates agree that drugs are bad for your body). In language arts, children can solve problems find in all types of children's literature. Charting favorite books, calculating ages of characters in stories, and drawing maps of the setting(s) of books are some beginning examples of ways to connect the two subjects. There are also numerous exciting books written with a mathematical basis which can be used to cover both subjects in a fun manner.

Problem solving can involve many different aspects and is not always limited to the basic operations of addition, subtraction, multiplication and division. It is important to remember to incorporate all different types of problem solving. No matter the skill area, the idea of making predictions, drawing conclusions, developing appropriate language constructs and providing accurate detailed descriptions are all important problem solving strategies.

Some examples of nontraditional problem solving include:

- **Patterns-** Having the students determine how to add a pattern to an art project, find patterns in the school, finish patterns, add missing elements to patterns or even create their own patterns are examples ways to include patterning into problem solving. Remember for the very young children patterns may involve shapes, colors or objects, but as they increase in age the patterns might involve number patterns or other more complex concepts of patterns.
- **Geometric Concepts-** Exposing children to a variety of shapes and activities from shape sorters for the young to tessellations or tiling situations for the older students can help them begin to learn to solve problems with geometric reasoning. Comparing objects, using Venn diagrams, building patterns, and drawing conclusions are additional methods for building geometric concepts.
- **Spatial Reasoning** – Using tangrams, pantomimes, and tessellations will help students begin to solve problems involving spatial reasoning. Additionally, it is important to incorporate real world language and locations within the physical world are other ways to increase spatial reasoning within your students.

Skill 6.5 Demonstrate knowledge of approaches and activities for integrating learning experiences in mathematics with learning experiences in other content areas.

Teaching students how subjects connect and are interrelated. Bridging the gaps between various subjects by integration of learning helps students in numerous ways. Integration of content provides a clearer understanding of real life situations. In reality, students will not have a separate math, reading, and science time at the grocery store or other venues. Instead they will be expected to incorporate all of their information together into one process to complete the task.

One of the easiest ways to incorporate real life mathematical activities is to bring real life activities into the classroom. Working as a class to prepare food where the students need to measure different ingredients before/after completing lessons on fractions is an excellent way for the students to understand the importance of the learning, especially if you make a food the children enjoy. Other mixing activities which involve measuring math skills involve: making play dough, making slime, and creating the perfect bubble blowing mixture. Cooking and mixture activities also have a direct connection to the sciences and allow the teacher to combine subject areas into one lesson.

Other methods to incorporate math activities into more regular parts of students' lives and other subject areas include:

- Charting/graphing the weather on a regular basis
- Predicting temperatures based on a pattern or other information
- Helping students keep track of the score of a sporting event using tally marks
- Finding the age of other family members or characters in stories
- Building race cars or straw structures to represent buildings from stories or having your own race, similar to a NASCAR event
- Redesigning the layout of the classroom/cafeteria
- Playing card, dice, and board games with the students (the popular games like Pokemon involve a lot of math if played correctly)
- Timing activities or determining how long until a special event will occur
- In the home living area, provide muffin tins and play food muffins to match one-to-one. Have placemats, plates, plastic forks, etc. so that students can set the table – again one-to-one.
- In the Science area, provide a simple balance to compare the weight of groups of blocks, etc.
- Provide number word/concept math books in the reading area. Have number puzzles and shape sorters.

COMPETENCY 7.0 UNDERSTAND FUNDAMENTAL SCIENTIFIC CONCEPTS AND PROCESSES AND HOW TO PROMOTE YOUNG CHILDREN'S DEVELOPMENT OF SCIENTIFIC KNOWLEDGE AND SKILLS, INCLUDING THEIR USE OF SCIENTIFIC THINKING, REASONING, AND INQUIRY.

Skill 7.1 Demonstrate knowledge of the process of scientific inquiry and reasoning

Science may be defined as a body of knowledge that is systematically derived from study, observations and experimentation. Its goal is to identify and establish principles and theories that may be applied to solve problems.

Scientific inquiry begins with observation. Observation is a very important skill by itself, since it leads to experimentation and finally communicating the experimental findings to the society / public. After observing, a question is formed, which starts with "why" or "how." To answer these questions, experimentation is necessary. Between observation and experimentation, there are three more important steps. These are gathering information (or researching about the problem), developing a hypothesis, and designing the experiment.

As much information as possible is collected from various sources including the internet, books, journals, knowledgeable people, newspapers, etc. This lays a solid foundation for formulating a hypothesis. The third step is hypothesizing. This is making a statement about the problem with the knowledge acquired and using the two important words 'if' and 'when'. This is an educated guess about the answer to the problem or question. The 'best guess' is your hypothesis.

Designing an experiment is involves identifying a control, constants, independent variables and dependent variables. A control or standard is something we compare our results with at the end of the experiment. It is a reference. Constants are the factors we have to keep constant in an experiment to get reliable results. Independent variables are factors we change in an experiment. It is very important to bear in mind that there should be more constants than variables to obtain reproducible results in an experiment.

Classifying is grouping items according to their similarities. It is important for students to realize relationships and similarity as well as differences to reach a reasonable conclusion in a lab experience. After the experiment is done, it is repeated and results are graphically presented. The results are then analyzed and conclusions drawn. It is the responsibility of the scientists to share the knowledge they obtain through their research.

After the conclusion is drawn, the final step is communication. In this age, lot of emphasis is put on the way and the method of communication. The conclusions must be communicated by clearly describing the information using accurate data, visual presentation like graphs (bar/line/pie), tables/charts, diagrams, artwork, and other appropriate media like power point presentation. Modern technology must be used whenever it is necessary. The method of communication must be suitable to the audience. Written communication is as important as oral communication.

Skill 7.2   Demonstrate knowledge of fundamental concepts and principles related to Earth and space science, the life sciences, the physical sciences, and the environmental sciences

Physical Science

Everything in our world is made up of **matter**, whether it is a rock, a building, an animal, or a person. Matter is defined by its characteristics: It takes up space and it has mass.

Mass is a measure of the amount of matter in an object. Two objects of equal mass will balance each other on a simple balance scale no matter where the scale is located. For instance, two rocks with the same amount of mass that are in balance on Earth will also be in balance on the Moon. They will feel heavier on Earth than on the Moon because of the gravitational pull of the Earth. So, although the two rocks have the same mass, they will have different weight.

Weight is the measure of the Earth's pull of gravity on an object. It can also be defined as the pull of gravity between other bodies. The units of weight measurement commonly used are the pound (English measure) and the kilogram (metric measure).

Physical properties and chemical properties of matter describe the appearance or behavior of a substance. A **physical property** can be observed without changing the identity of a substance. For instance, you can describe the color, mass, shape, and volume of a book. **Chemical properties** describe the ability of a substance to be changed into new substances. Baking powder goes through a chemical change as it changes into carbon dioxide gas during the baking process.

Matter constantly changes. A **physical change** is a change that does not produce a new substance. The freezing and melting of water is an example of physical change. A **chemical change** (or chemical reaction) is any change of a substance into one or more other substances. Burning materials turn into smoke; a seltzer tablet fizzes into gas bubbles.

The **phase of matter** (solid, liquid, or gas) is identified by its shape and volume. A **solid** has a definite shape and volume. A **liquid** has a definite volume, but no shape. A **gas** has no shape or volume because it will spread out to occupy the entire space of whatever container it is in.

Energy is the ability to cause change in matter. Applying heat to a frozen liquid changes it from solid back to liquid. Continue heating it and it will boil and give off steam, a gas. **Evaporation** is the change in phase from liquid to gas. **Condensation** is the change in phase from gas to liquid.

A **magnet** is a material or object that attracts certain metals, such as cobalt, nickel, and iron and can also repel or attract another magnet. All magnets have poles: a North-seeking (N) and a South-seeking (S). In a compass, the side marked N will point toward the Earth's North magnetic pole, which is different from the North Pole (they are actually several hundred miles apart). If you cut a magnet into parts, each part will have both North and South poles. If you place magnets near each other, the opposite poles will attract and the like poles will repel each other. Therefore, a North pole will repel a North pole and attract a South pole.

The first true application of a magnet was the compass, which not only helps in navigation but also can help in detecting small magnetic fields. Magnets are also found in loudspeakers, electrical generators, and electrical motors. A very common use of magnets is to stick things to the refrigerator.

A **magnetic field** is made up of imaginary lines of flux resulting from moving or spinning electrically charged particles. These lines of magnetic flux move from one end of a magnetic object to the other, or rather, from the North-seeking pole to the South-seeking pole.

Magnetic and electric fields are similar in that in electricity, like charges repel, and in magnetism, like poles repel. They are different in that a magnet must have two poles, but an electrical charge, positive or negative, can stand alone.

Heat and temperature are different physical quantities. **Heat** is a measure of energy. **Temperature** is the measure of how hot (or cold) a body is with respect to a standard object.

We can not rely on our sense of touch to determine temperature because the heat from a hand may be conducted more efficiently by certain objects, making them feel colder. **Thermometers** are used to measure temperature. A small amount of mercury in a capillary tube will expand when heated. The thermometer and the object whose temperature it is measuring are put in contact long enough for them to reach thermal equilibrium. Then the temperature can be read from the thermometer scale. Three temperature scales are used. These are Celsius, Fahrenheit, and Kelvin.

Life Science

All organisms are adapted to life in their unique habitat. The habitat includes all the components of their physical environment and is a necessity for the species' survival. Below are several key components of a complete habitat that all organisms require.

Food and water

Because all biochemical reactions take place in aqueous environments, all organisms must have access to clean water, even if only infrequently. Organisms also require two types of food: a source of energy (fixed carbon) and a source of nutrients. Autotrophs can fix carbon for themselves, but must have access to certain inorganic precursors. These organisms must also be able to obtain other nutrients, such as nitrogen, from their environment. Hetertrophs, on the other hand, must consume other organisms for both energy and nutrients. The species these organisms use as a food source must be present in their habitat.

Sunlight and air

This need is closely related to that for food and water because almost all species derive some needed nutrients from the sun and atmosphere. Plants require carbon dioxide to photosynthesize and oxygen is required for cellular respiration. Sunlight is also necessary for photosynthesis and is used by many animals to synthesize essential nutrients (i.e. vitamin D).

Shelter and space

The need for shelter and space vary greatly between species. Many plants do not need shelter, per se, but must have adequate soil to spread their roots and acquire nutrients. Certain invasive species can threaten native plants by out-competing them for space. Other types of plants and many animals also require protection from environmental hazards. These locations may facilitate reproduction (for instance, nesting sites) or provide seasonal shelter (for examples, dens and caves used by hibernating species).

Life Cycles

A diagram of an organism's life cycle simply reveals the various stages through which it progresses from the time it is conceived until it reaches sexual maturity and reproduces, starting the cycle over again. However, the various types of animals pass through very different phases of life. The different species may either lay eggs or give live birth, pass through metamorphosis or be born in a form similar to that of an adult, and have aquatic and terrestrial phases or spend their entire lives on land. Some classic examples are outlined here.

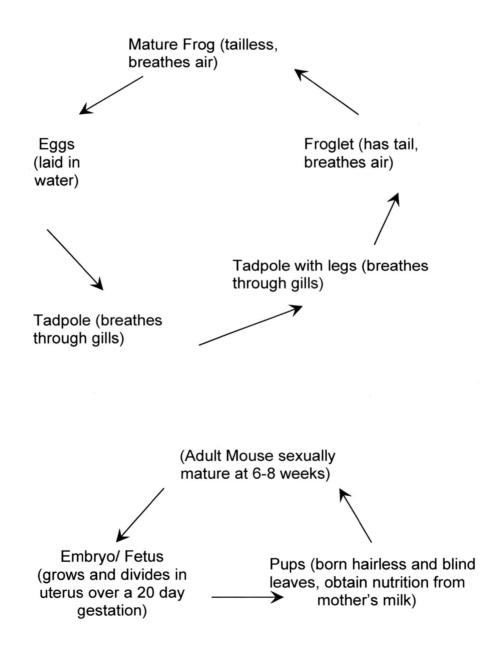

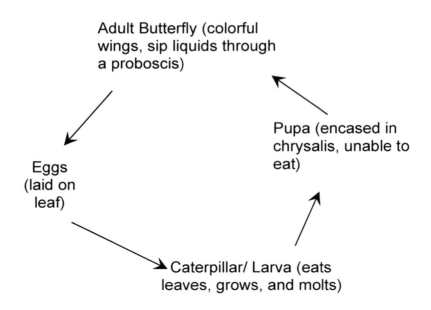

Trophic levels are based on the feeding relationships that determine energy flow and chemical cycling.

Autotrophs are the primary producers of the ecosystem. **Producers** mainly consist of plants. **Primary consumers** are the next trophic level. The primary consumers are the herbivores that eat plants or algae. **Secondary consumers** are the carnivores that eat the primary consumers. **Tertiary consumers** eat the secondary consumer. These trophic levels may go higher depending on the ecosystem. **Decomposers** are consumers that feed off animal waste and dead organisms. This pathway of food transfer is known as the food chain.

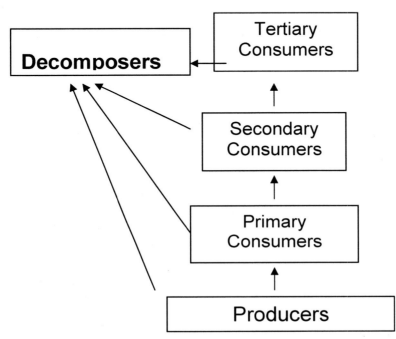

Space Science

Satellites

An artificial satellite is any object placed into orbit by human endeavor. A satellite revolves around a planet in a circular or elliptical path. Most man-made satellites are useful objects placed in orbit purposely to perform some specific mission or task. Such satellites may include weather satellites, communication satellites, navigational satellites, reconnaissance satellites and scientific study satellites. Satellites are placed into orbit by first riding on a rocket or in the cargo bay of a space shuttle that is launched into space. Once the vessel has reached the satellite's destination, the satellite is released into space and remains in orbit due to the Earth's gravitational pull. The largest artificial satellite currently orbiting the Earth is the International Space Station. Currently, there are approximately 23,000 items of space junk—objects large enough to track with radar that were inadvertently placed in orbit or have outlived their usefulness—floating above Earth.

Airplanes

Airplanes or fixed-wing aircraft are heavier than aircraft that utilize the laws of physics to achieve flight. Airplanes achieve flight using the concepts of lift, weight, thrust and drag. Lift pushes the plane upward, and is created by the design of aircraft wings, which have flat bottoms and slightly rounded tops. As the aircraft is propelled forward by thrust from the engines, air moves faster over the top of the wings, and slower under the bottom. The slower airflow beneath the wing generates more pressure, while the faster airflow above generates less. This difference in pressure results in upward lift. Weight is Earth's gravity pulling down on a plane. Planes are designed to remain level, with equal weight in the front and back of the plane. Drag is the opposite force that slows a plane. Planes minimize drag with aerodynamic design.

Humankind's interest in flight is documented as far back as Greek mythology. The first real study of flight, however, is attributed to Leonardo da Vinci, who designed a craft called the orthinopter, on which the modern day helicopter is based. The first successful flight was achieved by the Wright Brothers off the outer banks of North Carolina. Their craft was developed by first studying many early attempts at flight, and then testing their own theories using balloons and kites. The brothers designed gliders to understand craft control and wind effects. Using a wind tunnel, the Wright Brothers tested many different wing and tail shapes. After determining a glider shape that consistently passed flight tests, they began to develop a propulsion system capable of creating lift. Eventually, the brothers constructed an engine capable of generating almost 12 horsepower. On December 17, 1903, the Wright Brother's craft known as the "Flyer" lifted from ground level piloted by brother Orville, and traveled one hundred and twenty feet.

Natural Objects in the sky

There are eight established planets in our solar system. These are Mercury, Venus, Earth, Mars, Jupiter, Saturn, Uranus, and Neptune. Pluto was known as an established planet in our solar system, but as of summer 2006, its status is being reconsidered. The planets are divided into two groups based on their distance from the Sun. The inner planets include: Mercury, Venus, Earth, and Mars. The outer planets include: Jupiter, Saturn, Uranus, and Neptune.

Mercury – is the closest planet to the Sun. Its surface has craters and rocks. The atmosphere is composed of hydrogen, helium and sodium. Mercury was named after the Roman messenger god.

Venus - has a slow rotation when compared to Earth. Venus and Uranus rotate in opposite directions from the other planets. This opposite rotation is called retrograde rotation. The surface of Venus is not visible due to the extensive cloud cover. The atmosphere is composed mostly of carbon dioxide. Sulfuric acid droplets in the dense cloud cover give Venus a yellow appearance. Venus has a greater greenhouse effect than observed on Earth. The dense clouds combined with carbon dioxide trap heat. Venus was named after the Roman goddess of love.

Earth – is considered a water planet with 70% of its surface covered by water. Gravity holds the masses of water in place. The different temperatures observed on earth allow for the different states (solid, liquid, gas) of water to exist. The atmosphere is composed mainly of oxygen and nitrogen. Earth is the only planet that is known to support life.

Mars – The surface contains numerous craters, active and extinct volcanoes, ridges, and valleys with extremely deep fractures. Iron oxide found in the dusty soil makes the surface seem rust colored and the skies seem pink in color. The atmosphere is composed of carbon dioxide, nitrogen, argon, oxygen and water vapor. Mars has polar regions with ice caps composed of water. Mars has two satellites and was named after the Roman war god.

Jupiter – is the largest planet in the solar system. Jupiter has 16 moons. The atmosphere is composed of hydrogen, helium, methane and ammonia. There are white colored bands of clouds indicating rising gas and dark colored bands of clouds indicating descending gases. The gas movement is caused by heat resulting from the energy of Jupiter's core. Jupiter has a Great Red Spot that is thought to be a hurricane type cloud. Jupiter has a strong magnetic field.

Saturn – is the second largest planet in the solar system. Saturn has rings of ice, rock, and dust particles circling it. Saturn's atmosphere is composed of hydrogen, helium, methane, and ammonia. Saturn has 20 plus satellites and was named for the Roman god of agriculture.

Uranus – is the second largest planet in the solar system with retrograde revolution. Uranus is a gaseous planet. It has 10 dark rings and 15 satellites. Its atmosphere is composed of hydrogen, helium, and methane. Uranus was named after the Greek god of the heavens.

Neptune – is another gaseous planet with an atmosphere consisting of hydrogen, helium, and methane. Neptune has 3 rings and 2 satellites. Neptune was named after the Roman sea god because its atmosphere is the same color as the seas.

Pluto – was once considered the smallest planet in the solar system; its status as a planet is being reconsidered. Pluto's atmosphere probably contains methane, ammonia, and frozen water. Pluto has 1 satellite. Pluto revolves around the Sun every 250 years. Pluto was named after the Roman god of the underworld.

Astronomers believe that rocky fragments may have been the remains of the birth of the solar system that never formed into a planet. **Asteroids** are found in the region between Mars and Jupiter.

Comets are masses of frozen gases, cosmic dust, and small rocky particles. Astronomers think that most comets originate in a dense comet cloud beyond Pluto. Comet consists of a nucleus, a coma, and a tail. A comet's tail always points away from the sun. The most famous comet, **Halley's Comet,** is named after the person whom first discovered it in 240 B.C. It returns to the skies near earth every 75 to 76 years.

Meteoroids are composed of particles of rock and metal of various sizes. When a meteoroid travels through the earth's atmosphere, friction causes its surface to heat up and it begins to burn. The burning meteoroid falling through the earth's atmosphere is called a **meteor** (also known as a "shooting star").

Meteorites are meteors that strike the earth's surface. A physical example of a meteorite's impact on the earth's surface can be seen in Arizona. The Barringer Crater is a huge meteor crater. There are many other meteor craters throughout the world.

Astronomers use groups or patterns of stars called **constellations** as reference points to locate other stars in the sky. Familiar constellations include Ursa Major (also known as the big bear) and Ursa Minor (known as the little bear). Within the Ursa Major, the smaller constellation, The Big Dipper is found. Within the Ursa Minor, the smaller constellation, The Little Dipper is found.

Different constellations appear as the Earth continues its revolution around the sun with the seasonal changes. Magnitude stars are 21 of the brightest stars that can be seen from earth. These are the first stars noticed at night. There are 15 commonly observed first magnitude stars in the Northern Hemisphere.

A vast collection of stars is defined as a **galaxy**. Galaxies are classified as irregular, elliptical, and spiral. An irregular galaxy has no real structured appearance; most are in their early stages of life. An elliptical galaxy consists of smooth ellipses, containing little dust and gas, but composed of millions or trillion stars. Spiral galaxies are disk-shaped and have extending arms that rotate around its dense center. Earth's galaxy is found in the Milky Way and it is a spiral galaxy.

Earth Science

Seasonal change on Earth is caused by the orbit and axial tilt of the planet in relation to the Sun's Ecliptic: the rotational path of the Sun. These factors combine to vary the degree of insolation (distribution of solar energy) at a particular location and thereby change the seasons.

World weather patterns are greatly influenced by ocean surface currents in the upper layer of the ocean. These currents continuously move along the ocean surface in specific directions. Surface currents are caused by winds and classified by temperature. Cold currents originate in the Polar regions and flow through surrounding water that is measurably warmer. Those currents with a higher temperature than the surrounding water are called warm currents and can be found near the **equator**. These currents follow swirling routes around the ocean basins and the equator. The Gulf Stream and the California Current are the two main surface currents that flow along the coastlines of the United States. The California Current is a cold current that originates in the Arctic regions and flows southward along the western coast of the United States.

A **thunderstorm** is a brief, local storm produced by the rapid upward movement of warm, moist air within a cumulonimbus cloud. Thunderstorms always produce lightning and thunder, and are accompanied by strong wind gusts and heavy rain or hail.

A severe storm with swirling winds that may reach speeds of hundreds of km per hour is called a **tornado**. Such a storm is also referred to as a "twister". The sky is covered by large cumulonimbus clouds and violent thunderstorms; a funnel-shaped swirling cloud may extend downward from a cumulonimbus cloud and reach the ground. Tornadoes are storms that leave a narrow path of destruction on the ground.

Hurricanes are storms that develop when warm, moist air carried by trade winds rotates around a low-pressure "eye". A large, rotating, low-pressure system accompanied by heavy precipitation and strong winds is called a tropical cyclone (better known as a hurricane). In the Pacific region, a hurricane is called a typhoon.

Storms that occur only in the winter are known as blizzards or ice storms. A **blizzard** is a storm with strong winds, blowing snow and frigid temperatures. An **ice storm** consists of falling rain that freezes when it strikes the ground, covering everything with a layer of ice.

Minerals

Minerals are natural, non-living solids with a definite chemical composition and a crystalline structure. **Ores** are minerals or rock deposits that can be mined for a profit. **Rocks** are earth materials made of one or more minerals. A **Rock Facies** is a rock group that differs from comparable rocks (as in composition, age, or fossil content).

There are over 3000 minerals in Earth's crust. Minerals are classified by composition. The major groups of minerals are silicates, carbonates, oxides, sulfides, sulfates, and halides. The largest group of minerals is the silicates. Silicates are made of silicon, oxygen, and one or more other elements. This is the most abundant class of minerals on Earth and includes quartz, garnets, micas, and feldspars.

Rocks

Rocks are simply aggregates of minerals. Rocks are classified by their differences in chemical composition and mode of formation. Generally, three classes are recognized: igneous, sedimentary, and metamorphic. However, it is common that one type of rock is transformed into another and this is known as the rock cycle.

Igneous rocks are formed from molten magma. There are two types of igneous rock: volcanic and plutonic. As the name suggests, volcanic rock is formed when magma reaches the Earth's surface as lava. Plutonic rock is also derived from magma, but it is formed when magma cools and crystallizes beneath surface of the Earth. Thus, both types of igneous rock are magma that has cooled either above (volcanic) or below (plutonic) the Earth's crust. Examples of this type of rock include granite and obsidian glass.

Sedimentary rocks are formed by the layered deposition of inorganic and/or organic matter. Layers, or strata, of rock are laid down horizontally to form sedimentary rocks. Sedimentary rocks that form as mineral solutions (i.e., sea water) evaporate are called precipitate. Those that contain the remains of living organisms are termed biogenic. Finally, those that form from the freed fragments of other rocks are called clastic. Because the layers of sedimentary rocks reveal chronology and often contain fossils, these types of rock have been key in helping scientists understand the history of the earth. Chalk, limestone, sandstone, and shale are all examples of sedimentary rock.

Metamorphic rocks are created when rocks are subjected to high temperatures and pressures. The original rock, or protolith, may have been igneous, sedimentary or even an older metamorphic rock. The temperatures and pressures necessary to achieve transformation are higher than those observed on the Earth's surface and are high enough to alter the minerals in the protolith. Because these rocks are formed within the Earth's crust, studying metamorphic rocks gives us clues to conditions in the Earth's mantle. In some metamorphic rocks, different colored bands are apparent. These result from strong pressures being applied from specific directions and is termed foliation. Examples of metamorphic rock include slate and marble.

Fossil: The trace or remains of any once living organism. The preservation of fossils in the environment is not all that common an occurrence. Although there is no formally set time limit to be considered a fossil, the term is not usually applied to remains less than 100 years old. Although soft tissues can be fossilized, they are very rare. If preserved, the fossil is usually found as hard points. Bones and shells are the most fossilized parts of the organism. Rapid burial is a major factor in fossilization. It helps to keep scavengers at bay and bacterial decay at a minimum. 99% of all fossils are found in sedimentary rock. The heat present in forming Igneous and Metamorphic rock generally obliterates organic remains.

Water

The unique properties of water are partially responsible for the development of life on Earth. Many of the unique qualities of water stem from the hydrogen bonds that form between the molecules. Hydrogen bonds are particularly strong dipole-dipole interactions that form between the H-atom of one molecule and an F, O, or N atom of an adjacent molecule. The partial positive charge on the hydrogen atom is attracted to the partial negative charge on the electron pair of the other atom. The hydrogen bond between two water molecules is shown as the dashed line below:

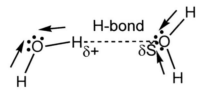

Erosion is the inclusion and transportation of surface materials by another moveable material, usually water, wind, or ice. The most important cause of erosion is running water. Streams, rivers, and tides are constantly at work removing weathered fragments of bedrock and carrying them away from their original location.

A stream erodes bedrock by the grinding action of the sand, pebbles and other rock fragments. This grinding against each other is called abrasion. Streams also erode rocks by dissolving or absorbing their minerals. Limestone and marble are readily dissolved by streams.

The breaking down of rocks at or near to the Earth's surface is known as **weathering**. Weathering breaks down these rocks into smaller and smaller pieces. There are two types of weathering: physical weathering and chemical weathering.

Physical weathering is the process by which rocks are broken down into smaller fragments without undergoing any change in chemical composition. Physical weathering is mainly caused by the freezing of water, the expansion of rock, and the activities of plants and animals.

Frost wedging is the cycle of daytime thawing and refreezing at night. This cycle causes large rock masses, especially the rocks exposed on mountain tops, to be broken into smaller pieces.

Chemical weathering is the breaking down of rocks through changes in their chemical composition. An example would be the change of feldspar in granite to clay. Water, oxygen, and carbon dioxide are the main agents of chemical weathering. When water and carbon dioxide combine chemically, they produce a weak acid that breaks down rocks.

Deposition, also known as sedimentation, is the term for the process by which material from one area are slowly deposited into another area. This is usually due to the movement of wind, water, or ice containing particles of matter. When the rate of movement slows down, particles filter out and remain behind, causing a build up of matter. Note that this is a result of matter being eroded and removed from another site.

Skill 7.3   **Demonstrate understanding of strategies for encouraging young children's natural curiosity about their world and for promoting their respect for living organisms and appreciation of the environment**

Learning can be broadly divided into two kinds - active and passive. Active learning involves, as the name indicates, a learning atmosphere full of action whereas in passive learning students are taught in a non-stimulating and inactive atmosphere. Active learning involves and draws students into it, thereby interesting them to the point of participating and purposely engaging in learning.

It is crucial that students are actively engaged, not entertained. They should be taught the answers for "How" and "Why" questions and encouraged to be inquisitive and interested. Active learning is conceptualized as follows:

A Model of Active Learning

Experience of	Dialogue with
Doing	Self
Observing	Others

This model suggests that all learning activities involve some kind of experience or some kind of dialogue. The two main kinds of dialogue are "Dialogue with self" and "Dialogue with others". The two main kinds of experience are "Observing" and "Doing".

Dialogue with self: This is what happens when a learner thinks reflectively about a topic. They ask themselves a number of things about the topic.

Dialogue with others: When the students are listening to a book being read by another student or when the teacher is teaching, a partial dialogue takes place because the dialogue is only one sided. When they are listening to an adult and when there is an exchange of ideas back and forth, it is said to be a dialogue with others.

Observing: This is a most important skill in science. This occurs when a learner is carefully watching or observing someone else doing an activity or experiment. This is a good experience, although it is not quite like doing it for themselves.

Doing: This refers to any activity where a learner actually does something, giving the learner a firsthand experience that is very valuable.

The scientific attitude is to be curious, open to new ideas, and skeptical. In science, there is always new research, new discoveries, and new theories proposed. Sometimes, old theories are disproved. To view these changes rationally, one must have such openness, curiosity, and skepticism. (Skepticism is a Greek word, meaning a method of obtaining knowledge through systematic doubt and continual testing. A scientific skeptic is one who refuses to accept certain types of claims without subjecting them to a systematic investigation.) The students may not have these attitudes inherently, but it is the responsibility of the teacher to encourage, nurture, and practice these attitudes so that your students will have a good role model.

Because biology is the study of living things, we can easily apply the knowledge of biology to daily life and personal decision-making. For example, biology greatly influences the health decisions humans make everyday. What foods to eat, when and how to exercise, and how often to bathe are just three of the many decisions we make everyday that are based on our knowledge of biology.

If learning is connected to everyday life, students are motivated because they can easily see its relevance. If they are taught about something remote, they will not be able to relate, and the result is decreased interest, decreased motivation to study, and a general decrease in learning.

Skill 7.4 **Identify developmentally appropriate activities and learning opportunities that encourage young children to conduct experiments, solve problems, apply the scientific process, and incorporate safety precautions.**

Science is an exciting field. It is one of the areas of study in which students can readily explore cause and effect relationships.

The quintessential experiment for a chemical reaction is the volcano experiment. The addition of vinegar to baking soda in a contained area will cause a chemical reaction similar to an erupting volcano. Children love this as it gives them a visual representation of the abstract idea of a chemical reaction.

An idea for changes of state (these represent a physical change not a chemical change) would be the freezing and melting of water/ice. If you do this on a large enough scale, you can literally go back and forth between states every few days without too much loss of water (due to evaporation).

Growth is an important concept in science. Because it is such a central concept there are many appropriate experiments. Some familiar ideas include the peeling apart of a seed or bean to study its various parts. Left over seeds not dissected can be planted. Students enjoy seeing their seeds grow. However, if you set a few aside and change the conditions you can examine experimental variables (lack of sunlight, drought conditions, etc.) Continuing on the idea of growth, children can create a growth chart of themselves. This can be a literal growth chart in inches over the course of the school year or a developmental chart of their youth (parent input required).

Hatching and/or housing animals in your classroom teaches children valuable lessons about respect for the Earth and its inhabitants. If you choose to hatch an organism (popular choices are tadpoles and butterflies), students can be introduced to the concept of life cycle. The duration of each stage in the life cycle can be tracked, tallied, and displayed in a graph format. Housing animals teaches children about responsibility and humane treatment. Animals should always be fed, watered, and cleaned appropriately and cared for adequately over school vacations. Be particularly careful about the temperature of the classroom.

While not an experiment, it sets a good example to keep a recycling bin in your classroom for recyclable materials (where recycling capabilities exist). It is never too early to teach a child to respect the Earth.

Disclaimer: Experiments involving young children should never include toxic or harmful materials. The ideas listed above are generally considered safe. With that said, use appropriate discretion when conducting experiments and never leave your students unattended.

Skill 7.5 Recognize activities for fostering young children's ability to apply scientific concepts and principles and explore the interconnectedness of the sciences in everyday environments

There are two important things in teaching science. The first is theory- explaining the lesson and answering why, how, when, what and which (out of these five, why and how are the most important and useful to gain knowledge). The second is practical exploration, which implies doing an activity and gaining knowledge by experimentation. Both need to be balanced. Only then will a student fully understand science properly. Specific ideas for fun and engaging science activities are discussed in Skill 7.4.

Linking of ideas is important because the students' prior knowledge is taken into consideration. Based on the prior knowledge of the students, the next step of instruction is planned. When students do not have the expected grade level knowledge, action must be taken to remedy the situation. Otherwise, the students will not be able to benefit. In science each lesson builds upon the next and previous comprehension is critical. For example, students studying life science can not understand organ systems if they do not understand that cells make up tissue, tissue makes up organs, and organs work together in systems.

Inquiry based instruction is becoming popular because the students have questions which must be answered. They need to be encouraged to ask questions and create opportunities to find answers for those questions. The best way to find answers for some of their questions is to let them investigate, experiment and discover for themselves the answers to their questions.

Skill 7.6 **Demonstrate knowledge of the relationships among the sciences; the relationships among science, technology, and society in historical and contemporary contexts; and activities for integrating learning experiences in science with learning experiences in other content areas**

The following are the concepts and processes generally recognized as common to all scientific disciplines:

- Systems, order, and organization
- Evidence, models, and explanation
- Constancy, change, and measurement
- Evolution and equilibrium
- Form and function

Systems, order, and organization

Because the natural world is so complex, the study of science involves the **organization** of items into smaller groups based on interaction or interdependence. These groups are called **systems**. Examples of organization are the periodic table of elements and the five-kingdom classification scheme for living organisms. Examples of systems are the solar system, cardiovascular system, Newton's laws of force and motion, and the laws of conservation.

Order refers to the behavior and measurability of organisms and events in nature. The arrangement of planets in the solar system and the life cycle of bacterial cells are examples of order.

Evidence, models, and explanations

Scientists use **evidence** and **models** to form **explanations** of natural events. Models are miniaturized representations of a larger event or system. Evidence is anything that furnishes proof.

Constancy, change, and measurement

Constancy and **change** describe the observable properties of natural organisms and events. Scientists use different systems of **measurement** to observe change and constancy. For example, the freezing and melting points of given substances and the speed of sound are constant under constant conditions. Growth, decay, and erosion are all examples of natural change.

Evolution and equilibrium

Evolution is the process of change over a long period of time. While biological evolution is the most common example, one can also classify technological advancement, changes in the universe, and changes in the environment as evolution.

Equilibrium is the state of balance between opposing forces of change. Homeostasis and ecological balance are examples of equilibrium.

Form and function

Form and **function** are properties of organisms and systems that are closely related. The function of an object usually dictates its form and the form of an object usually facilitates its function. For example, the form of the heart (e.g. muscle, valves) allows it to perform its function of circulating blood through the body.

Science and technology

Science and technology, while distinct concepts, are closely related. Science attempts to investigate and explain the natural world, while technology attempts to solve human adaptation problems. Technology often results from the application of scientific discoveries, and advances in technology can increase the impact of scientific discoveries. For example, Watson and Crick used science to discover the structure of DNA and their discovery led to many biotechnological advances in the manipulation of DNA. These technological advances greatly influenced the medical and pharmaceutical fields. The success of Watson and Crick's experiments, however, was dependent on the technology available. Without the necessary technology, the experiments would have failed.

Math, science and technology have common themes in how they are applied and understood. All three use models, diagrams, and graphs to simplify a concept for analysis and interpretation. Patterns observed in these systems lead to predictions. Another common theme among these three systems is equilibrium. Equilibrium is a state in which forces are balanced, resulting in stability. Static equilibrium is stability due to a lack of changes and dynamic equilibrium is stability due to a balance between opposite forces. Scale is a ratio of size. For example, a map may have a scale of true miles per every inch drawn on the map. A model drawn to scale is a representation of something that is larger or smaller than its actual size. There is also the very literal interpretation of scale. In this context the scale would be used to measure mass, and would often be called a balance.

The knowledge and use of basic mathematical concepts and skills is a necessary aspect of scientific study. Science depends on data and the manipulation of data requires knowledge of mathematics. As children grow and increase their math competency, an understanding of basic statistics, graphs, charts, and algebra will be expected. For now, studying and creating patterns, identifying the tens, hundreds, and thousands places, basic math, and an introduction to graphing would be appropriate.

The fundamental relationship between the natural and social sciences is the use of the scientific method and the rigorous standards of proof that both disciplines require. This emphasis on organization and evidence separates the sciences from the arts and humanities. Natural science, particularly biology, is closely related to social science, the study of human behavior. Biological and environmental factors often dictate human behavior and accurate assessment of behavior requires a sound understanding of biological factors.

When teaching science, it is a good policy to use an approach called 'paired literature'. This mode of teaching involves reading a book about the topic prior to its instruction, or relating it back to literature previously read. This helps to link science learning to the subjects of language and literacy.

COMPETENCY 8.0 UNDERSTAND FUNDAMENTAL CONCEPTS, SKILLS, AND MODES OF INQUIRY IN THE SOCIAL SCIENCES AND HOW TO PROMOTE YOUNG CHILDREN'S DEVELOPMENT OF KNOWLEDGE AND SKILLS IN THIS AREA.

Skill 8.1 Demonstrate understanding of geographic concepts and phenomena; major ideas, eras, themes, developments, and turning points in the history of Illinois, the United States and the world; rights and responsibilities of citizenship in the United States; basic economic concepts and major features of the U.S. economic system; and concepts related to the structure and organization of human societies, including social, economic, cultural, and political elements and their relationships

U.S. and World History

Ancient civilizations were those cultures that developed to a greater degree and were considered advanced. These included the following with their major accomplishments.

The culture of **Mesopotamia** was definitely autocratic in nature. The various civilizations that criss-crossed the Fertile Crescent were very much top-heavy, with a single ruler at the head of the government and, in many cases, also the head of the religion. The people followed his strict instructions or faced the consequences, which were usually dire and often life-threatening.

The civilizations of the Sumerians, Amorites, Hittites, Assyrians, Chaldeans, and Persians controlled various areas of the land we call Mesopotamia. With few exceptions, tyrants and military leaders controlled the vast majority of aspects of society, including trade, religions, and the laws. Each Sumerian city-state (and there were a few) had its own god, with the city-state's leader doubling as the high priest of worship of that local god. Subsequent cultures had a handful of gods as well, although they had more of a national worship structure, with high priests centered in the capital city as advisers to the tyrant.

Trade was vastly important to these civilizations, since they had access to some but not all of the things that they needed to survive. Some trading agreements led to occupation, as was the case with the Sumerians, who didn't bother to build walls to protect their wealth of knowledge. Egypt and the Phoenician cities were powerful and regular trading partners of the various Mesopotamian cultures.

Legacies handed down to us from these people include:

- The first use of writing, the wheel, and banking (Sumeria)
- The first written set of laws (Code of Hammurabi)
- The first epic story (*Gilgamesh*)
- The first library dedicated to preserving knowledge (instituted by the Assyrian leader Ashurbanipal)
- The Hanging Gardens of Babylon (built by the Chaldean Nebuchadnezzar)

The ancient civilization of the Sumerians invented the wheel; developed irrigation through use of canals, dikes, and devices for raising water; devised the system of cuneiform writing; learned to divide time; and built large boats for trade. The Babylonians devised the famous Code of Hammurabi, a code of laws.

Egypt made numerous significant contributions including construction of the great pyramids; development of hieroglyphic writing; preservation of bodies after death; making paper from papyrus; contributing to developments in arithmetic and geometry; the invention of the method of counting in groups of 1-10 (the decimal system); completion of a solar calendar; and laying the foundation for science and astronomy.

The earliest historical record of **Kush** is in Egyptian sources. They describe a region upstream from the first cataract of the Nile as "wretched." This civilization was characterized by a settled way of life in fortified mud-brick villages. They subsisted on hunting and fishing, herding cattle, and gathering grain. Skeletal remains suggest that the people were a blend of Negroid and Mediterranean peoples. This civilization appears to be the second oldest in Africa (after Egypt).

In government, the king ruled through a law of custom that was interpreted by priests. The king was elected from the royal family. Descent was determined through the mother's line (as in Egypt). But in *an unparalleled innovation*, the Kushites were ruled by a series of female monarchs. The Kushite religion was polytheistic, including all of the primary Egyptian gods. There were, however, regional gods that were the principal gods in their regions. Derived from other African cultures, there was also a lion warrior god. This civilization was vital through the last half of the first millennium BC, but it suffered about 300 years of gradual decline until they were conquered by the Nuba people.

The ancient **Assyrians** were warlike and aggressive due to a highly organized military and used horse drawn chariots.

The **Hebrews**, also known as the ancient Israelites instituted "monotheism," which is the worship of one God, Yahweh, and combined the 66 books of the Hebrew and Christian Greek scriptures into the Bible we have today.

The **Minoans** had a system of writing using symbols to represent syllables in words. They built palaces with multiple levels containing many rooms, water and sewage systems with flush toilets, bathtubs, hot and cold running water, and bright paintings on the walls.

The **Mycenaeans** changed the Minoan writing system to aid their own language and used symbols to represent syllables.

The **Phoenicians** were sea traders well known for their manufacturing skills in glass and metals and the development of their famous purple dye. They became so very proficient in the skill of navigation that they were able to sail by the stars at night. Further, they devised an alphabet using symbols to represent single sounds, which was an improved extension of the Egyptian principle and writing system.

In **India**, the caste system was developed, the principle of zero in mathematics was discovered, and the major religion of Hinduism was begun.

China is considered by some historians to be the oldest, uninterrupted civilization in the world and was in existence around the same time as the ancient civilizations founded in Egypt, Mesopotamia, and the Indus Valley. The Chinese studied nature and weather; stressed the importance of education, family, and a strong central government; followed the religions of Buddhism, Confucianism, and Taoism; and invented such things as gunpowder, paper, printing, and the magnetic compass.

China began building the Great Wall; practiced crop rotation and terrace farming; increased the importance of the silk industry, and developed caravan routes across Central Asia for extensive trade. Also, they increased proficiency in rice cultivation and developed a written language based on drawings or pictographs (no alphabet symbolizing sounds as each word or character had a form different from all others). Ancient China was a land in constant turmoil. Tribes warred with one another almost from the first, with the Great Wall of China being a consolidation of walls built to keep out invaders. The Great Wall was built at the direction of China's emperor, and the idea of an emperor or very strong "government of one" was the rule of law until the twentieth century. Chinese people became very proficient at producing beautiful artworks and exporting them, along with silk, to the rest of the world along the Silk Road. China was also the birthplace of many of the world's most familiar inventions, including paper, printing, paper money, and gunpowder

The ancient **Persians** developed an alphabet; contributed the religions/philosophies of Zoroastrianism, Mithraism, and Gnosticism; and allowed conquered peoples to retain their own customs, laws, and religions.

The classical civilization of **Greece** reached the highest levels in man's achievements based on the foundations already laid by such ancient groups as the Egyptians, Phoenicians, Minoans, and Mycenaeans. Among the more important contributions of Greece were the Greek alphabet derived from the Phoenician letters that formed the basis for the Roman alphabet and our present-day alphabet. Extensive trading and colonization resulted in the spread of the Greek civilization. The love of sports, with emphasis on a sound body, led to the tradition of the Olympic Games. Greece was responsible for the rise of independent, strong city-states. Note the complete contrast between independent, freedom-loving Athens with its practice of pure democracy i.e. direct, personal, active participation in government by qualified citizens and the rigid, totalitarian, militaristic Sparta. Other important areas that the Greeks are credited with influencing include drama, epic and lyric poetry, fables, myths centered on the many gods and goddesses, science, astronomy, medicine, mathematics, philosophy, art, architecture, and recording historical events.

The conquests of Alexander the Great spread Greek ideas to the areas he conquered and brought to the Greek world many ideas from Asia. Above all, the value of ideas, wisdom, curiosity, and the desire to learn as much about the world as possible, satisfied Alexander's thirst for knowledge.

The ancient civilization of **Rome** lasted approximately 1,000 years including the periods of republic and empire, although its lasting influence on Europe and its history was for a much longer period. There was a very sharp contrast between the curious, imaginative, inquisitive Greeks and the practical, simple, down-to-earth, no-nonsense Romans, who spread and preserved the ideas of ancient Greece and other culture groups. The contributions and accomplishments of the Romans are numerous but their greatest included language, engineering, building, law, government, roads, trade, and the **Pax Romana**. Pax Romana was the long period of peace enabling free travel and trade, spreading people, cultures, goods, and ideas all over a vast area of the known world.

In **India**, Hinduism was a continuing influence along with the rise of Buddhism. Industry and commerce developed along with extensive trading with the Near East. Outstanding advances in the fields of science and medicine were made along with being one of the first to be active in navigation and maritime enterprises during this time.

The civilizations in Africa south of the Sahara were developing the refining and use of iron, especially for farm implements and later for weapons. Trading was overland using camels and at important seaports. The Arab influence was extremely important, as was their later contact with Indians, Christian Nubians, and Persians. In fact, their trading activities were probably the most important factor in the spread of and assimilation of different ideas and stimulation of cultural growth.

The people who lived in the Americas before Columbus arrived had a thriving, connected society. The civilizations in North America tended to spread out more and were in occasional conflict but maintained their sovereignty, for the most part. The South American civilizations, however, tended to migrate into empires, with the strongest city or tribe assuming control of the lives and resources of the rest of the nearby peoples.

Native Americans in North America had a spiritual and personal relationship with the various Spirits of Nature and a keen appreciation of the ways of woodworking and metalworking. Various tribes dotted the landscape of what is now the U.S. They struggled against one another for control of resources such as food and water but had no concept of ownership of land, since they believed that they were living on the land with the permission of the Spirits. The North Americans mastered the art of growing many crops and, to their credit, were willing to share that knowledge with the various Europeans who eventually showed up. Artwork made of hides, beads, and jewels were popular at this time.

The most well known empires of South America were the Aztec, Inca, and Maya. Each of these empires had a central capital in which lived the emperor, who controlled all aspects of the lives of his subjects. The empires traded with other peoples; and if the relations soured, the results were usually absorption of the trading partners into the empire. These empires, especially the Aztecs, had access to large numbers of metals and jewels, and they created weapons and artwork that continue to impress historians today. The Inca Empire stretched across a vast period of territory down the western coast of South America and was connected by a series of roads.

The Mayas are most well known for their famous pyramids and calendars, as well as their language, which still stumps archaeologists.

The ancient **Israelites** and **Christians** created a powerful legacy of political and philosophical traditions, much of which survives to this day. In law and religion, especially, we can draw a more or less straight line from then to now.

Israel was not the first ancient civilization to have a series of laws for its people to follow. However, thanks to the staggering popularity of the Ten Commandments, we think of the Israelites in this way. This simple set of laws, some of which are not laws at all but societal instructions, maintains to this day a central role in societies the world over. Such commandments as the ones that prohibit stealing and killing were revolutionary in their day because they applied to everyone, not just the disadvantaged. In many ancient cultures, the rich and powerful were above the law because they could buy their way out of trouble and because it wasn't always clear what the laws were. Echoing the Code of Hammurabi and preceding Rome's Twelve Tables, the Ten Commandments provided a written record of laws, so all knew what was prohibited.

The civilization of Israel is also known as the first to assume a worship of just one god. The Christian communities built on this tradition, and both faiths exist and are expanding today, especially in western countries. Rather than a series of gods, each of which was in charge of a different aspect of nature or society, the ancient Israelites and Christians believed in just one god, called Yahweh or God, depending on which religion you look at. This divine being was, these peoples believed, the "one, true god," lord over all. This worship of just one god had more of a personal nature to it, and the result was that the believers thought themselves able to talk (or, more properly, pray) directly to their god, whereas the peoples of Mesopotamia and Egypt thought the gods distant and unapproachable.

The civilization in **Japan** appeared during this time having borrowed much of their culture from China. It was the last of these classical civilizations to develop. Although they used, accepted, and copied Chinese art, law, architecture, dress, and writing, the Japanese refined these into their own unique way of life, including incorporating the religion of Buddhism into their culture. Early Japanese society focused on the emperor and the farm, in that order. The Sea of Japan protected Japan from more than Chinese invasion, including the famous Mongol one that was blown back by the "divine wind." The power of the emperor declined as it was usurped by the era of the Daimyo and his loyal soldiers, the Samurai. Japan flourished economically and culturally during many of these years, although the policy of isolation the country developed kept the rest of the world from knowing such things. Buddhism and local religions were joined by Christianity in the sixteenth century, but it wasn't until the mid-nineteenth century that Japan rejoined the world community.

African civilizations during these centuries were few and far between. Most of northern coastal Africa had been conquered by Moslem armies. The preponderance of deserts and other inhospitable lands restricted African settlements to a few select areas. The city of Zimbabwe became a trading center in south-central Africa in the 5th century but didn't last long. More successful was Ghana, a Muslim-influenced kingdom that arose in the 9th century and lasted for nearly 300 years. Ghanaians had large farming areas and also raised cattle and elephants. They traded with people from Europe and the Middle East. Eventually overrunning Ghana was Mali, whose trade center Timbuktu survived its own empire's demise and blossomed into one of the world's caravan destinations.

Iron, tin, and leather came out of **Mali** with a vengeance. The succeeding civilization of the Songhai had relative success in maintaining the success of their predecessors. Religion in all of these places was definitely Muslim; and even after extended contact with other cultures, technological advancements were few and far between.

The **Scientific Revolution** and the **Enlightenment** were two of the most important movements in the history of civilization, resulting in a new sense of self-examination and a wider view of the world than ever before. The Scientific Revolution was, above all, a shift in focus from belief to evidence. Scientists and philosophers wanted to see the proof, not just believe what other people told them. It was an exciting time, if you were a forward-looking thinker.

A Polish astronomer, **Nicolaus Copernicus**, began the Scientific Revolution. He crystallized a lifetime of observations into a book that was published about the time of his death. In this book, Copernicus argued that the Sun, not the Earth, was the center of a solar system and that other planets revolved around the Sun, not the Earth. This flew in the face of established (Church-mandated) doctrine. The Church still wielded tremendous power at this time, including the power to banish people or sentence them to prison or even death.

The Danish astronomer **Tycho Brahe** was the first to catalog his observations of the night sky, of which he made thousands. Building on Brahe's data, German scientist Johannes Kepler instituted his theory of planetary movement, embodied in his famous Laws of Planetary Movement. Using Brahe's data, Kepler also confirmed Copernicus's observations and argument that the Earth revolved around the Sun.

The most famous defender of this idea was **Galileo Galilei,** an Italian scientist who conducted many famous experiments in the pursuit of science. He is most well known, however, for his defense of the heliocentric (sun-centered) idea. He wrote a book comparing the two theories, but most readers could tell easily that he favored the new one. He was convinced of this mainly because of what he had seen with his own eyes. He had used the relatively new invention of the telescope to see four moons of Jupiter. They certainly did not revolve around the Earth, so why should everything else? His ideas were not at all favored with the Church, which continued to assert its authority in this and many other matters. The Church was still powerful enough at this time, especially in Italy, to order Galileo to be placed under house arrest.

Galileo died under house arrest, but his ideas didn't die with him. Picking up the baton was an English scientist named **Isaac Newton**, who became perhaps the most famous scientist of all. He is known as the discoverer of gravity and a pioneering voice in the study of optics (light), calculus, and physics.

More than any other scientist, Newton argued for (and proved) the idea of a mechanistic view of the world: You can see how the world works and prove how the world works through observation; if you can see these things with your own eyes, they must be so. Up to this time, people believed what other people told them; this is how the Church was able to keep control of people's lives for so long. Newton, following in the footsteps of Copernicus and Galileo, changed all that.

This naturally led to the Enlightenment, a period of intense self-study that focused on ethics and logic. More so than at any time before, scientists and philosophers questioned cherished truths, widely held beliefs, and their own sanity in an attempt to discover why the world worked—from within. "I think, therefore I am" was one of the famous sayings of that or any day. It was uttered by **Rene Descartes,** a French scientist-philosopher whose dedication to logic and the rigid rules of observation were a blueprint for the thinkers who came after him.

One of the giants of the era was England's **David Hume.** A pioneer of the doctrine of empiricism (believing things only when you've seen the proof for yourself), Hume was also a prime believer in the value of skepticism; in other words, he was naturally suspicious of things that other people told him to be true and constantly set out to discover the truth for himself. These two related ideas influenced a great many thinkers after Hume, and his writings (of which there are many) continue to inspire philosophers to this day.

The Enlightenment thinker who might be the most famous is **Immanuel Kant** of Germany. He was both a philosopher and a scientist, and he took a definite scientific view of the world. He wrote the movement's most famous essay, "Answering the Question: What Is Enlightenment?" and he answered his famous question with the motto "Dare to Know." For Kant, the human being was a rational being capable of hugely creative thought and intense self-evaluation. He encouraged all to examine themselves and the world around them. He believed that the source of morality lay not in nature of in the grace of God but in the human soul itself. He believed that man believed in God for practical, not religious or mystical, reasons.

Also prevalent during the Enlightenment was the idea of the "social contract," the belief that government existed because people wanted it to, that the people had an agreement with the government that they would submit to it as long as it protected them and didn't encroach on their basic human rights. This idea was first made famous by the Frenchman Jean-Jacques Rousseau but was also adopted by England's John Locke and America's Thomas Jefferson.
John Locke was one of the most influential political writers of the seventeenth century who put great emphasis on human rights and put forth the belief that when governments violate those rights people should rebel. Locke wrote the book "***Two Treatises of Government***' in 1690, which had tremendous influence on political thought in the American colonies and helped shaped the U.S. Constitution and Declaration of Independence.

The word **Renaissance** literally means "rebirth", and signaled the rekindling of interest in the glory of ancient classical Greek and Roman civilizations. It was the period in human history marking the start of many ideas and innovations leading to our modern age. The Renaissance began in Italy with many of its ideas starting in Florence, controlled by the infamous Medici family. Education, especially for some of the merchants, required reading, writing, math, the study of law, and the writings of classical Greek and Roman writers.

Most famous are the Renaissance artists, first and foremost Leonardo, Michelangelo, and Raphael but also Titian, Donatello, and Rembrandt. All of these men pioneered a new method of painting and sculpture—that of portraying real events and real people as they really looked, not as the artists imagined them to be. One needs look no further than Michelangelo's David to illustrate this.

Literature was a focus as well during the Renaissance. Humanists Petrarch, Boccaccio, Erasmus, and Sir Thomas More advanced the idea of being interested in life here on earth and the opportunities it can bring, rather than constantly focusing on heaven and its rewards. The monumental works of Shakespeare, Dante, and Cervantes found their origins in these ideas as well as the ones that drove the painters and sculptors. All of these works, of course, owe much of their existence to the invention of the printing press, which occurred during the Renaissance.

The Renaissance changed music as well. No longer just a religious experience, music could be fun and composed for its own sake, to be enjoyed in fuller and more humanistic ways than in the Middle Ages. Musicians worked for themselves, rather than for the churches, as before, and so could command good money for their work, increasing their prestige. Science advanced considerably during the Renaissance, especially in the area of physics and astronomy. Copernicus, Kepler, and Galileo led a Scientific Revolution in proving that the earth was round and certainly not perfect, an earth-shattering revelation to those who clung to medieval ideals of a geocentric, church-centered existence.

Until the early years of the twentieth century **Russia** was ruled by a succession of Czars. The Czars ruled as autocrats or, sometimes, despots. Society was essentially feudalistic and was structured in three levels. The Czar held the top level. The second level was composed of the rich nobles who held government positions and owned vast tracts of land. The third level of the society was composed of the remaining people who lived in poverty as peasants or serfs. There was discontent among the peasants. There were several unsuccessful attempts to revolt during the nineteenth century, but they were quickly suppressed. The revolutions of 1905 and 1917, however, were quite different.

The causes of the 1905 Revolution were:

- Discontent with the social structure
- Discontent with the living conditions of the peasants
- Discontent with working conditions despite industrialization
- The general discontent was aggravated by the Russo-Japanese War (1904-1905) with inflation, rising prices, etc. Peasants who had been able to eke out a living began to starve.
- Many of the fighting troops were killed in battles Russia lost to Japan because of poor leadership, lack of training, and inferior weaponry.
- Czar Nicholas II refused to end the war despite setbacks
- In January 1905, Port Arthur fell.

A trade union leader, Father Gapon, organized a protest to demand an end to the war, industrial reform, more civil liberties, and a constituent assembly. Over 150,000 peasants joined a demonstration outside the Czar's Winter Palace. Before the demonstrators even spoke, the palace guard opened fire on the crowd. This destroyed the people's trust in the Czar. Illegal trade unions and political parties formed and organized strikes to gain power. The strikes eventually brought the Russian economy to a halt. This led Czar Nicholas II to sign the October Manifesto that created a constitutional monarchy, extended some civil rights, and gave the parliament limited legislative power. In a very short period of time, the Czar disbanded the parliament and violated the promised civil liberties, contributing to the 1917 Revolution.

The causes of the 1917 Revolution were:

- The violation of the October Manifesto.
- Defeats on the battlefields during WWI caused discontent, loss of life, and a popular desire to withdraw from the war.
- The Czar continued to appoint unqualified people to government posts and handle the situation with general incompetence.
- The Czar also listened to his wife's (Alexandra) advice. She was strongly influenced by Rasputin. This caused increased discontent among all level of the social structure.
- WWI had caused another surge in prices and scarcity of many items. Most of the peasants could not afford to buy bread.

The most significant differences between the 1905 and 1917 revolutions were the formation of political parties and their use of propaganda and the support of the military and some of the nobles in 1917.

The first organized **genocide** in the 1900s was the Armenian genocide, an attempted extermination of a huge number of Armenians at the hands of the Young Turks who inherited Turkey from the Ottoman Empire. More than one million Armenian people (nearly half of their population) died between 1915 and 1917. The government blamed the Armenians for early defeats at the hands of Russia and its allies. Armenians were forcibly moved and kept in harsh conditions elsewhere. A total of 25 concentration camps are believed to have existed. Turkish authorities claimed that the Armenian people had agitated for separation from the Ottoman Empire and that the relocation was pursuant to the goals of both peoples. Others disagree. Some sources blame other causes for these deaths; most scholars, however, agree that it was a determined attempt to exterminate an entire group of people.

World War I: 1914 to 1918
In Europe, war broke out in 1914, eventually involving nearly 30 nations, and ended in 1918. One of the major causes of the war was the tremendous surge of nationalism during the 1800s and early 1900s. People of the same nationality or ethnic group sharing a common history, language or culture began uniting or demanding the right of unification, especially in the empires of Eastern Europe, such as Russian Ottoman and Austrian-Hungarian Empires. Getting stronger and more intense were the beliefs of these peoples in loyalty to common political, social, and economic goals considered to be before any loyalty to the controlling nation or empire. Other causes included the increasing strength of military capabilities, massive colonization for raw materials needed for industrialization and manufacturing, and military and diplomatic alliances. The initial spark, which started the conflagration, was the assassination of Austrian Archduke Francis Ferdinand and his wife in Sarajevo.

In Europe, Italy and Germany were each totally united into one nation from many smaller states. There were revolutions in Austria and Hungary, the Franco-Prussian War, the dividing of Africa among the strong European nations, interference and intervention of Western nations in Asia, and the breakup of Turkish dominance in the Balkans.

In Africa, France, Great Britain, Italy, Portugal, Spain, Germany, and Belgium controlled the entire continent except Liberia and Ethiopia. In Asia and the Pacific Islands, only China, Japan, and present-day Thailand (Siam) kept their independence. The others were controlled by the strong European nations.

Under the administration of Theodore Roosevelt, the U.S. Armed Forces were built up, greatly increasing its strength. Roosevelt's foreign policy was summed up in the slogan of "Speak softly and carry a big stick," backing up the efforts in diplomacy with a strong military. During the years before the outbreak of World War I, evidence of U.S. emergence as a world power could be seen in a number of actions. Using the Monroe Doctrine of non-involvement of Europe in the affairs of the Western Hemisphere, President Roosevelt forced Italy, Germany, and Great Britain to remove their blockade of Venezuela; gained the rights to construct the Panama Canal by threatening force; assumed the finances of the Dominican Republic to stabilize it and prevent any intervention by Europeans; and in 1916 under President Woodrow Wilson, to keep order, U.S. troops were sent to the Dominican Republic.

World War I saw the introduction of such warfare as use of tanks, airplanes, machine guns, submarines, poison gas, and flamethrowers. Fighting on the Western front was characterized by a series of trenches that were used throughout the war until 1918. U.S. involvement in the war did not occur until 1916. When it began in 1914, President Woodrow Wilson declared that the U.S. was neutral and most Americans were opposed to any involvement anyway. In 1916, Wilson was reelected to a second term based on the slogan proclaiming his efforts at keeping America out of the war. For a few months after, he put forth most of his efforts to stopping the war but German submarines began unlimited warfare against American merchant shipping.

The kind of nationalism that Europe saw in the nineteenth century spilled over into the mid-twentieth century, with former colonies of European powers declaring themselves independent all the time, especially in Africa. India, a longtime British protectorate, also achieved independence at this time. With independence, these countries continued to grow.

There were 28 nations involved in the war, not including colonies and territories. It began July 28, 1914 and ended November 11, 1918 with the signing of the Treaty of Versailles. Economically, the war cost a total of $337 billion; increased inflation and huge war debts; and caused a loss of markets, goods, jobs, and factories.

Politically, old empires collapsed; many monarchies disappeared; smaller countries gained temporary independence; Communists seized power in Russia; and, in some cases, nationalism increased. Socially, total populations decreased because of war casualties and low birth rates. There were millions of displaced persons and villages and farms were destroyed. Cities grew while women made significant gains in the work force and the ballot box. There was less social distinction and classes. Attitudes completely changed and old beliefs and values were questioned. The peace settlement established the League of Nations to ensure peace, but it failed to do so.

The most well known genocide of the twentieth century is the **Holocaust** of Jews before and during World War II. Much of this took place in Germany, although the practice increased throughout German-occupied countries throughout the war. German authorities capitalized on hundreds of years of distrust of Jewish people and invented what they saw as "the Final Solution of the Jewish Question": extermination of the Jewish people. Germans in charge of this "Final Solution" constructed a vast, complicated system of transport systems and concentration camps, where Jews were imprisoned, forced to work, and killed in increasingly large numbers.

This Holocaust was known especially for its efficiency and its record-keeping, which was extensive. Thousands of pages of documents describe in excruciating detail how thorough and determined Nazi authorities were in pursuing their goals. The number of Jews killed during the Holocaust is generally said to be 6 million. This figure includes people from all over Europe. The Holocaust didn't kill just Jews, however. Gypsies, communists, homosexuals, Jehovah's Witnesses, Catholics, psychiatric patients, and even common criminals were systematically incarcerated and, in many cases, killed for being "enemies of the state." The number of concentration camps in Nazi-controlled lands during World War II was more than 40. Not all of them were death camps. The most famous ones, including Auschwitz, were. The Holocaust ended with Germany's defeat in World War II. The liberating troops of the West and East uncovered the concentration camps and the killing that the Nazis wrought. Much of the meticulous record keeping was intact, preserving the horrors that these people had wrought.

Pre-war empires lost tremendous amounts of territories as well as the wealth of natural resources in them. New, independent nations were formed and some predominately ethnic areas came under control of nations of different cultural backgrounds. Some national boundary changes overlapped and created tensions and hard feelings as well as political and economic confusion. The wishes and desires of every national or cultural group could not possibly be realized and satisfied, resulting in disappointments for both; those who were victorious and those who were defeated. Germany received harsher terms than expected from the treaty that weakened its post-war government and, along with the worldwide depression of the 1930s, set the stage for the rise of Adolf Hitler and his Nationalist Socialist Party and **World War II**.

The world after World War II was a complicated place. The Axis powers were defeated, but the Cold War had sprung up in its place. Many countries struggled to get out of the debt and devastation that their Nazi occupiers had wrought. The American Marshall Plan helped the nations of Western Europe get back on their feet. The Soviet Union helped the Eastern European nations return to greatness, with Communist governments at the helm. The nations of Asia were rebuilt as well, with Communism taking over China and Americanization taking over Japan and Taiwan. East and West struggled for control in this arena, especially in Korea and Southeast Asia. When Communism fell in the USSR and Eastern Europe, it remained in China, North Korea, and Vietnam; Vietnam's neighbors, however, set their own path to government.

In America, President Wilson lost in his efforts to get the U.S. Senate to approve the peace treaty. The Senate at the time was a reflection of American public opinion and its rejection of the treaty was a rejection of Wilson. The approval of the treaty would have made the United States a member of the League of Nations, but Americans had just come off a bloody war to ensure that democracy would exist throughout the world. Americans just did not want to accept any responsibility that resulted from its new position of power and were afraid that membership in the League of Nations would embroil the U.S. in future disputes in Europe.

One of the major political movements in the twentieth century was **communism**. Communism has a rigid theology, and a bible (*Das Capital*) that sees Communism emerging as a result of almost cosmic laws. Modern socialism is much closer to the ground. It too sees change in human society and hopes for improvement, but there is no unchanging millennium at the end of the road. Communism is sure that it will achieve the perfect state and in this certainty it is willing to use any and all means, however ruthless, to bring it about.

Communist states controlled nearly every aspect of society, including religion and economics. The government owned factories and ports, machines and ships; this means that the income from goods produced therein went into the state-controlled coffers. This kind of economic theory was in stark contrast to the famous laissez faire attitude that occupied much of the Western nations during the 1700s, 1800s, and 1900s.

The **United Nations**, a more successful successor to the League of Nations (which couldn't prevent World War II), began in the waning days of the war. It brought the nations of the world together to discuss their problems, rather than fight about them. Another successful method of keeping the peace since the war has been the atomic bomb. On a more pacific note, UNICEF, a worldwide children's fund, has been able to achieve great things in just a few decades of existence. Other peace-based organizations like the Red Cross and Doctors without Borders have seen their membership and their efficacy rise during this time as well.

The Cold War was, more than anything else, an ideological struggle between proponents of democracy and those of communism. The two major players were the United States and the Soviet Union, but other countries were involved as well. It was a "cold" war because no large-scale fighting took place directly between the two big protagonists.

The Soviet Union kept much more of a tight leash on its supporting countries, including all of Eastern Europe, which made up a military organization called the Warsaw Pact. The Western nations responded with a military organization of their own, NATO. Another prime battleground was Asia, where the Soviet Union had allies in China, North Korea, and North Vietnam and the U.S. had allies in Japan, South Korea, Taiwan, and South Vietnam. The Korean War and Vietnam War were major conflicts in which both big protagonists played big roles but didn't directly fight each other. The main symbol of the Cold War was the arms race, a continual buildup of missiles, tanks, and other weapons that became ever more technologically advanced and increasingly more deadly. The ultimate weapon, which both sides had in abundance, was the nuclear bomb. Spending on weapons and defensive systems eventually occupied great percentages of the budgets of the U.S. and the U.S.S.R. and some historians argue that this high level of spending played a large part in the end of the latter.

The war was a cultural struggle as well. Adults brought up their children to hate "the Americans" or "the Communists." Cold War tensions spilled over into many parts of life in countries around the world. The ways of life in countries on either side of the divide were so different that they served entirely foreign to outside observers.

The Cold War continued to varying degrees from 1947 to 1991, when the Soviet Union collapsed. Other Eastern European countries had seen their communist governments overthrown by this time as well, marking the shredding of the "Iron Curtain."

Illinois History

Key points of reference in the history of Illinois include the following:

- 1673 Father Jacques Marquette and Louis Jolliet, French explore Illinois territory.
- 1675-1700 French establish settlements in Illinois
- 1717 Illinois is recognized as a French colony as part of the Louisiana territory.
- 1763 French and Indian War ends. Illinois becomes property of England.
- The end of the Revolutionary War and the Treaty of Paris makes Illinois a territory of the United States and part of Virginia
- Illinois is ceded to the United States from Virginia.
- 1788 Arthur St. Clair becomes Governor of the Northwest Territory which includes Illinois
- 1800 Through an act of Congress the Indiana territory is created which includes Illinois.
- 1803 Fort Dearborn is established in the Chicago area
- The Illinois territory is established
- 1818 The twenty-first state, Illinois is established. Kaskaskia is the capital. Slave owners are permitted to retain slaves, but no new slaves permitted to be brought into the State.
- 1820 Vandalia designated capital.
- Chicago is chartered.
- Springfield is designated capital of the State.
- 1844 Mormon leaders Joseph and Hyrum Smith were murdered which prompted the Mormon move to Salt Lake City, Utah.
- 1847 McCormick reaper plant established in Chicago.
- 1855 Illinois establishes public school system.
- Illinois resident Abraham Lincoln is elected President.
- The start of the Civil War.
- 1864 President Lincoln reelected.
- 1865 Chicago Stock Yards opened. President Lincoln assassinated.
- 1867 Pullman Palace Car Company manufacturing railroad cars established in Chicago.
- Illinois resident Ulysses S. Grant elected President of the United States.
- 1871 Chicago fire.
- 1873 Women Christian Temperance League founded in Illinois. Barb wire is patented.
- 1886 Bombing at Haymarket Square in Chicago and labor riots.
- 1888 Melville Fuller of Chicago appointed Chief Justice of the U.S. Supreme Court
- 1889 Jane Addams opens Hull House.

- 1896 Illinois resident William Jennings Bryan is defeated for President after receiving nomination. He would be defeated in 3 Presidential elections.
- 1903 Representative Joseph Cannon elected Speaker of the House.
- 1931 Jane Addams awarded Nobel Peace Prize.
- 1942 First nuclear reaction achieved by University of Chicago scientists.
- 1949 Airport in Chicago renamed O'Hare Field.
- 1952 Governor Adlai Stevenson nominated for President loses to Dwight Eisenhower.
- 1959 Senator Everett Dirksen elected to Republican Senate Leader.
- 1968 Demonstration breaks out at Democratic Convention in Chicago.
- 1976 Chicago resident Saul Bellow achieves Nobel Prize in literature.
- 1980 Former Illinois resident Ronald Reagan is elected President.
- 1992 Carol Moseley Braun becomes first African American women elected to Senate.
- 1999 Dennis Hastert elected Speaker of U. House of Representatives.

Human Societies

Spatial organization is a description of how things are grouped in a given space. In geographical terms, this can describe people, places, and environments anywhere and everywhere on Earth.

The most basic form of spatial organization for people is where they live. The vast majority of people live near other people, in villages and towns and cities and settlements. These people live near others in order to take advantage of the goods and services that naturally arise from cooperation. These villages and towns and cities and settlements are, to varying degrees, near bodies of water, since water is a staple of survival for every person on the planet and is also a good source of energy for factories and other industries as well as a form of transportation for people and goods.

Another way to describe where people live is by the geography and topography around them. The vast majority of people on the planet live in areas that are very hospitable. Yes, people live in the Himalayas and in the Sahara, but the populations in those areas are small indeed when compared to the plains of China, India, Europe, and the United States. People naturally want to live where they won't have to work really hard just to survive, and world population patterns reflect this.

Most places in the world are in some manner close to agricultural land as well. Food makes the world go round, and some cities are more agriculturally inclined than others. Rare is the city, however, that grows absolutely no crops. The kind of food grown is almost entirely dependent on the kind of land available and the climate surrounding that land. Rice doesn't grow well in the desert, for instance, nor do bananas grow well in snowy lands. Certain crops are easier to transport than others as well, and the ones that aren't are usually grown nearer ports or other areas of export.

The one thing that changes all of these things, of course, is the airplane. Flight has made possible global commerce and goods exchange on a level never before seen. Foods from all around the world can be flown literally around the world and, with the aid of refrigeration techniques, be kept fresh enough to sell in markets nearly everywhere. The same is true of medicine and, unfortunately, weapons.

Human communities subsisted initially as **gatherers** – gathering berries, leaves, etc. With the invention of tools it became possible to dig for roots, hunt small animals, and catch fish from rivers and oceans. Humans observed their environments and soon learned to plant seeds and harvest crops. As people migrated to areas in which game and fertile soil were abundant, communities began to develop. When people had the knowledge to grow crops and the skills to hunt game, they began to understand division of labor. Some of the people in the community tended to agricultural needs while others hunted game.

As habitats attracted larger numbers of people, environments became crowded and there was competition. The concept of division of labor and sharing of food soon came, in more heavily populated areas, to be managed. Groups of people focused on growing crops while others concentrated on hunting. Experience led to the development of skills and of knowledge that make the work easier. Farmers began to develop new plant species and hunters began to protect animal species from other predators for their own use. This ability to manage the environment led people to settle down, to guard their resources, and to manage them.

Camps soon became villages. Villages became year-round settlements. Animals were domesticated and gathered into herds that met the needs of the village. With the settled life it was no longer necessary to "travel light." Pottery was developed for storing and cooking food.

By 8000 BCE, culture was beginning to evolve in these villages. Agriculture was developed for the production of grain crops, which led to a decreased reliance on wild plants. Domesticating animals for various purposes decreased the need to hunt wild game. Life became more settled. It was then possible to turn attention to such matters as managing water supplies, producing tools, making cloth, etc. There was both the social interaction and the opportunity to reflect upon existence. Mythologies arose and various kinds of belief systems. Rituals arose that re-enacted the mythologies that gave meaning to life.

As farming and animal husbandry skills increased, the dependence upon wild game and food gathering declined. With this change came the realization that a larger number of people could be supported on the produce of farming and animal husbandry.

Two things seem to have come together to produce **cultures and civilizations**: a society and culture based on agriculture and the development of centers of the community with literate social and religious structures. The members of these hierarchies then managed water supply and irrigation, ritual and religious life, and exerted their own right to use a portion of the goods produced by the community for their own subsistence in return for their management.

Sharpened skills, development of more sophisticated tools, commerce with other communities, and increasing knowledge of their environment, the resources available to them, and responses to the needs to share good, order community life, and protect their possessions from outsiders led to further division of labor and community development.

As trade routes developed and travel between cities became easier, trade led to specialization. Trade enables a people to obtain the goods they desire in exchange for the goods they are able to produce. This, in turn, leads to increased attention to refinements of technique and the sharing of ideas. The knowledge of a new discovery or invention provides knowledge and technology that increases the ability to produce goods for trade. As each community learns the value of the goods it produces and improves its ability to produce the goods in greater quantity, industry is born.

Sociologists have identified five different types of institutions around which societies are structured: family, education, government, religion and economy. These institutions provide a framework for members of a society to learn about and participate in a society, and allow for a society to perpetuate its beliefs and values to succeeding generations.

The **family** is the primary social unit in most societies. It is through the family that children learn the most essential skills for functioning in their society such as language and appropriate forms of interaction. The family is connected to ethnicity, which is partly defined by a person's heritage.

Education is an important institution in a society, as it allows for the formal passing on of a culture's collected knowledge. The institution of education is connected to the family, as that is where a child's earliest education takes place. The United States has a public school system administered by the states that ensures a basic education and provides a common experience for most children.

A society's **governmental** institutions often embody its beliefs and values. Laws, for instance, reflect a society's values by enforcing its ideas of right and wrong. The structure of a society's government can reflect a society's ideals about the role of an individual in his society. The American form of democracy emphasizes the rights of the individual, but in return expects individuals to respect the rights of others, including those of ethnic or political minorities.

Religion is frequently the institution from which springs a society's primary beliefs and values, and can be closely related to other social institutions. Many religions have definite teachings on the structure and importance of the family, for instance. The U.S. Constitution guarantees the free practice of religion, which has led to a large number of denominations practicing in the U.S. today.

A society's **economic** institutions define how an individual can contribute and receive economic reward from his society. The United States has a capitalist economy motivated by free enterprise. While this system allows for economic advancement for the individual, it can also produce areas of poverty and economic depression.

Sociologists have identified three main types of norms, or ways that cultures define behavioral expectations, each associated with different consequences if they are violated. These norms are called folkways, mores and laws.

Folkways are the informal rules of etiquette and behaviors that a society follows in day-to-day practice. Forming a line at a shop counter or holding a door open for an elderly person are examples of folkways in many societies. Someone who violates a folkway - by pushing to the front of a line, for instance - might be seen as rude, but is not thought to have done anything immoral or illegal.

Mores are stronger than folkways in the consequences they carry for not observing them. Examples of mores might include honesty and integrity. Cheating on a test or lying might violate a social more, and a person who does so may be considered immoral.

Laws are formal adoptions of norms by a society with formal punishment for their violation. Laws are usually based on the mores of a society. The more that it is wrong to kill is codified in a law against murder, for example. Laws are the most formal types of social norm, as their enforcement is specifically provided for. The fellow members of a society, on the other hand, primarily enforce folkways and mores, informally.

The folkways, mores and laws of a society are based on the prevailing beliefs and values of that society. Beliefs and values are similar and interrelated systems. **Beliefs** are those things that are thought to be true. Beliefs are often associated with religion, but beliefs can also be based on political or ideological philosophies. "All men are created equal," is an example of an ideological belief.

Values are what a society thinks are right and wrong, and are often based on and shaped by beliefs. The value that every member of the society has a right to participate in his government might be considered to be based on the belief that "All men are created equal," for instance.

The **family** is the primary social unit in most societies. It is through the family that children learn the most essential skills for functioning in their society such as language and appropriate forms of interaction. The size of the family unit varies among cultures, with some including grandparents, aunts, uncles and cousins as part of the basic family, who may all live together. The family is also related to a society's economic institutions, as families often purchase and consume goods as a unit. A family that works to produce its own food and clothing, as was the case historically in many societies, is also a unit of economic production.

Economics

Economics is the study of how a society allocates its scarce resources to satisfy what are basically unlimited and competing wants. A fundamental fact of economics is that resources are scarce and that wants are infinite. The fact that scarce resources have to satisfy unlimited wants means that choices have to be made. If society uses its resources to produce good A then it doesn't have those resources to produce good B. More of good A means less of good B. This trade-off is referred to as the opportunity cost, or the value of the sacrificed alternative.

Economic systems refer to the arrangements a society has devised to answer what are known as the Three Questions: What goods to produce, How to produce the goods, and For Whom are the goods being produced, or how is the allocation of the output determined. Different economic systems answer these questions in different ways. These are the different "isms" that exist that define the method of resource and output allocation. A **market economy** answers these questions in terms of demand and supply and the use of markets. **Demand** is based on consumer preferences and satisfaction and refers to the quantities of a good or service that buyers are willing and able to buy at different prices during a given period of time. **Supply** is based on costs of production and refers to the quantities that sellers are willing and able to sell at different prices during a given period of time. The determination of market equilibrium price is where the buying decisions of buyers coincide with the selling decision of sellers

Consumers vote for the products they want with their dollar spending. Goods acquiring enough dollar votes are profitable, signaling to the producers that society wants their scarce resources used in this way. This is how the "What" question is answered. The producer then hires inputs in accordance with the goods consumers want, looking for the most efficient or lowest cost method of production. The lower the firm's costs for any given level of revenue, the higher the firm's profits. This is the way in which the "How" question is answered in a market economy. The "For Whom" question is answered in the marketplace by the determination of the equilibrium price. Price serves to ration the good to those who can and will transact at the market price of better. Those who can't or won't are excluded from the market. This mechanism results in market efficiency or obtaining the most output from the available inputs that are consistent with the preferences of consumers. Society's scarce resources are being used the way society wants them to be used.

Free enterprise, individual entrepreneurship, competitive markets and consumer sovereignty are all parts of a market economy. Individuals have the right to make their own decisions as to what they want to do as a career. The financial incentives are there for individuals who are willing to take the risk. A successful venture earns profit. It is these financial incentives that that serve to motivate inventors and small businesses. The same is true for businesses. They are free to determine what production technique they want to use and what output they want to produce within the confines of the legal system. They can make investments based on their own decisions. Nobody is telling them what to do. Competitive markets, relatively free from government interference are also a manifestation of the freedom that the U.S. economic system is based on. These markets function on the basis of supply and demand to determine output mix and resource allocation. There is no commissar dictating what is produced and how. Since consumers buy the goods and services that give them satisfaction, this means that, for the most part, they don't buy the goods and services that they don't want that don't give them satisfaction. Consumers are, in effect, voting for the goods and services that they want with the dollars or what is called dollar voting. Consumers are basically signaling firms as to how they want society's scarce resources used with their dollar votes. A good that society wants acquires enough dollar votes for the producer to experience profits – a situation where the firm's revenues exceed the firm's costs. The existence of profits indicates to the firm that it is producing the goods and services that consumers want and that society's scarce resources are being used in accordance with consumer preferences. When a firm does not have a profitable product, it is because that product is not tabulating enough dollar votes of consumers. Consumers don't want the good or service and they don't want society's scarce resources being used in its production.

This process where consumers vote with their dollars is called consumer sovereignty. Consumers are basically directing the allocation of scarce resources in the economy with the dollar spending. Firms, who are in business to earn profit, then hire resources, or inputs, in accordance with consumer preferences. This is the way in which resources are allocated in a market economy. This is the manner in which society achieves the output mix that it desires.

Civics

Many of the core values in the U.S. democratic system can be found in the opening words of the Declaration of Independence, including the belief in equality, and the rights of citizens to "life, liberty and the pursuit of happiness."

The Declaration was a condemnation of the British king's tyrannical government, and these words emphasized the American colonists' belief that a government received its authority to rule from the people, and its function should not be to suppress the governed, but to protect the rights of the governed, including protection from the government itself. These two ideals, **popular sovereignty** and the **rule of law** are basic core values.

Popular sovereignty grants citizens the ability to directly participate in their own government by voting and running for public office. This ideal is based on a belief of **equality** that holds that all citizens have an equal right to engage in their own governance. The ideal of equality has changed over the years, as women and non-white citizens were not always allowed to vote or bring suit in court. Now all U.S citizens above the age of 18 are allowed to vote. This expansion of rights since the adoption of the Constitution demonstrates an American value of **respect for minority rights.**

The democratic system of election and representation is based on **majority rule**. In the case of most public elections, the candidate receiving the most votes is awarded the office. Majority rule is also used to pass legislation in Congress. Majority rule is meant to ensure that authority cannot be concentrated in one small group of people.

The rule of law is the ideal that the law applies not only to the governed, but to the government as well. This core value gives authority to the justice system, which grants citizens protection from the government by requiring that any accusation of a crime be proved by the government before a person is punished. This is called **due process** and ensures that any accused person will have an opportunity to confront his accusers and provide a defense. Due process follows from the core value of a right to liberty. The government cannot take away a citizen's liberty without reason or without proof. The correlating ideal is also a core value - that someone who does harm another or break a law will receive **justice** under the democratic system. The ideal of justice holds that a punishment will fit the crime, and that any citizen can appeal to the judicial system if he feels he has been wronged.

Central to the ideal of justice is an expectation that citizens will act in a way that promotes the **common good**, that they will treat one another with **honesty** and respect and will exercise **self-discipline** in their interactions with others. These are among the basic responsibilities of a citizen of a democracy.

The terms "civil liberties" and "civil rights" are often used interchangeably, but there are some fine distinctions between the two terms. The term "civil liberties" is more often used to imply that the state has a positive role to play. It assures that citizens will have equal protection and justice under the law with equal opportunities to exercise their privileges of citizenship and to participate fully in the life of the nation, regardless of race, religion, sex, color or creed. The term civil rights is used more often to refer to rights that may be described as guarantees that are specified as against the state authority implying limitations on the actions of the state to interfere with citizens' liberties. Although the term "civil rights" has thus been identified with the ideal of equality and the term "civil liberties" with the idea of freedom, the two concepts are really inseparable and interacting. Equality implies the proper ordering of liberty in a society so that one individual's freedom does not infringe on the rights of others.

The beginnings of civil liberties and the idea of civil rights in the United States go back to the ideas of the Greeks. The experience of the early British struggles for civil rights and to the very philosophies that led people to come to the New World in the first place. Religious freedom, political freedom, and the right to live one's life as one sees fit are basic to the American ideal. These were embodied in the ideas expressed in the Declaration of Independence and the Constitution.

All these ideas found their final expression in the United States Constitution's first ten amendments, known as the **Bill of Rights**. In 1789, the first Congress passed these first amendments and by December 1791, three-fourths of the states at that time had ratified them. The Bill of Rights protects certain liberties and basic rights. James Madison who wrote the amendments said that the Bill of Rights does not give Americans these rights. People, Madison said, already have these rights. They are natural rights that belong to all human beings. The Bill of Rights simply prevents the governments from taking away these rights.

To summarize:

The first amendment guarantees the basic rights of freedom of religion, freedom of speech, freedom of the press, and freedom of assembly.

The next three amendments came out of the colonists' struggle with Great Britain. For example, the third amendment prevents Congress from forcing citizens to keep troops in their homes. Before the Revolution, Great Britain tried to coerce the colonists to house soldiers.

Amendments five through eight protect citizens who are accused of crimes and are brought to trial. Every citizen has the right to due process of law since the government must follow the same fair rules for everyone brought to trial. These rules include the right to a trial by an impartial jury, the right to be defended by a lawyer, and the right to a speedy trial.

The last two amendments limit the powers of the federal government to those that are expressly granted in the Constitution, any rights not expressly mentioned in the Constitution, thus, belong to the states or to the people.

In regards to specific guarantees:

Freedom of Religion: Religious freedom has not been seriously threatened in the United States historically. The policy of the government has been guided by the premise that church and state should be separate. But when religious practices have been at cross purposes with attitudes prevailing in the nation at particular times, there has been restrictions placed on these practices. Some of these have been restrictions against the practice of polygamy that is supported by certain religious groups. The idea of animal sacrifice that is promoted by some religious beliefs is generally prohibited. The use of mind-altering illegal substances that are used in religious rituals has been restricted. In the United States, all recognized religious institutions are tax-exempt in following the idea of separation of church and state, and therefore, there have been many quasi-religious groups that have in the past tried to take advantage of this fact. All of these issues continue, and most likely will continue to occupy both political and legal considerations for some time to come.

Freedom of Speech, Press, and Assembly: These rights historically have been given wide latitude in their practices, though there has been instances when one or the other have been limited for various reasons. The classic limitation, for instance, in regards to freedom of speech, has been the famous precept that an individual is prohibited from yelling "Fire!" in a crowded theatre. This prohibition is an example of the state saying that freedom of speech does not extend to speech that might endanger other people. There is also a prohibition against **slander,** or the knowingly stating of a deliberate falsehood against one party by another. Also there are many regulations regarding freedom of the press, the most common example are the various laws against **libel,** (or the printing of a known falsehood). In times of national emergency, various restrictions have been placed on the rights of press, speech and sometimes assembly.

The legal system in recent years has also undergone a number of serious changes, or challenges, with the interpretation of some constitutional guarantees.

SEE also Skill 8.2

Skill 8.2 Demonstrate understanding of relationships among the social sciences and ways in which geography, history, civics, and economics relate to everyday experiences

The social sciences are built upon the philosophy that human movements and interactions can be measured, studied, and ultimately predicted using a variety of methods and research techniques. By studying how humans act individually and within their societies, the social sciences seek to discover and explain common motivations and reactions among humans.

The body of knowledge generated by the social sciences has great influence on both the individual and societal levels. Methods of individual psychological treatment, for instance, are based on ongoing research in the social science of psychology. In the larger scheme, a country bases its foreign policy largely on the analysis of political scientists and other social research.

Geography involves studying location and how living things and earth's features are distributed throughout the earth. The term geography is defined as the study of earth's features and living things as to their location, relationship with each other, how they came to be there, and why so important. It includes where animals, people, and plants live and the effects of their relationship with earth's physical features. Geographers also explore the locations of earth's features, how they got there, and why it is so important. Another way to describe where people live is by the **geography** and **topography** around them. The vast majority of people on the planet live in areas that are very hospitable. Yes, people live in the Himalayas and in the Sahara, but the populations in those areas are small indeed when compared to the plains of China, India, Europe, and the United States. People naturally want to live where they will not have to work really hard just to survive, and world population patterns reflect this. The six themes of geography are:

Location - including relative and absolute location. A relative location refers to the surrounding geography, e.g., "on the banks of the Mississippi River." Absolute location refers to a specific point, such as 41 degrees North latitude, 90 degrees West longitude, or 123 Main Street.

Every point on Earth has a specific **location** that is determined by an imaginary grid of lines denoting latitude and longitude. Parallels of latitude measure distances north and south of the line called the Equator. Meridians of longitude measure distances east and west of the line called the Prime Meridian. Geographers use latitude and longitude to pinpoint a place's absolute, or exact, location.

To know the absolute location of a place is only part of the story. It is also important to know how that place is related to other places—in other words, to know that place's relative location. Relative location deals with the interaction that occurs between and among places. It refers to the many ways—by land, by water, even by technology—that places are connected.

All places have characteristics that give them meaning and character and distinguish them from other places on earth. Geographers describe places by their physical and human characteristics. Physical characteristics include such elements as animal life. Human characteristics of the landscape can be noted in architecture, patterns of livelihood, land use and ownership, town planning, and communication and transportation networks.

Languages, as well as religious and political ideologies, help shape the character of a place. Studied together, the physical and human characteristics of places provide clues to help students understand the nature of places on the earth.

A basic unit of geographic study is the region, an area on the earth's surface that is defined by certain unifying characteristics. The unifying characteristics may be physical, human, or cultural. In addition to studying the unifying characteristics of a region, geographers study how a region changes over times. Using the theme of regions, geographers divide the world into manageable units for study.

Spatial organization is a description of how things are grouped in a given space. In geographical terms, this can describe people, places, and environments anywhere and everywhere on Earth. The most basic form of spatial organization for people is where they live. The vast majority of people live near other people, in villages and towns and cities and settlements. These people live near others in order to take advantage of the goods and services that naturally arise from cooperation. These villages and towns and cities and settlements are, to varying degrees, near bodies of water.

Place - A place has both human and physical characteristics. Physical characteristics include features such as mountains, rivers, deserts, etc. Human characteristics are the features created by human interaction with their environment such as canals and roads.

Human-Environmental Interaction - The theme of human-environmental interaction has three main concepts: humans adapt to the environment (wearing warm clothing in a cold climate, for instance,) humans modify the environment (planting trees to block a prevailing wind, for example,) and humans depend on the environment (for food, water and raw materials.)

Movement - The theme of movement covers how humans interact with one another through trade, communications, emigration and other forms of interaction.

Regions - A region is an area that has some kind of unifying characteristic, such as a common language, a common government, etc. There are three main types of regions. Formal regions are areas defined by actual political boundaries, such as a city, county, or state. Functional regions are defined by a common function, such as the area covered by a telephone service. Vernacular regions are less formally defined areas that are formed by people's perception, e.g. "the Middle East," and "the South."

Absolute location is the exact whereabouts of a person, place, or thing, according to any kind of geographical indicators you want to name. For example, Paris is at 48 degrees north longitude and 2 degrees east latitude.

Relative location, on the other hand, is *always* a description that involves more than one thing. When you describe a relative location, you tell where something is by describing what is around it. The same description of where the nearest post office is in terms of absolute location might be this: "It's down the street from the supermarket, on the right side of the street, next to the dentist's office

Physical locations of the earth's surface features include the four major hemispheres and the parts of the earth's continents in them. Political locations are the political divisions, if any, within each continent. Both physical and political locations are precisely determined in two *ways:* (1) Surveying is done to determine boundary lines and distance from other features. (2) Exact locations are precisely determined by imaginary lines of latitude (parallels) and longitude (meridians). The intersection of these lines at right angles forms a grid, making it impossible to pinpoint an exact location of any place using any two grip coordinates.

The Eastern Hemisphere, located between the North and South Poles and between the Prime Meridian (0 degrees longitude) east to the International Date Line at 180 degrees longitude, consists of most of Europe, all of Australia, most of Africa, and all of Asia, except for a tiny piece of the easternmost part of Russia that extends east of 180 degrees longitude.

The Western Hemisphere, located between the North and South Poles and between the Prime Meridian (0 degrees longitude) west to the International Date Line at 180 degrees longitude, consists of all of North and South America, a tiny part of the easternmost part of Russia that extends east of 180 degrees longitude, and a part of Europe that extends west of the Prime Meridian (0 degrees longitude).

The Northern Hemisphere, located between the North Pole and the Equator, contains all of the continents of Europe and North America and parts of South America, Africa, and most of Asia.

The Southern Hemisphere, located between the South Pole and the Equator, contains all of Australia, a small part of Asia, about one-third of Africa, most of South America, and all of Antarctica.

Of the seven continents, only one contains just one entire country and is the only island continent, Australia. Its political divisions consist of six states and one territory: Western Australia, South Australia, Tasmania, Victoria, New South Wales, Queensland, and Northern Territory.

Africa is made up of 54 separate countries, the major ones being Egypt, Nigeria, South Africa, Zaire, Kenya, Algeria, Morocco, and the large island of Madagascar.

Asia consists of 49 separate countries, some of which include China, Japan, India, Turkey, Israel, Iraq, Iran, Indonesia, Jordan, Vietnam, Thailand, and the Philippines.

Europe's 43 separate nations include France, Russia, Malta, Denmark, Hungary, Greece, Bosnia and Herzegovina.

North America consists of Canada and the United States of America and the island nations of the West Indies and the "land bridge" of Middle America, including Cuba, Jamaica, Mexico, Panama, and others.

Thirteen separate nations together occupy the continent of South America, among them such nations as Brazil, Paraguay, Ecuador, and Suriname.

The continent of Antarctica has no political boundaries or divisions but is the location of a number of science and research stations managed by nations such as Russia, Japan, France, Australia, and India.

Physical geography is concerned with the locations of such earth features as climate, water, and land; how these relate to and affect each other and human activities; and what forces shaped and changed them. All three of these earth features affect the lives of all humans having a direct influence on what is made and produced, where it occurs, how it occurs, and what makes it possible. The combination of the different climate conditions and types of landforms and other surface features work together all around the earth to give the many varied cultures their unique characteristics and distinctions.

Cultural geography studies the location, characteristics, and influence of the physical environment on different cultures around the earth. Also included in these studies are comparisons and influences of the many varied cultures. Ease of travel and up-to-the-minute, state-of-the-art communication techniques ease the difficulties of understanding cultural differences making it easier to come in contact with them.

The earth's surface is made up of 70% water and 30% land. Physical features of the land surface include mountains, hills, plateaus, valleys, and plains. Other minor landforms include deserts, deltas, canyons, mesas, basins, foothills, marshes and swamps. Earth's water features include oceans, seas, lakes, rivers, and canals.

Mountains are landforms with rather steep slopes at least 2,000 feet or more above sea level. Mountains are found in groups called mountain chains or mountain ranges. At least one range can be found on six of the earth's seven continents. North America has the Appalachian and Rocky Mountains; South America the Andes; Asia the Himalayas; Australia the Great Dividing Range; Europe the Alps; and Africa the Atlas, Ahaggar, and Drakensburg Mountains.

Hills are elevated landforms rising to an elevation of about 500 to 2000 feet. They are found everywhere on earth including Antarctica where they are covered by ice.

Plateaus are elevated landforms usually level on top. Depending on location, they range from being an area that is very cold to one that is cool and healthful. Some plateaus are dry because they are surrounded by mountains that keep out any moisture. Some examples include the Kenya Plateau in East Africa, which is very cool. The plateau extending north from the Himalayas is extremely dry while those in Antarctica and Greenland are covered with ice and snow.

Plains are described as areas of flat or slightly rolling land, usually lower than the landforms next to them. Sometimes called lowlands (and sometimes located along **seacoasts)** they support the majority of the world's people. Some are found inland and many have been formed by large rivers. This resulted in extremely fertile soil for successful cultivation of crops and numerous large settlements of people. In North America, the vast plains areas extend from the Gulf of Mexico north to the Arctic Ocean and between the Appalachian and Rocky Mountains. In Europe, rich plains extend east from Great Britain into central Europe on into the Siberian region of Russia. Plains in river valleys are found in China (the Yangtze River valley), India (the Ganges River valley), and Southeast Asia (the Mekong River valley).

Valleys are land areas found between hills and mountains. Some have gentle slopes containing trees and plants; others have steep walls and are referred to as canyons. One example is Arizona's Grand Canyon of the Colorado River.

Deserts are large dry areas of land receiving ten inches or less of rainfall each year. Among the better known deserts are Africa's large Sahara Desert, the Arabian Desert on the Arabian Peninsula, and the desert Outback covering roughly one third of Australia.

Deltas are areas of lowlands formed by soil and sediment deposited at the mouths of rivers. The soil is generally very fertile and most fertile river deltas are important crop-growing areas. One well-known example is the delta of Egypt's Nile River, known for its production of cotton.

Mesas are the flat tops of hills or mountains usually with steep sides. Sometimes plateaus are also called mesas. Basins are considered to be low areas drained by rivers or low spots in mountains. Foothills are generally considered a low series of hills found between a plain and a mountain range. Marshes and swamps are wet lowlands providing growth of such plants as rushes and reeds.

Oceans are the largest bodies of water on the planet. The four oceans of the earth are the **Atlantic Ocean**, one-half the size of the Pacific and separating North and South America from Africa and Europe; the **Pacific Ocean**, covering almost one-third of the entire surface of the earth and separating North and South America from Asia and Australia; the **Indian Ocean**, touching Africa, Asia, and Australia; and the ice-filled **Arctic Ocean,** extending from North America and Europe to the North Pole. The waters of the Atlantic, Pacific, and Indian Oceans also touch the shores of Antarctica.

Seas are smaller than oceans and are surrounded by land. Some examples include the Mediterranean Sea found between Europe, Asia, and Africa; and the Caribbean Sea, touching the West Indies, South and Central America. A lake is a body of water surrounded by land. The Great Lakes in North America are a good example.

Rivers, considered a nation's lifeblood, usually begin as very small streams, formed by melting snow and rainfall, flowing from higher to lower land, emptying into a larger body of water, usually a sea or an ocean. Examples of important rivers for the people and countries affected by and/or dependent on them include the Nile, Niger, and Zaire Rivers of Africa; the Rhine, Danube, and Thames Rivers of Europe; the Yangtze, Ganges, Mekong, Hwang He, and Irrawaddy Rivers of Asia; the Murray-Darling in Australia; and the Orinoco in South America. River systems are made up of large rivers and numerous smaller rivers or tributaries flowing into them. Examples include the vast Amazon Rivers system in South America and the Mississippi River system in the United States.

Canals are man-made water passages constructed to connect two larger bodies of water. Famous examples include the **Panama Canal** across Panama's isthmus connecting the Atlantic and Pacific Oceans and the **Suez Canal** in the Middle East between Africa and the Arabian Peninsula connecting the Red and Mediterranean Seas.

Weather is the condition of the air which surrounds the day-to-day atmospheric conditions including temperature, air pressure, wind and moisture or precipitation which includes rain, snow, hail, or sleet.

Climate is average weather or daily weather conditions for a specific region or location over a long or extended period of time. Studying the climate of an area includes information gathered on the area's monthly and yearly temperatures and its monthly and yearly amounts of precipitation. In addition, a characteristic of an area's climate is the length of its growing season. Four reasons for the different climate regions on the earth are differences in:

- Latitude,
- The amount of moisture,
- Temperatures in land and water, and
- The earth's land surface.

There are many different climates throughout the earth. It is most unusual if a country contains just one kind of climate. Regions of climates are divided according to latitudes:

0 - 23 1 /2 degrees are the "low latitudes"
23 1/2 - 66 1/2 degrees are the "middle latitudes"
66 1/2 degrees to the Poles are the "high latitudes"

The **low latitudes** are comprised of the rainforest, savanna, and desert climates. The tropical rainforest climate is found in equatorial lowlands and is hot and wet. There is sun, extreme heat and rain--everyday. Although daily temperatures rarely rise above 90 degrees F, the daily humidity is always high, leaving everything sticky and damp. North and south of the tropical rainforests are the tropical grasslands called "savannas," the "lands of two seasons"--a winter dry season and a summer wet season. Further north and south of the tropical grasslands or savannas are the deserts. These areas are the hottest and driest parts of the earth receiving less than 10 inches of rain a year. These areas have extreme temperatures between night and day. After the sun sets, the land cools quickly dropping the temperature as much as 50 degrees F.

The **middle latitudes** contain the Mediterranean, humid-subtropical, humid-continental, marine, steppe, and desert climates. Lands containing the Mediterranean climate are considered "sunny" lands found in six areas of the world: lands bordering the Mediterranean Sea, a small portion of southwestern Africa, areas in southern and southwestern Australia, a small part of the Ukraine near the Black Sea, central Chile, and Southern California. Summers are hot and dry with mild winters. The growing season usually lasts all year and what little rain falls are during the winter months. What is rather unusual is that the Mediterranean climate is located between 30 and 40 degrees north and south latitude on the western coasts of countries.

The humid **subtropical climate** is found north and south of the tropics and is moist indeed. The areas having this type of climate are found on the eastern side of their continents and include Japan, mainland China, Australia, Africa, South America, and the United States--the southeastern coasts of these areas. An interesting feature of their locations is that warm ocean currents are found there. The winds that blow across these currents bring in warm moist air all year round. Long, warm summers; short, mild winters; a long growing season allow for different crops to be grown several times a year. All contribute to the productivity of this climate type which supports more people than any of the other climates.

Most places in the world are in some manner close to agricultural land as well. Food makes the world go round and some cities are more agriculturally inclined than others. Rare is the city, however, that grows absolutely no crops. The kind of food grown is almost entirely dependent on the kind of land available and the climate surrounding that land. Rice doesn't grow well in the desert, for instance, nor do bananas grow well in snowy lands. Certain crops are easier to transport than others and the ones that aren't are usually grown near ports or other areas of export.

Settlements begin in areas that offer the natural resources to support life – food and water. With the ability to manage the environment one finds a concentration of populations. With the ability to transport raw materials and finished products, comes mobility. With increasing technology and the rise of industrial centers, comes a migration of the workforce.

Cities are the major hubs of human settlement. Almost half of the population of the world now lives in cities. These percentages are much higher in developed regions. Established cities continue to grow. The fastest growth, however, is occurring in developing areas. In some regions there are "metropolitan areas" made up of urban and sub-urban areas. In some places cities and urban areas have become interconnected into "megalopoli" (e.g., Tokyo-Kawasaki-Yokohama).

The concentrations of populations and the divisions of these areas among various groups that constitute the cities can differ significantly. North American cities are different from European cities in terms of shape, size, population density, and modes of transportation. While in North America, the wealthiest economic groups tend to live outside the cities, the opposite is true in Latin American cities.

There are significant differences among the cities of the world in terms of connectedness to other cities. While European and North American cities tend to be well linked both by transportation and communication connections, there are other places in the world in which communication between the cities of the country may be inferior to communication with the rest of the world.

Rural areas tend to be less densely populated due to the needs of agriculture. More land is needed to produce crops or for animal husbandry than for manufacturing, especially in a city in which the buildings tend to be taller. Rural areas, however, must be connected via communication and transportation in order to provide food and raw materials to urban areas.

Civics

Citizenship in a democracy bestows on an individual certain rights, foremost being the right to participate in one's own government. Along with these rights come responsibilities, including the responsibility of a citizen to participate.

The most basic form of participation is the vote. Those who have reached the age of 18 in the U.S. are eligible to vote in public elections. With this right comes the responsibility to be informed before voting, and not to sell or otherwise give away one's vote. Citizens are also eligible to run for public office. Along with the right to run for office comes the responsibility to represent the electors as fairly as possible and to perform the duties expected of a government representative.

In the United States, citizens are guaranteed the right to free speech; the right to express an opinion on public issues. In turn, citizens have the responsibility to allow others to speak freely. At the community level, this might mean speaking at a city council hearing while allowing others with different or opposing viewpoints to have their say without interruption or comment.

The U.S. Constitution also guarantees freedom of religion. This means that the government may not impose an official religion on its citizens, and that people are free to practice their religion. Citizens are also responsible for allowing those of other religions to practice freely without obstruction. Occasionally, religious issues will be put before the public at the state level in the form of ballot measures or initiatives. To what extent it should be acceptable for religious beliefs to be expressed in a public setting, such as a public school, is an issue that has been debated recently.

In making decisions on matters like these, the citizen is expected to take responsibility to become informed of the issues involved and to make his vote based on his own opinion. Being informed of how one's government works and what the effects of new legislation will be is an essential part of being a good citizen.

The U.S. Constitution also guarantees that all citizens be treated equally by the law. In addition, federal and state laws make it a crime to discriminate against citizens based on their sex, race, religion and other factors. To ensure that all people are treated equally, citizens have the responsibility to follow these laws.

These rights and responsibilities are essentially the same whether one is voting in a local school board race, for the passage of a new state law, or for the President of the United States. Being a good citizen means exercising one's own rights while allowing others to do the same.

A person who lives in a democratic society theoretically has an entire laundry list guaranteed to him or her by the government. In the United States, this is the Constitution and its Amendments. Among these very important rights are:

- the right to speak out in public;
- the right to pursue any religion;
- the right for a group of people to gather in public for *any* reason that doesn't fall under a national security cloud;
- the right *not* to have soldiers stationed in your home;
- the right *not* to be forced to testify against yourself in a court of law;
- the right to a speedy and public trial by a jury of your peers;
- the right *not* to the victim of cruel and unusual punishment;
- and the right to avoid unreasonable search and seizure of your person, your house, and your vehicle.

The terms "civil liberties" and "civil rights" are often used interchangeably, but there are some fine distinctions between the two terms. The term civil liberties is used to imply that the state has a positive role to play in assuring that all its' citizens will have equal protection and justice under the law. The term implies equal opportunities to exercise their privileges of citizenship and to participate fully in the life of the nation, regardless of race, religion, sex, color or creed. The term civil rights is used more often to refer to rights that may be described as guarantees that are specified as against the state authority implying limitations on the actions of the state to interfere with citizens' liberties. Although the term "civil rights" has thus been identified with the ideal of equality and the term "civil liberties" with the idea of freedom, the two concepts are really inseparable and interacting. Equality implies the proper ordering of liberty in a society so that one individual's freedom does not infringe on the rights of others.

The beginnings of civil liberties and the idea of civil rights in the United States go back to the ideas of the Greeks. The early British struggle for civil rights and to the very philosophies that led people to come to the New World in the first place. Religious freedom, political freedom, and the right to live one's life as one sees fit are basic to the American ideal. These were embodied in the ideas expressed in the Declaration of Independence and the Constitution.

All these ideas found their final expression in the United States Constitution's first ten amendments, known as the Bill of Rights. In 1789, the first Congress passed these first amendments and by December 1791, three-fourths of the states at that time had ratified them. The Bill of Rights protects certain liberties and basic rights. James Madison who wrote the amendments said that the Bill of Rights does not give Americans these rights. People, Madison said, already have these rights. They are natural rights that belong to all human beings. The Bill of Rights simply prevents the governments from taking away these rights.

Federal laws are passed by the Congress, and can originate in either the House of Representatives or the Senate. The first step in the passing of a law is for the proposed law to be introduced in one of the houses of Congress. A proposed law is called a **bill** while it is under consideration by Congress. A bill can be introduced, or sponsored, by a member of Congress by giving a copy to the clerk or by placing a copy in a special box called a hopper.

Once a bill is introduced, copies are printed and it is assigned to one of several standing committees of the house in which it was introduced. The committee studies the bill and performs research on the issues it would cover. Committees may call experts to testify on the bill and gather public comments. The committee may revise the bill. Finally, the committee votes on whether to release the bill to be voted on by the full body. A committee may also lay aside a bill so that it cannot be voted on. Once a bill is released, it can be debated and amended by the full body before being voted on. If it passes by a simple majority vote, the bill is sent to the other house of Congress, where the process begins again.

Once a bill has passed both the House of Representatives and the Senate, it is assigned to a conference committee that is made up of members of both houses. The conference committee resolves differences between the House and Senate versions of a bill, if any, and then sends it back to both houses for final approval. Once a bill receives final approval, it is signed by the Speaker of the House and the Vice President, who is also the President of the Senate, and sent to the President for consideration. The President may either sign the bill or **veto** it. If he vetoes the bill, his veto may be overruled if two-thirds of both the Senate and the House vote to do so. Once the President signs it the bill becomes a law.

Federal laws are enforced by the executive branch and its departments. The Department of Justice, led by the United States Attorney General is the primary law enforcement department of the federal government. The Justice Department is aided by other investigative and enforcement departments such as the Federal Bureau of Investigation (FBI) and the U.S. Postal Inspectors.

The U.S. Constitution and Congressional laws provide basic as well as additional rights to American citizens. These civil rights include freedom of religion, assembly, speech, voting, holding public office, and traveling throughout the country. U.S. citizens have the right to live in America and cannot be forced to leave. American citizenship is guaranteed and will not be taken away for any reason, unless one commits certain serious actions. Civil rights have limitations such as minimum age for voting and limited free speech, forbidding the damage to someone's reputation by slander and lying.

Popular sovereignty grants citizens the ability to directly participate in their own government by voting and running for public office. This ideal is based on a belief of equality that holds that all citizens have an equal right to engage in their own governance, and is established in the United States Constitution. The Constitution also contains a list of specific rights that citizens have, and which the government cannot infringe upon. Popular sovereignty also allows for citizens to change their government if they feel it is necessary. This was the driving ideal behind the Declaration of Independence and is embodied in the governmental structure laid out in the Constitution.

The **rule of law** is the ideal that the law applies not only to the governed, but to the government as well. This core value gives authority to the justice system, which grants citizens protection from the government by requiring that any accusation of a crime be proved by the government before a person is punished. This is called due process and ensures that any accused person will have an opportunity to confront his accusers and provide a defense. Due process follows from the core value of a right to liberty. The government cannot take away a citizen's liberty without reason or without proof. The correlating ideal is also a core value - that someone who does harm another or break a law will receive justice under the democratic system. The ideal of justice holds that a punishment will fit the crime, and that any citizen can appeal to the judicial system if he feels he has been wronged.

Citizens' duties also vary from nation to nation. Duties demanded by law (also considered civic responsibilities) include paying taxes, obeying laws, and defending the country. Although some governments require jury duty, in the United States this would be a duty not required by law along with voting, doing volunteer work to help others, and becoming aware of public problems.

Citizenship is granted one of two ways: either by birth or by naturalization. Some Americans hold dual citizenship.

Historical concepts are movements, belief systems or other phenomena that can be identified and examined individually or as part of a historical theme. Capitalism, communism, democracy, racism and globalization are all examples of historical concepts. Historical concepts can be interpreted as part of larger historical themes and provide insight into historical events by placing them in a larger historical context.

Almost all representative democracies in the world guarantee similar rights to their citizens, and expect them to take similar responsibilities to respect the rights of others. As a citizen of the world one is expected to respect the rights of other nations, and the people of those nations, in the same way.

Social studies provide an opportunity for students to broaden their general academic skills in many areas. By encouraging students to ask and investigate questions, they gain skill in making meaningful inquiries into social issues. Providing them with a range of sources requires students to make judgments about the best sources for investigating a line of inquiry and develops the ability to determine authenticity among those sources. Collaboration develops the ability to work as part of a team and to respect the viewpoints of others.

Historic events and social issues cannot be considered only in isolation. People and their actions are connected in many ways, and events are linked through cause and effect over time. Identifying and analyzing these social and historic links is a primary goal of the social sciences. The methods used to analyze social phenomena borrow from several of the social sciences. Interviews, statistical evaluation, observation and experimentation are just some of the ways that people's opinions and motivations can be measured. From these opinions, larger social beliefs and movements can be interpreted, and events, issues and social problems can be placed in context to provide a fuller view of their importance.

Skill 8.3   **Demonstrate knowledge of social science skills (e.g., gathering, organizing, interpreting, and presenting information; creating and using maps) used in various contexts**

We use **illustrations** of various sorts because it is often easier to demonstrate a given idea visually instead of orally. Sometimes it is even easier to do so with an illustration than a description. This is especially true in the areas of education and research because humans are visually stimulated. It is a fact that any idea presented visually in some manner is always easier to understand and to comprehend than simply getting an idea across verbally, by hearing it or reading it. Among the more common illustrations used are various types of **maps, graphs and charts**.

Photographs and globes are useful as well, but as they are limited in what kind of information that they can show, they are rarely used. Unless, as in the case of a photograph, it is of a particular political figure or a time that one wishes to visualize.

Although maps have advantages over globes and photographs, they do have a major disadvantage. This problem must be considered as well. The major problem of all maps comes about because most maps are flat and the Earth is a sphere. It is impossible to reproduce exactly on a flat surface an object shaped like a sphere. In order to put the earth's features onto a map they must be stretched in some way. This stretching is called **distortion.**

Distortion does not mean that maps are wrong it simply means that they are not perfect representations of the Earth or its parts. **Cartographers,** or mapmakers, understand the problems of distortion. They try to design them so that there is as little distortion as possible in the maps.

The process of putting the features of the Earth onto a flat surface is called **projection**. All maps are really map projections. There are many different types. Each one deals in a different way with the problem of distortion. Map projections are made in a number of ways. Some are done using complicated mathematics. However, the basic ideas behind map projections can be understood by looking at the three most common types:

(1) **Cylindrical Projections** - These are done by taking a cylinder of paper and wrapping it around a globe. A light is used to project the globe's features onto the paper. Distortion is least where the paper touches the globe. For example, suppose that the paper was wrapped so that it touched the globe at the equator, the map from this projection would have just a little distortion near the equator. However, in moving north or south of the equator, the distortion would increase as you moved further away from the equator. The best known and most widely used cylindrical projection is the **Mercator Projection.** It was first developed in 1569 by Gerardus Mercator, a Flemish mapmaker.

(2) **Conical Projections** - The name for these maps come from the fact that the projection is made onto a cone of paper. The cone is made so that it touches a globe at the base of the cone only. It can also be made so that it cuts through part of the globe in two different places. Again, there is the least distortion where the paper touches the globe. If the cone touches at two different points, there is some distortion at both of them. Conical projections are most often used to map areas in the **middle latitudes**. Maps of the United States are most often conical projections. This is because most of the country lies within these latitudes.

(3) **Flat-Plane Projections** – These are made with a flat piece of paper. It touches the globe at one point only. Areas near this point show little distortion. Flat-plane projections are often used to show the areas of the north and south poles. One such flat projection is called a **Gnomonic Projection**. On this kind of map all meridians appear as straight lines, Gnomonic projections are useful because any straight line drawn between points on it forms a **Great-Circle Route**.

Great-Circle Routes can best be described by thinking of a globe and when using the globe the shortest route between two points on it can be found by simply stretching a string from one point to the other. However, if the string was extended in reality, so that it took into effect the globe's curvature, it would then make a great-circle. A Great-Circle is any circle that cuts a sphere, such as the globe, into two equal parts. Because of distortion, most maps do not show great-circle routes as straight lines, Gnomonic projections, however, do show the shortest distance between the two places as a straight line, because of this they are valuable for navigation. They are called Great-Circle Sailing Maps.

To properly analyze a given map one must be familiar with the various parts and symbols that most modern maps use. For the most part, this is standardized, with different maps using similar parts and symbols, these can include:

The Title - All maps should have a title, just like all books should. The title tells you what information is to be found on the map.

The Legend - Most maps have a legend. A legend tells the reader about the various symbols that are used on that particular map and what the symbols represent, (also called a *map key)*.

The Grid - A grid is a series of lines that are used to find exact places and locations on the map. There are several different kinds of grid systems in use, however, most maps do use the longitude and latitude system, known as the **Geographic Grid System**.

Directions - Most maps have some directional system to show which way the map is being presented. Often on a map, a small compass will be present, with arrows showing the four basic directions, north, south, east, and west.

The Scale - This is used to show the relationship between a unit of measurement on the map versus the real world measure on the Earth. Maps are drawn to many different scales. Some maps show a lot of detail for a small area. Others show a greater span of distance, whichever is being used one should always be aware of just what scale is being used. For instance the scale might be something like 1 inch = 10 miles for a small area or for a map showing the whole world it might have a scale in which 1 inch = 1,000 miles. The point is that one must look at the map key in order to see what units of measurements the map is using.

Maps have four main properties. They are (1) the size of the areas shown on the map. (2) The shapes of the areas, (3) Consistent scales, and (4) Straight line directions. A map can be drawn so that it is correct in one or more of these properties. No map can be correct in all of them.

Equal areas - One property which maps can have is that of equal areas, In an equal area map, the meridians and parallels are drawn so that the areas shown have the same proportions as they do on the Earth. For example, Greenland is about 1eighteenth the size of South America, thus it will be show as 1eighteenth the size on an equal area map. The **Mercator projection** is an example of a map that does not have equal areas. In it, Greenland appears to be about the same size of South America. This is because the distortion is very bad at the poles and Greenland lies near the North Pole.

Conformality - A second map property is conformality, or correct shapes. There are no maps which can show very large areas of the earth in their exact shapes. Only globes can really do that, however Conformal Maps are as close as possible to true shapes. The United States is often shown by a Lambert Conformal Conic Projection Map.

Consistent Scales - Many maps attempt to use the same scale on all parts of the map. Generally, this is easier when maps show a relatively small part of the earth's surface. For example, a map of Florida might be a Consistent Scale Map. Generally maps showing large areas are not consistent-scale maps. This is so because of distortion. Often such maps will have two scales noted in the key. One scale, for example, might be accurate to measure distances between points along the Equator. Another might be then used to measure distances between the North Pole and the South Pole.

Maps showing physical features often try to show information about the elevation or *relief* of the land. *Elevation* is the distance above or below the sea level. The elevation is usually shown with colors, for instance, all areas on a map which are at a certain level will be shown in the same color.

Relief Maps - Show the shape of the land surface, flat, rugged, or steep. Relief maps usually give more detail than simply showing the overall elevation of the land's surface. Relief is also sometimes shown with colors, but another way to show relief is by using *contour lines*. These lines connect all points of a land surface which are the same height surrounding the particular area of land.

Thematic Maps - These are used to show more specific information, often on a single *theme*, or topic. Thematic maps show the distribution or amount of something (population density, climate, economic information, cultural, political information, etc.) over a certain given area.

Information can be gained looking at a map that might take hundreds of words to explain otherwise. Maps reflect the great variety of knowledge covered by political science. To show such a variety of information maps are made in many different ways. Because of this variety, maps must be understood in order to make the best sense of them.

Spatial organization is a description of how things are grouped in a given space. In geographical terms, this can describe people, places, and environments anywhere and everywhere on Earth.

The most basic form of spatial organization for people is where they live. The vast majority of people live near other people, in villages and towns and cities and settlements. These people live near others in order to take advantage of the goods and services that naturally arise from cooperation. These villages and towns and cities and settlements are, to varying degrees, near bodies of water. Water is a staple of survival for every person on the planet and is also a good source of energy for factories and other industries, as well as a form of transportation for people and goods.

Another way to describe where people live is by the **geography** and **topography** around them. The vast majority of people on the planet live in areas that are very hospitable. Yes, people live in the Himalayas and in the Sahara, but the populations in those areas are small indeed when compared to the plains of China, India, Europe, and the United States. People naturally want to live where they won't have to work really hard just to survive, and world population patterns reflect this.

We can examine the spatial organization of the places where people live. For example, in a city, where are the factories and heavy industry buildings? Are they near airports or train stations? Are they on the edge of town, near major roads? What about housing developments? Are they near these industries, or are they far away? Where are the other industry buildings? Where are the schools and hospitals and parks? What about the police and fire stations? How close are homes to each of these things? Towns and especially cities are routinely organized into neighborhoods, so that each house or home is near to most things that its residents might need on a regular basis. This means that large cities have multiple schools, hospitals, grocery stores, fire stations, etc.

Demography is the branch of science of statistics most concerned with the social well being of people. **Demographic tables** may include: (1) Analysis of the population on the basis of age, parentage, physical condition, race, occupation and civil position, giving the actual size and the density of each separate area. (2) Changes in the population as a result of birth, marriage, and death. (3) Statistics on population movements and their effects and their relations to given economic, social and political conditions. (4) Statistics of crime, illegitimacy and suicide. (5) Levels of education and economic and social statistics.

Such information is also similar to that area of science known as **vital statistics** and as such is indispensable in studying social trends and making important legislative, economic, and social decisions. Such demographic information is gathered from census, and registrar reports and the like, and by state laws such information, especially the vital kind, is kept by physicians, attorneys, funeral directors, member of the clergy, and similar professional people. In the United States such demographic information is compiled, kept and published by the Public Health Service of the United States Department of Health, Education, and Welfare.

The most important element of this information is the so-called **rate**, which customarily represents the average of births and deaths for a unit of 1000 population over a given calendar year. These general rates are called **crude rates**, which are then sub-divided into *sex, color, age, occupation, locality, etc.* They are then known as **refined rates**.

In examining **statistics** and the sources of statistical data one must also be aware of the methods of statistical information gathering. For instance, there are many good sources of raw statistical data. Books such as *The Statistical Abstract of the United States,* published by the United States Chamber of Commerce, *The World Fact Book,* published by the Central Intelligence Agency or *The Monthly Labor Review* published by the United States Department of Labor are excellent examples that contain much raw data. Many such yearbooks and the like on various topics are readily available from any library, or from the government itself. However, knowing how that data and information was gathered is at least equally as important as the figures themselves.

By having knowledge of statistical language and methodology, can one really be able to gauge the usefulness of any given piece of data presented. Thus we must first understand just what statistics are and what they can and cannot, tell us. The social sciences are built upon the philosophy that human movements and interactions can be measured, studied, and ultimately predicted using a variety of methods and research techniques. By studying how humans act individually and within their societies, the social sciences seek to discover and explain common motivations and reactions among humans.

The body of knowledge generated by the social sciences has great influence on both the individual and societal levels. Methods of individual psychological treatment, for instance, are based on ongoing research in the social science of psychology. In the larger scheme, a country bases its foreign policy largely on the analysis of political scientists and other social research.

There are many different ways to find ideas for **research problems**. One of the most common ways is through experiencing and assessing relevant problems in a specific field. Researchers are often involved in the fields in which they choose to study, and thus encounter practical problems related to their areas of expertise on a daily basis. The can use their knowledge, expertise and research ability to examine their selected research problem. For students, all that this entails is being curious about the world around them. Research ideas can come from one's background, culture, education, experiences etc. Another way to get research ideas is by exploring literature in a specific field and coming up with a question that extends or refines previous research.

Once a **topic** is decided, a research question must be formulated. A research question is a relevant, researchable, feasible statement that identifies the information to be studied. Once this initial question is formulated, it is a good idea to think of specific issues related to the topic. This will help to create a hypothesis. A research **hypothesis** is a statement of the researcher's expectations for the outcome of the research problem. It is a summary statement of the problem to be addressed in any research document. A good hypothesis states, clearly and concisely, the researchers expected relationship between the variables that they are investigating. Once a hypothesis is decided, the rest of the research paper should focus on analyzing a set of information or arguing a specific point. Thus, there are two types of research papers: analytical and argumentative.

The scientific method is the process by which researchers over time endeavor to construct an accurate (that is, reliable, consistent and non-arbitrary) representation of the world. Recognizing that personal and cultural beliefs influence both our perceptions and our interpretations of natural phenomena, standard procedures and criteria minimize those influences when developing a theory.

The scientific method has four steps:
1. Observation and description of a phenomenon or group of phenomena.
2. Formulation of a hypothesis to explain the phenomena.
3. Use of the hypothesis to predict the existence of other phenomena or to predict quantitatively the results of new observations.
4. Performance of experimental tests of the predictions by several independent experimenters and properly performed experiments.

While the researcher may bring certain biases to the study, it's important that bias not be permitted to enter into the interpretation. It's also important that data that doesn't fit the hypothesis not be ruled out. This is unlikely to happen if the researcher is open to the possibility that the hypothesis might turn out to be null. Another important caution is to be certain that the methods for analyzing and interpreting are flawless. Abiding by these mandates is important if the discovery is to make a contribution to human understanding.

The Internet and other research resources provide a wealth of information on thousands of interesting topics for students preparing presentations or projects. Using search engines like Google, Microsoft and Infotrac allow students to search multiple Internet resources or databases on one subject search. Students should have an outline of the purpose of a project or research presentation that includes:

- Purpose - identity the reason for the research information
- Objective - having a clear thesis for a project will allow the students opportunities to be specific on Internet searches
- Preparation - when using resources or collecting data, students should create folders for sorting through the information. Providing labels for the folders will create a system of organization that will make construction of the final project or presentation easier and less time consuming
- Procedure - organized folders and a procedural list of what the project or presentation needs to include will create A+ work for students and A+ grading for teachers
- Visuals or artifacts - choose data or visuals that are specific to the subject content or presentation. Make sure that poster boards or Power Point presentations can be visually seen from all areas of the classroom. Teachers can provide laptop computers for Power Point presentations.

Skill 8.4   Demonstrate knowledge of strategies for providing developmentally appropriate opportunities for young children to explore and apply concepts and skills in geography, history, civics, economics, and culture

The importance of a quality early childhood educational experience in shaping a child's development in future years has long been recognized. Approaches to achieve the desired level of quality vary greatly. A quality preschool experience prepares the child for Kindergarten and elementary school. The early grades prepare the students for more advanced forms of learning. The research recognizes that the sooner a learning disability is recognized, the greater likelihood a successful intervention can occur.

Alternative learning strategies, creating quality learning environments, intervention strategies for slower learners, helping children to transition and succeed in the education system are among some of the common areas of research. Research indicates that active learning strategies are effective in helping students to comprehend social studies skills. The early years are essential in shaping socializations, reducing prejudices and accepting diversity.

Varying Learning Materials

There are many resources available for the teaching of social science concepts. The resources used should be appropriate to the learning objectives specified. The teacher wants to use different kinds of resources in order to make the subject matter more interesting to the student and to appeal to different learning styles. First of all a good textbook is required. This gives the student something that they can refer to and something to study from. Students generally like to have a text to refer to.

The use of audio-video aides is also beneficial in the classroom environment. Most people are visual learners and will retain information better when it is in visual form. Audio-visual presentations, like movies, give them concepts in pictures that they will easily retain.

Library projects are good for students also. The library has an abundance of resources that students should become familiar with at an early age, so they learn to use the library. There are books and magazines that they can look through and read to expand their knowledge beyond the textbooks. Younger children, particularly, like to look at pictures.

The computer also offers abundant opportunities as a teaching tool and resource. The Internet provides a wealth of information on all topics and something can be found that is suitable for any age group. Children like to play game, so presenting the material in a game-like format is also a good teaching tool. Making little puzzles for vocabulary or letting them present the information in the form of a story or even a play helps them learn and retain various concepts.

Field trips, if possible, are also a good way to expose children to various aspects of social science. Today's world of technology makes a myriad of resources available to the teacher. The teacher should make use of as many of them as possible to keep the material more interesting for the student and to aide in their retention of the material.

Maximizing the Social Science Learning Opportunities

At the early childhood level, social science themes permeate almost every aspect of a school's curriculum. Opportunities for students to explore and apply the concepts of social science should be easily found in good interdisciplinary units. Below are some examples of lesson ideas and activities that can be used as springboards for creating effective interdisciplinary social science programs:

Civics

Discuss the role of the president, but include child-friendly topics such as his family, pets, etc.

- Provide fun reference materials on the nation's capital, including landmarks, to create a travel brochure

- Discuss different civic occupations to create a game where students match the worker to their occupation's tools

Geography

Take a magic carpet ride to travel around the globe, exploring new regions and countries and tracking your travel on a world map

- Explore cultural diversity in your neighborhood or city to write a story about how meeting new people is fun

- Create storybook characters that come from different parts of the world by using information about the countries to build the character

History

Read a book about an American holiday (e.g., Fourth of July, Thanksgiving, etc) or event (e.g., Pilgrims landing in Plymouth) to create their own poster or project utilizing the historical information

- Learn about modern day heroes and how they contributed to a better world, and have students come up with one thing they can do to improve their community

- Research and discuss a world civilization (e.g., the Mayans) and construct a duplicate icon from their history (e.g., build a pyramid from sugar cubes)

Economics

Design a fundraiser (e.g., used book sale, lemonade stand) and sketch out a simple plan to execute the fundraiser

- To explore commercialism and advertising, have students brainstorm economic wants vs. needs (e.g., new video game vs. a coat) and how advertising targets an audience

Culture

- Make a food from a foreign culture and/or organize a cultural food festival

- Examine a variety of cultural celebrations and find their similarities and differences

- Explore clothing or other artifacts from various cultures and have students design their own

For more examples, visit http://www.pbs.org/teachers/socialstudies/

Skill 8.5 **Demonstrate knowledge of how to promote young children's understanding of social science phenomena (e.g., communities; families; relationships among people; interdependence of people, places, and regions; roles of individuals and groups in society; effects of stereotyping; relationship of the self to others and to social, economic, cultural, and political activities and institutions)**

Early childhood education prepares the students for a lifetime of learning, functioning and succeeding in a diverse global environment. Young learners are building a base of understanding of the world around them. Concepts like location and community are important in building not only a geographic base for future learning but also an understanding of the basic community institutions which shape our world and how they interrelate. A community involves much more than a location. It involves social systems, economics, politics, services, government providing a means of examining the various elements of social science in an integrated way.

Location and community offer wonderful topics to help children explore the world in which we live and to begin to integrate knowledge from various disciplines. Community involves all aspects of living from employment to family to institutions. Recognizing location offers an opportunity to explore a variety to topics including countries, addresses, people, as well as community aspects. The location theme becomes one of the building blocks to geographic awareness.

The National Council for Social Studies identifies 10 themes essential to social science instruction including (www.socialstudies.org/standards/strands/):

1. Culture
2. Time, Continuity and Change
3. People, Places and Environments
4. Individual development and identity
5. Individuals, Groups and Institutions
6. Power, Authority and Governance
7. Production, Distribution and Consumption
8. Science, Technology and Society
9. Global Connections
10. Civic Ideals and Practices

Additionally national and State organizations establish standards for early childhood instruction. History standards include organizing events, knowledge of historic inquiry, understanding societal change and diversity, knowledge of science, technology, religion and philosophies, and political institutions.

Geography standards include knowledge of maps and other geographic tools, recognition of physical processes, regions, and human characteristics, people, places and environment, as well as interdependence of societies.

Economic standards include understanding of scarcity, use of resources and how different economic systems allocate resources, as well as basic economic principles including trade, exchange, business and individual behavior.

Civics standards for early childhood include describing purpose of government, understanding law and order, and the constitution framework.

Various national organizations such as the Center for Civic Education, the National Council for the Social Studies, National Geographic Society, and the National Council on Economic Education have developed national standard for the education of students

Alternative learning strategies, creating quality learning environments, intervention strategies for slower learners, helping children to transition and succeed in the education system are among some of the common areas of research. Research indicates that active learning strategies are effective in helping students to comprehend social studies skills. The early years are essential in shaping socializations, reducing prejudices and accepting diversity.

The integration of social science knowledge and the interdisciplinary nature of the topics require an interactive approach to teaching which exposes the students to a variety of tools, documents and the contrasts which exist globally.

The National Council for the Social Sciences identifies 5 elements of successful social science education:

"Social Studies Teaching and Learning are powerful when they are meaningful; Social Science Teaching and Learning are powerful when they are integrated; Social Science Teaching and Learning are powerful when they are value-based; Social Science Teaching and Learning are powerful when they are challenging; Social Science Teaching and Learning are powerful when they are active."
(*A Vision of Powerful Teaching and Learning in the Social Studies;* National Council for the Social Studies)

The complexity of the ideas of social studies is best taught through an active interaction between teacher and students, requiring preparation and reflection. The integrative nature of social studies through interaction can help students to grasp the focus of the various disciplines of the area. Values form the basis of many of the ideas of the disciplines and require an objective exploration to help students to comprehend. Challenging the minds of students through interactions aids the understanding of the material and concepts. Social studies provide opportunities for active learning both individually and in groups. The various topics of social studies offer tremendous opportunities to expose students to a variety of documents to aid the learning process.

Using themes in lesson plans which build on themes of every day life provides the student with useful information and exposure to important social awareness. Unlike other disciplines, social studies is evolving and changing daily with events around the world, new discoveries and the constant debate and reevaluation of issues. For the young learner, the relating of the various themes to events in the world developing around the school helps the student to associate the relevance of social studies to everyday life.

Many of the skills of social studies are preparing the student for their future responsibilities as a citizen. Using everyday (current) events make the social studies relevant to the student, and help them understand the events of the world.

Integrating disciplines provides an opportunity for the student to learn broader perspectives and also utilizes available educational time more efficiently. Particularly during the early years as students learn basic reading, mathematics and writing skills, time available for development of social studies proficiencies is limited. Integrating social studies with the learning of other skills allows students to gain a greater understanding of the world in which we live.

Within the social sciences an integrated approach allows a theme to be explored across the social sciences including anthropology, geography, economics and history among others, while learning math, reading, or other important skills. As a result greater mastery of the topic occurs.

American classrooms contain students from different races, classes, and ethnic groups. They begin the education process with different values, attitudes and abilities. Expanding the child's appreciation and respect for human diversity is important to be able to function in a diverse world and a diverse educational experience. Inappropriate perceptions of diversity limit the students' ability to function within the educational experience and later in life. Students need to recognize and respect the individual behaviors and values of a diverse population.

Recognizing the diverse culture and the rights which our democracy provides to all citizens begins early in the education process and continues throughout a lifetime. The education process contributes to the building of society's acceptance of diversity and prepares the student for success within a diverse democracy. Not only does a school's curriculum shape this learning, but its hiring practices reflecting diversity is important as well. Ideally, cultural education should extend beyond the classroom and be part of the entire school learning environment. Providing training opportunities for teachers to improve skills in teaching diversity is also important.

Integrating cultural education throughout the various disciplines helps the student to recognize contributions from various cultures. Teachers help students to recognize the contributions of multiple cultures to the development of our current state of knowledge and this helps to reduce the belief that one culture is superior or inferior. Helping students to recognize the difference practices of various cultures helps with the acceptance process. Identifying examples of successful people should maintain a diverse character. Holidays and special events provide an important opportunity to explore diversity in greater detail.

The early years of the education process offers an opportunity to begin the shaping of a student's mind to function of a diverse global environment. Beyond student education, the educational system can help to change the values and attitudes of the population as a whole.

Interdependence of People, Places and Regions
See also Skill 8.1 and Skill 8.2

Related to this is the distance between cities, towns, villages, or settlements. In certain parts of the United States and definitely in many countries in Europe, the population settlement patterns achieve megalopolis standards, with no clear boundaries from one town to the next. Other, more sparsely populated areas have towns that are few and far between and have relatively few people in them. Some exceptions to this exist, of course, like oases in the deserts; for the most part, however, population centers tend to be relatively near one another or at least near smaller towns.

The growth of urban areas is often linked to the advantages provided by its geographic location. Before the advent of efficient overland routes of commerce such as railroads and highways, water provided the primary means of transportation of commercial goods. Most large American cities are situated along bodies of water.

As transportation technology advanced, the supporting infrastructure was built to connect cities with one another and to connect remote areas to larger communities. The railroad, for example, allowed for the quick transport of agricultural products from rural areas to urban centers. This newfound efficiency not only further fueled the growth of urban centers, it changed the economy of rural America. Where once farmers had practiced only subsistence farming – growing enough to support one's own family – the new infrastructure meant that one could convert agricultural products into cash by selling them at market.

For urban dwellers, improvements in building technology and advances in transportation allowed for larger cities. Growth brought with it a new set of problems unique to each location. The bodies of water that had made the development of cities possible in their early days also formed natural barriers to growth. Further infrastructure in the form of bridges, tunnels and ferry routes were needed to connect central urban areas with outlying communities.

As cities grew in population, living conditions became more crowded. As roads and bridges became better, and transportation technology improved, many people began to look outside the city for living space. Along with the development of these new suburbs came the infrastructure to connect them to the city in the form of commuter railroads and highways. In the case of New York City, which is situated mainly on islands, a mass transit system became crucial early on to bring essential workers from outlying areas into the commercial centers.

The growth of suburbs had the effect in many cities of creating a type of economic segregation. Working class people who could not afford new suburban homes and perhaps an automobile to carry them to and from work were relegated to closer, more densely populated areas. Frequently, these areas had to be passed through by those on their way to the suburbs, and rail lines and freeways sometimes bisected these urban communities.

In the modern age, advancements in telecommunications infrastructure may have an impact on urban growth patterns as information can pass instantly and freely between almost any two points on the globe, allowing access to some aspects of urban life to those in remote areas. Flight has made possible global commerce and goods exchange on a level never before seen. Foods from all around the world can be flown literally around the world and, with the aid of refrigeration techniques, be kept fresh enough to sell in markets nearly everywhere. The same is true of medicine and, unfortunately, weapons.

The priorities and culture of a society are shaped by the contributions of individuals and groups. Individuals are socialized to the values of the society beginning early in life through the educational system, families and other institutions. Society depends on the contributions of its members to function properly. Individuals organize into groups of shared common values and to achieve a specific goal or a series of goals. Groups often form to protect the interests including the security interests of individual members. Groups can take various forms and adopt a variety of leadership structures. Individuals often are part of multiple groups and associations.

Stereotyping behavior occurs all throughout the society. Often groups of individuals are stereotyped because of a practice, behavior or characteristic of a group or individual member. Unfortunately, stereotyping is often based on the prejudices of an individual or another group. Stereotyping is usually based on race, religion, sexual orientation or other characteristics including professions. Laws have been created to protect individuals from the harmful aspects of prejudices and stereotyping behavior which limits ability to fully benefit from the economic system.

Skill 8.6   Demonstrate knowledge of approaches and activities for integrating learning experiences in the social sciences with learning experiences in other content areas

The interdisciplinary curriculum planning approach to student learning creates a meaningful balance inclusive of curriculum depth and breadth. Take for instance the following scenario: Mrs. Jackson presents her Language Arts class with an assignment for collaborative group work. She provides them with the birth date and death of the famous author Ernest Hemingway and asks them to figure how old he was when he died. She gives them five minutes as a group to work on the final answer. After five minutes, she asked each group for their answer and wrote the answers on the board. Each group gave a different answer. When Mrs. Jackson came to the last group, a female student stated, "Why do we have to do math in a Language Arts class?"

The application of knowledge learned from a basic math class would have problem-solved the Language Arts' question. Given the date of his birth and the date of his death, all students needed to do was subtract his birth from his death year to come up with a numerical answer = age when he died. Providing students with a constructivist modality of applying knowledge to problem-solve pertinent information for a language arts' class should be an integral part of instructional practice and learning in an interdisciplinary classroom.

Historically, previous centuries of educational research have shown a strong correlation between the need for interdisciplinary instruction and cognitive learning application. Understanding how students process information and create learning was the goal of earlier educators. Earlier researchers looked at how the brain connected information pieces into meaning and found that learning takes place along intricate neural pathways that formulate processing and meaning from data input into the brain. The implications for student learning are vast in that teachers can work with students to break down subject content area into bits of information that can be memorized and applied to a former learning experience and then processed into integral resources of information.

It is important for teachers to consider students' development and readiness when deciding instructional decisions. If an educational program is child-centered, then it will surely address the developmental abilities and needs of the students because it will take its cues from students' interests, concerns, and questions. Making an educational program child-centered involves building on the natural curiosity children bring to school, and asking children what they want to learn.

Teachers help students to identify their own questions, puzzles, and goals, and then structure for them widening circles of experience and investigation of those topics. Teachers manage to infuse all the skills, knowledge, and concepts that society mandates into a child-driven curriculum. This does not mean passive teachers who respond only to students' explicit cues. Teachers also draw on their understanding of children's developmentally characteristic needs and enthusiasms to design experiences that lead children into areas they might not choose, but that they do enjoy and that engage them. Teachers also bring their own interests and enthusiasms into the classroom to share and to act as a motivational means of guiding children.

Implementing such a child-centered curriculum is the result of very careful and deliberate planning. Planning serves as a means of organizing instruction and influences classroom teaching. Well thought-out planning includes specifying behavioral objectives, specifying students' entry behavior (knowledge and skills), selecting and sequencing learning activities so as to move students from entry behavior to objective, and evaluating the outcomes of instruction in order to improve planning.

COMPETENCY 9.0   **UNDERSTAND THE ROLE OF MOVEMENT AND PHYSICAL ACTIVITY IN YOUNG CHILDREN'S HEALTH AND FITNESS; INTERACTIONS AMONG PHYSICAL, EMOTIONAL, AND SOCIAL WELL-BEING; AND WAYS TO PROVIDE YOUNG CHILDREN WITH OPPORTUNITIES TO PARTICIPATE IN HEALTH AND FITNESS ACTIVITIES AND TO HELP THEM LEARN TO MAKE HEALTH-RELATED DECISIONS**

Skill 9.1   **Demonstrate knowledge of basic principles and practices of personal, interpersonal, and community health and safety, including those related to the prevention and treatment of illness and injury**

The effect of factors such as gender, age, environment, nutrition, heredity and substance abuse is also crucial in understanding adolescent fitness performance. Girls mature earlier than boys do, but boys quickly catch up and grow larger and stronger. Age, combined with maturity level, influences a child's physical strength, flexibility, and coordination. Good nutrition positively influences the quality of a child's physical activity level, while poor nutrition has the opposite effect. Adverse environmental conditions such as high heat or poor air quality strongly affect activity level. Students that inherit favorable physical characteristics will perform better and with more ease than those who aren't so fortunate. Substance abuse of any sort – alcohol, tobacco, or drugs – is a detriment to physical performance.

Dealing with factors that are out of the teacher's control requires both structure and flexibility. When necessary, make adjustments amongst the students and/or the activity. For example, when teaching how to throw a softball, don't hesitate to pair girls with boys if their maturity and strength levels are similar. If the distance is too far for some pairs, move them closer. If some pairs are more advanced, challenge them by increasing the partner's distance while continuing to work on accuracy and speed. Add a personal challenge to see how many times they can toss without dropping the ball. Finally, having more advanced students teach their peers that aren't as competent will benefit all students.

A variety of influences affects a student's motor development, growth, and fitness level:

Psychological – Psychological influences on motor development and fitness include a student's mental well-being, perceptions of fitness activities, and level of comfort in a fitness-training environment (both alone and within a group). Students experiencing psychological difficulties, such as depression, will tend to be apathetic and lack both the energy and inclination to participate in fitness activities. As a result, their motor development and fitness levels will suffer. Factors like the student's confidence level and comfort within a group environment, related to both the student's level of popularity within the group and the student's own personal insecurities, are also significant. It is noteworthy, though, that in the case of psychological influences on motor development and fitness levels, there is a more reciprocal relationship than with other influences. While a student's psychology may negatively affect their fitness levels, proper fitness training has the potential to positively affect the student psychologically, thereby reversing a negative cycle.

Cultural – Culture is a significant and sometimes overlooked influence on a student's motor development and fitness, especially in the case of students belonging to minority groups. Students may not feel motivated to participate in certain physical activities, either because they are not associated with the student's sense of identity or because the student's culture discourages these activities. For example, students from cultures with strict dress codes may not be comfortable with swimming activities. On the same note, students (especially older children) may be uncomfortable with physical activities in inter-gender situations. Educators must keep such cultural considerations in mind when planning physical education curricula.

Economic – The economic situation of students can affect their motor development and fitness because lack of resources can detract from the ability of parents to provide access to extra-curricular activities that promote development, proper fitness training equipment (ranging from complex exercise machines to team sport uniforms to something as simple as a basketball hoop), and even adequate nutrition.

Familial – Familial factors that can influence motor development and fitness relate to the student's home climate concerning physical activity. A student's own feelings toward physical activity often reflect the degree to which caregivers and role models (like older siblings) are athletically inclined and have a positive attitude towards physical activity. It isn't necessary for the parents to be athletically inclined, so much as it is important for them to encourage their child to explore fitness activities that could suit them.

Environmental and Health – Genetic make-up (i.e. age, gender, ethnicity) has a big influence on growth and development. Various physical and environmental factors directly affect one's personal health and fitness. Poor habits, living conditions, and afflictions such as disease or disability can impact a person in a negative manner. A healthy lifestyle with adequate conditions and minimal physical or mental stresses will enable a person to develop towards a positive, healthy existence. A highly agreed upon motor development theory is the relationship between one's own heredity and environmental factors.

Instructors should place students in rich learning situations, regardless of previous experience or personal factors, which provide plenty of positive opportunities to participate in physical activity. For example, prior to playing a game of softball, have students practice throwing by tossing the ball to themselves, progress to the underhand toss, and later to the overhand toss.

Identify Common Signs of Stress

Emotional signs of stress include: depression, lethargy, aggressiveness, irritability, anxiety, edginess, fearfulness, impulsiveness, chronic fatigue hyper excitability, inability to concentrate, frequent feelings of boredom, feeling overwhelmed, apathy, impatience, pessimism, sarcasm, humorlessness, confusion, helplessness, melancholy, alienation, isolation, numbness, purposelessness, isolation, numbness, self-consciousness; inability to maintain an intimate relationship.

Behavioral signs of stress include: elevated use of substances (alcohol, drugs; tobacco), crying, yelling, insomnia or excessive sleep, excessive TV watching, school/job burnout, panic attacks, poor problems solving capability, avoidance of people, aberrant behavior, procrastination, accident proneness, restlessness, loss of memory, indecisiveness, aggressiveness, inflexibility, phobic responses, tardiness, disorganization; sexual problems.

Physical signs of stress: pounding heart, stuttering, trembling/nervous tics, excessive perspiration, teeth grinding, gastrointestinal problems (constipation, indigestion, diarrhea, queasy stomach), dry mouth, aching lower back, migraine/tension headaches, stiff neck, asthma attacks, allergy attacks, skin problems, frequent colds or low grade fevers, muscle tension, hyperventilation, high blood pressure, amenorrhea, nightmares; cold intolerance.

Identify Both Positive and Negative Coping Strategies for Individuals under Stress

Positive coping strategies to cope with stress include using one's social support system, spiritual support, managing time, initiating direct action, re-examining priorities, active thinking, acceptance, meditation, imagery, biofeedback, progressive relaxation, deep breathing, massage, sauna, Jacuzzi, humor, recreation and diversions, and exercise.

Negative coping strategies to cope with stress include: using alcohol or other mind altering substances, smoking, excessive caffeine intake, poor eating habits, negative "self-talk;" expressing feelings of distress, anger, and other feelings in a destructive manner.

Skill 9.2   Demonstrate knowledge of motor development, human body systems, concepts and practices of health-related fitness, and relationships between fitness and body systems

In order for a child to write correctly, they must first develop fine motor skills. Before being required to manipulate a pencil, children should have dexterity and strength in their fingers, which helps them to gain more control of small muscles.

These hands-on activities are excellent for practicing fine motor skills and will build strength in their fingers and hands, which will aid in the development of a child's writing skills:

Tearing

- Tear newspaper into strips and then crumple them into balls. Use the balls to stuff a Halloween pumpkin or other art creation.

Cutting

- Cut pictures from magazines
- Cut a fringe on the edge of a piece of construction paper

Puzzles

- Have children put together a puzzle with large puzzles pieces. This will help to develop proper eye-hand coordination

Clay

- Manipulating play dough into balls strengthens a child's grasp. Let the children explain to what they created from their play dough objects

Finger Painting

- Many times when a child has not developed fine motor skills yet, it helps to trace the pattern with his finger before he tries it with a pencil. Have the child trace a pattern in sand, cornmeal, finger paint, etc.

Drawing

- Draw at an easel with a large crayon. Encourage children to practice their name or letters of the alphabet

The most important factors of learning to write are the grip on the writing instrument, the position of the arm and wrist, and the position of the writing paper.

Gross Motor Development

Gross motor skills refer to the movements of the large muscles of the body. The development of these skills is important for children to move about freely, such as in jumping, running, climbing stairs, etc. It is necessary to build activities for this development into the curriculum of early childhood classes. However, some of these should be developed by the time children reach school age. They include:

- Running
- Walking in a straight line
- Jumping up and down and over obstacles
- Hopping on one foot
- Walking down stairs using one foot after the other
- Marching
- Standing on one foot for at least 10 seconds
- Walking backwards
- Throwing a ball
- Sliding

Play as part of the classroom routine is essential in the development of gross motor skills. The toys used should be age appropriate and there should be an open space in the classroom. Outside activities as well as those in the school gymnasium help to develop the skills the children need.

Concept of Body Awareness Applied to Physical Education Activities

Body awareness is a person's understanding of his or her own body parts and their capability of movement.

Instructors can assess body awareness by playing and watching a game of "Simon Says" and asking the students to touch different body parts. You can also instruct students to make their bodies into various shapes, from straight to round to twisted, and varying sizes, to fit into different sized spaces.

In addition, you can instruct children to touch one part of their body to another and to use various body parts to stamp their feet, twist their neck, clap their hands, nod their heads, wiggle their noses, snap their fingers, open their mouths, shrug their shoulders, bend their knees, close their eyes, bend their elbows, or wiggle their toes.

Concept of Spatial Awareness Applied to Physical Education Activities

Spatial awareness is the ability to make decisions about an object's positional changes in space (i.e. awareness of three-dimensional space position changes). Developing spatial awareness requires two sequential phases: 1) identifying the location of objects in relation to one's own body in space, and 2) locating more than one object in relation to each object and independent of one's own body. Plan activities using different size balls, boxes, or hoops and have children move towards and away; under and over; in front of and behind; and inside, outside, and beside the objects.

Concepts of Space, Direction, and Speed Related to Movement of Concepts

Research shows that the concepts of space, direction, and speed are interrelated with movement concepts. Such concepts and their understanding are extremely important for students, as they need to relate movement skills to direction in order to move with confidence and avoid collisions.

A student or player in motion must take the elements of space, direction, speed, and vision into consideration in order to perform and understand a sport. A player must decide how to handle their space as well as numerous other factors that arise on the field.

For a player, the concepts are all interlinked. He has to understand how to maintain or change pathways with speed. This ability allows him to change motion and perform well in space (or the area that the players occupy on the field).

Skill 9.3 **Demonstrate understanding of ways in which participation in movement activities provides young children with opportunities to develop skills for resolving conflicts, communicating positively, cooperating, and showing respect for differences among individuals**

For most people, the development of social roles and appropriate social behaviors occurs during childhood. Physical play between parents and children, as well as between siblings and peers, serves as a strong regulator in the developmental process. Chasing games, roughhousing, wrestling, or practicing sport skills such as jumping, throwing, catching, and striking, are some examples of childhood play. These activities may be competitive or non-competitive and are important for promoting social and moral development of both boys and girls. Unfortunately, fathers will often engage in this sort of activity more with their sons than their daughters. Regardless of the sex of the child, both boys and girls enjoy these types of activities.

Physical play during infancy and early childhood is central to the development of social and emotional competence. Research shows that children who engage in play that is more physical with their parents, particularly with parents who are sensitive and responsive to the child, exhibited greater enjoyment during the play sessions and were more popular with their peers. Likewise, these early interactions with parents, siblings, and peers are important in helping children become more aware of their emotions and to learn to monitor and regulate their own emotional responses. Children learn quickly through watching the responses of their parents which behaviors make their parents smile and laugh and which behaviors cause their parents to frown and disengage from the activity.

If children want the fun to continue, they engage in the behaviors that please others. As children near adolescence, they learn through rough-and-tumble play that there are limits to how far they can go before hurting someone (physically or emotionally), which results in termination of the activity or later rejection of the child by peers. These early interactions with parents and siblings are important in helping children learn appropriate behavior in the social situations of sport and physical activity.

Children learn to assess their social competence (i.e., ability to get along with and acceptance by peers, family members, teachers and coaches) in sport through the feedback received from parents and coaches. Initially, authority figures teach children, "You can't do that because I said so." As children approach school age, parents begin the process of explaining why a behavior is right or wrong because children continuously ask, "Why?"

Similarly, when children engage in sports, they learn about taking turns with their teammates, sharing playing time, and valuing rules. They understand that rules are important for everyone and without these regulations, the game would become unfair. The learning of social competence is continuous as we expand our social arena and learn about different cultures. A constant in the learning process is the role of feedback as we assess the responses of others to our behaviors and comments.

In addition to the development of social competence, sports participation can help youth develop other forms of self-competence. Most important among these self-competencies is self-esteem. Self-esteem is how we judge our worth and indicates the extent to which an individual believes he is capable, significant, successful and worthy. Educators have suggested that one of the biggest barriers to success in the classroom today is low self-esteem.

Children develop self-esteem by evaluating abilities and by evaluating the responses of others. Children actively observe the responses of parents and coaches to their performances, looking for signs of approval or disapproval of their behavior. Children often interpret feedback and criticism as either a negative or a positive response to the behavior. In sports, research shows that the coach is a critical source of information that influences the self-esteem of children.

Little League baseball players whose coaches use a "positive approach" to coaching (e.g. more frequent encouragement, positive reinforcement for effort and corrective, instructional feedback), had significantly higher self-esteem ratings over the course of a season than children whose coaches used these techniques less frequently. The most compelling evidence supporting the importance of coaches' feedback was found for those children who started the season with the lowest self-esteem ratings and increased considerably their self-assessment and self-worth. In addition to evaluating themselves more positively, low self-esteem children evaluated their coaches more positively than did children with higher self-esteem who played for coaches who used the "positive approach." Moreover, studies show that 95 percent of children who played for coaches trained to use the positive approach signed up to play baseball the next year, compared with 75 percent of the youth who played for untrained adult coaches.

We cannot overlook the importance of enhanced self-esteem on future participation. A major part of the development of high self-esteem is the pride and joy that children experience as their physical skills improve. Children will feel good about themselves as long as their skills are improving. If children feel that their performance during a game or practice is not as good as that of others, or as good as they think mom and dad would want, they often experience shame and disappointment.

Some children will view mistakes made during a game as a failure and will look for ways to avoid participating in the task if they receive no encouragement to continue. At this point, it is critical that adults (e.g., parents and coaches) intervene to help children to interpret the mistake or "failure." We must teach children that a mistake is not synonymous with failure. Rather, a mistake shows us that we need a new strategy, more practice, and/or greater effort to succeed at the task.

Goal Setting

Goal setting is an effective way of achieving progress. In order to preserve and/or increase self-confidence, you and your students must set goals that are frequently reachable. One such way of achieving this is to set several small, short-term goals to attain one long-term goal. Be realistic in goal setting to increase fitness levels gradually. As students reach their goals, set more in order to continue performance improvement. Keep in mind that maintaining a current fitness level is an adequate goal provided the individual is in a healthy state. Reward your students when they reach goals. Rewards serve as motivation to reach the next goal. Also, be sure to prepare for lapses. Try to get back on track as soon as possible.

Skill 9.4   Demonstrate knowledge of developmentally appropriate procedures for promoting young children's understanding of principles and practices of personal, interpersonal, and community health and safety

Factors that Affect Family Health

The primary factors that affect family health include environmental conditions such as pollution and proximity to industrial areas, smoking and drinking habits of family members, economic conditions that affect nutritional factors, and general levels of education among family members as related to an understanding of healthy living habits.

The relative levels of pollution in the family's area can significantly contribute to family health. For example, proximity to industrial areas, which may be releasing carcinogenic emissions, can be dangerous. Similarly, a smoking habit within the home environment is highly detrimental, as it will negatively affect the respiratory and circulatory systems of all members of the household. A drinking habit can also pose a risk both to the individual and to those in proximity to him or her.

Economic conditions can affect family health in that lower economic means can lead to neglect of some nutritional factors (which are critical to healthy living and proper physical and cognitive development). Similarly, families with two working parents may not have as much time to spend with children to monitor their eating habits. Education levels among family members as related to an understanding of healthy living habits are also significant. Even with all of the required financial means, parents/caregivers may not have the requisite knowledge to direct them to habits for healthy living.

Strategies for Promoting Environmental Health

Environmental health demonstrates concern about environmental issues. Examples of environmental issues include outdoor air pollution, indoor air pollution, noise pollution, water contamination, radiation exposure, disposal of hazardous wastes, and recycling.

Air pollution is a primary environmental health hazard. Various air pollutants are highly dangerous. Examples of air pollutants include motor vehicle emissions such as carbon monoxide, sulfur oxide, nitrogen oxide, hydrocarbons, and airborne lead. The Clean Air Act of 1979 reduced some motor vehicle emissions; however, the levels remain dangerously high due to large numbers of vehicles on the road, long commutes, and oversized vehicles. Carpooling and the use of smaller vehicles could significantly decrease the amount of motor vehicle emissions.

Another type of pollution is indoor air pollution. The most dangerous types of indoor pollution are tobacco smoke, carbon monoxide, asbestos, radon, and lead. To prevent indoor air pollution, avoid tobacco smoking indoors and ensure that indoor areas have adequate ventilation with fresh outdoor air. Remove the sources of any pollutants. Keep appliances and heating systems in good condition and follow the regular maintenance schedule. Homes should have at least one carbon monoxide detector located near the sleeping area. Check homes for asbestos, lead, and radon. When detected, safely remove them.

Noise is an additional environmental concern. To protect the ears, keep headphones at a low level, sit at a safe distance from the speakers at concerts, and wear earplugs when exposed to loud sounds.

Yet another major environmental hazard is water pollution. Water pollution can cause dysentery (a severe intestinal infection), increases in hypertension (due to increased sodium content), and chemical poisoning (such as mercury poisoning). The Safe Water Drinking Act passed in 1974 requires water treatment facilities to notify consumers when they violate safe drinking water requirements; however, this regulation is not strictly enforced. To ensure safe drinking water, consumers should not assume that their facility is following the regulations. They should contact their individual facility to determine the contaminant levels in their drinking water. Additionally, consumers should avoid dumping garbage or chemicals in lakes, rivers, on the ground, or down the drain. Instead, take chemicals to a hazardous waste disposal center. Finally, everyone should practice water conservation. Methods of water conservation include installing a low-flow showerhead, running the dishwasher and washing machine only when completely full, turning off the water while brushing teeth and washing hands, taking quick showers, and watering the lawn at the coolest time of the day. Radiation exposure is also an environmental concern. Application of a thirty SPF sunscreen every hour and the use of ultraviolet-ray-blocking sunglasses can minimize the effects of ultraviolet radiation exposure.

One final environmental concern is the proper disposal of hazardous wastes. Consumers should always read and follow label information regarding the proper disposal of household products. Recycling is the process of breaking down products to their fundamental elements for use in another product. Recycling can help reduce air, water, and soil contaminants. Consumers should buy recycled products and recycle their own household materials. Additionally, consumers should avoid one-use products, especially disposable products made of plastic, paper, and foam.

Technology

The technology market is rapidly changing. Consumers are progressively turning to technology for a healthier life. Consumer-focused healthcare information technology helps patients handle the significant demands of healthcare management.

Healthcare information technology is a term describing the broad digital resources that are available to promote community health and proper health care for consumers. Healthcare information technology empowers patients to direct their healthcare and to advocate for themselves and their families as they use health care services. Healthcare information technology enables consumers, patients, and informal caregivers to gather facts, make choices, communicate with healthcare providers, control chronic disease, and participate in other health-related activities. Consumers should take caution when reviewing healthcare information on the internet, as much information is invalid. Consumers need to be educated in regards to website evaluation before using information from the internet in making healthcare decisions.

Healthcare information technology functions in numerous ways. The functions include providing general health information, supporting behavior change, providing tools to self-manage health, providing access to online groups, providing decision-making assistance, aiding in disease control, and providing access to healthcare tools. Information technology has the power to bring patients into full partnership with their healthcare providers. Specifically, instead of waiting for a return phone call, patients can simply e-mail the physician regarding his or her non-urgent condition. Healthcare providers can then respond to patient e-mails.

Many healthcare facilities are also moving towards complying with the executive order mandating electronic personal healthcare records. At some point in the near future, all healthcare facilities will link personal healthcare records. Consumers can also utilize computerized re-ordering systems for prescription refills. Many pharmacies and physicians are also moving towards electronic prescriptions. The increasingly widespread use of electronic personal healthcare records and computerized prescriptions will decrease the number of medical errors.

Peer Pressure

Peer pressure can cause children to make decisions, both positive and negative. For example, a child that interacts with other children that practice poor health behaviors such as drug use are more likely to mimic such behaviors. On the other hand, interacting with children that are committed to exercise may encourage a previously inactive child to become physically active.

Media

Media-based expectations influence the development of self-concept by setting media-based role models as the benchmarks against which students will measure their traits. Self-concept is a set of statements describing the child's own cognitive, physical, emotional, and social self-assessment. These statements will usually tend to be fairly objective ("good at baseball" or "has red hair"), media-based expectations can change the statements to be measurements against role models ("athletic like this actor" or "tall like that pop star").

SEE also Skill 9.1

General Classroom Safety

In the modern classroom, there is a great deal of furniture, equipment, supplies, appliances, and learning aids to help the teacher teach and students learn. The classroom should contain furnishings that fit the purpose of the classroom, and it is the responsibility of the administration to see these materials are maintained. However, it is the keen teacher's eye that can spot safety issues at their earliest appearance.

Whatever the arrangement of furniture and equipment may be the teacher must provide for adequate traffic flow. Rows of desks must have adequate space between them for students to move and for the teacher to circulate. All areas must be open to line-of-sight supervision by the teacher.

Local fire and safety codes dictate entry and exit standards. In addition, all corridors and classrooms should be wheelchair accessible for students and others who use them. It is the teachers' responsibility to educate themselves on their district's fire safety codes.

Another consideration is adequate ventilation and climate control. Specialty classes such as science require specialized hoods for ventilation. Physical Education classes have the added responsibility for shower areas and specialized environments that must be heated such as pool or athletic training rooms.

In all cases, proper care must be taken to ensure student safety. Furniture and equipment should be situated safely at all times. No equipment, materials, boxes, etc. should be placed where there is danger of falling over. Doors must have entry and exit accessibility at all times.

Skill 9.5 **Identify strategies for providing young children with developmentally appropriate opportunities to participate in movement activities in a variety of contexts, explore health related concepts, and make decisions related to their health and safety**

Locomotor Skills

Locomotor skills move an individual from one point to another.

1. **Walking** - with one foot contacting the surface at all times, walking shifts one's weight from one foot to the other while legs swing alternately in front of the body.

2. **Running** - an extension of walking that has a phase where the body is propelled with no base of support (speed is faster, stride is longer, and arms add power).

3. **Jumping** - projectile movements that momentarily suspend the body in midair.

4. **Vaulting** - coordinated movements that allow one to spring over an obstacle.

5. **Leaping** - similar to running, but leaping has greater height, flight, and distance.

6. **Hopping** - using the same foot to take off from a surface and land.

7. **Galloping** - forward or backward advanced elongation of walking combined and coordinated with a leap.

8. **Sliding** - sideward stepping pattern that is uneven, long, or short.

9. **Body Rolling** - moving across a surface by rocking back and forth, by turning over and over, or by shaping the body into a revolving mass.

10. **Climbing** - ascending or descending using the hands and feet with the upper body exerting the most control.

Nonlocomotor Skills

Nonlocomotor skills are stability skills where the movement requires little or no movement of one's base of support and does not result in change of position.

1. **Bending** - movement around a joint where two body parts meet.

2. **Dodging** - sharp change of direction from original line of movement such as away from a person or object.

3. **Stretching** - extending/hyper-extending joints to make body parts as straight or as long as possible.

4. **Twisting** - rotating body/body parts around an axis with a stationary base.

5. **Turning** - circular moving the body through space releasing the base of support.

6. **Swinging** - circular/pendular movements of the body/body parts below an axis.

7. **Swaying** - same as swinging but movement is above an axis.

8. **Pushing** - applying force against an object or person to move it away from one's body or to move one's body away from the object or person.

9. **Pulling** - executing force to cause objects/people to move toward one's body.

Manipulative Skills

Manipulative skills use body parts to propel or receive an object, controlling objects primarily with the hands and feet. Two types of manipulative skills are receptive (catch + trap) and propulsive (throw, strike, kick).

1. **Bouncing/Dribbling** - projecting a ball downwards.

2. **Catching** - stopping momentum of an object (for control) using the hands.

3. **Kicking** - striking an object with the foot.

4. **Rolling** - initiating force to an object to instill contact with a surface.

5. **Striking** - giving impetus to an object with the use of the hands or an object.

6. **Throwing** - using one or both arms to project an object into midair away from the body.

7. **Trapping** - without the use of the hands, receiving and controlling a ball

Knowledge of activities for body management skill development

Sequential development and activities for locomotor skills acquisition = crawl, creep, walk, run, jump, hop, gallop, slide, leap, skip, step-hop.

- **Activities to develop walking skills** include walking slower and faster in place; walking forward, backward, and sideways with slower and faster paces in straight, curving, and zigzag pathways with various lengths of steps; pausing between steps; and changing the height of the body.

- **Activities to develop running skills** include having students pretend they are playing basketball, trying to score a touchdown, trying to catch a bus, finishing a lengthy race, or running on a hot surface.

- **Activities to develop jumping skills** include alternating jumping with feet together and feet apart, taking off and landing on the balls of the feet, clicking the heels together while airborne, and landing with a foot forward and a foot backward.

- **Activities to develop galloping skills** include having students play a game of Fox and Hound, with the lead foot representing the fox and the back foot the hound trying to catch the fox (alternate the lead foot).

- **Activities to develop sliding skills** include having students hold hands in a circle and sliding in one direction, then sliding in the other direction.

- **Activities to develop hopping skills** include having students hop all the way around a hoop and hopping in and out of a hoop reversing direction. Students can also place ropes in straight lines and hop side-to-side over the rope from one end to the other and change (reverse) the direction.

- **Activities to develop skipping skills** include having students combine walking and hopping activities leading up to skipping.

- **Activities to develop step-hopping skills** include having students practice stepping and hopping activities while clapping hands to an uneven beat.

Sequential development and activities for nonlocomotor skill acquisition = stretch, bend, sit, shake, turn, rock and sway, swing, twist, dodge, and fall.

- **Activities to develop stretching** include lying on the back and stomach and stretching as far as possible; stretching as though one is reaching for a star, picking fruit off a tree, climbing a ladder, shooting a basketball, or placing an item on a high self; waking and yawning.

- **Activities to develop bending** include touching knees and toes then straightening the entire body and straightening the body halfway; bending as though picking up a coin, tying shoes, picking flowers/vegetables, and petting animals of different sizes.

- **Activities to develop sitting** include practicing sitting from standing, kneeling, and lying positions without the use of hands.

- **Activities to develop falling skills** include first collapsing in one's own space and then pretending to fall like bowling pins, raindrops, snowflakes, a rag doll, or Humpty Dumpty.

Sequential development and activities for manipulative skill development = striking, throwing, kicking, ball rolling, volleying, bouncing, catching, and trapping.

- **Activities to develop striking** begin with the striking of stationary objects by a participant in a stationary position. Next, the person remains still while trying to strike a moving object. Then, both the object and the participant are in motion as the participant attempts to strike the moving object.

- **Activities to develop throwing** include throwing yarn/foam balls against a wall, then at a big target, and finally at targets decreasing in size.

- **Activities to develop kicking** include alternating feet to kick balloons/beach balls, then kicking them under and over ropes. Change the type of ball as proficiency develops.

- **Activities to develop ball rolling** include rolling different size balls to a wall, then to targets decreasing in size.

- **Activities to develop volleying** include using a large balloon and, first, hitting it with both hands, then one hand (alternating hands), and then using different parts of the body. Change the object as students progress (balloon, to beach ball, to foam ball, etc.)

- **Activities to develop bouncing** include starting with large balls and, first, using both hands to bounce and then using one hand (alternate hands).

- **Activities to develop catching** include using various objects (balloons, beanbags, balls, etc.) to catch and, first, catching the object the participant has thrown him/herself, then catching objects someone else threw, and finally increasing the distance between the catcher and the thrower.

- **Activities to develop trapping** include trapping slow and fast rolling balls; trapping balls (or other objects such as beanbags) that are lightly thrown at waist, chest, and stomach levels; trapping different size balls.

SEE also Skill 9.4

Skill 9.6   Demonstrate knowledge of approaches and activities for integrating learning experiences related to health and movement with learning experiences in other content areas

Physical education is a key component of an interdisciplinary learning approach because not only does it draw from, but also it contributes to many other curriculum areas. Instructors can relate concepts from the physical sciences, mathematics, natural sciences, social sciences, and kinesiology to physical education activities.

Physical science is a term for the branches of science that study non-living systems. However, the term "physical" creates an unintended, arbitrary distinction, since many branches of physical science also study biological phenomena. Topics in physical science such as movement of an object through space and the effect of gravity on moving objects are of great relevance to physical education. Physical sciences allow us to determine the limits of physical activities.

Mathematics is the search for fundamental truths in pattern, quantity, and change. Examples of mathematical applications in sport include measuring speed, momentum, and height of objects; measuring distances and weights; scorekeeping; and statistical computations.

Natural science is the study of living things. Content areas in the natural sciences of great importance to physical education include physiology, nutrition, anatomy, and biochemistry. For example, a key component of physical education is an understanding of proper nutrition and the affect of food on the body.
The social sciences are a group of academic disciplines that study the human aspects of the world. Social scientists engage in research and theorize about both aggregate and individual behaviors. For example, a basic understanding of psychology is essential to the discussion of human patterns of nutrition and attitudes toward exercise and fitness. In addition, sport psychology is a specialized social science that explores the mental aspects of athletic performance.

Finally, kinesiology encompasses human anatomy, physiology, neuroscience, biochemistry, biomechanics, exercise psychology, and sociology of sport. Kinesiologists also study the relationship between the quality of movement and overall human health. Kinesiology is an important part of physical therapy, occupational therapy, chiropractics, osteopathy, exercise physiology, kinesiotherapy, massage therapy, ergonomics, physical education, and athletic coaching. The purpose of these applications may be therapeutic, preventive, or high-performance. The application of kinesiology can also incorporate knowledge from other academic disciplines such as psychology, sociology, cultural studies, ecology, evolutionary biology, and anthropology. The study of kinesiology is often part of the physical education curriculum and illustrates the truly interdisciplinary nature of physical education.

COMPETENCY 10.0 **UNDERSTAND THE FINE ARTS (INCLUDING THE VISUAL ARTS, MUSIC, DRAMA, AND DANCE) AS MEDIA FOR COMMUNICATION, INQUIRY, AND INSIGHT, AND UNDERSTAND HOW TO PROVIDE YOUNG CHILDREN WITH LEARNING OPPORTUNITIES THAT ENCOURAGE THEM TO EXPRESS THEMSELVES THROUGH THE ARTS**

Skill 10.1 **Demonstrate knowledge of elements, concepts, tools, techniques, and materials in the visual arts; the cultural dimensions of the visual arts; and relationships between the visual arts and other art forms**

Students should have an early introduction to the principles of visual art and should become familiar with the basic level of the following terms:

abstract
an image that reduces a subject to its essential visual elements, such as lines, shapes, and colors.

background
portions or areas of composition that are behind the primary or dominant subject matter or design areas

balance
the arrangement of one or more elements in a work of art so that they appear symmetrical or asymmetrical in design and proportion

contrast
juxtaposing one or more elements in opposition, to show their differences

emphasis
making one or more elements in a work of art stand out in such a way as to appear more important or significant

sketch
an image-development strategy; a preliminary drawing

texture
the way something feels by representation of the tactile character of surfaces

unity
the arrangement of one or more of the elements used to create a coherence of parts and a feeling of completeness or wholeness

After learning the above terms and how they relate to the use of line, color, value, space, texture and shape, an excellent opportunity is to have students create an "art sample book." Such books could include a variety of materials that would serve as examples, such as sandpaper and cotton balls to represent texture elements. Samples of square pieces of construction paper designed into various shapes could represent shape. String samples could represent the element of lines.

The sampling of art should also focus clearly on colors necessary for the early childhood student. Color can be introduced more in-depth when discussing **intensity**, the strength of the color, and **value**, the lightness or darkness of the colors. Another valuable tool regarding color is the use of a color wheel, and allowing students to experiment with the mixing of colors to create their own art experience.

It is vital that students learn to identify characteristics of visual arts that include materials, techniques and processes necessary to establish a connection between art and daily life. Early ages should begin to experience art in a variety of forms. It is important to reach many areas at an early age to establish a strong artistic foundation for young students. Students should be introduced to the simple recognition of simple patterns found in the art environment. They must also identify art materials such as clay, paint and crayons. Each of these types of material should be introduced and explained for use in daily lessons with young children.

Young students may need to be introduced to items that are developmentally appropriate for their age and for their fine motor skills. Many Pre-Kindergarten and Kindergarten students use oversized pencils and crayons for the first semester. Typically, after this first semester, development occurs to enable children to gradually develop into using smaller sized materials.

Students should begin to explore artistic expression at this age using colors and mixing. The color wheel is a vital lesson for young children and students begin to learn the uses of primary colors and secondary colors. By the middle of the school year students should be able to explain this process. For example, a student needs orange paint, but only has a few colors. Students should be able to determine that by mixing red and yellow that orange is created.

Teachers should begin to plan and use variation using line, shape, texture and many different principles of design. By using common environmental figures such as people, animals and buildings teachers can base many art lessons on characteristics of readily available examples. Students should be introduced to as many techniques as possible to ensure that all strands of the visual arts and materials are experienced at a variety of levels.

By using original works of arts students should be able to identify visual and actual textures of art and based their judgments of objects found in everyday scenes. Other examples that can be described as subjects could include landscapes, portraits and still life.

The major areas that young students should experience should include the following:

1. Painting-using tempra or watercolors.
2. Sculpture-typically using clay or play-dough.
3. Architecture-building or structuring design using 3D materials such as cardboard and poster board to create a desired effect.
4. Ceramics- another term for pottery using a hollow clay sculpture and pots made from clay and fired in a kiln using high temperature to strengthen them.
5. Metalworking-another term for engraving or cutting design or letters into metal with a sharp tool printmaking.
6. Lithography is an example of planographics, where a design is drawn on a surface and then the print is lifted from the surface.

Visual arts provide historical proof of various cultures. Andy Warhol's Campbell's Soup Can of the 1960's is a comment on American society and a glimpse of life at the time in the United States. Prehistoric Venus figurines combine art and religion and show us about the beliefs of a particular culture. Visual art is also used to enhance and strengthen music, dance and drama, by providing a beautiful backdrop or aesthetic surroundings to portray a specific time or place.

Skill 10.2   **Recognize elements, concepts, techniques, and materials for producing, listening to, and responding to music; the cultural dimensions of music; and relationships between music and other art forms**

Melody, harmony, rhythm, timbre, dynamics and texture are some of the basic components of music.

Melody is the tune – a specific arrangement of sounds in a pleasing pattern. Melody is often seen as the horizontal aspect of music, because melodic notes on a page travel along horizontally.

Harmony refers to the vertical aspect of music, or the musical chords related to a melody. So, when looking at a piece of music, the harmony notes are the ones lined up below each note of the melody, providing a more complex, fuller sound to a piece of music.

Rhythm refers to the duration of musical notes. Rhythms are patterns of long and short music note durations. A clear way to describe rhythm to young students is through percussion instruments. A teacher creates a rhythmic pattern of long and short drum beats and asks the students to repeat the rhythm.

Timbre is the quality of a sound. If a clarinet and a trumpet play the same exact note, they will still have a different timbre, or unique quality of sound. You can also describe different timbres using the same instrument. You may have two singers, but one has a harsh timbre and the other has a warm or soothing timbre to their voice. Timbre is subjective and lends itself to a number of creative exercises for early childhood students to describe what they hear in terms of the timbre of the sound.

Dynamics refer to the loudness or softness of music. Early Childhood students should develop a basic understanding of music vocabulary for dynamics. Piano describes soft music. Forte describes loud music. Pianissimo is very soft music. Double Forte refers to very loud music. Mezzo piano is kind of soft, while mezzo forte is kind of loud. These definitions can be organized on a continuum of soft to loud, with music examples for each.

Texture in music usually refers to the number of separate components making up the whole of a piece. A monophonic texture is a single melody line, such as a voice singing a tune. Polyphonic texture denotes two or more music lines playing at the same time. A single melodic line with harmonic accompaniment is called homophonic texture.

Music is an integral part of dance and is also often included in dramatic productions, either as background or as a central element in the story. Music is a terrific historian, as well, and much may be learned of cultures by listening to their popular music. American history is charted by the styles of music brought to the United States and then combined into new musical forms as people from different countries and cultures learn to live together.

Skill 10.3   Demonstrate knowledge of elements, concepts, techniques, and materials related to drama and dance; the cultural dimensions of drama and dance; and relationships between drama and dance and other art forms

Dance is an artistic form of self expression that uses the various elements of dance, such as use of **space**, **time**, **levels**, and **force**, to form a composition.

The primary grades have a gross understanding of their motor movements whereas older children are more apt to have a refined concept of their bodies. Individual movements are developed by the instructor when attention is given to various aspects such as:

- the range of movement or gestures through **space**
- the **direction** of the action or imaginary lines the body flows through space
- the **timing** of when movements form the dramatic effects
- the awareness of the **planes** formed by any two areas such as height and width or width and depth
- **levels** that are introduced so that the composition incorporates sit, stand, and kneeling, etc.
- The **elevation** or the degree of lift as in leaping and the movements that are done under that allusion of suspension
- the **force** and energy of dance that reflects the music, such as adagio (slow music) or allegro (quickening steps).

Rhythm is the basis of dance. A child can sit in a chair and clap or tap their hands on their legs to express thoughts of rhythm. With older children, imagery enables a dancer to visualize and internalize the particular qualities of a specific movement.

Because the younger child is more unsteady the initial level emphasis is not on gracefulness but rather to develop **body awareness**. The uniqueness of dance is that it is self-expression that can be guided through instruction. The student is taught the elements that are available such as **time and space.** Therefore, the student is incorporating **listening skills** to develop a sense of tempo.

Creative dance is the one that is most natural to a young child. Creative dance depicts feelings through movement. It is the initial reaction to sound and movement. The older elementary student will incorporate mood and expressiveness. Stories can be told to release the dancer into imagination.

Isadora Duncan is credited with being the mother of modern dance. **Modern dance** today refers to a concept of dance where the expressions of opposites are developed such as fast-slow, contract- release, vary height and level to fall and recover. Modern dance is based on four principles which are substance, dynamism, metakinesis, and form.

Drama

Drama comes from the Greek word "dran", meaning "to do." Therefore, drama is the acting out of a written story. Theater itself has several aspects, such as speech, gesture, dance, music, sound and spectacle. This art form combines many of the arts into a single live performance.

The basic elements of drama include:

Acting - Acting requires the student to demonstrate the ability to effectively communicate using skillful speaking, movement, rhythm, and sensory awareness.

Directing - Direction requires the management skills to produce and perform an onstage activity. This requires guiding and inspiring students as well as script and stage supervision.

Designing - Designing involves creating and initiating the onsite management of the art of acting.

Scriptwriting - Scriptwriting demands that a leader be able to produce original material and staging an entire production through the writing and designing a story that has performance value.

Each of the above mentioned skills should be incorporated in daily activities with young children. It is important that children are exposed to character development through stories, role-play, and modeling through various teacher guided experiences. Some of the experiences that are age appropriate for early childhood level include puppet theatre, paper dolls, character sketches, storytelling, and re-telling of stories in a student's own words.

Drama and dance both tell stories, and they are often combined as art forms. Drama and dance provide clues to cultures. Through the dances and the stories that unfold in dramas, we discover what is important to a particular culture, what they value, what they enjoy, what issues they face. Music and visual arts are also very often intertwined in drama and dance. Dance is certainly greatly enhanced by music, and visual backdrops and decorations displayed in a dramatic presentation help audience members to better imagine the artistic creation or representation before them.

Skill 10.4 Demonstrate understanding of the interrelationships of the fine arts and how the fine arts have been represented in past and present society

The evolution of how and why artworks are created is complicated, but in general historical terms, arts were originally part of religious ritual. Early religious artworks are evident in the cave drawings from the Paleolithic Era in Chauvet-Pont-d'Arc in France.

As time progressed, dance, theatre, music and visual arts were used to commemorate events, such as the ordination of a king. George F. Handel composed four coronation anthems in 1727 for the coronation of King George II, and these anthems are still widely performed today.

Courtly dances of the Renaissance period were an art form that reflected values in society and provided entertainment and romance. This example of the arts combined dance and music.

The arts are often used to record or comment on a time in history. We receive much of our knowledge of history from surviving artworks. The portrait "American Gothic," by Grant Wood, is one of the most familiar depictions of American regionalism from the 1930s. The musical "South Pacific" by Rogers & Hammerstein, written in 1949, depicts life in the U.S. Navy during World War II. Theatre often combines all of the arts into one performance. Music, dance, drama and the visual arts in the backdrops and scenery come together into one experience in American Musical Theatre.

Additionally, the arts provide social commentary, tell a story or convey intense emotion. Artworks are also created simply to provide something that is pleasing to the senses. Whatever the reason why artworks are created, they have become an interpreter of the world around us. The arts provide a unique language to express individual and societal values and reflect on culture.

The process of creating art is a discovery process. As soon as early childhood students are exposed to the basic elements of the arts, the process of discovery begins. As students increase their knowledge base, they question their basic assumptions, and the creative process evolves with each new creation. Fingers and toes are added to stick figures; what once was a melody, now also includes harmony; basic movements are coordinated into a dance combination; pretending to be an old woman evolves to a storytelling piece about an old woman who lives in a house by the sea and makes dolls for little children. Students begin to use the arts as a language to reflect on the world as they see it.

Creating, performing and responding are three points of an artistic triangle, which flow from one to the other. The artist creates, the performer brings the creation to an audience, and the audience responds, giving the feedback to the creator and commenting on what that particular work of art means to them.

Skill 10.5 **Demonstrate knowledge of strategies and tools for providing young children with developmentally appropriate opportunities to explore visual media, music, drama, and dance in a variety of contexts and to use visual media, music, drama, and dance to communicate ideas, experiences, and stories**

Visual Arts

Students are expected to fine tune observation skills and be able to identify and recreate the experiences that teachers provide for them as learning tools. For example, students may walk as a group on a nature hike taking in the surrounding elements and then begin to discuss the repetition found in the leaves of trees, or the bricks of the sidewalk, or the size and shapes of the buildings and how they may relate. They may also use such an experience to describe lines, colors, shapes, forms and textures. Beginning elements of perspective are noticed at an early age. The questions of why buildings look smaller when they are at a far distance and bigger when they are closer are sure to spark the imagination of early childhood students. Students can then take their inquiry to higher level of learning with some hands-on activities such as building three dimensional buildings and construction using paper and geometric shapes. Eventually students should acquire higher level thinking skills such as analysis, in which they will begin to question artists, art work, and analyze many different aspects of visual art.

An excellent opportunity is to have students create an "art sample book." Such books could include a variety of materials that would serve as examples, such as sandpaper and cotton balls to represent texture elements. Samples of square pieces of construction paper designed into various shapes could represent shape. String samples could represent the element of lines.

The sampling of art should also focus clearly on colors necessary for the early childhood student. Color can be introduced more in-depth when discussing **intensity**, the strength of the color, and **value**, the lightness or darkness of the colors. Another valuable tool regarding color is the use of a color wheel, and allowing students to experiment with the mixing of colors to create their own art experience.

Music

Core skills such as reading and writing music notation; composing, arranging and improvising music are continuously improved and complimented by other musical activities and information. Students become part of the musical process by ascertaining the natural evolution of their capabilities by the experience the teacher provides.

The increase of substance in the students' performance, both instrumental and vocal, is connected to the context provided by the teacher. Relating the students' musical inclinations to a working context of existing and current musical production creates a viable pathway for motivation and progress.

Amplifying the context in which music is performed through exercises and analysis that is grounded through knowledge of the historical and cultural context; aesthetic value; connections, relationships and applications of music lends the broad appreciation that is intrinsic in successfully interpreting the performer's role. Success in the music industry is appreciated according to the knowledge absorbed about the function of music in the social and cultural environment.

Movement
Dance is an artistic form of self expression that uses the various elements of dance, such as use of space, time, levels, and force, to form a composition.

The primary grades have a gross understanding of their motor movements whereas older children are more apt to have a refined concept of their bodies. Individual movements are developed by the instructor when attention is given to various aspects such as:

- the range of movement or gestures through space
- the direction of the action or imaginary lines the body flows through space
- the timing of when movements form the dramatic effects
- the awareness of the planes formed by any two areas such as height and width or width and depth
- levels that are introduced so that the composition incorporates sit, stand, and kneeling, etc.
- The elevation or the degree of lift as in leaping and the movements that are done under that allusion of suspension
- the force and energy of dance that reflects the music, such as adagio (slow music) or allegro (quickening steps).

Drama

Students come to the classroom with a basic knowledge of drama through their own games of make-believe. Extending that game of pretend or make-believe through improvisation is a starting point in building knowledge, language and concepts related to drama.

The **ten elements of acting** can be incorporated immediately into improvisation exercises. These elements begin with the questions: Who? What? Where? When? Why? Then, rounding out the ten elements are the senses: sight, hearing, smell, taste and touch. Discussing the ten elements within acting exercises begins a pattern of thought or a checklist for the students.

In a sample exercise, the students pretend to be at the beach. What do they see? What do they smell? Who are they? Why are they there? After these guided questions become more familiar, the student will take the ten elements and apply them to future dramatic creations. The ten elements will also be used as a barometer to critique dramatic performances. Do you know where that actor is located? What are they doing? Why? Did they hear something? What do you think they heard? Who are they?

The teacher further builds the drama language of a student by setting up an improvisation and placing actors **center stage**, **downstage** or **upstage** to begin the exercise. The teacher may also use drama vocabulary such as **stage left**, **stage right** when guiding actors. Incorporating the language of drama into hands-on activities, where the students are up and moving around, helps to cement the new vocabulary.

The next step for students is to increase their roles from actors to directors, script writers, set designers and audience members. Each one of these roles will build knowledge of drama and the various aspects that come together to create a dramatic piece, as well as reinforce the language of drama. Directors must tell their actors to move downstage or stage right. Audience members must sit quietly until the end of the exercise or performance and then clap for their fellow students to show appreciation. What materials do set designers use to create the illusion of a particular place or time? How does a script writer put into words what they would like the actors to portray?

Encouraging students with exercises such as writing their own scripts and performing them for each other is a hands-on activity that builds knowledge of the elements of acting, reinforces the language of theatre through writing down stage directions and dialogue, and adds a piece of the puzzle that will come together as a dramatic production.

Skill 10.6   Demonstrate knowledge of approaches and activities for integrating learning experiences in the fine arts with learning experiences in other content areas

The arts provide essential opportunities to explore connections among all disciplines. Content areas are unique, but they share common themes and terms and ideas. Skills developed in the arts enhance learning across content areas. Conversely, increased knowledge in curriculum content areas enhance the depth of knowledge and experience in the arts.

Charles Fowler effectively argues in his book, *Strong Arts, Strong Schools: the Promising Potential and Shortsighted Disregard of the Arts in American Schooling,* that the best schools have the best arts programs. He explains that we need to utilize every possible way to represent and interpret our world, and that means combining content areas, not isolating them. Science, Math, Literature, History or the Arts by themselves only convey a part of the subject. Charles Fowler believes that integrating these programs to provide students with a more complete picture is crucial. He uses the Grand Canyon as an example. A teacher can discuss mathematically the dimensions of the Grand Canyon or the science behind how it was formed, but this lesson is taken a step further by providing examples of artistic renderings of the Grand Canyon or asking students to write a poem describing the canyon. This integration provides a more three dimensional understanding of the subject.

Using African cultural history as another example, a teacher begins with a short history lesson on select African cultures. Geography may also come into play in the lesson, as the teacher chooses a specific region, such as Senegal-Gambia in West Africa, to describe to the children what an area of Africa looks like. This may be expanded to a music lesson on African musical styles and how they influenced Western music, such as gospel, jazz, spirituals, hip hop and rap. The teacher can introduce various African instruments, and discuss what the instruments are made of and how they are played. Students will learn several drum techniques and experiment with creating their own unique drum beats. Again, at the end of this lesson students have experienced Africa through an integrated teaching approach, and they come away with a more complete understanding.

Lynn Hallie Najem provides further evidence of the importance of integrating the arts into standard curriculum in her research article, "Sure It's Fun, But Why Bother With It During the School Day? The Benefits of Using Drama with Primary Students" A copy of this article may be found on the following website: http://www.madison.k12.wi.us/ . In her research, she found that integrating the arts into primary school curriculum had a very positive effect on the self-esteem of students and opened them up to learning in all subject areas.

SUBAREA III.   DIVERSITY, COLLABORATION, AND
                    PROFESSIONALISM IN THE EARLY CHILDHOOD

COMPETENCY 11.0   UNDERSTAND HUMAN DEVELOPMENT AND
                    DIVERSITY IN CHILDREN FROM BIRTH THROUGH
                    GRADE THREE AND CONDITIONS AND FACTORS
                    THAT AFFECT YOUNG CHILDREN'S GROWTH AND
                    LEARNING

Skill 11.1   Demonstrate knowledge of characteristics and processes
              associated with young children's development in various
              domains (e.g., physical, cognitive, social, emotional, linguistic,
              aesthetic) from birth through grade three

The teacher of students in early childhood should have a broad knowledge and
understanding of the phases of development which typically occur during this
stage of life. And the teacher must be aware of how receptive children are to
specific methods of instruction and learning during each period of development.
A significant premise in the study of child development holds that all domains of
development (physical, social, and academic) are integrated. Development in
each dimension is influenced by the others. Equally important to the teacher's
understanding of the process is the knowledge that developmental advances
within the domains occur neither simultaneously nor parallel to one another,
necessarily.

Physical Development

It is important for the teacher to be aware of the physical stages of development
and how changes to the child's physical attributes (which include internal
developments, increased muscle capacity, improved coordination and other
attributes as well as obvious growth) affect the child's ability to learn. Factors
determined by the physical stage of development include: ability to sit and attend,
the need for activity, the relationship between physical coordination and self-
esteem, and the degree to which physical involvement in an activity (as opposed
to being able to understand an abstract concept) affects learning and the child's
sense of achievement. By the time children reach school age there are certain
physical activities they should be able to do. Careful observation of children when
they first start school with regard to these activities should alert the teacher that
there may be a problem with the child's physical development. These include:
  • Being able to ride a tricycle
  • Throwing, catching and holding a ball
  • Being able to dress oneself, but still needing help with zippers and buttons
  • Being able to walk on tiptoe
  • Being able to use scissors to cut paper
  • Being active at play outdoors and in the classroom

Cognitive (Academic) Development

Children go through patterns of learning beginning with pre-operational thought processes and move to concrete operational thoughts. Eventually, they begin to acquire the intellectual ability to contemplate and solve problems independently, when they mature enough to manipulate objects symbolically. Students in early childhood can use symbols such as words and numbers to represent objects and relations, but they need concrete reference points. Successful acquisition of the skills taught in early childhood, through the fourth grade, will progressively prepare the student for more advanced problem solving and abstract thinking in the later grades. The content of curriculum for younger students must be relevant for their stage of development (accessible and comprised of acquirable skills), engaging, and meaningful to the students.

It is important for teachers of the early childhood grades to be aware of the warning signs of cognitive delay in children, although most of these are apparent before the children come to school. In order for a child to be diagnosed as having impairment in cognitive development, there must be a deficiency in at least two of the following:
- Speech and communication
- Self-care
- Social and Interpersonal skills
- Functional academic skills for the grade level

Social Development

Children progress through a variety of social stages beginning with an awareness of self and self-concern. They soon develop an awareness of peers but demonstrate a lack of concern for their presence. For a time, young children engage in "parallel" activities, playing alongside their peers without directly interacting with one another.

During the primary years, children develop an intense interest in peers. They establish productive, positive, social and working relationships with one another. This area of social growth will continue to increase in significance throughout the child's academic career. The foundation for the students' successful development in this area is established through the efforts of the classroom teacher to plan and develop positive peer group relationships and to provide opportunities and support for cooperative small group projects that not only develop cognitive ability, but promote peer interaction. The ability to work and relate effectively with peers contributes greatly to the child's sense of competence. In order to develop this sense of competence, children need to be successful in acquiring the information base and social skill sets which promote cooperative effort to achieve academic and social objectives.

High expectations for student achievement, which are age-appropriate and focused, provide the foundation for a teacher's positive relationship with young students and are consistent with effective instructional strategies. It is equally important to determine what is appropriate for specific individuals in the classroom, and approach classroom groups and individual students with an understanding and respect for their emerging capabilities. Those who study childhood development recognize that young students grow and mature in common, recognizable patterns, but at different rates which cannot be effectively accelerated. This can result in variance in the academic performance of different children in the same classroom. With the establishment of inclusion as a standard in the classroom, it is necessary for all teachers to understand that variation in development among the student population is another aspect of diversity within the classroom. And this has implications for the ways in which instruction is planned and delivered and the ways in which students learn and are evaluated.

Children may exhibit behaviors that alert the teacher to a problem involving a delay in social development. Before children enter school, they may not be in the presence of children their own age for long periods of time and so these behaviors may not be noticed. Children who fight with the other children or hit them for no reason show signs of not having the popper social skills for the age or grade level. This may be the result of being the only child or one that is pampered at home. It can also be a warning sign that the child is emulating the behavior of the parents.

Language Development

Learning approach
Early theories of language development were formulated from learning theory research. The assumption was that language development evolved from learning the rules of language structures and applying them through imitation and reinforcement. This approach also assumed that language, cognitive, and social developments were independent of each other. Thus, children were expected to learn language from patterning after adults who spoke and wrote Standard English. No allowance was made for communication through child jargon, idiomatic expressions, or grammatical and mechanical errors resulting from too strict adherence to the rules of inflection (childs instead of children) or conjugation (runned instead of ran). No association was made between physical and operational development and language mastery.

Linguistic approach

Studies spearheaded by Noam Chomsky in the 1950s formulated the theory that language ability is innate and develops through natural human maturation as environmental stimuli trigger acquisition of syntactical structures appropriate to each exposure level. The assumption of a hierarchy of syntax downplayed the significance of semantics. Because of the complexity of syntax and the relative speed with which children acquire language, linguists attributed language development to biological rather than cognitive or social influences.

Cognitive approach

Researchers in the 1970s proposed that language knowledge derives from both syntactic and semantic structures. Drawing on the studies of Piaget and other cognitive learning theorists, supporters of the cognitive approach maintained that children acquire knowledge of linguistic structures after they have acquired the cognitive structures necessary to process language. For example, joining words for specific meaning necessitates sensory motor intelligence. The child must be able to coordinate movement and recognize objects before she can identify words to name the objects or word groups to describe the actions performed with those objects. Children must have developed the mental abilities for organizing concepts as well as concrete operations, predicting outcomes, and theorizing before they can assimilate and verbalize complex sentence structures, choose vocabulary for particular nuances of meaning, and examine semantic structures for tone and manipulative effect.

Socio-cognitive approach

Other theorists in the 1970s proposed that language development results from sociolinguistic competence. Language, cognitive, and social knowledge are interactive elements of total human development. Emphasis on verbal communication as the medium for language expression resulted in the inclusion of speech activities in most language arts curricula.

Unlike previous approaches, the socio-cognitive allowed that determining the appropriateness of language in given situations for specific listeners is as important as understanding semantic and syntactic structures. By engaging in conversation, children at all stages of development have opportunities to test their language skills, receive feedback, and make modifications. As a social activity, conversation is as structured by social order as grammar is structured by the rules of syntax. Conversation satisfies the learner's need to be heard and understood and to influence others. Thus, choices of vocabulary, tone, and content are dictated by the ability to assess the language knowledge of the listeners. The learner is constantly applying cognitive skills to using language in a social interaction. If the capacity to acquire language is inborn, without an environment in which to practice language, a child would not pass beyond grunts and gestures as did primitive man.

Of course, the varying degrees of environmental stimuli to which children are exposed at all age levels create a slower or faster development of language. Some children are prepared to articulate concepts and recognize symbolism by the time they enter fifth grade because they have been exposed to challenging reading and conversations with well-spoken adults at home or in their social groups. Others are still trying to master the sight recognition skills and are not yet ready to combine words in complex patterns.

Emotional Development

In an era of academic accountability, all teachers must remember that they are still teaching children, who are whole individuals. While teachers are not substitutes for parents, they certainly do have a responsibility to look out for the well-being of their students. In early elementary school, children are particularly affected by emotional upsets in family structure, and they are particularly susceptible to emotional harm when they are not cared for in an appropriate manner at home.

While it would be too easy to say that teachers should look out for children who show signs of emotional abuse or emotional neglect, whenever a teacher does notice something unusual in a child's behavior, it might be a good idea to look into it. A note of caution, though—teachers should remember that a student's privacy is extremely important. Furthermore, teachers should remember that all schools, districts, and states have very specific procedures and laws about the reporting of concerns.

When children are emotionally neglected or have recently endured family upsets, what sorts of things would this impact in a child? Well, first, the level of attention toward school will be greatly reduced. While children may actually think about these things, they may also show signs of jealousy of other children, or they may feel a sense of anger toward other children, the teacher, or their parents. Aggression is a very common behavior of emotionally-neglected children.

When a child has had little verbal interaction, the symptoms can be rather similar to the symptoms of abuse or neglect. The child might have a "deer in the headlights" look and maintain a very socially awkward set of behaviors. In general, such a child will have a drastically reduced ability to express him or herself in words, and often, aggression can be a better tool for the child to get his or her thoughts across.

Although cognitive ability is not lost due to such circumstances (abuse, neglect, emotional upset, lack of verbal interaction), the child will most likely not be able to provide as much intellectual energy as the child would if none of these things were present. But, also, note that the classroom can be seen as a "safe" place by a child, so it is imperative that teachers be attentive to the needs and emotions of their students.

Teachers need to be aware of any traumatic events in a student's life. What may seem trivial to an adult can be very emotionally upsetting for a child. Talk is a great therapy for emotional events and children need time to talk about their problems. This does take time for the teacher, who does have many things to do, but it is essential to provide the time a child needs to talk. However, if a teacher knows something about any emotional event in a child's life, the child should not be forced to talk about it. This should occur naturally.

Eric Erikson articulated a theory that humans go through eights stages of development as they go from infancy to adulthood. Here are the stages that pertain to early childhood programs:

- Infancy to 12 months
  During this phase the young child develops the ideas of trust and mistrust. This is evident when the child can't lose sight of the mother or cries when strangers get too close. One has to slowly approach a baby of this age in order to let the child learn whether or not the person is to be trusted.

- Young Childhood - Ages 1 to 3
  During this stage, the child develops feelings of shame and doubt along with learning about autonomy. The child wants to be independent and if denied, this could translate into temper tantrums as he tests the adults in charge. Play of all kinds is very important as the child learns the language and self-control.

- Early Childhood – Ages 3 – 5
  Here the child learns how to initiate tasks and carry them out. However, the child also learns the quality of guilt in this stage when tasks are not completed. He/She learns how to dream about goals associated with adult life. During this stage the child will begin playing with other children and become aware of the differences between the sexes. There is also some moral development taking place as well.

- Middle Childhood – Ages 6 – 10
  The child begins to take pride in work and has a sense of achievement. Friendships develop during this stage as well as learning skills. The child also learns how to act as part of a team.

Skill 11.2 **Demonstrate understanding of the significance of play and active involvement in activities for young children's development in various domains**

Too often, recess and play is considered peripheral or unimportant to a child's development. It's sometimes seen as a way to allow kids to just get physical energy out or a "tradition" of childhood. The truth is, though, that play is very important to human development. First, an obvious point, in this country, even though we are very industrious, we believe strongly that all individuals deserve time to relax and enjoy the "fruits of our labors."

But even more importantly, for the full development of children (who will soon be active citizens of our democracy, parents, spouses, friends, colleagues, and neighbors), play is an activity that helps teach basic values such as sharing and cooperation. It also teaches that taking care of oneself (as opposed to constantly working) is good for human beings and further creates a more enjoyable society.

The stages of play development do indeed move from solitary (particularly in infancy stages) to cooperative (in early childhood), but even in early childhood, children should be able to play on their own and entertain themselves from time to time. Children who do not know what to do with themselves when they are bored should be encouraged to think about particular activities that might be of interest.

But it is also extremely important that children play with peers. While the emerging stages of cooperative play may be awkward (as children will at first not want to share toys, for example), with some guidance and experience, children will learn how to be good peers and friends.

Play—both cooperative and solitary—helps to develop very important attributes in children. For example, children learn and develop personal interests and practice particular skills. The play that children engage in may even develop future professional interests.

Finally, playing with objects helps to develop motor skills. The objects that children play with should be varied and age appropriate. For example, playing with a doll can actually help to develop hand-eye coordination. Sports, for both boys and girls, can be equally valuable. Parents and teachers, though, need to remember that sports at young ages should only be for the purpose of development of interests and motor skills—not competition. Many children will learn that they do not enjoy sports, and parents and teachers should be respectful of these decisions.

In general, play is an appropriate place of children to learn many things about themselves, their world, and their interests. Children should be encouraged to participate in different types of play, and they should be watched over as they encounter new types of play.

Skill 11.3 Demonstrate knowledge of young children's health, nutrition, and safety needs and appropriate procedures for maintaining health, safety, and good nutrition for infants, toddlers, and young children and for responding to childhood illnesses and communicable diseases

Day-to-day issues, such as lack of sufficient sleep or nutrition, can harm children in a more temporal fashion. While a child who has had sleep disruptions or insufficient nutrition can bounce back easily when these things are attended to, it is often the case that children living in environments where sleep and proper nutrition are not available will continue through childhood to struggle for these things. Through federal and local funds, many schools are able to provide free or reduced-price breakfasts and lunches for children, however, consider that if this is a necessity, such children may not get a decent dinner, and during weekends and holidays, may struggle even more.

Symptoms of a lack of nutrition and sleep most notably include a lack of concentration, particularly in the classroom. Furthermore, children who lack sufficient sleep or nutrition may become agitated more easily than other children.

Young children need ample time to exercise to help them develop as they should. Along with providing time in the classroom for children to move about, they should also be experience dance and exercises as part of the Physical Education classes. During these classes, they will be exposed to rules of age appropriate sports and safety when running about. Outside activities with the children playing on the playground and engaging in physical exercise also gives them the fresh air that they need instead of keeping all play indoors.

It is important for children to get at least 10 hours of sleep a night. Children who are sleepy in school may not be getting the sleep they need and this should be a cause of concern for the teacher. A meeting may need to be called with the parents who do not have a regular bedtime for their children explaining to them that during sleep the child's brain and body becomes revitalized for the next day. Children who are tired and sleepy in class cannot learn at the correct rate and therefore may lag behind their peers.

There are also environmental conditions that can affect young children. Air pollution can cause respiratory problems and this will affect how children learn and how much school they miss due to illness. The air pollution could be the result of factories in the town, but it could also be the result of secondhand smoke in the home.

The temperature of the classroom has to be closely monitored to ensure that it is neither too hot nor too cold for the children. During warmer weather, an air conditioner or fan in the classroom can help keep temperature to the correct level.

The Components of Nutrition

The components of nutrition are **carbohydrates, proteins, fats, vitamins, minerals, and water.**

Carbohydrates – the main source of energy (glucose) in the human diet. The two types of carbohydrates are simple and complex. Complex carbohydrates have greater nutritional value because they take longer to digest, contain dietary fiber, and do not excessively elevate blood sugar levels. Common sources of carbohydrates are fruits, vegetables, grains, dairy products, and legumes.

Proteins – are necessary for growth, development, and cellular function. The body breaks down consumed protein into component amino acids for future use. Major sources of protein are meat, poultry, fish, legumes, eggs, dairy products, grains, and legumes.

Fats – a concentrated energy source and important component of the human body. The different types of fats are saturated, monounsaturated, and polyunsaturated. Polyunsaturated fats are the healthiest because they may lower cholesterol levels, while saturated fats increase cholesterol levels. Common sources of saturated fats include dairy products, meat, coconut oil, and palm oil. Common sources of unsaturated fats include nuts, most vegetable oils, and fish.

Vitamins and minerals – organic substances that the body requires in small quantities for proper functioning. People acquire vitamins and minerals in their diets and in supplements. Important vitamins include A, B, C, D, E, and K. Important minerals include calcium, phosphorus, magnesium, potassium, sodium, chlorine, and sulfur.

Water – makes up 55 – 75% of the human body. It is essential for most bodily functions and can be attained through foods and liquids.

Determine the adequacy of diets in meeting the nutritional needs of students

Nutritional requirements vary from person to person. General guidelines for meeting adequate nutritional needs are: no more than 30% total caloric intake from fats (preferably 10% from saturated fats, 10% from monounsaturated fats, 10% from polyunsaturated fats), no more than 15% total caloric intake from protein (complete), and <u>at least</u> 55% of caloric intake from carbohydrates (mainly complex carbohydrates).

Exercise and diet help maintain proper body weight by equalizing caloric intake and caloric output.

Body Composition Management

It is vital to analyze procedures, activities, resources, and benefits involved in developing and maintaining healthy levels of body composition. Maintaining a healthy body composition allows an individual to move freely and to obtain a certain pattern that is necessary for a specific activity. Furthermore, maintaining a healthy body composition is positively related with long-term health and resistance to disease and sickness.

The total weight of an individual is a combination of bones, ligaments, tendons, organs, fluids, muscles and fat. Because muscle weighs three times more than fat per unit of volume, a person who exercises often gains muscle. This could cause an individual to be smaller physically, but weigh more than he/she appears to weigh.

The only proven method for maintaining a healthy body composition is following a healthy diet and engaging in regular exercise. A healthy diet emphasizes fruits, vegetables, whole grains, unsaturated fats, and lean protein, and minimizes saturated fat and sugar consumption. Such a program of nutrition and exercise helps balance caloric intake and output, thus preventing excessive body fat production.

In summary, it is always a good idea for teachers to pay attention to the abnormalities in behavior of children, or even sudden drop-offs in achievement or attention, and notify superiors at the school with concerns.

Dealing with Childhood Illnesses & Diseases

It is common to have outbreaks of childhood illnesses and communicable diseases in school because young children do not always cover their mouths and noses when they cough or sneeze, they do not always use tissues and they must constantly be reminded to wash their hands. The school nurse will have a list of precautions regarding the outbreak of illnesses and pamphlets to send home to the parents telling them when they should keep their children home from school. Sometimes, it may be necessary to report diseases and illnesses to the school nurse for further investigation when there are large numbers of children absent from school.

In addition to the common cold, common childhood illnesses and communicable diseases include the following:

- Chickenpox – The child may have a slight fever and runny nose and/or headache. Spots appear on the skin, alone or in clusters, and they have raised centers. The child will be scratching because these spots are itchy, but may not be visible to the teacher because they tend to develop on areas of the skin covered by clothing. Chicken pox is a communicable disease spread through the air and by direct contact with blister fluid, saliva or phlegm. It is infectious for 1-5 days after the first symptoms appear, but another child may not develop any symptoms until 11- 21 days after coming into contact with the disease. The child should stay home for the first few days, but can return to school upon feeling better whether or not all the blisters have healed.

- Conjunctivitis (Pink Eye) – The child will have red and swollen eyes and may have some itchiness or discomfort. This disease is spread through touching anything that has come in contact with the discharge from the eyes. A child can have pink eye in only one eye or in both at the same time. It will take 24-72 hours for the condition to develop after coming in contact with it and it will not get better until it is treated by a doctor – usually with eye drops. Once the child gets treatment, it is possible to return to school or the parent may choose to keep the child home until the whites of the eyes are clear and there is no further crusting.

- Fifth's Disease – This is characterized by a noticeable reddening of the face followed in a few days with an itchy or irritating rash on the truck and legs. It can be spread through coughing and sneezing, but once the rash develops, the disease is no longer "catching". Children do not usually stay home with this disease unless they are not feeling well.

- Gastroenteritis – The child will be generally unwell with stomach cramps, diarrhea, and vomiting. It is usually spread through poor hygiene habits. A child with this illness should stay home for at least 48 hours, and preferably until there are no further symptoms.

- Impetigo – This is a communicable disease with sores around the nose and mouth. They are different from ordinary cold sores and take longer to heal. It is spread by touching anything belonging to the infected child and remains contagious until the sores are dry or 24-48 hours after the child starts taking antibiotics. The child should stay home from school until all the sores have dried up or the school is confident that the child is under a doctor's treatment.

- Measles – With the inset of this disease the child has a fever, cough, red eyes and runny nose. After a few days red blotches will appear on the skin, beginning with the face, and lasts about 4 to 7 days. It is spread by coming in contact with saliva or phlegm of the infected child, but the virus is also airborne. The disease is contagious from 4 days before the rash develops to 4 days afterwards so a child with measles should be home from school for at least four days.

- Meningitis (Bacterial and Viral) – The child will have a sudden headache and fever, have a stiff neck and may be nauseous or vomiting. This remains contagious until 24 hours after taking antibiotics and it is then that the child can return to school.

- Mumps – The child will have a general feeling of being unwell and possibly have a headache r chills. The glands in the neck swell and the child will have difficulty swallowing or chewing. It is spread by not covering the nose and mouth when sneezing and coughing. It usually takes about 18 days for mumps to develop when the child has been in contact with the disease and remains contagious up to 9 days after the swelling occurs. Therefore, it is important that the parents be informed about this and keep the child home from school.

- Head Lice – A child with head lice may be constantly scratching the scalp. The lice will move from head to head when the children have their heads together. When a child in the classroom has lice, all parents should be informed that it is a possibility their children are infected. The treatment is to wash the child's hair with a special shampoo.

- Whooping Cough – It is normal for children to have a cough associated with a cold, but the whooping cough is a prolonged cough with a high-pitched whoop or a crowing sound. It is contagious and is spread by airborne or direct contact with saliva or phlegm (such as on toys, or clothing). It takes about 7-10 days for the whooping cough to appear once the child has been exposed to it and remains contagious up to 5 days after the start of antibiotics. The child should remain home from school until 5 days after the treatment starts.

- Scabies (Also called The Itch) – There is a fine rash in between the fingers and toes, but it may be hard to see because of the redness caused by the intense scratching due to the extreme itchiness of this disease. It can be spread by just touching the rash or from sleeping in the same bed as the infected child. The treatment is to bathe in a solution that kills the mites causing the disease, but the clothes must also be washed in boiling water or frozen. The child can return to school after the solution has been applied.

- Scarlet fever – The child will have a sore throat, swollen glands and a fever as well as a fine red rash. It is spread by coughing or sneezing without covering the mouth and nose. It is contagious until 24 hours after the child starts taking antibiotics. The child should stay home until the ill feeling is gone once the treatment starts.

Skill 11.4 **Demonstrate knowledge of factors and conditions that affect young children's development and learning (e.g., linguistic variations, specific disabilities, biological and environmental factors, family conflict, stressful or traumatic events or circumstances, teacher expectations and practices, peer relationships, nutrition)**

Generally, teachers and parents should know what specific attributes develop over time in children. There is usually no cause for alarm, as many children do develop later in childhood (and certain domains may be developed later than others). Concern regarding intervention might arise when teachers notice that certain functions or attributes seem abnormally absent. In such a case, certain tasks may be very difficult for a child. Later in childhood, a large concern of teasing and bullying may arise, and the teacher may want to ensure that the child is fully protected.

When in doubt, though, the teacher should privately discuss the concern with a special education teacher or school psychologist first. That professional may be able to assist the teacher in determining whether it would be important to evaluate the child, or whether it would be important to contact the parent to ask questions, seek clarification, or point out a potential delay.

Very often, though, parents will be aware of the delay, and the child will be able to receive special accomodations in the classroom. Teachers should be forewarned about this by the special education personnel prior to the beginning of the schoolyear.

Emotional Factors

In early elementary school, children are particularly affected by emotional upsets in family structure, and they are particularly susceptible to emotional harm when they are not cared for in an appropriate manner at home. While it would be too easy to say that teachers should look out for children who show signs of emotional abuse or emotional neglect, whenever a teacher does notice something unusual in a child's behavior, it might be a good idea to look into it. However, teachers should remember that a student's privacy is also extremely important. All schools, districts, and states have very specific procedures and laws about the reporting of concerns, and teachers should follow these procedures.

When children are emotionally neglected or have recently endured family upsets, what sorts of things would this impact in a child? Well, first, the level of attention toward school will be greatly reduced. While children may actually think about these things, they may also show signs of jealousy of other children, or they may feel a sense of anger toward other children, the teacher, or their parents. Aggression is a very common behavior of emotionally-neglected children.

When a child has had little verbal interaction, the symptoms can be rather similar to the symptoms of abuse or neglect. The child might have a "deer in the headlights" look and maintain a very socially awkward set of behaviors. In general, such a child will have a drastically reduced ability to express him or herself in words, and often, aggression can be a better tool for the child to get his or her thoughts across.

Cognitive Factors

Although cognitive ability is not lost due to such circumstances (abuse, neglect, emotional upset, lack of verbal interaction), the child will most likely not be able to provide as much intellectual energy as the child would if none of these things were present. But, also, note that the classroom can be seen as a "safe" place by a child, so it is imperative that teachers be attentive to the needs and emotions of their students.

Behavioral Factors

The home environment and even the neighborhood can have an affect on the development of children and cause them to come to school with behavior problems. Recent studies indicate that children from neighborhoods where there are few affluent families tend to exhibit more behavioral issues in school than those who do, such as not paying attention, fighting and in general causing disturbances in the class.

There are also issues that do cause children to have behavior problems, such as the mother consuming alcohol while pregnant and an exposure to violence in the home. The teacher has to be very observant of how children behave towards one another in the classroom to rule out any possibilities that some children may be bringing their frustrations with the home environment into the school setting.

Environmental Factors

Environmental factors that can cause delays in the development of some children could include:
- Lead poisoning
- Exposure to contaminants in water, food and air

Because children are exposure to contaminants can be more harmful for them that it is for adults. The body's systems and organs are still developing and due to the fact that children often out foreign objects in their mouths only adds to the amount of exposure for them.

Biological Factors

Children develop at rapidly different rates. However, there are certain impairments and delays that should cause concern. Generally, one might divide delays into cognitive delays (which could delays in verbal communication, mathematical reasoning, logical reasoning, visual processing, auditoring processing, memorization, etc.), physical delays (which could include a lack of motor skills, the inability to stand up straight, walk normally, play simple sport-like activities, hold a pencil; in very young children, it could include not being able to walk or sit up, for example), and social delays (which could include a child's inability to relate to other children). The potential delays or impairments are endless.

They might relate to specific disabilities that can stay with a child the rest of his or her life (everything from problems with eyesight to autism) or learning disabilities (everything from attention deficit disorder to dyslexia). They might also be things that fade as a child gets older (such as problems with motor skills).

Social Factors

A positive self-concept for a child or adolescent is a very important element in terms of the students' ability to learn and to be an integral member of society. If students think poorly of themselves or have sustained feelings of inferiority, they probably will not be able to optimize their potentials for learning. It is therefore part of the teacher's task to ensure that each student develops a positive self-concept.

A positive self-concept does not imply feelings of superiority, perfection, or competence/efficacy. Instead, a positive self-concept involves self-acceptance as a person, and having a proper respect for oneself. The teacher who encourages these factors has contributed to the development of a positive self-concept in students.

Teachers may take a number of approaches to enhancement of self-concept among students. An approach that targets the enhancement of self concept is designated Invitational Education. According to this approach, teachers and their behaviors may be inviting or they may be disinviting. Inviting behaviors enhance self-concept among students, while disinviting behaviors diminish self-concept.

Disinviting behaviors include those that demean students, as well as those that may be chauvinistic, sexist, condescending, thoughtless, or insensitive to student feelings. Inviting behaviors are the opposite of these, and characterize teachers who act with consistency and sensitivity. Inviting teacher behaviors reflect an attitude of "doing with" rather than "doing to." Students are "invited" or "disinvited" depending on the teacher behaviors.

Invitational teachers exhibit the following skills (Biehler and Snowman, 394):

a) reaching each student (e.g., learning names, having one-to-one contact)
b) listening with care (e.g., picking up subtle cues)
c) being real with students (e.g., providing only realistic praise, "coming on straight")
d) being real with oneself (e.g., honestly appraising your own feelings and disappointments)
e) inviting good discipline (e.g., showing students you have respect in personal ways)
f) handling rejection (e.g., not taking lack of student response in personal ways)
g) inviting oneself (e.g., thinking positively about oneself)

Physiological Factors

Anyone who has been in a Kindergarten to grade four classroom knows that students do not sit still and focus on one thing for too long. Some people joke that the age of a person equals the amount of time the person is willing to sit and listen for any one time. So, a kindergartener, under this premise, would only be able to sit and concentrate on one thing for 5 to 6 minutes. Many kindergarten teachers would agree with this. But think about someone at age 30 to 50: most adults don't want to sit and listen for longer than one hour. So, there may be some truth to this, unscientific as it is!

The bottom line is this: young children do not concentrate for long periods of time, and good teachers know how to capitalize on the need of children to move and change topics. Generally, young children should be changing academic activities every 15-20 minutes. This means that if a teacher wants to fill a block of two hours for literacy learning in the morning, the teacher should have about 6-8 activities planned. Here's an example:

1. Teacher has students write something to access background knowledge. In kindergarten, this might include just a picture. In grade four, this might include a paragraph.
2. Teacher might spend a few minutes asking students what they wrote about in a large group.
3. Teacher might introduce a new book by doing a "book walk"—looking at the title, the pictures, etc.
4. Teacher reads book aloud as students follow along.
5. Students do a pair-share where they turn to their neighbors to discuss a question.
6. Students return to desks to do a comprehension activity on their own.
7. Whole class discussion of what they wrote.
8. Students go to centers to practice specific skills as teacher works with small groups of students.
9. Teacher conducts a vocabulary activity with the whole class.

Teachers who change activities often are more likely to keep their students' attention, engage their students more, and have fewer discipline problems. When children get bored, they obviously will start to not pay attention, and many will become disruptive.

Teacher Expectations

Prior experiences that children have with caregivers and/or teachers can directly impact their attitude towards learning in school. Caregivers/parents who lead the child to believe that education is not important can be a great factor in this especially if the child has a feeling of attachment to that person. A child that comes to school not being familiar with books may have come from a home where reading is not considered important and may not display an active interest in reading.

Teachers who tended to be strict with the child in the past or did not sure a lot of caring in helping the child to understand how to correct mistakes could leave the child with the thought that all teachers act in this way. This is especially true if the child is experiencing problems with learning or the tasks assigned and does not get needed help and support.

It is a fact of life that everyone does not get along in a classroom. However, a teacher that gives a child the impression of not being liked or wanted in the classroom could be seriously impeding that child's attitude for future school years. Teachers do need to take am impartial approach when dealing with students who do not get along, yet it is important to demonstrate caring to each and every one of them.

Familial Factors

The student's capacity and potential for academic success within the overall educational experience are products of her or his total environment: classroom and school system; home and family; neighborhood and community in general. All of these segments are interrelated and can be supportive, one of the other, or divisive, one against the other.

As a matter of course, the teacher will become familiar with all aspects of the system, the school and the classroom pertinent to the students' educational experience. This would include not only process and protocols but also the availability of resources provided to meet the academic, health and welfare needs of students. But it is incumbent upon the teacher to look beyond the boundaries of the school system to identify additional resources as well as issues and situations which will effect (directly or indirectly) a student's ability to succeed in the classroom.

Examples of Resources

1. Libraries, museums, zoos, planetariums, etc.
2. Clubs, societies and civic organizations, community outreach programs of private businesses and corporations and of government agencies–
   These can provide a variety of materials and media as well as possible speakers and presenters
3. Departments of social services operating within the local community–
   These can provide background and program information relevant to social issues which may be impacting individual students.

Initial contacts for resources outside of the school system will usually come from within the system itself: from administration; teacher organizations; department heads; and other colleagues.

Examples of Issues/Situations

1. Students from multicultural backgrounds:

Curriculum objectives and instructional strategies may be inappropriate and unsuccessful when presented in a single format which relies on the student's understanding and acceptance of the values and common attributes of a specific culture which is not his or her own.

2. Parental/family influences: Attitude, resources and encouragement available in the home environment may be attributes for success or failure.

Families with higher incomes are able to provide increased opportunities for students. Students from lower income families will need to depend on the resources available from the school system and the community. This should be orchestrated by the classroom teacher in cooperation with school administrators and educational advocates in the community.

Family members with higher levels of education often serve as models for students, and have high expectations for academic success. And families with specific aspirations for children (often, regardless of their own educational background) encourage students to achieve academic success, and are most often active participants in the process.

A family in crisis (caused by economic difficulties, divorce, substance abuse, physical abuse, etc.) creates a negative environment which may profoundly impact all aspects of a student's life, and particularly his or her ability to function academically. The situation may require professional intervention. It is often the classroom teacher who will recognize a family in crisis situation and instigate an intervention by reporting on this to school or civil authorities.

Regardless of the positive or negative impacts on the students' education from outside sources, it is the teacher's responsibility to ensure that all students in the classroom have an equal opportunity for academic success. This begins with the teacher's statement of high expectations for every student, and develops through planning, delivery and evaluation of instruction which provides for inclusion and ensures that all students have equal access to the resources necessary for successful acquisition of the academic skills being taught and measured in the classroom.

SEE also Skill 11.6

For information on linguistic factors, **SEE** Skill 11.1

For information on nutrition, **SEE** Skill 11.3

Skill 11.5 **Demonstrate knowledge of principles, procedures, and experiences that support and enhance young children's physical, cognitive, social, emotional, linguistic, and aesthetic development**

Knowledge of age-appropriate expectations is fundamental to the teacher's positive relationship with students and effective instructional strategies. Equally important is the knowledge of what is individually appropriate for the specific children in a classroom. Developmentally oriented teachers approach classroom groups and individual students with a respect for their emerging capabilities.

Developmentalists recognize that kids grow in common patterns, but at different rates which usually cannot be accelerated by adult pressure or input. Developmentally oriented teachers know that variance in the school performance of different children often results from differences in their general growth. With the establishment of inclusionary classes throughout the schools, it is vital for all teachers to know the characteristics of students' exceptionalities and their implications on learning.

The effective teacher selects learning activities based on specific learning objectives. Ideally, teachers should not plan activities that fail to augment the specific objectives of the lesson. Learning activities should be planned with a learning objective in mind. Objective driven learning activities tend to serve as a tool to reinforce the teacher's lesson presentation. Additionally, selected learning objectives should be consistent with state and district educational goals that focus on National educational goals (Goals 2000) and the specific strengths and weaknesses of individual students assigned to the teacher's class.

The effective teacher takes care to select appropriate activities and classroom situations in which learning is optimized. The classroom teacher should manipulate instructional activities and classroom conditions in a manner that enhances group and individual learning opportunities. For example, the classroom teacher can organize group learning activities in which students are placed in a situation in which cooperation, sharing ideas, and discussion occurs. Cooperative learning activities can assist students in learning to collaborate and share personal and cultural ideas and values in a classroom learning environment.

The effective teacher plans his/her learning activities to introduce them in a meaningful instructional sequence. Teachers should combine instructional activities as to reinforce information by providing students with relevant learning experiences through instructional activities.

If an educational program is child-centered, then it will surely address the abilities and needs of the students because it will take its cues from students' interests, concerns, and questions. Making an educational program child-centered involves building on the natural curiosity children bring to school, and asking children what they want to learn.

Teachers help students to identify their own questions, puzzles, and goals, and then structure for them widening circles of experience and investigation of those topics. Teachers manage to infuse all the skills, knowledge, and concepts that society mandates into a child-driven curriculum. This does not mean passive teachers who respond only to students' explicit cues. Teachers also draw on their understanding of children's developmentally characteristic needs and enthusiasms to design experiences that lead children into areas they might not choose, but that they do enjoy and that engage them. Teachers also bring their own interests and enthusiasms into the classroom to share and to act as a motivational means of guiding children.

Implementing such a child-centered curriculum is the result of very careful and deliberate planning. Planning serves as a means of organizing instruction and influences classroom teaching. Well thought-out planning includes specifying behavioral objectives, specifying students' entry behavior (knowledge and skills), selecting and sequencing learning activities so as to move students from entry behavior to objective, and evaluating the outcomes of instruction in order to improve planning.

Planning for instructional activities entails identification or selection of the activities the teacher and students will engage in during a period of instruction. Planning is a multifaceted activity which includes the following considerations: the determination of the order in which activities will be completed; the specification of the component parts of an activity, including their order; the materials to be used for each part, and the particular roles of the teacher and students; decisions about the amount of time to be spent on a given activity and the number of activities to be completed during a period of instruction; judgment of the appropriateness of an activity for a particular situation; and specifications of the organization of the class for the activity.

Attention to learner needs during planning is foremost and includes identification of that which the students already know or need to know; the matching of learner needs with instructional elements such as content, materials, activities, and goals; and the determination of whether or not students have performed at an acceptable level, following instruction.

Skill 11.6 **Recognize the importance of understanding young children within the context of family, culture, and society and of using strategies that build on family priorities, strengths, and values**

Effective teaching and learning for students begins with teachers who can demonstrate sensitivity for diversity in teaching and relationships within school communities. Student portfolios include work that has a multicultural perspective and inclusion where students share cultural and ethnic life experiences in their learning. Teachers are responsive to including cultural and diverse resources in their curriculum and instructional practices. Exposing students to culturally sensitive room decorations and posters that show positive and inclusive messages is one way to demonstrate inclusion of multiple cultures.

Teachers should also continuously make cultural connections that are relevant and empowering for all students and communicate academic and behavioral expectations. Cultural sensitivity is communicated beyond the classroom with parents and community members to establish and maintain relationships.

Teachers must establish a classroom climate that is culturally respectful and engaging for students. In a culturally sensitive classroom, teachers maintain equity and fairness in student interactions and curriculum implementation. Assessments include cultural responses and perspectives that become further learning opportunities for students.

Other artifacts that could reflect teacher/student sensitivity to diversity might consist of the following:

- Student portfolios reflecting multicultural/multiethnic perspectives
- Journals and reflections from field trips/ guest speakers from diverse cultural backgrounds
- Printed materials and wall displays from multicultural perspectives
- Parent/guardian letters in a variety of languages reflecting cultural diversity
- Projects that include cultural history and diverse inclusions
- Disaggregated student data reflecting cultural groups
- Classroom climate of professionalism that fosters diversity and cultural inclusion

COMPETENCY 12.0   UNDERSTAND THE EARLY CHILDHOOD
CURRICULUM AND HOW TO PLAN INSTRUCTION
AND ASSESSMENT THAT IS BASED ON
KNOWLEDGE OF YOUNG CHILDREN, THEIR
FAMILIES AND COMMUNITIES, AND CURRICULAR
GOALS

Skill 12.1   Demonstrate understanding of the implications of young
children's developmental characteristics for curriculum
development and the features of a conceptually sound and
meaningful curriculum for young children

Jean Piaget, a European scientist who died in the late 20th Century, developed
many theories about the way humans learn. Most famously, he developed a
theory about the stages of the development of human minds. It's very simple.
The first stage is the "sensory-motor" stage that lasts until a child is in the toddler
years. In this stage, children begin to understand their senses.

The next stage, called the "pre-operational" stage, is where children begin to
understand symbols. For example, as they learn language, they begin to realize
that words are symbols of thoughts, actions, items, and other elements in the
world. This stage lasts into early elementary school.

The third stage is referred to as the "concrete operations" stage. This lasts until
late elementary school. In this stage, children go one step beyond learning what
a symbol is. They learn how to manipulate symbols, objects, and other elements.
A common example of this stage is the displacement of water. In this stage, they
can reason that a wide and short cup of water poured into a tall and thin cup of
water can actually have the same amount of water.

The next stage is called the "formal operations" stage. It usually starts in
adolescence or early teen years and it continues on into adulthood. This stage is
what allows critical thinking, hypothesis, systematic organization of knowledge,
etc.

Generally, when we say that children move from a stage of concrete thinking to
logical and abstract thinking, we mean that they are moving from the "pre-
operational" and "concrete" stage TO the "formal operations" stage. But as
anyone who spends time with children knows, there are many bumps in the way
to a person's ability to be a strong critical thinker. And remember, just because a
child has moved into a particular stage does not mean that they will be able to
complete function at the specified level. For example, adolescents may be able
to think critically, but they need plenty of instruction and assistance to do so at an
adequate level. This does not necessarily mean that critical thinking skills should
be taught out of context; rather, through all lessons, teachers should work to
instill components that help develop the thinking of children.

The development of children does move in a predicted progression, but there are no definite times when certain events or changes occur. All children develop at different rates. Development is not just physical; it is also cognitive and emotional. However, all aspects of development—physical, cognitive, and emotional—impact learning and performance.

While physical changes are indeed important, they are by no means the most impressive changes. From early childhood to grade four, children are able to move from highly concrete ways of thinking to more abstract ways of thinking. All children by grade four cannot be expected to perform at adult levels of critical thinking, but by fourth grade, many students will have gained many important critical thinking skills, and those skills will continue to develop each year.

One of the most significant changes in academic skill that occurs from early childhood through grade four is the development of reading ability. From early childhood to grade four, children go from not knowing how to read to reading for pleasure and new knowledge. The old saying is that kids go from "learning to read" to "reading to learn" in this critical time period.

Children will start with basic book skills (such as knowing how to hold a book) and move to phonetic skills (phonics, phonemic awareness) within the first couple years of school. By fourth grade, students typically should not have to work with phonics any longer. By that time, they should focus on learning how to read and make sense of informational texts, functional texts, and more complicated fictional texts.

Lending to the literacy development is physical, cognitive, and emotional development. This serves as an example of how human development impacts academic development. As a child develops physically, his or her ability to focus on letters and words increases. Children are able to hold and use pencils, thereby increasing their ability to learn letters by practicing the writing of them. And as children read stories, they use their emotions and their cognition to make sense of complex ideas.

In general, all areas of human development assist in the academic development of children. It is amazing to see how quick changes occur in children; often when one area of development occurs, many others follow suit quickly.

Skill 12.2 **Identify characteristics, benefits, and limitations of types of instructional strategies (e.g., play, small-group projects, open-ended questioning, group discussion, problem solving, cooperative learning, learning centers, inquiry experiences), and demonstrate knowledge of how to use instructional strategies to create and modify activities for all young children, including young children with disabilities, developmental delays, and special abilities**

Public education should be concerned with much more than academic standards. School is a place where children can learn skills of good citizenship, time management, goal setting, and decision-making. But teachers must be deliberate about teaching these skills. Like most good teaching, though, students will have much more success learning these things if they get the opportunity to practice them. That is why a classroom should be like a little "community" where children get opportunities to help with chores and maintain responsibility for certain things. Some of the ways teachers can do this include setting up stations and centers throughout the classroom. With a classroom that contains various centers, student desks consist of only one physical component of the classroom. Teachers can set up student mailboxes to store certain materials. They can also arrange manipulatives and other classroom objects in various places where students are required to maintain and keep clean.

A technique many teachers use is rotating various chores each week. One student might be responsible for ensuring that materials get distributed to students. Another student might supervise clean-up time. Another student might assist with preparation of manipulatives. Not only does this type of activity improve time management and organizational skills in students, it creates a type of classroom community that is motivating to students. In a way, it causes students to feel safer and more included in their classroom environment.

In addition to physical classroom arrangement and student responsibility, teachers should focus on teaching children skills for time management and goal setting. Teachers can use a variety of materials and expectations to do this. For example, many teachers have students write down class-time agendas each morning and then set personal goals for the school-day. Then, they might have their students reflect on whether or not they met these goals and whether or not they successfully completed all agenda items.

Longer-term goals can be discussed, as well. Teachers might work with students on an individual basis to set personal academic goals for students. Students should be encouraged to come up with their own goals, but with the assistance of teachers. Teachers can help students focus on goals that might be related to current performance and/or interests. Then, students should get opportunities quite often to reflect on their goals, consider their work toward those goals, and alter goals as they go along.

Finally, learning centers, although usually used for the purpose of teaching content-area skills, can be great tools for teaching responsibility and independence. Teachers can use this time particularly to work independently with students. While they do so, students, in small groups, travel from one center to another, completing various learning activities. For example, one center might ask students to read a story together and answer a few questions. Another center might have computers and require students to complete various computer-based learning activities. Doing this promotes independent and group learning skills and gives students opportunities to set and monitor short-term goals.

The effective teacher is aware of students' individual learning styles and human growth and development theory and applies these principles in the selection and implementation of appropriate instructional activities. In regards to the identification and implementation of appropriate learning activities, effective teachers select and implement instructional activities consistent with principles of human growth and development theory.

Learning activities selected for younger students (below age eight) should focus on short time frames in highly simplified form. The nature of the activity and the content in which the activity is presented affects the approach that the students will take in processing the information. Younger children tend to process information at a slower rate than older children (age eight and older).

Skill 12.3 Identify instructional strategies for integrating various developmental domains (e.g., physical, cognitive, social, emotional, linguistic, aesthetic) and for promoting young children's intellectual curiosity, problem-solving skills, and decision-making processes

Child development does not occur in a vacuum. Each element of development impacts other elements of development. For example, as cognitive development progresses, social development often follows. The reason for this is that all areas of development are fairly inter-related. People laugh about how adolescents often develop slower in the physical domain than they do in the social or cognitive domain (e.g., they may think like teenagers, but they still look like children), however, the truth is that even in such cases, physical development is under progress—just not as evident on the surface. And as children develop physically, they develop the dexterity to demonstrate cognitive development, such as writing something on a piece of paper (in this case, this is cognitive development that only can be demonstrated by physical development). Or, as they develop emotionally, they learn to be more sensitive to others and therefore enhance social development.

What does this mean for teachers? The concept of latent development is particularly important. While teachers may not see some aspects of development present in their students, other areas of development may give clues as to a child's current or near-future capabilities. For example, as students' linguistic development increases, observable ability may not be present (i.e., a student may know a word but cannot quite use it yet). As the student develops emotionally and socially, the ability to use more advanced words and sentence structures develops because the student will have a greater need to express him or herself.

In general, by understanding that developmental domains are not exclusive, teachers can identify current needs of students better, and they can plan for future instructional activities meant to assist students as they develop into adults.

SEE also Skill 12.2

Skill 12.4   **Identify techniques and skills for conducting and participating in family-centered assessments and strategies for involving families in assessment and planning for individual young children**

Research proves that the more families are involved in a child's educational experience, the more that child will succeed academically. The problem is that often teachers assume that involvement in education simply means that the parents show up to help at school events or participate in parental activities on campus. With this belief, many teachers devise clever strategies to increase parental involvement at school. However, just because a parent shows up to school and assists with an activity does not mean that the child will learn more. Many parents work all day long and cannot assist in the school. Teachers, therefore, have to think of different ways to encourage parental and family involvement in the educational process.

Quite often, teachers have great success within involving families by just informing families of what is going on in the classroom. Newsletters are particularly effective at this. Parents love to know what is going on in the classroom, and this way, they'll feel included. In newsletters, for example, teachers can provide suggestions on how parents can help with the educational goals of the school. For example, teachers can recommend that parents read with their children for twenty minutes per day. To add effectiveness to that, teachers can also provide suggestions on what to do when their children come across difficult words or when they ask a question about comprehension. This gives parents practical strategies.

Parents often equate phone calls from teachers with news about misbehaviors of their children. Teachers can change that tone by calling parents with good news. Or they can send positive notes home with students. By doing this, when negative phone calls need to be made, teachers will have greater success.

Teachers can also provide very specific suggestions to individual parents. For example, let's say a student needs additional assistance in a particular subject. The teacher can provide tips to parents to encourage and increase deeper understandings in the subject outside of class.

Teachers today will deal with an increasingly diverse group of cultures in their classrooms. And while this is an exciting prospect for most teachers, it creates new challenges in dealing with a variety of family expectations for school and teachers.

First, teachers must show respect to all parents and families. They need to set the tone that suggests that their mission is to develop students into the best people they can be. And then they need to realize that various cultures have different views of how children should be educated.

Second, teachers will have better success when they talk personally about their children. Even though teachers may have many students, when they share personal things about each child, parents will feel more confident that their child will be "in the right hands."

Third, it is very important that teachers act like they are partners in the children's education and development. Parents know their children best, and it is important to get feedback, information, and advice from them.

Finally, teachers will need to be patient with difficult families, realizing that certain methods of criticism (including verbal attacks, etc.) are unacceptable. Such circumstances would require the teacher to get assistance from an administrator. This situation, however, is very unusual, and most teachers will find that when they really attempt to be friendly and personal with parents, the parents will reciprocate and assist in the educational program.

The support of the parent is an invaluable aid in the educational process. It is in the best interests of child, parent, and teacher for there to be cooperation and mutual support between parent and teacher. One of the teacher's professional responsibilities is to establish and maintain effective communication with parents. A few basic techniques to pursue are oral communication (phone calls), written communication in the form of general information classroom newsletters, notes to the parent of a particular child, and parent-teacher conferences.

Teachers should share items of interest with parents, including but not limited to, classroom rules and policies, class schedules and routines, homework expectations, communication procedures, conferences plans, and other similar information. Much of this can be done in a newsletter format sent home early in the school year. It is imperative that all such written communications be error free. It is a good idea to have another teacher read your letter before you send it out. Good writing and clear communication are learned skills and require time and effort to develop.

When you find it necessary to communicate (whether by phone, letter, or in person) with a parent regarding a concern about a student, allow yourself a "cooling off" period before making contact with the parent. It is important that you remain professional and objective. Your purpose for contacting the parent is to elicit support and additional information that may have a bearing on the student's behavior or performance. Be careful that you do not demean the child and do not appear antagonistic or confrontational. Be aware that the parent is likely to be quite uncomfortable with the bad news and will respond best if you take a cooperative, problem solving approach to the issue. It is also a nice courtesy to notify parents of positive occurrences with their children. The teacher's communication with parents should not be limited to negative items.

Skill 12.5   Demonstrate knowledge of principles and procedures for participating with others in assessment of young children with disabilities, developmental delays, and special abilities; for integrating assessment results into the development and implementation of Individualized Education Programs (IEPs) and Individualized Family Service Plans (IFSPs); and for interpreting and communicating assessment results responsibly and accurately

Children develop at rapidly different rates. However, there are certain impairments and delays that should cause concern. Generally, one might divide delays into cognitive delays (which could delays in verbal communication, mathematical reasoning, logical reasoning, visual processing, auditoring processing, memorization, etc.), physical delays (which could include a lack of motor skills, the inability to stand up straight, walk normally, play simple sport-like activities, hold a pencil; in very young children, it could include not being able to walk or sit up, for example), and social delays (which could include a child's inability to relate to other children). The potential delays or impairments are endless.

They might relate to specific disabilities that can stay with a child the rest of his or her life (everything from problems with eyesight to autism) or learning disabilities (everything from attention deficit disorder to dyslexia). They might also be things that fade as a child gets older (such as problems with motor skills).

Generally, teachers and parents should know what specific attributes develop over time in children. There is usually no cause for alarm, as many children do develop later in childhood (and certain domains may be developed later than others). Concern regarding intervention might arise when teachers notice that certain functions or attributes seem abnormally absent. In such a case, certain tasks may be very difficult for a child. Later in childhood, a large concern of teasing and bullying may arise, and the teacher may want to ensure that the child is fully protected.

When in doubt, though, the teacher should privately discuss the concern with a special education teacher or school psychologist first. That professional may be able to assist the teacher in determining whether it would be important to evaluate the child, or whether it would be important to contact the parent to ask questions, seek clarification, or point out a potential delay.

Very often, though, parents will be aware of the delay, and the child will be able to receive special accomodations in the classroom. Teachers should be forewarned about this by the special education personnel prior to the beginning of the schoolyear.

Inclusion, mainstreaming, and least restrictive environment

Inclusion, mainstreaming and least restrictive environment are interrelated policies under the IDEA, with varying degrees of statutory imperatives.
- Inclusion is the right of students with disabilities to be placed in the regular classroom.
- Least restrictive environment is the mandate that children be educated to the maximum extent appropriate with their non-disabled peers.
- Mainstreaming is a policy where disabled students can be placed in the regular classroom, as long as such placement does not interfere with the student's educational plan.

Adjusting Instruction

A teacher's job would be relatively easy if simply instructing students in current curriculum objectives was the primary responsibility. Today's educator must first assure that the students are able to come to school, are able to attend to the curriculum, have individual learning styles met, and are motivated to work to their fullest capacity.

A teacher's responsibility to students extends beyond the four walls of the school building. In addition to offering well-planned and articulately delivered lessons, the teacher must consider the effects of both body language and spoken language on students' learning.

Furthermore, today's educator must address the needs of diverse learners within a single classroom. The teacher is able to attain materials that may be necessary for the majority of the regular education students and some of the special needs children and, more and more frequently, one individual student. The "effective" teacher knows that there are currently hundreds of adaptive materials that could be used to help these students increase achievement and develop skills.

Student-centered classrooms contain not only textbooks, workbooks, and literature materials but also rely heavily on a variety of audio-visual equipment and computers. There are tape recorders, language masters, filmstrip projectors, and laser disc players to help meet the learning styles of the students.

Although most school centers cannot supply all the materials that special needs students require, each district more than likely has a resource center where teachers can check out special equipment. Most communities support agencies that offer assistance in providing the necessities of special needs people including students. Teachers must know how to obtain a wide range of materials including school supplies, medical care, clothing, food, adaptive computers and books (such as Braille), eye glasses, hearing aids, wheelchairs, counseling, transportation, etc.

Most special needs students have an Individual Educational Plan (IEP) or a 504 Plan. These documents clearly state the students' educational objectives and learning needs as well as persons responsible for meeting these objectives. A well-written (IEP) will contain evidence that the student is receiving resources from the school and the community that will assist in meeting the physical, social and academic needs of the student.

The challenges of meeting the needs of all students in the classroom require that the teacher is a lifelong learner. Ongoing participation in professional staff development, attendance at local, state, and national conferences, and continuing education classes help teachers grow in many ways including an awareness of resources available for students.

Whether a teacher is using criterion-referenced, norm-referenced or performance-based data to inform and impact student learning and achievement, the more important objective is ensuring that teachers know how to effectively use the data to improve and reflect upon existing teaching instructions.

Individualized Family Service Plans (IFSPs)

An IFSP is a legal document centered on helping the family of a child who has been diagnosed with a special need, such as hearing loss or other disability. This plan for helping the family can be put in place at age three and focuses on what the family needs to help themselves and the child. Services that come with an IFSP include visits to the home from a center-based program, classes that the parents or caregivers can attend and services of psychologists, speech pathologists or other health professionals that may need to be involved. From the age of 21/2 to 3 years, a transition plan is put in place to examine preschool options for the child.

Interpreting and communicating assessment results

When children are tested for developmental or cognitive delays when they enter school, the teacher first has to get the permission of the parents if testing outside the normal school testing is deemed necessary. The parents should be fully informed as to the reasons the teacher thinks this testing is necessary and be allowed to have input into the process. Once the tests results are final, there should be a meeting with the parents, teachers, school principal and the person who did the testing. The tester should be the person to deliver the report to the parents because of the detailed explanations of the results. Some parents may be upset when they find out that their child has a delay and the teacher has to be prepared to deal with this. However, it is important that the school support the parents in every way possible so that the child gets the needed help at an early age.

Skill 12.6 Demonstrate knowledge of ways to use systematic observation, documentation, and other effective assessment strategies in a responsible way

There are many ways to evaluate a child's knowledge and assess his/her learning needs. In recent years, the emphasis has shifted from "mastery testing" of isolated skills to authentic assessments of what children know. Authentic assessments allow the teacher to know more precisely what each individual student knows, can do, and needs to do. Authentic assessments can work for both the student and the teacher in becoming more responsible for learning.

One of the simplest most efficient ways for the teacher to get to know his/her students is to conduct an entry survey. This is a record that provides useful background information about the students as they enter a class or school. Collecting information through an entry survey will give valuable insights into a student's background knowledge and experience. Teachers can customize entry surveys according to the type of information considered valuable. Some of the information that may be incorporated include student's name and age, family members, health factors, special interests, strengths, needs, fears, etc., parent expectations, languages spoken in the home, what the child likes about school, etc.

At the beginning of each school term the teacher will likely feel compelled to conduct some informal evaluations in order to obtain a general awareness of his/her students. These informal evaluations should be the result of a learning activity rather than a "test" and may include classroom observations, collections of reading and writing samples, and notations about the students' cognitive abilities as demonstrated by classroom discussions and participation including the students' command of language. The value of these informal evaluations cannot be underestimated. These evaluations, if utilized effectively, will drive instruction and facilitate learning.

After initial informal evaluations have been conducted and appropriate instruction follows, teachers will need to fine tune individual evaluations in order to provide optimum learning experiences. Some of the same types of evaluations can be used on an ongoing basis to determine individual learning needs as were used to determine initial general learning needs. It is somewhat more difficult to choose an appropriate evaluation instrument for elementary-aged students than for older students. Therefore, teachers must be mindful of developmentally appropriate instruments. At the same time, teachers must be cognizant of the information that they wish to attain from a specific evaluation instrument. Ultimately, these two factors—students' developmental stage and the information to be derived—will determine which type of evaluation will be most appropriate and valuable. There are few commercially designed assessment tools that will prove to be as effective as the tool that is constructed by the teacher.

A simple-to-administer, information-rich evaluation of a child's reading strengths and weaknesses is the running reading record. "This technique for recording reading behavior is the most insightful, informative, and instructionally useful assessment procedure you can use for monitoring a child's progress in learning to read." (Traill, 1993) The teacher uses a simple coding system to record what a child does while reading text out loud. At a later time the teacher can go back to the record and assess what the child knows about reading and what the teacher needs to address in an effort to help the student become a better reader.

If the teacher is evaluating a child's writing, it is a good idea to discourage the child from erasing his/her errors and to train the child to cross out errors with a single line so that the teacher can actually see the process that the student went through to complete a writing assignment. This writing becomes an important means of getting to know about students' writing and is an effective, valuable writing evaluation.

One of the most valuable and effective assessment tools available to any teacher is the classroom observation. As instructional decision makers, teachers must base their instructional strategies upon students' needs. An astute observer of student behaviors and performance is most capable of choosing instructional strategies that will best meet the needs of the learners. Classroom observations take place within the context of the learning environment thus allowing the observer the opportunity to notice natural behaviors and performances.

Classroom observations should be sensitive and systematic in order to permit a constant awareness of student progress. One of the shortcomings of classroom observations is that they are often performed randomly and frequently are focused on those students whose behaviors are less than desirable. If the teacher establishes a focused observation process then observations become more valuable. It has been suggested that a teacher focus his/her observations on five or six students at a time for a period of one to two weeks.

In order for observations to truly be useful, teachers must record the information obtained from observations. When doing a formal behavioral observation, the teacher will write what the child is doing for a designated time period. At times the teacher will tally the occurrences of specific behaviors within a designated time period. When making focused observations that are ongoing, the teacher may simply use a blank piece of paper with only the student's name and date written on it and space for the teacher to write anecdotal notes. Other teachers might write on post-it notes and put the information in a student's file. If it is not possible to record the information as it occurs and is observed, it is critical that it be recorded as soon as possible in order to maintain accuracy.

Sometimes it is helpful to do an observation simply to watch for frequency of a specific behavior. An observation can answer questions such as: Is the student on-task during independent work time? Is the student interacting appropriately with peers? Is the student using materials appropriately? These behaviors can be tallied on a piece of paper with the student's name and date of observation.

Classroom observations can provide the teacher with one of the most comprehensive means of knowing their students. Teachers can observe students to see how they interact with their peers, to see which activities they choose, what they like to read, and how frequently they choose to work alone. "Everything you hear a child say and see a child do is a glimpse into a mind and a source of information to 'know' from." (Traill, 1993)

No two students are alike. It follows, then, that no students *learn* alike. To apply a one dimensional instructional approach and a strict tunnel vision perspective of testing is to impose learning limits on students. All students have the right to an education, but there cannot be a singular path to that education. A teacher must acknowledge the variety of learning styles and abilities among students within a class (and, indeed, the varieties from class to class) and apply multiple instructional and assessment processes to ensure that every child has appropriate opportunities to master the subject matter, demonstrate such mastery, and improve and enhance learning skills with each lesson.

Students' attitudes and perceptions about learning are the most powerful factors influencing academic focus and success. When instructional objectives center on students' interests and are relevant to their lives, effective learning occurs. Learners must believe that the tasks that they are asked to perform have some value and that they have the ability and resources to perform them. If a student thinks a task is unimportant, he/she will not put much effort into it.

If a student thinks he lacks the ability or resources to successfully complete a task, even attempting the task becomes too great a risk. Not only must the teacher understand the students' abilities and interests, she must also help students develop positive attitudes and perceptions about tasks and learning.

Alternative assessments

Alternative assessment is an assessment where students create an answer or a response to a question or task, as opposed to traditional, inflexible assessments where students choose a prepared response from among a selection of responses, such as matching, multiple-choice or true/false.

When implemented effectively, an alternative assessment approach will exhibit these characteristics, among others:

- Requires higher-order thinking and problem-solving
- Provides opportunities for student self-reflection and self-assessment
- Uses real world applications to connect students to the subject
- Provides opportunities for students to learn and examine subjects on their own, as well as to collaborate with their peers.
- Encourages students to continuing learning beyond the requirements of the assignment
- Clearly defines objective and performance goals

Students generally do not realize their own abilities and frequently lack self-confidence. Teachers can instill positive self-concepts in children and thereby enhance their innate abilities by providing certain types of feedback. Such feedback includes attributing students' successes to their effort and specifying what the student did that produced the success. Qualitative comments influence attitudes more than quantitative feedback such as grades.

Teachers must avoid teaching tasks that fit their own interests and goals and design activities that address the students' concerns. In order to do this, it is necessary to find out about students and to have a sense of their interests and goals. Teachers can do this by conducting student surveys and simply by questioning and listening to students. Once this information is obtained the teacher can link students' interests with classroom tasks.

A diverse classroom should also address children who are learning English, as well as those with disabilities and exceptionalities. The types of disabilities in children are very numerous. Some disabilities are entirely physical, while others are entirely related to learning and the mind or background. Some involve a combination of both. While it would be a disservice to say that all kids should display the same types of characteristics to be considered "normal," when abnormalities are noticed, such as a student's incredible ability to solve a math problem without working it out (a potential attribute of giftedness) or another student's extreme trouble with spelling (a potential attribute of dyslexia), a teacher may assume that a disability or exceptional ability is present.

Common learning disabilities include attention deficit hyperactivity disorder (where concentration can be very tough), auditory processing disorders (where listening comprehension is very difficult), visual processing disorders (where reading can be tough and visual memory may be impaired), dyslexia (where reading can be confusing), and many others. Physical disabilities include Down's Syndrome, where mental retardation may be a factor; cerebral palsy, where physical movement is impaired; and many others. Developmental disabilities might include the lack of ability to use fine motor skills.

When giftedness is observed, teachers should also concern themselves with ensuring that such children get the attention they need and deserve so that they can continue to learn and grow.

Below are some of the more common approaches used in today's K-12 classrooms for children still acquiring English. Cognitive approaches to language learning focus on concepts. While words and grammar are important, when teachers use the cognitive approach, they focus on using language for conceptual purposes—rather than learning words and grammar for the sake of simply learning new words and grammatical structures. This approach focuses heavily on students' learning styles, and it cannot necessarily be pinned down as having specific techniques. Rather, it is more of a philosophy of instruction.

Another very common motivational approach is Total Physical Response. This is a kinesthetic approach that combines language learning and physical movement. In essence, students learn new vocabulary and grammar by responding with physical motion to verbal commands. Some people say it is particularly effective because the physical actions create good brain connections with the words.

In general, the best methods do not treat students as if they have a language deficit. Rather, the best methods build upon what students already know, and they help to instill the target language as a communicative process rather than a list of vocabulary words that have to be memorized.

To ensure the maximum education for all diverse learners, teachers must plan accordingly to meet the needs of all their students. The target of diversity allows teachers a variety of opportunities to expand their experiences with students, staff, community members and parents from culturally diverse backgrounds, so that their experiences can be proactively applied in promoting cultural diversity inclusion in the classroom. Teachers are able to engage and challenge students to develop and incorporate their own diversity skills in building character and relationships with cultures beyond their own. In changing the thinking patterns of students to become more cultural inclusive in the 21st century, teachers are addressing the globalization of our world.

COMPETENCY 13.0 **UNDERSTAND PRINCIPLES AND PROCEDURES FOR CREATING AND MAINTAINING A SAFE, PRODUCTIVE LEARNING ENVIRONMENT FOR YOUNG CHILDREN THAT ENCOURAGES COMMUNICATION, SOCIAL SKILLS, RESPONSIBILITY, AND SELF-MOTIVATION**

Skill 13.1 **Demonstrate principles and procedures for designing learning environments that are physically and psychologically safe; that promote responsibility, equity, active learning, and positive social interactions; and that support the educational needs and interests of all young children**

A well organized classroom often begins with the room's physical arrangement – the arrangement of desks, the attractiveness of bulletin boards, and the storage of supplies and materials. By identifying various ways of organizing learning space teachers can create a caring and child-centered environment.

In the modern classroom, there is a great deal of furniture, equipment, supplies, appliances, and learning aids to help the teacher teach and students learn. The classroom should have furnishings that fit the purpose of the classroom. The kindergarten classroom may have a reading center, a playhouse, a puzzle table, student work desks/tables, a sandbox, and any other relevant learning/interest areas.

Teachers can create different learning areas within the classroom. For example, a quiet reading corner with pillows to relax on, listening stations where students can listen to music through the use of headphones while completing work, a large table for group projects, multimedia centers, several learning stations, and individual work areas. If supplies and materials are easily accessible, delays and confusion can be eliminated as students prepare for activities.

In the majority of classrooms, the largest amount of floor space is devoted to the organization of student desks. Some teachers like to arrange desks in groups of four, while others utilize a U-shaped arrangement, allowing every student to have front row seat. Most importantly, arrange the desks so that eye contact can be made with every student. If the arrangement of the room doesn't work, don't be afraid to make changes.

Environmental preferences such as lighting, noise level, and room temperature are factors that can affect students in various ways and are often directly related to individual learning styles. A number of students learn best in bright light, but others learn considerably better in low-lighted areas. Bright light can actually cause some students to become restless and hyperactive. Teachers can provide listening stations with headsets for children who need sound; and quiet, comfortable study areas for those who learn best in a silent environment.

Teachers should encourage students to dress according to their body's temperature; in order to assure that students are not uncomfortable and can concentrate fully on their schoolwork.

Classrooms with warmer subdued colors contribute to students' concentration on task items. Neutral hues for coloration of walls, ceiling, and carpet or tile are generally used in classrooms so distraction due to classroom coloration may be minimized.

The teacher has the responsibility to report any items of classroom disrepair to maintenance staff. Broken windows, falling plaster, exposed sharp surfaces, leaks in ceiling or walls, and other items of disrepair present hazards to students. Another factor which must be considered is adequate lighting. Report any inadequacies in classroom illumination. Florescent lights placed at acute angles often burn out faster. A healthy supply of spare tubes is a sound investment.

General Classroom Safety

In the modern classroom, there is a great deal of furniture, equipment, supplies, appliances, and learning aids to help the teacher teach and students learn. The classroom should contain furnishings that fit the purpose of the classroom, and it is the responsibility of the administration to see these materials are maintained. However, it is the keen teacher's eye that can spot safety issues at their earliest appearance.

Whatever the arrangement of furniture and equipment may be the teacher must provide for adequate traffic flow. Rows of desks must have adequate space between them for students to move and for the teacher to circulate. All areas must be open to line-of-sight supervision by the teacher.

Local fire and safety codes dictate entry and exit standards. In addition, all corridors and classrooms should be wheelchair accessible for students and others who use them. It is the teachers' responsibility to educate themselves on their district's fire safety codes.

Another consideration is adequate ventilation and climate control. Specialty classes such as science require specialized hoods for ventilation. Physical Education classes have the added responsibility for shower areas and specialized environments that must be heated such as pool or athletic training rooms.

In all cases, proper care must be taken to ensure student safety. Furniture and equipment should be situated safely at all times. No equipment, materials, boxes, etc. should be placed where there is danger of falling over. Doors must have entry and exit accessibility at all times.

A Community of Learners

A classroom is a community of learning, and when students learn to respect themselves and the members around them, learning is maximized.
A positive environment, where open, discussion-oriented, non-threatening communication among all students can occur, is a critical factor in creating an effective learning culture. The teacher must take the lead and model appropriate actions and speech, and intervene quickly when a student makes a misstep and offends (often inadvertently) another.

Communication issues that the teacher in a diverse classroom should be aware of include:

- Be sensitive to terminology and language patterns that may exclude or demean students. Regularly switch between the use of "he" and "she" in speech and writing. Know and use the current terms that ethnic and cultural groups use to identify themselves (e.g., "Latinos" (favored) vs. "Hispanics").
- Be aware of body language that is intimidating or offensive to some cultures, such as direct eye contact, and adjust accordingly.
- Monitor your own reactions to students to ensure equal responses to males and females, as well as differently-performing students.
- Don't "protect" students from criticism because of their ethnicity or gender. Likewise, acknowledge and praise all meritorious work without singling out any one student. Both actions can make all students hyper-aware of ethnic and gender differences and cause anxiety or resentment throughout the class.
- Emphasize the importance of discussing and considering different viewpoints and opinions. Demonstrate and express value for all opinions and comments and lead students to do the same.

Teachers should create a classroom climate that encourages extensive participation from the students. Collaborations and discussions are enhanced when students like and respect each other, and therefore, each student's learning can benefit. This is even truer when students engage in full participation. When everyone's thoughts and perspectives and ideas are offered, the class can consider each idea carefully in their discussion. The more students' participate, the more learning is gained through a more thorough examination of the topic.

To create this environment, teachers must first model how to welcome and consider all points of view for the students. The teacher should then positively affirm and reinforce students for offering their ideas in front of the other students. Even if somewhat amiss, the teacher should receive the idea while perhaps offering a modification or corrected statement (for more factual pieces of information). The idea is for students to feel confident and safe in being able to express their thoughts or ideas. Only then will students be able to engage in independent discussions that consider and respect everyone's statements. Student-student and teacher-student interactions play a significant role in a positive classroom climate. When interactions among classroom members are encouraging, learning becomes a more natural and genuine process. Cold or routine interactions discourage questioning, critical thinking and useful discussion. Teachers should make every effort to be available to their students, as well as provide natural, collaborative opportunities for students in order to strengthen classroom interactions. Reflection, observations and asking for feedback regarding one's classroom interactions (perhaps during a yearly observation) will help teachers to analyze the effectiveness of their classroom's interactions.

Skill 13.2   Demonstrate knowledge of how to create and modify learning environments to meet the needs of all young children (including young children with disabilities, developmental delays, and special abilities) and to integrate developmentally and culturally appropriate materials, equipment, and technology resources

Modifying Learning Environments

A teacher's job would be relatively easy if simply instructing students in current curriculum objectives was his/her primary responsibility. Today's educator must first assure that the students are able to come to school, are able to attend to the curriculum, have individual learning styles met, and are motivated to work to their fullest capacity.

Most special needs students have an Individual Educational Plan or a 504 Plan. These documents clearly state the students' educational objectives and learning needs as well as persons responsible for meeting these objectives. A well-written Individual Educational Plan will contain evidence that the student is receiving resources from the school and the community that will assist in meeting the physical, social and academic needs of the student.

Special needs children in a classroom may need special seating or may need to be seated in a specific place in the classroom. Adherence to the IEP or 504 Plan means that the teacher needs to do extra planning to accommodate these children to ensure that they are meeting the standards for the subject or grade. Some students may not be able to handle the paper and pencil tasks and may need to use a word processing program and others may need to have technologies to enable them to magnify the text so they can see it clearly. Students with developmental delays will need accommodations made to the class work so that they have longer time to complete the assignments, a shortened version of the work or less challenging work. Students with disabilities may also bring a teacher assistant with them, so the teacher in the class has to get used to having another person in the room at all times.

The challenges of meeting the needs of all students in the classroom require that the teacher is a lifelong learner. Ongoing participation in professional staff development, attendance at local, state, and national conferences, and continuing education classes help teachers grow in many ways including an awareness of resources available for students.

Integrating Culture

A teacher's responsibility to students extends beyond the four walls of the school building. In addition to offering well-planned and articulately delivered lessons, the teacher must consider the effects of both body language and spoken language on students' learning.

When planning instruction for a diverse group (or teaching about diversity, for that matter) incorporate teaching through the use of perspective. There is always more than one way to "see" or approach a problem, an example, a process, fact or event, or any learning situation. Varying approaches for instruction helps to maintain the students' interest in the material and enables the teacher to address the diverse needs of individuals to comprehend the material.

Furthermore, today's educator must address the needs of diverse learners within a single classroom. The teacher is able to attain materials that may be necessary for the majority of the regular education students and some of the special needs children and, more and more frequently, one individual student. The "effective" teacher knows that there are currently hundreds of adaptive materials that could be used to help these students increase achievement and develop skills.

Student-centered classrooms contain not only textbooks, workbooks, and literature materials but also rely heavily on a variety of audio-visual equipment and computers. There are tape recorders, language masters, filmstrip projectors, and laser disc players to help meet the learning styles of the students.

Although most school centers cannot supply all the materials that special needs students require, each district more than likely has a resource center where teachers can check out special equipment. Most communities support agencies which offer assistance in providing the necessities of special needs people including students. Teachers must know how to obtain a wide range of materials including school supplies, medical care, clothing, food, adaptive computers and books (such as Braille), eye glasses, hearing aids, wheelchairs, counseling, transportation, etc.

Skill 13.3 Demonstrate understanding of factors that can affect communication in the classroom (e.g., cultural, linguistic, or socioeconomic background) and apply communication strategies that are responsive to all young children's backgrounds and needs

Early childhood and elementary school educators provide the foundation for an individual's entire educational experience, ultimately influencing what that person will become in life. Teaching at this level requires many skills beyond subject matter mastery. Interpersonal skills, sensitivity, self-discipline and role modeling are but a few of the extra-curricular qualities which make for a successful teacher at this level. Essentially, the teacher develops goals, objectives and defines the necessary materials for teaching skill sets and incorporates these into lesson plans consistent with prescribed curriculum objectives. It is in the presentation of skill-based materials, the management of the classroom environment and the facilitation of learning by students as individuals and in groups, that all of the teacher's skills (and eventual experiences) come into play.

Students at this level are continually undergoing physical and emotional changes and development. Everything occurring to them is new, unfamiliar and sometimes discomforting. A student undergoing such a change may suddenly exhibit the disorientation and uneasiness more often seen in a child on his/her first day of school. As a result, a student may feel socially awkward, and this may be reflected in schoolwork and especially in classroom participation. The teacher must be sensitive to the issues of a developing child and aware of the impact this may have on student learning, classroom decorum and the cohesion among classmates which the teacher is trying to foster.

The teacher must be prepared to adapt and control the classroom environment to the degree possible, to ensure a safe and productive learning environment is established and maintained. However, some situations are more readily anticipated and incorporated than controlled or changed. Behavior modification, in the classroom, can often mean simply channeling existing energies and interests (of the students') into acceptable activities which provide a meaningful, educational experience as a positive outcome.

Younger students do not respond well to instruction which is singularly formatted (e.g., lectures, audio/video presentations, etc., which expend the entire class period). Multiple formats are preferable, and activities which provide direct involvement by the students are often most successful. It is within these planned activities that the teacher has the best opportunity to instruct on, and model, the concepts of sharing, cooperative endeavor, social involvement and communication skills. And the students have the opportunity to participate and practice these skills.

This, of course, requires continual monitoring by the teacher. While early childhood and elementary students are generally more easily controlled—often appearing better behaved and more responsive to authority—than older students, they still have a tendency to socialize and play just for the sake of play. This can quickly allow the classroom situation to deteriorate, replacing the learning environment with chaos. When the teacher is implementing a well-structured plan, with measurable milestones and specific objectives, he/she will quickly identify and redirect conversation and activity that is not relevant or supportive of the instructional objectives. A teacher may allow younger students a greater degree of latitude, but he/she must restrict their longitude.

Allowing for the differing needs of younger students does not mean abandoning classroom discipline and organized instruction. At this level, students need the reassurance of structure, organization and discipline. If the appropriate attitudes and responses to structure and discipline are internalized at an early age, they will serve the student throughout his/her educational experience and provide a solid foundation upon which the individual can develop the self-discipline necessary in later life. The teacher who can instill these values in a young student will have earned the gratitude and respect of all the teachers who instruct this student in the future.

And the time to implement organization and classroom discipline is not at a moment of crisis or chaos. This is an issue which will significantly effect the teacher's ability to teach and the student's ability to learn, day after day. A good deal of thought and preparation, on the part of the classroom teacher, should be devoted to this aspect of the educational experience. There are volumes of text available to the novice teacher, providing criteria and examples for structuring an organized, disciplined, classroom environment. Specific recommendations for discipline and organization in normal and in unusual classroom situations are available from experienced teachers in journals and on the Internet. Guidelines and structure may be made flexible to allow for certain contingencies, but they must be put into practice with specific limits provided, and the students must be made fully aware of the structure, the guidelines, their responsibilities and the consequences of their actions should they fail to observe these guidelines.

It is always beneficial for the teacher to remain current with the studies and findings published in numerous journals related to child and educational psychology and physical and intellectual development in early childhood. For classroom use, there are numerous resources (instructional videos, printed materials, instructional games) which provide for controlled interaction among the students and between teacher and students, and address issues of concern to young students. They are usually age and/or grade specific, activity-driven, and employ multimedia. Examples of pertinent topics, with stated educational goals, available for instructional use would include, "Listening to Others," "Caring," "Bullying," "Working Out Conflicts," "Controlling Anger," "Caring," "Fairness," "Saying No," "Dealing with Feelings," "Being Friends," "Appreciating Yourself," "Dealing with Disappointment."

Instructional objectives vary greatly from early childhood, where life-skills are introduced through play and activity, into kindergarten and early elementary where the fundamentals of academic subjects are introduced, through elementary where previously introduced skills are developed and new ones introduced. But it is often possible to include part or all of such instructional materials in a broader lesson plan which incorporates adopting life-skills with learning subject matter. The technology and varieties of media available to the teacher and the students, today, enable the teacher to provide a multifaceted, instructional experience in the classroom. The technology and other tools of the trade will continue to change and improve the means of education. It is the teacher's responsibility to the students to remain aware of these changes and exercise her or his professional judgment as to what is beneficial and when it should be introduced into the classroom environment.

Depending on the educational situation, team-teaching or the use of aids or assistants in the classroom, often serves to modify the behavior of students, positively. It is not just the presence of more authority figures, but a more diverse environment, more opportunity for individual attention and a perceived sense of increased security, which engenders a positive attitude among the students.

Monitoring of all the student's activities, skill acquisition, verbalization, socialization, etc., is particularly critical in these early years of development. Learning disabilities and social dysfunctions must be identified as soon as possible to ensure that each individual's needs are met and that every student has an equal opportunity to succeed, educationally.

SEE also Skill 13.2

COMPETENCY 14.0 UNDERSTAND THE IMPORTANCE OF COMMUNICATION, COLLABORATION, AND PROFESSIONALISM IN THE EARLY CHILDHOOD PROGRAM TO SUPPORT YOUNG CHILDREN'S LEARNING AND WELL-BEING

Skill 14.1   Demonstrate knowledge of the early childhood profession; its multiple historical, philosophical, and social foundations; and current issues, trends, and influences in early childhood education, including public policies affecting young children, families, and programs for young children

While the first kindergarten was established in the United States in 1855, it wasn't until the 1960's that America began to worry about the education of the young child. Piaget's and Bruner's work during that decade turned our attention to the importance of the early years before formal schooling. Studies at that time showed that one fourth of the children entering first grade were significantly behind academically. Research clearly demonstrated that children can master complex learning, such as the ability to read at a very early age, and parents became more concerned about the adequacy of preschool experiences. It was widely assumed that that the more a child learned as early as possible, the better his chances were that he would be able to meet college entrance requirements and secure a bright future

In 1965, the federal government provided unprecedented funds for the education of children from disadvantaged homes, especially preschool-age children. The Head Start program meant that large groups of preschool age children became readily available for research purposes concerning the effectiveness and improvement of programming for children of this age. The Head Start program also made educational programs available to **all** children, even children from poverty, for the first time.

The earliest preschool programs were places with relatively unstructured programs for young children. Whatever a child "happened" to learn was celebrated and these programs were not considered "real" schools. There were numerous experimental programs during the 60's and 70's, and they were almost all concerned with how children acquire specific knowledge. Proponents of this type of programming believed that there were basic elements of what a child is expected to know before entering a regular elementary school program, and proceeded to manipulate a child's environment to provide this knowledge base. There is still debate about whether this kind of learning is superior over learning that grows out of meaningful experience and results from the interests and needs of young children. Proponents of a child-centered philosophy for preschool programs seem to have lost popularity in today's "high accountability" era. As schools react to the new standards with national ratings based on student performance in core subject areas, there is even more pressure on early childhood programs to ensure that all children are acquiring cognitive skills at a "standard" rate.

With more mothers entering the work force in the late 60's and early 70's, the demand for quality preschool programs increased. The importance and value of education during the early childhood years is no longer questioned, but there is still no consensus about the best methods and curriculum to be used. We now know that language acquisition and cognitive development before age 6 is very important, but this learning can take place in the home setting as well. Government funding has been focused on providing opportunities for young children who have been deprived of normal early experiences to catch up before entering elementary school. In addition to Head Start, government funding provides preschool for four year olds from economically disadvantaged homes and for children whose home language is not English.

There are a diversity of current issues, trends, educational innovations, and legislation that impact elementary school communities. National assessments and local evaluations of student academic performance in the areas of reading, writing and math have shown that there are gaps in learning from one cultural group to another in classrooms. The issue of student learning and performance has become a national debate on whether providing additional educational funding will alleviate or create academic access for students identified as at risk in schools.

Current Trends

Differentiating Instruction

The effective teacher will seek to connect all students to the subject matter through multiple techniques, with the goal that each student, through their own abilities, will relate to one or more techniques and excel in the learning process. Differentiated instruction encompasses several areas:

1. <u>Content</u>: What is the teacher going to teach? Or, perhaps better put, what does the teacher want the students to learn? Differentiating content means that students will have access to content that piques their interest about a topic, with a complexity that provides an appropriate challenge to their intellectual development.

2. <u>Process</u>: A classroom management technique where instructional organization and delivery is maximized for the diverse student group. These techniques should include dynamic, flexible grouping activities, where instruction and learning occurs both as whole-class, teacher-led activities, as well peer learning and teaching (while teacher observes and coaches) within small groups or pairs.

3. <u>Product</u>: The expectations and requirements placed on students to demonstrate their knowledge or understanding. The type of product expected from each student should reflect each student's own capabilities.

Creating programs for literacy development and mathematical acquisition have become both the issues and the trends in the construct of new educational innovations. Differentiating instruction for learners who come to school in the pre-K grades has become a focus for educators seeking to increase the literacy and mathematical skills of its youngest learners. The development of effective programs and subsequent funding continue to be the goals of a legislative process dedicated to promoting educational equity for students.

Multiple Intelligence Theory & Brain-based Research

The Multiple Intelligence Theory, developed by Howard Gardner, suggests that students learn in (at least) seven different ways. These include visually/spatially, musically, verbally, logically/mathematically, interpersonally, intrapersonally, and bodily/kinesthetically.

Alternative Assessment

Alternative assessment is an assessment where students create an answer or a response to a question or task, as opposed to traditional, inflexible assessments where students choose a prepared response from among a selection of responses, such as matching, multiple-choice or true/false.

When implemented effectively, an alternative assessment approach will exhibit these characteristics, among others:

- Requires higher-order thinking and problem-solving
- Provides opportunities for student self-reflection and self-assessment
- Uses real world applications to connect students to the subject
- Provides opportunities for students to learn and examine subjects on their own, as well as to collaborate with their peers.
- Encourages students to continuing learning beyond the requirements of the assignment
- Clearly defines objective and performance goals

Inquiry-based learning is performance based learning where students are actively involved in the learning process and in the construction of new knowledge. When students engage in inquiry-based learning in order to understand the world around them, the learning process involves the formulation of questions that convert new information into an active application of knowledge.

Figure 1 shows the contextual and interactive component of inquiry-based learning for students:

Figure 1 Inquiry-based learning model

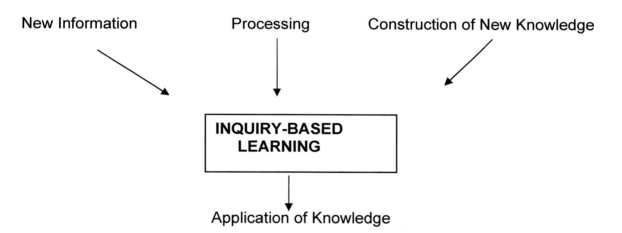

When students are given new information to process, inquiry based learning becomes a natural extension of knowledge acquisition and understanding. In traditional classrooms, the lecture becomes the mode of learning for students seeking to understand the context of mathematical application and real-life application of problem solving skills learned in the traditional math class. In an inquiry-based learning format, students are shown how to apply mathematical learning and actively involved in real-life application of newly constructed knowledge. Involving students in the active processing of mathematical learning increases their ability to construct frameworks of understanding into useful applications of new knowledge.

Legislation

Legislation issues of educational funding for teachers and program developments continue to impact existing educational implementations for students. With thousands of school communities failing to meet NCLB (No Child Left Behind) and AYP (Adequate Yearly Progress) standards, the cost of overhaul and providing additional financial support for effective school communities with over-capacity issues, is a major reason given for the decreased funding providing for current educational communities. Students who have been continually promoted from pre-K to higher elementary grade levels who have failed to attain the basic skills of reading, writing and math are becoming increasingly frustrated by school systems designed to promote rather than hold accountability for student learning and evaluation.

Other Current Issues

The cost of teacher turnover in school communities has been estimated to be in the range of 5-7 billion dollars which further impacts the legislature's ability to provide enough funding for all educational communities. Professional development training and required certification classes for teachers in elementary education also contribute to the comprehensive cost of educating students.

Early violence in elementary school communities coupled with classroom management issues have contributed to a reduction in teaching and instructional time for young learners. Providing young learners with ethical and social strategies to improve cooperative learning and communication will go a long way in reducing the time spent on conflict and increase the time spent on learning acquisition.

Educational innovations in technology and educational reform must address the issues that are creating conflicting issues which impact educational development and implementation of effective curriculum for young learners. Current educational reform must continue to focus on addressing educational issues that promote learning opportunities and professional development for both students and educators.

Skill 14.2   Demonstrate understanding of basic principles and practices for the administration, organization, and operation of early childhood programs (e.g., supervision of staff and volunteers), and the significance of local, state, and national standards and regulations regarding early childhood programs, educators, and environments

There are basic guiding principles and practices that should be adhered to in early childhood programs. The administrator of the program should first of all ensure that the teachers employed have the proper early childhood qualifications and police checks to ensure that they are suitable to work with young children. The curriculum of the program should meet the developmental needs of the children of each age group and be accessible for children with special needs and disabilities. Administration of early childhood programs also includes the following:

Organization

There should be plenty of space for young children to move about as they take part in the program. Desks and chairs should be low and small fitting the size of the children. There should be a designated play area that is carefully supervised so that children do not get hurt as they play. The timetable should be set so that staff, teachers and parents know what to expect during the day. Staff and volunteers need to follow behavior guidelines and be patient with the children. On times, when children act out, the appropriate punishment is to remove them from the setting for a "Time Out".

Operation

The day-to-day operation of the early childhood program includes careful monitoring of the children. Parents should sign out the children if they take them from the center before the scheduled time and should inform the center if the child will not be attending on a particular day.

When children are outside, they should be in an enclosed area from which they cannot wander off, but they still need to be supervised. For field trips, there should be enough staff and volunteers so that there is a ratio of at least 7:1 (seven children to one adult), but more volunteers will ensure better supervision. All adults who come to the center should sign in and wear a "Visitor" tag.

National, State and Local Standards

Adherence to national, state and local standards for early childhood programs is of utmost importance. These standards set out the curriculum by detailing what the children should be able to know at do at specific stages of development. Adherence to these standards can also give the teacher information about where some children may be lacking and need extra instruction or even testing by an outside agency. The standards set down for early childhood education programs prepare the children for Kindergarten and for the rest of their schooling. Making parents aware of these standards will help the children because the parents know what the child needs to know and can help at home.

Skill 14.3   Demonstrate knowledge of the roles of parents/guardians as primary caregivers and informal teachers of young children; the collaborative interactions between parents/guardians and teachers in early childhood programs; and strategies for maintaining communication and working supportively with families, including families with diverse backgrounds and those whose young children have special educational needs

Both the home and the school have important functions to serve in educating young children. Neither can work effectively without the understanding, support, and assistance of the other. Guiding the development of the child is a cooperative endeavor. Only by communicating with each other about how a child reacts in his life at home and at school can parents and teachers work to meet the needs of the whole child.

When teachers ask probing questions about a child's home life some parents are offended, not understanding that the teacher is interested in what the child does at home because it will assist her in working with the child at school.

Almost every day care center or preschool program requires some participation on the part of parents. It is not possible to mandate parent involvement, so it falls to the teacher to "win" parents over and make them comfortable interacting with the school. Parents often feel inferior to their child's teacher. Parents feel more comfortable if they know what is expected of them, so the teacher must utilize a variety of ways to keep them informed. Sending short notes home, weekly newsletters, home visits, parent conferences and even emails are ways to accomplish this. New advancements in technology allow some parents to view the preschool classroom activities via an internet connection, which makes parents feel connected to their child throughout the work day. Even though there are a variety of ways to connect and interact with parents, person-to-person and day-by-day relationships remain the most important and effective format, so that there will be no gaps between the school and the home. Communication between parents and teacher should be encouraged as the parent brings the child to school and picks the child up from school.

Good teachers realize the importance of identifying the special learning needs of children, and are sometimes the first ones to inform a parent of a possible learning difference or delay. While the teacher will do everything possible to include children with various delays or difficulties in the regular classroom, it may also fall to the teacher to "coach" the parent on how to gain outside help for the child, through referrals to physicians, counselors or therapists. This should always be done with sensitivity and without diagnosing. Teachers should leave diagnosis to trained professionals and instead should focus on helping parents know the "normal" developmental milestones and where their child falls in relation to them. If this is the first opportunity for the child to be grouped with other children his/her age, the parent may not realize that the child learns differently or is significantly delayed. Pediatricians are also trained to watch for these delays and to refer parents to early intervention programs from birth.

The most successful teacher is one who regards parents as partners and friends. Although all parents are different, they are alike in their desire to secure the best education for their child. Parents want to provide a chance for their own children to have a richer, more rewarding life than they themselves enjoyed.

Teachers today will deal with an increasingly diverse group of cultures in their classrooms. And while this is an exciting prospect for most teachers, it creates new challenges in dealing with a variety of family expectations for school and teachers.

First, teachers must show respect to all parents and families. They need to set the tone that suggests that their mission is to develop students into the best people they can be. And then they need to realize that various cultures have different views of how children should be educated. Second, teachers will have better success when they talk personally about their children. Even though teachers may have many students, when they share personal things about each child, parents will feel more confident that their child will be "in the right hands." Third, it is very important that teachers act like they are partners in the children's education and development. Parents know their children best, and it is important to get feedback, information, and advice from them. Finally, teachers will need to be patient with difficult families, realizing that certain methods of criticism (including verbal attacks, etc.) are unacceptable. Such circumstances would require the teacher to get assistance from an administrator. This situation, however, is very unusual, and most teachers will find that when they really attempt to be friendly and personal with parents, the parents will reciprocate and assist in the educational program.

One way of interacting with families includes the parent-teacher conference.

Parent conferences

The parent-teacher conference is generally for one of three purposes. First, the teacher may wish to share information with the parents concerning the performance and behavior of the child. Second, the teacher may be interested in obtaining information from the parents about the child. Such information may help answer questions or concerns that the teacher has. A third purpose may be to request parent support or involvement in specific activities or requirements. In many situations, more than one of the purposes may be involved.

Planning the conference

When a conference is scheduled, whether at the request of the teacher or parent, the teacher should allow sufficient time to prepare thoroughly. Collect all relevant information, samples of student work, records of behavior, and other items needed to help the parent understand the circumstances. It is also a good idea to compile a list of questions or concerns you wish to address. Arrange the time and location of the conference to provide privacy and to avoid interruptions.

Conducting the conference

Begin the conference by putting the parents as ease. Take the time to establish a comfortable mood, but do not waste time with unnecessary small talk. Begin your discussion with positive comments about the student. Identify strengths and desirable attributes, but do not exaggerate.

As you address issues or areas of concern, be sure to focus on observable behaviors and concrete results or information. Do not make judgmental statements about parent or child. Share specific work samples, anecdotal records of behavior, etc., which demonstrate clearly the concerns you have. Be a good listener and hear the parent's comments and explanations. Such background information can be invaluable in understanding the needs and motivations of the child.

Finally, end the conference with an agreed plan of action between parents and teacher (and, when appropriate, the child). Bring the conference to a close politely but firmly and thank the parents for their involvement.

After the conference

A day or two after the conference, it is a good idea to send a follow-up note to the parents. In this note, briefly and concisely reiterate the plan or step agreed to in the conference. Be polite and professional; avoid the temptation to be too informal or chatty. If the issue is a long term one such as the behavior or on-going work performance of the student, make periodic follow-up contacts to keep the parents informed of the progress.

Skill 14.4 **Demonstrate knowledge of how to use appropriate health appraisal procedures; make referrals to community health and social services when necessary; and link families of young children with a range of services based on identified resources, priorities, and concerns**

"Health is a state of physical, mental and social well being and depends upon the interaction of these dimensions. Health is influenced by the interaction of many hereditary and environmental factors and conditions over which the individual may exercise varying amounts of control. Some aspects of everyone's health can be improved."(Joint Committee on Health Problems in Education of the NEA and AMA, 1965)

Head Start

The Head Start Program is a federally funded program, which monitors the health of children from low-income families. Children in this program engage in educational and play activities in a safe environment. They are provided with nutritional meals and their health is monitored. At the same time, families receive the education they need to care for the child.

The curriculum and assessment techniques are carefully monitored to ensure that they are appropriate for the developmental age of each child. There Are classes for parents and caregivers to enable them to receive a High School Graduation certificate, and in areas such as child rearing, resources available to them in the community, job training and health and nutrition.

Skilled professionals work with the families to ensure that children with special needs receive the help and support they need. The program also ensures that all the children receive their immunization needles, have their hearing tested and receive dental care.

The health of young children has been identified as an area of special concern due to the research from Project Head Start that says a "child who is in poor health will function at a leave considerably lower than that of a well child." Effective early childhood programs will have policies that address the following areas:

1) Identifying health defects based on knowledge of developmental milestones for children at each stage of development
2) Providing or referring parents to preventive services (such as immunizations, dental checkups) to ensure a child's future health
3) Education for parents and children to improve the health of all members of the child's family

How Teachers Can Help

Alert supervision by the teacher and the parent is imperative in order to safeguard the health and safety of young children. This means careful observation of the child for signs of illness or abnormality, as well as removing safety hazards from the environment.

The teacher can help the parent by acquiring knowledge of resources available in the community to address health needs. There are doctors who provide services on a sliding scale basis, as well as free clinics, low cost immunizations, and community organizations who provide vouchers for free eyeglasses. Developing a list of these service providers, as well as advertising immunization clinics and other opportunities, is a way to connect parents to the resources needed for proper health care.

Many schools provide routine screenings for height, weight, vision and hearing. Trained volunteers can do these screenings and the school then communicates these results to parents who can seek further testing outside of school to determine the level of need. Schools should also communicate to parents about communicable diseases and establish policies about how long a child should stay out of school and on what authority the child can be readmitted to school after a contagious illness.

Schools must remember that they are role-models for parents and the community about proper health and safety procedures. The day-to-day cleanliness of the school environment, the nutritional value of food served, the safety of the school playground, and the appropriate focus on health concerns, teach parents and children more about good health practices than receiving such information by newsletters or conversations.

Linking Families of Young Children to Resources Available in the Community

Many families do not know that there are resources available in the community to help them with child rearing, health and nutrition. Teachers observe the children in the classroom and can discuss their needs with the parents. They can get the information for the parents as to what resources and skilled professionals are available for them and even set up meetings between the parents and these professionals.

Skill 14.5   Demonstrate knowledge of the use of personal and professional reflection to evaluate how choices and actions affect young children, families, and colleagues in the learning community

The very nature of the teaching profession—the yearly cycle of doing the same thing over and over again—creates the tendency to fossilize, to quit growing, to become complacent. The teachers who are truly successful are those who have built into their own approach to their jobs and to their lives safeguards against that. They see themselves as constant learners. They believe that learning never ends. They are careful never to teach their classes the same as they did the last time. They build in a tendency to reflect on what is happening to their students under their care or what happened this year as compared to last year. What worked the best? What didn't work so well? What can be changed to improve success rates? What about continuing education? Should they go for another degree or should they enroll in more classes?

There are several avenues a teacher might take in order to assess his or her own teaching strengths and weaknesses. Early indicators that a self-evaluation might be necessary include having several students that do not understand a concept. In such a case, a teacher might want to go over his or her lesson plans to make sure the topic is being covered thoroughly and in a clear fashion. Brainstorming other ways to tackle the content might also help. Speaking to other teachers, asking how they teach a certain skill, might give new insight to one's own teaching tactics.

Any good teacher will understand that he or she needs to self-evaluate and adjust his or her lessons periodically. Signing up for professional courses or workshops can also help a teacher assess his or her abilities by opening one's eyes to new ways of teaching.

Professional Development

Professional development opportunities for teacher performance improvement or enhancement in instructional practices are essential for creating comprehensive learning communities. In order to promote the vision, mission and action plans of school communities, teachers must be given the toolkits to maximize instructional performances. The development of student-centered learning communities that foster the academic capacities and learning synthesis for all students should be the fundamental goal of professional development for teachers.

The level of professional development may include traditional district workshops that enhance instructional expectations for teachers or the more complicated multiple day workshops given by national and state educational organizations to enhance the federal accountability of skill and professional development for teachers. Most workshops on the national and state level provide clock hours that can be used to renew certifications for teachers every five years. Typically, 150 clock hours is the standard certification number needed to provide a five year certification renewal, so teachers must attend and complete paperwork for a diversity of workshops that range from 1-50 clock hours according to the timeframe of the workshops.

Most districts and schools provide in-service professional development opportunities for teachers during the school year dealing with district objectives/expectations and relevant workshops or classes that can enhance the teaching practices for teachers. Clock hours are provided with each class or workshop and the type of professional development being offered to teachers determines clock hours. Each year, schools are required to report the number of workshops, along with the participants attending the workshops to the Superintendent's office for filing. Teachers collecting clock hour forms are required to file the forms to maintain certification eligibility and job eligibility.

The research by the National Association of Secondary Principals,' "Breaking Ranks II: Strategies for Leading High School Reform" created the following multiple listing of educational practices needed for expanding the professional development opportunities for teachers:

- Interdisciplinary instruction between subject areas
- Identification of individual learning styles to maximize student academic performance
- Training teachers in understanding and applying multiple assessment formats and implementations in curriculum and instruction
- Looking at multiple methods of classroom management strategies
- Providing teachers with national, federal, state and district curriculum expectations and performance outcomes
- Identifying the school communities' action plan of student learning objectives and teacher instructional practices
- Helping teachers understand how to use data to impact student learning goals and objectives
- Teaching teachers on how to disaggregate student data in improving instruction and curriculum implementation for student academic equity and access
- Develop leadership opportunities for teachers to become school and district trainers to promote effective learning communities for student achievement and success

In promoting professional development opportunities for teachers that enhance student achievement, the bottom line is that teachers must be given the time to complete workshops at no or minimal costs. School and district budgets must include financial resources to support and encourage teachers to engage in mandatory and optional professional development opportunities that create a "win-win" learning experience for students.

Whether a teacher is using criterion-referenced, norm-referenced or performance-based data to inform and impact student learning and achievement, the more important objective is ensuring that teachers know how to effectively use the data to improve and reflect upon existing teaching instructions. The goal of identifying ways for teachers to use the school data is simple, "Is the teacher's instructional practice improving student learning goals and academic success?"

School data can include demographic profiling, cultural and ethic academic trends, state and/or national assessments, portfolios, academic subject pre-post assessment and weekly assessments, projects, and disciplinary reports. By looking at trends and discrepancies in school data, teachers can ascertain whether they are meeting the goals and objectives of the state, national, and federal mandates for school improvement reform and curriculum implementation.

Assessments can be used to motivate students to learn and shape the learning environment to provide learning stimulation that optimizes student access to learning. Butler and McMunn (2006) have shown that "factors that help motivate students to learn are 1) Involving students in their own assessment, 2) Matching assessment strategies to student learning, and 3) Consider thinking styles and using assessments to adjust the classroom environment in order to enhance student motivation to learn." Teachers can shape the way students learn by creating engaging learning opportunities that promote student achievement.

The most effective teachers combine a clear understanding of learning theory with practical knowledge which can only be gained through actual classroom experience. Teachers should continually revise their teaching approaches as they reflect on their daily experiences with children and what has worked and not worked. While there are proven, research-based instructional strategies that work for every area of the curriculum, teaching also remains an art, as teachers utilize their toolbox of instructional practices to match each child's individual needs. Unfortunately there is not a comprehensive, master list of responses to children's unique needs. As teachers observe the individual student in the school setting, and then reflect on responses in the classroom, the effective teacher is able to craft a path for each child to succeed.

Teaching is complicated. After the teacher decides which objectives to teach, he/she must make instructional decisions minute by minute as she monitors and checks for understanding of the lesson content for each individual student. Teachers are also able to express their own professional choice (and academic freedom) while following the state or school expectations. This is contrast with many other professional careers, where a person's roles and responsibilities are dictated externally by the institution or employer.

Many views of teaching equate techniques or skills with the quality of teaching itself. But these are skills or techniques only–*tools* for reaching some other, valued end. Indeed, they may very well be used expertly and effectively. And a person with a larger repertoire of skills may have more possibilities open to them. Still, sheer mastery does not ensure that students learn, for example. Ultimately, each teacher must reflect and will find certain forms of teaching more suitable to his or her own goals, interactions with students, and personal dispositions.

Features of professional reflection

- It is grounded in, and develops your day-to-day professional practice and offers an opportunity for reflection on that practice through consideration of an issue relevant to your professional interests, experiences and context. It enables you to focus in-depth on an issue concerning pupil learning and the implications for teaching practice and school improvement
- It involves taking account of pupils' learning experiences and progress, including strategies to overcome individual barriers to learning.
- It can draw on pupil and classroom observations and other relevant data to inform your analysis of implications for improving teaching and learning.
- It will be informed by, and extend, your professional development and learning.

Outcomes from professional reflection should contribute to improved teaching and learning strategies, which have an impact on pupils' individual needs and achievements.

Examples of areas of focus for professional reflection

- Investigating the needs and experiences of an individual pupil (or pupils) with a specific Special Education need
- Evaluating appropriate and effective classroom practice to reach and teach children from diverse backgrounds and with special needs
- Understanding and designing effective supports to meet the needs of an individual student or a student who is at risk for school failure due to poverty, language acquisition, or other barriers to learning
- Developing strategies for Gifted and Talented students

- Exploring new developments in pedagogic practice and their application for teaching and learning in your classroom or school
- Assessing the range of behavior management policies and practices and their effectiveness in tackling student misbehavior

Professional development and training should always include this reflection-in-action component. Teachers gain theoretical understanding of practice as they engage in teaching and reflect upon it during and after its occurrence.

Post Test

Subarea I. Language and Literacy Development

1. A student who has difficulty pronouncing certain words or sounds may be demonstrating which speech and language disorder?
(Rigorous) (Skill 1.1)

   A. Apraxia

   B. Articulation Disorder

   C. Auditory Processing

   D. Dysarthria

2. A language-learning function exists in the brain that makes it easier for children to learn a language below age:
(Average rigor) (Skill 1.1)

   A. 2

   B. 7

   C. 10

   D. 14

3. A teacher reads a book to students. The students are then encouraged to ask who, what, where, when, and why questions. What is this activity designed to help develop?
(Rigorous) (Skill 1.2)

   A. Motor skills

   B. Social skills

   C. Higher cognitive skills

   D. Decision making skills

4. To enhance their students' effective listening skills, teachers can encourage which of the following strategies?
(Easy) (Skill 1.3)

   A. Associate

   B. Visualize

   C. Repeat

   D. All of the above

5. **The relationship between oral language and reading skills is best described as:**
    (Average rigor) (Skill 1.4)

    A. Reciprocal

    B. Inverse

    C. Opposite

    D. There is no relationship.

6. **During which stage of language acquisition would it be most inappropriate to ask a student to make a long speech?**
    (Average rigor) (Skill 1.5)

    A. Intermediate fluency

    B. Emergent speech

    C. Early production

    D. Advanced fluency

7. **Mr. Adams uses a short story about early train travel as part of a history lesson. This shows that literature:**
    (Average rigor) (Skill 1.6)

    A. Can be used to expand students' vocabulary

    B. Can be used to build students' communication skills

    C. Can be used to help students empathize

    D. Can be used to enhance other areas of the curriculum

8. **Which of the following is NOT a motivation behind providing reading activities, including reading aloud, to young children?**
    (Rigorous) (Skill 1.6)

    A. Developing word consciousness skills

    B. Developing functions of print skills

    C. Developing phonics skills

    D. Developing language skills

9. Jose moved to the United States last month. He speaks little to no English at this time. His teacher is teaching the class about habitats in science and has chosen to read a story about various habitats to the class. The vocabulary is difficult. What should Jose's teacher do with Jose?
    (Average rigor) (Skill 1.7)

    A. Provide Jose with additional opportunities to learn about habitats

    B. Read the story to Jose multiple times

    C. Show Jose pictures of habitats from his native country

    D. Excuse Jose from the assignment

10. Students who are learning English as a second language often require which of the following to process new information?
    (Average rigor) (Skill 1.7)

    A. Translators

    B. Reading tutors

    C. Instruction in their native language

    D. Additional time and repetitions

11. Which of the following demonstrates the difference between phonemic awareness and phonological awareness?
    (Rigorous) (Skill 2.1)

    A. Phonemic awareness is the understanding that words are made up of sounds, while phonological awareness is the understanding that letters are the representation of sounds.

    B. Phonemic awareness is the ability to rhyme and identify beginning sounds, while phonological awareness is the understanding that letters are the representation of sounds.

    C. Phonemic awareness is the ability to distinguish sounds, while phonological awareness is the understanding that letters are the representation of sounds.

    D. Phonemic awareness is the understanding that words are made up of sounds, while phonological awareness is the ability to distinguish sounds.

12. Ms. Smith hands each child in the classroom a letter of the alphabet. She then challenges each child to go around the classroom and find at least five things in the classroom which begin with that letter. What is Ms. Smith teaching the students? *(Rigorous) (Skill 2.1)*

 A. Phonemic awareness

 B. Vocabulary

 C. Meaning of print

 D. Letter identification

13. Which of the following areas correlate with a child's general language skills? *(Average rigor) (Skill 2.1)*

 A. Reading comprehension

 B. Phonics

 C. Phonemic awareness

 D. All of the above

14. Which of the following is NOT a core part of phonics instruction? *(Rigorous) (Skill 2.2)*

 A. Alphabetic principle

 B. Vowel Patterns

 C. Letter names

 D. Consonant Patterns

15. Which of the following explains a significant difference between phonics and phonemic awareness? *(Average rigor) (Skill 2.2)*

 A. Phonics involves print, while phonemic awareness involves language.

 B. Phonics is harder than phonemic awareness.

 C. Phonics involves sounds, while phonemic awareness involves letters.

 D. Phonics is the application of sounds to print, while phonemic awareness is oral.

16. Ms. Arnold has her first grade students sitting around her word wall. Which of the following activities would be inappropriate for her to use with this group of students? *(Rigorous) (Skill 2.3)*

 A. Having the students clap out the syllables of some of the displayed words

 B. Discussing word meanings

 C. Teaching new vocabulary words in isolation

 D. Finding all the words on the wall that meet certain criteria

17. **The basic features of the alphabetic principle include:** *(Average rigor) (Skill 2.4)*

    A.   Students need to be able to take spoken words apart and blend different sounds together to make new words

    B.   Students need to apply letter sounds to all their reading

    C.   The teaching of the alphabetic principle usually begins in Kindergarten

    D.   All of the above

18. **Which of these describes the best way to teach spelling?** *(Rigorous) (Skill 2.5)*

    A.   At the same time that grammar and sentence structure is taught.

    B.   Within the context of meaningful language experiences.

    C.   Independently so that students can concentrate on spelling.

    D.   In short lessons as students pick up spelling almost immediately.

19. **When students know that letters stand for a message, they are said to be in the_____ stage of spelling.** *(Rigorous) (Skill 2.5)*

    A.   Non-phonemic

    B.   Pre-phonemic

    C.   Early phonemic

    D.   Letter-name sounding

20. **A student can read spontaneously the words** *the, there, boy,* **and** *book.* **These words make up the student's:** *(Rigorous) (Skill 2.5)*

    A.   Personal vocabulary

    B.   Recognition vocabulary

    C.   Sight vocabulary

    D.   Working vocabulary

21. **To decode is to:** *(Easy) (Skill 3.1)*

    A.   Construct meaning

    B.   Sound out a printed sequence of letters

    C.   Use a special code to decipher a message

    D.   Revise for errors in grammar

22. Michael keeps using phrases such as "she go to the store." Which of the following areas should Michael's teacher work on to improve Michael's skills? *(Average rigor) (Skill 3.2)*

    A. Morphology

    B. Syntax

    C. Phonics

    D. Semantics

23. A teacher is showing students how to construct grammatically correct sentences. What is the teacher focusing on? *(Average rigor) (Skill 3.2)*

    A. Morphology

    B. Syntax

    C. Semantics

    D. Pragmatics

24. Vocabulary of children assessed at age six has been shown to be a strong prediction of which future skill at age 16?\ *(Rigorous) (Skill 3.4)*

    A. Reading Accuracy

    B. Reading Comprehension

    C. SAT scores

    D. Analogy Completion

25. Students are about to read a text that contains words that will need to be understood for the students to understand the text. When should the vocabulary be introduced to students? *(Rigorous) (Skill 3.4)*

    A. Before reading

    B. During reading

    C. After reading

    D. It should not be introduced.

26. Which of the following correctly describes the importance of developing fluent reading skills? *(Rigorous) (Skill 4.1)*

    A. Automaticity with text is necessary to be considered a reader.

    B. Fluency directly correlates to comprehension.

    C. Prosody allows students to sound better when reading aloud.

    D. Fluency is measured on high stakes tests.

27. Which of the following is NOT a component of reading fluency?
(Easy) (Skill 4.1)

A. Phoneme knowledge

B. Accuracy

C. Rate

D. Automaticity

28. Ms. Chomski is presenting a new story to her class of first graders. In the story, a family visits their grandparents where they all gather around a record player and listen to music. Many students do not understand what a record player is, especially some children for whom English is not their first language. Which of the following would Ms. Chomski be best to do?
(Rigorous) (Skill 4.1)

A. Discuss what a record player is with her students

B. Compare a record player with a CD player

C. Have students look up record player in a dictionary

D. Show the students a picture of a record player

29. George has read his second graders three formats of the story "The Three Little Pigs." One is the traditional version, one is written from the wolf's point of view, and the third is written from the first pig's point of view. As George leads a discussion on the three texts with his students, he is trying to help his students develop their ability to:
(Rigorous) (Skill 4.2)

A. Compare and contrast texts

B. Understand point of view

C. Recognize metaphors

D. Rewrite fictional stories

30. Mr. Stine put puppet making materials in his art center after he read the children a story. He asked the students who had chosen to make puppets to use them to retell the story he read in front of the class. Mr. Stine was helping the children:
(Rigorous) (Skill 4.2)

A. Improve their art skills

B. Respond to literature

C. Improve their oral presentation skills

D. Increase their listening skills

31. **What type of literature are characters, settings, and themes, interpretations, opinions, theories, and research usually found in?**
(Average rigor) (Skill 4.3)

   A.   Non-fiction

   B.   Fairy tale

   C.   Fiction

   D.   Folktales

32. **Teaching students how to interpret _____ involves evaluating a text's headings, subheadings, bolded words, and side notes.**
(Rigorous) (Skill 4.4)

   A.   Graphic organizers

   B.   Text structures

   C.   Textual marking

   D.   Summaries

33. **Which of the following types of children's literature would you be unlikely to utilize in a kindergarten classroom?**
(Easy) (Skill 4.6)

   A.   Fable

   B.   Science fiction

   C.   Epic

   D.   Fairy tale

34. **Which of the following is NOT a major genre of young children's literature?**
(Easy) (Skill 4.6)

   A.   Science fiction

   B.   Action and adventure

   C.   Current events

   D.   Biography

35. **Which of the following is an important criterion for evaluating children's literature?**
(Easy) (Skill 4.6)

   A.   Character development

   B.   Appropriate reading level

   C.   Cultural diversity

   D.   All of the above

36. **Which of the following is a defining characteristic of a fable?**
(Easy) (Skill 4.6)

   A.   Includes repetition and rhyme

   B.   Based on true events

   C.   Teaches a moral

   D.   Contains quotes and facts

37. Academically, appropriate literature primarily helps students to:
(Rigorous) (Skill 4.6)

   A. Become better readers

   B. See how the skills they learned are applied to writing

   C. Enjoy library time

   D. Increase academic skills in other content areas

38. Mrs. Gomez sends home book club order forms every month. Which of the following would explain why Mrs. Gomez feels this is so important?
(Easy) (Skill 4.7)

   A. To reduce the number of books the school needs to provide

   B. To earn items for her classroom at a discounted rate

   C. To increase student's enjoyment of reading

   D. To please parents who enjoy book clubs

39. What is the first step in developing writing skills?
(Easy) (Skill 5.1)

   A. Early writing

   B. Experimental writing

   C. Role play writing

   D. Conventional writing

40. A classroom activity involves students writing letters to a mayor to ask for more bike paths to be built. What type of discourse are the students engaged in?
(Easy) (Skill 5.2)

   A. Exposition

   B. Persuasion

   C. Narration

   D. Description

Subarea II. Learning Across the Curriculum

41. **What math principle is reinforced by matching numerals with number words?**
    (Rigorous) (Skill 6.1)

    A.   Sequencing

    B.   Greater than and less than

    C.   Number representations

    D.   Rote counting

42. **Each kindergarten child has a card with the word one, two, three, four, or five on it. As the teacher says a number, the children with the print word for that number stand. What math principle is being practiced?** *(Rigorous) (Skill 6.1)*

    A.   Rote counting

    B.   Number representations

    C.   Number sequencing

    D.   Addition or subtraction

43. **At snack time, three friends break a cracker into three equal parts. What portion of the original cracker does each part represent?** *(Easy) (Skill 6.1)*

    A.   One fourth

    B.   One half

    C.   One whole

    D.   One third

44. **Square is to cube as triangle is to:** *(Rigorous) (Skill 6.1)*

    A.   Sphere

    B.   Rectangle

    C.   Cone

    D.   Tetrahedron

45. **Recognizing if the word *fill* belongs in the word family of *bill, hill,* and *mill* or the word family of *king, sing,* and *wing* is an example of using what math principle?** *(Rigorous) (Skill 6.1)*

    A.   Pattern recognition

    B.   Letter counting

    C.   Counting by threes

    D.   Identity property

46. Third grade students are looking at a circle graph. Most of the graph is yellow. A small wedge of the graph is blue. Each colored section also has a number followed by a symbol. What are the students most likely learning about?
(Rigorous) (Skill 6.1)

A. Addition

B. Venn diagrams

C. Percent

D. Pictographs

47. When a student completes the following number sentence, which math concept is being learned?
(Rigorous) (Skill 6.1)

$15 - \square = 6$

A. Addition/subtraction and basic algebraic concepts

B. Counting and addition/subtraction

C. Counting and basic algebraic concepts

D. Counting and pattern recognition

48. Students are working with a set of rulers and various small objects from the classroom. Which concept are these students exploring?
(Average rigor) (Skill 6.1)

A. Volume

B. Weight

C. Length

D. Temperature

49. A teacher plans an activity that involves students calculating how many chair legs are in the classroom, given that there are 30 chairs and each chair has 4 legs. This activity is introducing the ideas of:
(Average rigor) (Skill 6.1)

A. Probability

B. Statistics

C. Geometry

D. Algebra

50. Students are making three-dimensional figures by folding a net made up of four equilateral triangles. What three-dimensional figure are the students making?
(Rigorous) (Skill 6.1)

A. Cube

B. Tetrahedron

C. Octahedron

D. Cone

51. Students using a measuring cylinder are exploring what concept?
(Average rigor) (Skill 6.1)

A. Volume

B. Weight

C. Length

D. Temperature

52. The term *millimeters* indicates which kind of measurement?
(Easy) (Skill 6.1)

A. Volume

B. Weight

C. Length

D. Temperature

53. Which of the following types of graphs would be best to use to record the eye color of the students in the class?
(Average rigor) (Skill 6.1)

A. Bar graph or circle graph

B. Pictograph or bar graph

C. Line graph or pictograph

D. Line graph or bar graph

54. What type of graph would be best to use to show changes in the height of a plant over the course of a month?
(Average rigor) (Skill 6.1)

A. Circle graph

B. Bar graph

C. Line graph

D. Pictograph

55. A teacher completes a survey of student hair color. The teacher then creates a graph so students can compare how many students have each hair color. What type of graph should be used?
(Rigorous) (Skill 6.1)

A. Bar graph

B. Pictograph

C. Circle graph

D. Line graph

56. **Scientific inquiry begins with:**
(Easy) (Skill 7.1)

   A. A hypothesis

   B. An observation

   C. A conclusion

   D. An experiment

57. **Which of the following can be a source of bias in scientific experiments?**
(Easy) (Skill 7.1)

   A. Investigators

   B. Samples

   C. Instruments

   D. All of the above

58. **Which of the following is a vector quantity that refers to the rate at which an object changes its position?**
(Rigorous) (Skill 7.1)

   A. Speed

   B. Momentum

   C. Velocity

   D. Motion

59. **What is a change that produces new material known as?**
(Average rigor) (Skill 7.2)

   A. Physical change

   B. Chemical change

   C. Phase change

   D. Reversible change

60. **What is a large, rotating, low-pressure system accompanied by heavy precipitation and strong winds known as?**
(Average rigor) (Skill 7.2)

   A. A hurricane

   B. A tornado

   C. A thunderstorm

   D. A tsunami

61. **What is the main benefit of teaching science in a context where it is relevant to the lives of students?**
(Average rigor) (Skill 7.3)

   A. It reduces costs for the school.

   B. It allows science to be integrated with other subjects.

   C. It increases student motivation.

   D. It promotes independence.

62. Which of the following is defined as the identification and application of knowledge to solve a problem?
(Average rigor) (Skill 7.6)

A. Scientific method

B. Technological design

C. Applied science

D. Reverse engineering

63. In which year did the pilgrims arrive on the *Mayflower*?
(Rigorous) (Skill 8.1)

A. 1602

B. 1614

C. 1620

D. 1625

64. What does the First Amendment to the U.S. constitution describe?
(Average rigor) (Skill 8.1)

A. The right to bear arms

B. Right to free speech

C. Freedom of religion

D. Security from the quartering of troops in home

65. What does geography include the study of?
(Easy) (Skill 8.1)

A. Location

B. Distribution of living things

C. Distribution of the earth's features

D. All of the above

66. What term is applied to the process by which humans learn the expectations their society has for their behavior, in order that they might successfully function within that society?
(Rigorous) (Skill 8.1)

A. Cultural diffusion

B. Socialization

C. Assimilation

D. Naturalization

67. The division of a society into different levels based on factors such as race, religion, economic standing, or family heritage is known as:
(Average rigor) (Skill 8.1)

A. Social stratification

B. Class distinction

C. The caste system

D. Assimilation

68. Young children are taught geography skills using which of the following primary types of illustrations? *(Average rigor) (Skill 8.4)*

   A. Legend, grid, scale

   B. Maps, charts, graphs

   C. Topography and demography

   D. Consistent scales and conformality

69. A teacher is giving students a set budget and asking them to assess the different ways they could spend the money. Which subject does this activity help students learn about? *(Average rigor) (Skill 8.4)*

   A. History

   B. Geography

   C. Economics

   D. Politics

70. A student who is observed to often collide with other people while taking part in physical education probably has poor awareness of: *(Rigorous) (Skill 9.1)*

   A. Balance

   B. Space

   C. Speed

   D. Force

71. Which nonlocomotor skill involves a sharp change of direction from the original line of movement? *(Average rigor) (Skill 9.1)*

   A. Bending

   B. Dodging

   C. Pushing

   D. Swaying

72. What is the main target of flexibility training? *(Average rigor) (Skill 9.2)*

   A. Tendons

   B. Ligaments

   C. Joints

   D. Muscles

73. **Which of the following benefits can physical education provide?**
(Easy) (Skill 9.3)

   A.   A sense of belonging

   B.   Increased self-esteem

   C.   Appreciation of beauty

   D.   All of the above

74. **Which of the following activities incorporates physical science with physical education?**
(Rigorous) (Skill 9.6)

   A.   Analyzing how runners can reduce friction

   B.   Studying the use of statistics in sport

   C.   Researching how athletes use sports psychology

   D.   Considering the biochemistry of producing energy

75. **A student art sample book would include cotton balls and sand paper to represent:**
(Easy) (Skill 10.1)

   A.   Color

   B.   Lines

   C.   Texture

   D.   Shape

76. **When discussing color, the intensity of a color refers to the color's:**
(Average rigor) (Skill 10.1)

   A.   Strength

   B.   Value

   C.   Lightness or darkness

   D.   Associated emotions

77. **Which term refers to the juxtaposition of one or more elements in opposition?**
(Average rigor) (Skill 10.1)

   A.   Balance

   B.   Contrast

   C.   Emphasis

   D.   Unity

78. **What should be the first thing taught when introducing dance?**
(Easy) (Skill 10.3)

   A.   Rhythm

   B.   Feelings

   C.   Empathy

   D.   Texture

79. **What would the viewing of a dance company performance be most likely to promote?** *(Average rigor) (Skill 10.5)*

    A. Critical-thinking skills

    B. Appreciation of the arts

    C. Improvisation skills

    D. Music vocabulary

80. **Which activity would be most suitable for beginning students of visual arts?** *(Rigorous) (Skill 10.5)*

    A. Analyzing famous works of arts

    B. Reflecting on the possible meanings of art work

    C. Observing the shapes and forms of common objects

    D. Using blocks to construct three dimensional shapes

Subarea III. Diversity, Collaboration, and Professionalism in the Early Childhood Program

81. **What developmental patterns should a professional teacher assess to meet the needs of each student?** *(Average rigor) (Skill 11.1)*

    A. Academic, regional, and family background

    B. Social, physical, and academic

    C. Academic, physical, and family background

    D. Physical, family, and ethnic background

82. **According to Erikson's theory of psychosocial development, what is the cause of temper tantrums in children aged 1 to 3?** *(Rigorous) (Skill 11.1)*

    A. A desire to be independent
    B. A lack of empathy

    C. A sense of general confusion

    D. An increase in feelings of guilt

83. Why is Kohlberg's theory important to classroom teachers?
(Rigorous) *(Skill 11.1)*

A. It is a theory that explains how language is acquired.

B. It is a theory that explains how complex and logical thought is developed.

C. It is a theory that explains the stages of moral development in a child.

D. It is a theory that explains how higher mental functions develop in a child.

84. Which of the following best explains why emotional upset and emotional abuse can reduce a child's classroom performance?
(Rigorous) *(Skill 11.1)*

A. They reduce the energy that students put towards schoolwork.

B. They lead to a reduction in cognitive ability.

C. They contribute to learning disorders such as dyslexia.

D. They result in the development of behavioral problems.

85. Which of the following is a true statement?
(Rigorous) *(Skill 11.2)*

A. Recess is not important to a child's development.

B. Playtime is only provided in schools to help children release energy.

C. Play has an important and positive role in child development.

D. Solitary play is always an indication that a child has development issues.

86. The stages of play development from infancy stages to early childhood includes a move from:
(Rigorous) *(Skill 11.2)*

A. Cooperative to solitary

B. Solitary to cooperative

C. Competitive to collaborative

D. Collaborative to competitive

87. While children develop at different rates, which of the following can cause learning difficulties?
(Average rigor) (Skill 11.4)

   A.   Lack of sleep

   B.   Poor nutrition

   C.   Prenatal exposure to nicotine

   D.   All of the above

88. A child exhibits the following symptoms: inability to appreciate humor, indifference to physical contact, abnormal social play, and abnormal speech. What is the likely diagnosis for this child?
(Average rigor) (Skill 11.4)

   A.   Separation anxiety

   B.   Mental retardation

   C.   Autism

   D.   Hypochondria

89. What type of disability does a student who talks incessantly using bizarre words most likely have?
(Easy) (Skill 11.4)

   A.   Attention deficit hyperactivity disorder

   B.   Severe emotional stress

   C.   Schizophrenia

   D.   Dyslexia

90. What is a student who has extreme trouble spelling most likely to be identified as?
(Average rigor) (Skill 11.4)

   A.   Dyslexic

   B.   Gifted

   C.   Autistic

   D.   Hyperactive

91. How many stages of intellectual development does Piaget define?
(Easy) (Skill 12.1)

   A.   Two

   B.   Four

   C.   Six

   D.   Eight

92. **A learning activity for students below age eight should focus on:**
(Rigorous) (Skill 12.2)

   A. Complex activities

   B. Applying the information

   C. Short time frames

   D. Challenging students

93. **Providing instruction from various points of view, not only helps students academically, but it also allows them to:**
(Rigorous) (Skill 12.3)

   A. Work cooperatively and contribute to a team

   B. Develop the personal skill of being able to view situations from multiple viewpoints

   C. Become problem solvers with the ability to apply creative thinking to common problems

   D. Develop tolerance and patience

94. **What criteria are used to assess whether a child qualifies for services under IDEA?**
(Rigorous) (Skill 12.5)

   A. Having a disability only

   B. Having a disability and demonstrating educational need only

   C. Demonstrating educational need only

   D. Having a disability, demonstrating educational need, and having financial support

95. **Under the IDEA, Congress provides safeguards for students against schools' actions, including the right to sue in court, and encourages states to develop hearing and mediation systems to resolve disputes. This is known as:**
(Rigorous) (Skill 12.5)

   A. Due process

   B. Mediation

   C. Safe Schools Initiative

   D. Parent involvement

96. **Which type of assessment is the least structured?**
    (Easy) (Skill 12.6)

    A. Observation

    B. Informal continuous assessment

    C. Formal assessment

    D. Standardized testing

97. **Which of the following is the best method for a teacher to use to get to know the students initially?**
    (Average rigor) (Skill 12.6)

    A. Running reading record

    B. Entry survey

    C. Norm-referenced test

    D. Oral presentations

98. **Which type of test is most likely to be a true indication of the content knowledge of ESOL students?**
    (Average rigor) (Skill 12.6)

    A. Oral test

    B. Written test

    C. Timed test

    D. Practical test

99. **Which of the following best explains why teachers should consider carefully observations recorded by other teachers?**
    (Average rigor) (Skill 12.6)

    A. Teachers may be manipulative.

    B. Teachers may be biased.

    C. Teachers may be dishonest.

    D. Teachers may be indifferent.

100. **What are tests, exams, and a science project all examples of?**
    (Easy) (Skill 12.6)

    A. Observation

    B. Informal assessment

    C. Formal assessment

    D. Norm-referenced assessment

101. Which type of assessment would be used to determine if students are meeting national and state learning standards?
(Average rigor) (Skill 12.6)

    A.   Norm-referenced assessments

    B.   Criterion-referenced assessments

    C.   Performance-based assessments

    D.   Observation-based assessments

102. Why are student records often a good indicator of student progress?
(Easy) (Skill 12.6)

    A.   They contain information from several people.

    B.   They show changes over time.

    C.   They contain information gathered over a period of time.

    D.   All of the above

103. Which type of assessment is most likely to be used to assess student interest and motivation?
(Average rigor) (Skill 12.6)

    A.   Rating scales

    B.   Questioning

    C.   Portfolio assessment

    D.   Anecdotal records

104. What are the most powerful factors influencing student's academic focus and success?
(Average rigor) (Skill 12.6)

    A.   Teachers' knowledge and training

    B.   Teachers' preparation and planning

    C.   Students' attitudes and perceptions

    D.   Students' interests and goals

105. **What is an effective way to help a non-English speaking student succeed in class?** *(Rigorous) (Skill 12.6)*

    A. Refer the child to a specialist

    B. Maintain an encouraging, success-oriented atmosphere

    C. Help them assimilate by making them use English exclusively

    D. Help them cope with the content materials you presently use

106. **Teachers must create personalized learning communities where every student is a valued member and contributor of the classroom experiences. Which of the following are effects of a personalized learning environment?** *(Rigorous) (Skill 13.1)*

    A. Decreased drop-out rates among marginalized students

    B. Increased learning affect for students

    C. Decreased unproductive student behavior

    D. All of the above

107. **Which of the following is NOT a communication issue related to diversity within the classroom?** *(Average rigor) (Skill 13.1)*

    A. Learning disorders

    B. Sensitive terminology

    C. Body language

    D. Discussing differing viewpoints and opinions

108. **Which of the following is the most important reason for integrating the curriculum?** *(Average rigor) (Skill 13.2)*

    A. It increases ease of lesson planning.

    B. It meets the needs of diverse students.

    C. It breaks down barriers between subjects.

    D. It narrows the focus of study.

109. **The three areas of differentiated instruction are content, process, and:** *(Easy) (Skill 14.1)*

    A. Application

    B. Product

    C. Assessment

    D. Structure

110. **A teacher attempting to create a differentiated classroom should focus on incorporating activities that:**
(Rigorous) (Skill 14.1)

   A.   Favor academically advanced students

   B.   Challenge special education students to achieve more

   C.   Are suitable for whichever group of students is the majority

   D.   Meet the needs of all the students in the class

111. **What area of differentiated instruction is a teacher focusing on when planning how to teach the material?**
(Average rigor) (Skill 14.1)

   A.   Content

   B.   Process

   C.   Product

   D.   Assessment

112. **When developing lessons, it is important that teachers provide equity in pedagogy so that:**
(Rigorous) (Skill 14.1)

   A.   Unfair labeling of students will not occur

   B.   Student experiences will be positive

   C.   Students will achieve academic success

   D.   All of the above

113. **Which of the following is a widely known curriculum model for early childhood programs?**
(Easy) (Skill 14.1)

   A.   Montessori method

   B.   DISTAR method

   C.   Success for All

   D.   Voyager

114. **What is the most important factor in raising academic outcomes for all students as required in the NCLB law?** *(Rigorous) (Skill 14.1)*

    A.   The curriculum model used

    B.   The quality of instruction in the classroom

    C.   The location of the school

    D.   The number of years of experience the teacher has

115. **Which of the following is NOT one of Gardner's Multiple Intelligences?** *(Average rigor) (Skill 14.1)*

    A.   Intrapersonal

    B.   Musical

    C.   Technological

    D.   Logical/mathematical

116. **Which of the following is NOT a right of parents?** *(Average rigor) (Skill 14.3)*

    A.   To be informed of the teacher's concerns about their child

    B.   To require the teacher to use a certain teaching method

    C.   To administer discipline to their child in the classroom

    D.   Both B and C

117. **When is it appropriate for a teacher to talk to parents about another student's performance?** *(Rigorous) (Skill 14.3)*

    A.   When the parents of the student have been invited to participate

    B.   When the student is having a negative impact on other students

    C.   When the student is performing well and only positive information will be communicated

    D.   When permission to discuss the student has been given by the principal

118. **Which of the following statements would not be appropriate in an anecdotal record about a student?**
(Rigorous) (Skill 14.3)

   A. Jasmine completed only half of the homework assigned.

   B. Jasmine contributed only slightly to class discussions.

   C. Jasmine was not interested in learning the material.

   D. Jasmine did not volunteer to answer any questions.

119. **What should a teacher begin a parent-teacher conference with?**
(Average rigor) (Skill 14.3)

   A. Student weaknesses

   B. Positive comments

   C. Entertaining anecdotes

   D. Issues of concern

120. **Tommy is a student in your class. His parents are deaf. Tommy is struggling with math and you want to contact the parents to discuss the issues. How should you proceed?**
(Rigorous) (Skill 14.3)

   A. Limit contact due to the parents' inability to hear

   B. Use a TTY phone to communicate with the parents

   C. Talk to your administrator to find an appropriate interpreter to help you communicate with the parents personally

   D. Both B and C but not A

121. **You receive a phone call from a parent who is angry about the grade their child receives on the report card. As the conversation continues, the parent becomes verbally abusive and uses curse words. What should you do?**
(Rigorous) (Skill 14.3)

A. Raise your voice to establish your authority.

B. Hang up and get assistance from your administrator.

C. Blame the parent for the poor grade.

D. Apologize over and over and hope that the parent will calm down and stop cursing.

122. **What is the most important factor in improving the developmental and educational gains for students with language delays?**
(Average rigor) (Skill 14.3)

A. Varied teaching procedures

B. The social environment

C. Early intervention

D. Encouraging independence

123. **Because teachers today will deal with an increasingly diverse group of cultures in their classrooms, they must:**
(Average rigor) (Skill 14.3)

A. Ignore the cultures represented

B. Show respect to all parents and families

C. Provide a celebration for each culture represented

D. Focusing on teaching the majority

124. **If child abuse is suspected, what action should a teacher take?**
(Average rigor) (Skill 14.4)

A. Wait to see if the child talks about it again

B. Talk to your supervisor about your concerns

C. Call the child's parent

D. Take no action unless there is proof

125. What is the most important factor in improving the developmental and educational gains for an exceptional child?
(Average rigor) (Skill 14.5)

    A.   Varied teaching procedures

    B.   The social environment

    C.   Early intervention

    D.   Encouraging independence

Post Test: Answer Key

1.	B	43.	D	85.	C
2.	B	44.	D	86.	B
3.	C	45.	A	87.	D
4.	D	46.	C	88.	C
5.	A	47.	A	89.	C
6.	C	48.	C	90.	A
7.	D	49.	D	91.	B
8.	C	50.	B	92.	C
9.	A	51.	A	93.	B
10.	D	52.	C	94.	B
11.	D	53.	B	95.	A
12.	C	54.	C	96.	A
13.	A	55.	A	97.	B
14.	C	56.	B	98.	A
15.	D	57.	D	99.	B
16.	B	58.	C	100.	C
17.	D	59.	B	101.	B
18.	B	60.	A	102.	D
19.	B	61.	C	103.	A
20.	C	62.	B	104.	C
21.	B	63.	C	105.	B
22.	B	64.	C	106.	D
23.	B	65.	D	107.	A
24.	B	66.	B	108.	C
25.	A	67.	A	109.	B
26.	B	68.	B	110.	D
27.	A	69.	C	111.	B
28.	D	70.	B	112.	D
29.	A	71.	B	113.	A
30.	B	72.	D	114.	B
31.	A	73.	D	115.	C
32.	B	74.	A	116.	D
33.	C	75.	C	117.	A
34.	C	76.	A	118.	C
35.	D	77.	B	119.	B
36.	C	78.	A	120.	D
37.	B	79.	B	121.	B
38.	C	80.	C	122.	C
39.	C	81.	B	123.	B
40.	B	82.	A	124.	B
41.	C	83.	C	125.	C
42.	B	84.	A		

Post Test: Rigor Table

	Easy 20%	Average rigor 40%	Rigorous 40%
Question #	4, 21, 27, 33, 34, 35, 36, 38, 39, 40, 43, 52, 56, 57, 65, 73, 75, 78, 89, 91, 96, 100, 102, 109, 113	2, 5, 6, 7, 9, 10, 13, 15, 17, 22, 23, 31, 48, 49, 51, 53, 54, 59, 60, 61, 62, 64, 67, 68, 69, 71, 72, 76, 77, 79, 81, 87, 88, 90, 97, 98, 99, 101, 103, 104, 107, 108, 111, 115, 116, 119, 122, 123, 124, 125	1, 3, 8, 11, 12, 14, 16, 18, 19, 20, 24, 25, 26, 28, 29, 30, 32, 37, 41, 42, 44, 45, 46, 47, 50, 55, 58, 63, 66, 70, 74, 80, 82, 83, 84, 85, 86, 92, 93, 94, 95, 105, 106, 110, 112, 114, 117, 118, 120, 121

Post Test: Rationales with Sample Questions

Subarea I. Language and Literacy Development

1. **A student who has difficulty pronouncing certain words or sounds may be demonstrating which speech and language disorder? (Rigorous) (Skill 1.1)**

    A.   Apraxia
    B.   Articulation Disorder
    C.   Auditory Processing
    D.   Dysarthria

Answer B: Articulation Disorder

When children have difficulty pronouncing specific sounds, they may have an articulation disorder. It is important to remember that certain sounds are not expected to develop until certain ages. In these cases, the errors are age-appropriate and not any sort of disorder.

2. **A language-learning function exists in the brain that makes it easier for children to learn a language below age: (Average rigor) (Skill 1.1)**

    A.   2
    B.   7
    C.   10
    D.   14

Answer B: 7

The most important concept to remember regarding the difference between learning a first language and a second one is that if the learner is approximately age seven or older, learning a second language will occur very differently in the learner's brain than it will had the learner been younger. The reason for this is that there is a language-learning function that exists in young children that appears to go away as they mature. Learning a language prior to age seven is almost guaranteed, with relatively little effort.

3. **A teacher reads a book to students. The students are then encouraged to ask who, what, where, when, and why questions. What is this activity designed to help develop?**
(Rigorous) (Skill 1.2)

   A. Motor skills
   B. Social skills
   C. Higher cognitive skills
   D. Decision making skills

Answer C: Higher cognitive skills

Teaching the art of questioning is one activity that can be used to promote language development. This involves reading a book to the students and allowing them to ask curiosity questions (who, what, why, when and where). This encourages the students to develop higher cognitive skills through questions.

4. **To enhance their students' effective listening skills, teachers can encourage which of the following strategies?**
(Easy) (Skill 1.3)

   A. Associate
   B. Visualize
   C. Repeat
   D. All of the above

Answer D: All of the above

Associating, visualizing, repeating and concentrating are four listed strategies to increase listening skills in students.

5. **The relationship between oral language and reading skills is best described as:**
(Average rigor) (Skill 1.4)

   A. Reciprocal
   B. Inverse
   C. Opposite
   D. There is no relationship.

Answer A: Reciprocal

A highly developed oral language vocabulary helps to build reading skills comprehension. The inverse is true as well, with highly developed reading and comprehension skills helping to develop oral language skills.

6.   During which stage of language acquisition would it be most inappropriate to ask a student to make a long speech?
(*Average rigor*) (*Skill 1.5*)

A.   Intermediate fluency
B.   Emergent speech
C.   Early production
D.   Advanced fluency

Answer C: Early production

The second phase of language acquisition is early production. This is where the student can actually start to produce the target language. It is quite limited, and teachers most likely should not expect students to produce eloquent speeches during this time.

7.   Mr. Adams uses a short story about early train travel as part of a history lesson. This shows that literature:
(*Average rigor*) (*Skill 1.6*)

A.   Can be used to expand students' vocabulary
B.   Can be used to build students' communication skills
C.   Can be used to help students empathize
D.   Can be used to enhance other areas of the curriculum

Answer D: Can be used to enhance other areas of the curriculum

"Learning across the curriculum" can be enhanced by using literature as another means to convey essential information. Using a short story with a subject related to history could be used to enhance the learning of history.

8.   Which of the following is NOT a motivation behind providing reading activities, including reading aloud, to young children?
(*Rigorous*) (*Skill 1.6*)

A.   Developing word consciousness skills
B.   Developing functions of print skills
C.   Developing phonics skills
D.   Developing language skills

Answer C: Developing phonics skills

There are almost unlimited positive reasons for encouraging adults to provide reading activities for young children. While it can be true that reading aloud may improve the phonics skills for some students, it is not a motivation for providing such activities to students.

9. Jose moved to the United States last month. He speaks little to no English at this time. His teacher is teaching the class about habitats in science and has chosen to read a story about various habitats to the class. The vocabulary is difficult. What should Jose's teacher do with Jose?
(Average rigor) (Skill 1.7)

A. Provide Jose with additional opportunities to learn about habitats
B. Read the story to Jose multiple times
C. Show Jose pictures of habitats from his native country
D. Excuse Jose from the assignment

Answer A: Provide Jose with additional opportunities to learn about habitats

Students who are learning English should be exposed to a variety of opportunities to learn the same concepts as native speakers. Content should not be changed, but the manner in which it is presented and reinforced should be changed.

10. Students who are learning English as a second language often require which of the following to process new information?
(Average rigor) (Skill 1.7)

A. Translators
B. Reading tutors
C. Instruction in their native language
D. Additional time and repetitions

Answer D: Additional time and repetitions

While there are varying thoughts and theories into the most appropriate instruction for ESL students, much ground can be gained by simply providing additional repetitions and time for new concepts. It is important to include visuals and the other senses into every aspect of this instruction.

11. **Which of the following demonstrates the difference between phonemic awareness and phonological awareness?**
(Rigorous) (Skill 2.1)

    A.   Phonemic awareness is the understanding that words are made up of sounds, while phonological awareness is the understanding that letters are the representation of sounds.
    B.   Phonemic awareness is the ability to rhyme and identify beginning sounds, while phonological awareness is the understanding that letters are the representation of sounds.
    C.   Phonemic awareness is the ability to distinguish sounds, while phonological awareness is the understanding that letters are the representation of sounds.
    D.   Phonemic awareness is the understanding that words are made up of sounds, while phonological awareness is the ability to distinguish sounds.

Answer D: Phonemic awareness is the understanding that words are made up of sounds, while phonological awareness is the ability to distinguish sounds.

The concept of phonemic awareness and phonological awareness are often misunderstand and confused. It is important to understand clearly the difference and realize they cannot and should not be used interchangeably.

12. **Ms. Smith hands each child in the classroom a letter of the alphabet. She then challenges each child to go around the classroom and find at least five things in the classroom which begin with that letter. What is Ms. Smith teaching the students?**
(Rigorous) (Skill 2.1)

    A.   Phonemic awareness
    B.   Vocabulary
    C.   Meaning of print
    D.   Letter identification

Answer C: Meaning of print

Connecting letters to objects or sounds helps the students begin to recognize that print has meaning. This is an essential foundation skill for students to develop before phonics instruction is begun.

13. **Which of the following areas correlate with a child's general language skills?**
    (Average rigor) (Skill 2.1)

    A. Reading comprehension
    B. Phonics
    C. Phonemic awareness
    D. All of the above

Answer A: Reading comprehension

It has been found that a child's overall general language skills have a direct correlation between his/her reading comprehension skills. This demonstrates the relationship between language skills and literacy skills.

14. **Which of the following is NOT a core part of phonics instruction?**
    (Rigorous) (Skill 2.2)

    A. Alphabetic principle
    B. Vowel Patterns
    C. Letter names
    D. Consonant Patterns

Answer C: Letter names

While it is consistent and regular instruction in early childhood classrooms, the names in and of themselves are not direct phonics instruction. Tying the sound and symbol is phonics.

15. **Which of the following explains a significant difference between phonics and phonemic awareness?**
    (Average rigor) (Skill 2.2)

    A. Phonics involves print, while phonemic awareness involves language.
    B. Phonics is harder than phonemic awareness.
    C. Phonics involves sounds, while phonemic awareness involves letters.
    D. Phonics is the application of sounds to print, while phonemic awareness is oral.

Answer D: Phonics is the application of sounds to print, while phonemic awareness is oral.

Both phonics and phonemic awareness activities involve sounds, but it is with phonics that the application of these sounds is applied to print. Phonemic awareness is an oral activity

16. **Ms. Arnold has her first grade students sitting around her word wall. Which of the following activities would be inappropriate for her to use with this group of students?**
    (Rigorous) (Skill 2.3)

    A.   Having the students clap out the syllables of some of the displayed words
    B.   Discussing word meanings
    C.   Teaching new vocabulary words in isolation
    D.   Finding all the words on the wall that meet certain criteria

Answer B: Discussing word meanings

While brief discussions of meanings might be used during word wall activities, it is not the purpose of a word wall. Meanings should be discussed in context rather than in the isolation of word walls. It might be appropriate to develop a vocabulary board, where words, pictures and meanings are connected instead.

17. **The basic features of the alphabetic principle include:**
    (Average rigor) (Skill 2.4)

    A.   Students need to be able to take spoken words apart and blend different sounds together to make new words
    B.   Students need to apply letter sounds to all their reading
    C.   The teaching of the alphabetic principle usually begins in Kindergarten
    D.   All of the above

Answer D: All of the above

All the stated answers above are features of the alphabetic principle. Another one not mentioned in the list above is that teachers need to use a systematic, effective program in order to teach children to read.

18. **Which of these describes the best way to teach spelling?**
    (Rigorous) (Skill 2.5)

    A.   At the same time that grammar and sentence structure is taught.
    B.   Within the context of meaningful language experiences.
    C.   Independently so that students can concentrate on spelling.
    D.   In short lessons as students pick up spelling almost immediately.

Answer B: Within the context of meaningful language experiences.

Spelling should be taught within the context of meaningful language experiences. Giving a child a list of words to learn to spell and then testing the child on the words every Friday will not aid in the development of spelling. The child must be able to use the words in context and they must have some meaning for the child. The assessment of how well a child can spell or where there are problems also has to be done within a meaningful environment.

19. **When students know that letters stand for a message, they are said to be in the_____ stage of spelling.**
    (Rigorous) (Skill 2.5)

    A.   Non-phonemic
    B.   Pre-phonemic
    C.   Early phonemic
    D.   Letter-name sounding

Answer B: Pre-phonemic

The pre-phonemic stage of spelling is the first stage of spelling where the students know that letters stand for a message, but they cannot link the spelling to meaningful pronunciation yet. In the early phonemic stage, students are beginning to understand spelling and can start to write letters. Finally, letter-name spelling is when students spell some words correctly, and they are developing a sight vocabulary. There is no non-phonemic stage of spelling.

20. **A student can read spontaneously the words *the*, *there*, *boy*, and *book*. These words make up the student's:**
    (Rigorous) (Skill 2.5)

    A. Personal vocabulary
    B. Recognition vocabulary
    C. Sight vocabulary
    D. Working vocabulary

Answer C: Sight vocabulary

Sight words are words that the reader learns to read spontaneously either because of frequency or lack of conformity to orthographic rules. For example, words like 'the', 'what', and 'there' because they don't conform to rules, and words like 'boy', 'girl', and 'book' because they are seen very frequently in early reading texts.

21 **To decode is to:**
    (Easy) (Skill 3.1)

    A. Construct meaning
    B. Sound out a printed sequence of letters
    C. Use a special code to decipher a message
    D. Revise for errors in grammar

Answer B: Sound out a printed sequence of letters

Decoding is the process students use to figure out unknown words when reading.

22. **Michael keeps using phrases such as "she go to the store." Which of the following areas should Michael's teacher work on to improve Michael's skills?**
    (Average rigor) (Skill 3.2)

    A. Morphology
    B. Syntax
    C. Phonics
    D. Semantics

Answer B: Syntax

Syntax is the understanding of the rules of the English language to put words together in a grammatically appropriate manner. Michael is having difficulty with this concept and could benefit from some more instruction in this area.

23. **A teacher is showing students how to construct grammatically correct sentences. What is the teacher focusing on?**
(Average rigor) (Skill 3.2)

A. Morphology
B. Syntax
C. Semantics
D. Pragmatics

Answer B: Syntax

Syntax refers to the rules or patterned relationships that correctly create phrases and sentences from words. When readers develop an understanding of syntax, they begin to understand the structure of how sentences are built, and eventually the beginning of grammar.

24. **Vocabulary of children assessed at age six has been shown to be a strong prediction of which future skill at age 16?**
(Rigorous) (Skill 3.4)

A. Reading Accuracy
B. Reading Comprehension
C. SAT scores
D. Analogy Completion

Answer B: Reading Comprehension

The correlation between vocabulary in young children and future reading comprehension skills provides further evidence of the importance of building vocabulary and oral language skills in the early childhood years.

25. **Students are about to read a text that contains words that will need to be understood for the students to understand the text. When should the vocabulary be introduced to students?**
(Rigorous) (Skill 3.4)

A. Before reading
B. During reading
C. After reading
D. It should not be introduced.

Answer A: Before reading

Vocabulary should be introduced before reading if there are words within the text which are definitely keys necessary for reading comprehension.

26. **Which of the following correctly describes the importance of developing fluent reading skills?**
   (Rigorous) (Skill 4.1)

   A. Automaticity with text is necessary to be considered a reader.
   B. Fluency directly correlates to comprehension.
   C. Prosody allows students to sound better when reading aloud.
   D. Fluency is measured on high stakes tests.

Answer B: Fluency directly correlates to comprehension.

Research over the years has shown a correlation between adequate rates of fluency and student's comprehension. It is important to know appropriate reading rates at different grade levels and to realize that fluency has different levels: letter fluency, sound fluency, word fluency, phrase fluency, and finally oral reading fluency.

27. **Which of the following is NOT a component of reading fluency?**
   (Easy) (Skill 4.1)

   A. Phoneme knowledge
   B. Accuracy
   C. Rate
   D. Automaticity

Answer A: Phoneme knowledge

Accuracy, rate, prosody, and automaticity are the main components of reading fluency. Phoneme knowledge allows students to better decode and read basic words. This will eventually help with reading fluency, but is more of a subcomponent of a student's accuracy in reading.

28. **Ms. Chomski is presenting a new story to her class of first graders. In the story, a family visits their grandparents where they all gather around a record player and listen to music. Many students do not understand what a record player is, especially some children for whom English is not their first language. Which of the following would Ms. Chomski be best to do?**
(Rigorous) (Skill 4.1)

    A.   Discuss what a record player is with her students
    B.   Compare a record player with a CD player
    C.   Have students look up record player in a dictionary
    D.   Show the students a picture of a record player

Answer D: Show the students a picture of a record player

The most effective method for ensuring adequate comprehension is through direct experience. Sometimes this is not able to be completed and therefore it is necessary to utilize pictures or other visual aids to provide the students with experience in another mode besides oral language.

29. **George has read his second graders three formats of the story "The Three Little Pigs." One is the traditional version, one is written from the wolf's point of view, and the third is written from the first pig's point of view. As George leads a discussion on the three texts with his students, he is trying to help his students develop their ability to:**
(Rigorous) (Skill 4.2)

    A.   Compare and contrast texts
    B.   Understand point of view
    C.   Recognize metaphors
    D.   Rewrite fictional stories

Answer A: Compare and contrast texts

George understands the importance of developing critical thinking skills in young children. He has read three different formats of the same story in order to help his students develop their ability to compare texts.

30. **Mr. Stine put puppet making materials in his art center after he read the children a story. He asked the students who had chosen to make puppets to use them to retell the story he read in front of the class. Mr. Stine was helping the children:**
(Rigorous))(Skill 4.2)

   A.   Improve their art skills
   B.   Respond to literature
   C.   Improve their oral presentation skills
   D.   Increase their listening skills

Answer B: Respond to literature

31. **What type of literature are characters, settings, and themes, interpretations, opinions, theories, and research usually found in?**
(Average rigor) (Skill 4.3)

   A.   Non-fiction
   B.   Fairy tale
   C.   Fiction
   D.   Folktales

Answer A: Non-fiction

In fiction, students can generally expect to see plot, characters, setting, and themes. In nonfiction, students may see a plot, characters, settings, and themes, but they will also experience interpretations, opinions, theories, research, and other elements.

32. **Teaching students how to interpret _____ involves evaluating a text's headings, subheadings, bolded words, and side notes.**
(Rigorous) (Skill 4.4)

   A.   Graphic organizers
   B.   Text structures
   C.   Textual marking
   D.   Summaries

Answer B: Text structures

Studying text structures, including the table of contents, glossary, index, headings, etc., is an excellent way for students to increase comprehension of a text. Knowledge of these tools helps students to understand the organization and flow of their reading.

33. **Which of the following types of children's literature would you be unlikely to utilize in a kindergarten classroom?** *(Easy) (Skill 4.6)*

   A. Fable
   B. Science fiction
   C. Epic
   D. Fairy tale

Answer C: Epic

It would be unlikely that you would use a full epic in a kindergarten classroom. The complexity of a combination poem and story to the extent of an epic story would be difficult for this particular age range to understand.

34. **Which of the following is NOT a major genre of young children's literature?** *(Easy) (Skill 4.6)*

   A. Science fiction
   B. Action and adventure
   C. Current events
   D. Biography

Answer C: Current events

The major themes of young children's literature can be classified into seven major genres. They are: science fiction; fantasy; horror and ghost stories; action and adventure; historical fiction; biography; and educational books.

35. **Which of the following is an important criterion for evaluating children's literature?**
(Easy) (Skill 4.6)

 A. Character development
 B. Appropriate reading level
 C. Cultural diversity
 D. All of the above

Answer D: All of the above

In selecting appropriate literature for children, teachers must consider several factors. Primary among these factors is the composition of the class (including diversity) and the preferences of the children. Children love to identify with the characters in books; therefore it is important to select books with characters that provide positive role models for children. Books should be chosen at an appropriate reading level and should be challenging enough to promote vocabulary growth.

36. **Which of the following is a defining characteristic of a fable?**
(Easy) (Skill 4.6)

 A. Includes repetition and rhyme
 B. Based on true events
 C. Teaches a moral
 D. Contains quotes and facts

Answer C: Teaches a moral

The common characteristics of fables are animals that act like humans, a focus on revealing human foibles, and teaching a moral or lesson.

37. **Academically, appropriate literature primarily helps students to:**
    (Rigorous) (Skill 4.6)

    A. Become better readers
    B. See how the skills they learned are applied to writing
    C. Enjoy library time
    D. Increase academic skills in other content areas

Answer B: See how the skills they learned are applied to writing

When students are exposed to appropriate literature selections, as well as are taught to select appropriate texts for themselves, they are able to observe how the reading and writing skills they learn in classroom mini-lessons are applied to published writing. Published works are an excellent place for students to see not only proper conventions of grammar, but "real-life" examples of imagery and figurative language.

38. **Mrs. Gomez sends home book club order forms every month. Which of the following would explain why Mrs. Gomez feels this is so important?**
    (Easy) (Skill 4.7)

    A. To reduce the number of books the school needs to provide
    B. To earn items for her classroom at a discounted rate
    C. To increase student's enjoyment of reading
    D. To please parents who enjoy book clubs

Answer C: To increase student's enjoyment of reading

In the case of book clubs, students can pick books that spark their interest. Mrs. Gomez understands that it is important for students to enjoy reading and wants to provide as many opportunities as possible for this to happen within her classroom.

39. **What is the first step in developing writing skills?**
    (Easy) (Skill 5.1)

    A. Early writing
    B. Experimental writing
    C. Role play writing
    D. Conventional writing

Answer C: Role play writing

Children develop writing skills through a series of steps. These steps are: role play writing, experimental writing, early writing, and then conventional writing. In the role play writing stage, the child writes in scribbles and assigns a message to the symbols. Even though an adult would not be able to read the writing, the child can read what is written although it may not be the same each time the child reads it. S/he will be able to read back the writing because of prior knowledge that print carries a meaning.

40. **A classroom activity involves students writing letters to a mayor to ask for more bike paths to be built. What type of discourse are the students engaged in?**
    (Easy) (Skill 5.2)

    A. Exposition
    B. Persuasion
    C. Narration
    D. Description

Answer B: Persuasion

Persuasion is a piece of writing, a poem, a play, a speech whose purpose is to change the minds of the audience members or to get them to do something. A letter to a mayor asking for a bike path to be built is being writing to convince the mayor to do something.

Subarea II. Learning Across the Curriculum

41. **What math principle is reinforced by matching numerals with number words?**
(Rigorous) (Skill 6.1)

   A. Sequencing
   B. Greater than and less than
   C. Number representations
   D. Rote counting

Answer C: Number representations

The students are practicing recognition that a numeral (such as 5) has a corresponding number word (five) that represents the same math concept. They are not putting numbers in order (sequencing), and they are not comparing two numbers for value (greater than or less than). In this activity, students are also not counting in order just for the sake of counting (rote counting).

42. **Each kindergarten child has a card with the word one, two, three, four, or five on it. As the teacher says a number, the children with the print word for that number stand. What math principle is being practiced?**
(Rigorous) (Skill 6.1)

   A. Rote counting
   B. Number representations
   C. Number sequencing
   D. Addition or subtraction

Answer B: Number representations

In this activity, students are practicing different ways to represent numbers (verbal word, printed word). They are not rote counting (counting without meaning). They are not arranging numbers in order (sequencing), and they are not adding or subtracting two numbers.

43. **At snack time, three friends break a cracker into three equal parts. What portion of the original cracker does each part represent?**
    (Easy) (Skill 6.1)

    A. One fourth
    B. One half
    C. One whole
    D. One third

Answer D: One third

If the cracker is broken into three equal parts, each part represents one third of the whole.

44. **Square is to cube as triangle is to:**
    (Rigorous) (Skill 6.1)

    A. Sphere
    B. Rectangle
    C. Cone
    D. Tetrahedron

Answer D: Tetrahedron

A square is a two-dimensional polygon, and a cube is a three-dimensional solid made up of squares. A triangle is a two-dimensional polygon, and a tetrahedron is a three-dimensional solid made up of triangles.

45. **Recognizing if the word *fill* belongs in the word family of *bill, hill,* and *mill* or the word family of *king, sing,* and *wing* is an example of using what math principle?**
    (Rigorous) (Skill 6.1)

    A. Pattern recognition
    B. Letter counting
    C. Counting by threes
    D. Identity property

Answer A: Pattern recognition

To understand which is the correct word family for *fill*, the student must recognize the pattern *i-l-l* as opposed to the pattern *i-n-g*.

46. **Third grade students are looking at a circle graph. Most of the graph is yellow. A small wedge of the graph is blue. Each colored section also has a number followed by a symbol. What are the students most likely learning about?**
    (Rigorous) (Skill 6.1)

    A. Addition
    B. Venn diagrams
    C. Percent
    D. Pictographs

Answer C: Percent

The symbol after the numbers of the sections indicates that students are learning about percents instead of an exact number.

47. **When a student completes the following number sentence, which math concept is being learned?**
    (Rigorous) (Skill 6.1)

    $15 - \square = 6$

    A. Addition/subtraction and basic algebraic concepts
    B. Counting and addition/subtraction
    C. Counting and basic algebraic concepts
    D. Counting and pattern recognition

Answer A: Addition/subtraction and basic algebraic concepts

Students may use basic addition or subtraction by rearranging the numbers. They are also demonstrating the algebraic concept of finding the value of a missing number.

48. **Students are working with a set of rulers and various small objects from the classroom. Which concept are these students exploring?**
    (Average rigor) (Skill 6.1)

    A. Volume
    B. Weight
    C. Length
    D. Temperature

Answer C: Length

The use of a ruler indicates that the activity is based on exploring length.

49. A teacher plans an activity that involves students calculating how many chair legs are in the classroom, given that there are 30 chairs and each chair has 4 legs. This activity is introducing the ideas of: *(Average rigor) (Skill 6.1)*

    A.   Probability
    B.   Statistics
    C.   Geometry
    D.   Algebra

Answer D: Algebra

This activity involves recognizing patterns. It could also involve problem-solving by developing an expression that represents the problem. Activities such as this do not introduce the terms of algebra, but they introduce some of the ideas of algebra.

50. Students are making three-dimensional figures by folding a net made up of four equilateral triangles. What three-dimensional figure are the students making?
(Rigorous) (Skill 6.1)

    A.   Cube
    B.   Tetrahedron
    C.   Octahedron
    D.   Cone

Answer B: Tetrahedron

A net is a two-dimensional figure that can be cut out and folded up to make a three-dimensional solid. A tetrahedron is made by folding a net made up of four equilateral triangles.

51. Students using a measuring cylinder are exploring what concept?
(Average rigor) (Skill 6.1)

    A.   Volume
    B.   Weight
    C.   Length
    D.   Temperature

Answer A: Volume

The amount of liquid in a cylinder would be a measure of volume. A balance or scale would be used to measure weight. A ruler or meter stick would be used to measure length. A thermometer would be used to measure temperature.

52. **The term *millimeters* indicates which kind of measurement?**
    (Easy) (Skill 6.1)

    A.   Volume
    B.   Weight
    C.   Length
    D.   Temperature

Answer C: Length

The term *millimeters* is a reference to length in the metric system.

53. **Which of the following types of graphs would be best to use to record the eye color of the students in the class?**
    (Average rigor) (Skill 6.1)

    A.   Bar graph or circle graph
    B.   Pictograph or bar graph
    C.   Line graph or pictograph
    D.   Line graph or bar graph

Answer B: Pictograph or bar graph

A pictograph or a line graph could be used. In this activity, a line graph would not be used because it shows change over time. Although a circle graph could be used to show a percentage of students with brown eyes, blue eyes, etc. that representation would be too advanced for early childhood students.

54. **What type of graph would be best to use to show changes in the height of a plant over the course of a month?**
    (Average rigor) (Skill 6.1)

    A.   Circle graph
    B.   Bar graph
    C.   Line graph
    D.   Pictograph

Answer C: Line graph

A line graph shows trends over time. A line graph would show how the plant's height changed over time.

55. **A teacher completes a survey of student hair color. The teacher then creates a graph so students can compare how many students have each hair color.   What type of graph should be used?**
    (Rigorous) (Skill 6.1)

    A. Bar graph
    B. Pictograph
    C. Circle graph
    D. Line graph

Answer A: Bar graph

Bar graphs are used to compare various quantities. In this case, the bar graph would show the number of students with each eye color. By looking at the graph, students would be able to compare how many students have each eye color.

56. **Scientific inquiry begins with:**
    (Easy) (Skill 7.1)

    A. A hypothesis
    B. An observation
    C. A conclusion
    D. An experiment

Answer B: An observation

Observations, however general they may seem, lead scientists to create a viable question and an educated guess (hypothesis) about what to expect. The hypothesis can be tested by an experiment, and a conclusion drawn based on the experiment.

57. **Which of the following can be a source of bias in scientific experiments?**
    (Easy) (Skill 7.1)

    A. Investigators
    B. Samples
    C. Instruments
    D. All of the above

Answer D: All of the above

Although bias related to the investigator, the sample, the method, or the instrument may not be completely avoidable in every case, it is important to know the possible sources of bias and how bias could affect the evidence. Moreover, scientists need to be attentive to possible bias in their own work as well as that of other scientists.

58. **Which of the following is a vector quantity that refers to the rate at which an object changes its position?**
    (Rigorous) (Skill 7.1)

    A. Speed
    B. Momentum
    C. Velocity
    D. Motion

Answer C: Velocity

Speed is a scalar quantity that refers to how fast an object is moving. Velocity is a vector quantity that refers to the rate at which an object changes its position.

59. **What is a change that produces new material known as?**
    (Average rigor) *(Skill 7.2)*

    A. Physical change
    B. Chemical change
    C. Phase change
    D. Reversible change

Answer B: Chemical change

Matter constantly changes. A physical change is a change that does not produce a new substance. The freezing and melting of water is an example of physical change. A chemical change (or chemical reaction) is any change of a substance into one or more other substances.

60. **What is a large, rotating, low-pressure system accompanied by heavy precipitation and strong winds known as?**
(Average rigor) (Skill 7.2)

A. A hurricane
B. A tornado
C. A thunderstorm
D. A tsunami

Answer A: A hurricane

Hurricanes are storms that develop when warm, moist air carried by trade winds rotates around a low-pressure "eye". These form a large, rotating, low-pressure system and are accompanied by heavy precipitation and strong winds. They are also known as tropical cyclones or typhoons.

61. **What is the main benefit of teaching science in a context where it is relevant to the lives of students?**
(Average rigor) (Skill 7.3)

A. It reduces costs for the school.
B. It allows science to be integrated with other subjects.
C. It increases student motivation.
D. It promotes independence.

Answer C: It increases student motivation.

If learning is connected to everyday life, students are motivated because they can easily see its relevance. If they are taught about something remote, they will not be able to relate, and the result is decreased interest, decreased motivation to study, and a general decrease in learning.

62. **Which of the following is defined as the identification and application of knowledge to solve a problem?**
(Average rigor) (Skill 7.6)

A. Scientific method
B. Technological design
C. Applied science
D. Reverse engineering

Answer B: Technological design

Technological design is the identification of a problem and the application of scientific knowledge to solve the problem.

63. **In which year did the pilgrims arrive on the *Mayflower*?**
    (Rigorous) (Skill 8.1)

    A. 1602
    B. 1614
    C. 1620
    D. 1625

Answer C: 1620

The real history of Massachusetts began in 1620 with the arrival of 102 pilgrims who arrived in search of a place that allowed them to worship as they chose. The *Mayflower* brought them to Plymouth, where they struggled against the elements to survive with little food. Almost half of the pilgrims died during their first winter in Massachusetts. The spring and summer allowed a bountiful harvest, and the first Thanksgiving Day was a great celebration.

64. **What does the First Amendment to the U.S. constitution describe?**
    (Average rigor) (Skill 8.1)

    A. The right to bear arms
    B. Right to free speech
    C. Freedom of religion
    D. Security from the quartering of troops in home

Answer C: Freedom of religion

The first ten amendments to the U.S. Constitution are also known as the Bill of Rights. They are summarized as follows:

1. Freedom of Religion.
2. Right To Bear Arms.
3. Security from the quartering of troops in homes.
4. Right against unreasonable search and seizures.
5. Right against self-incrimination.
6. Right to trial by jury, right to legal council.
7. Right to jury trial for civil actions.
8. No cruel or unusual punishment allowed.
9. These rights shall not deny other rights the people enjoy.
10. Powers not mentioned in the Constitution shall be retained by the states or the people.

65. **What does geography include the study of?**
     (Easy) (Skill 8.1)

     A.   Location
     B.   Distribution of living things
     C.   Distribution of the earth's features
     D.   All of the above

Answer D: All of the above

Geography involves studying location and how living things and earth's features are distributed throughout the earth. It includes where animals, people, and plants live and the effects of their relationship with earth's physical features.

66. **What term is applied to the process by which humans learn the**
     expectations their society has for their behavior, in order that they
     might successfully function within that society?
     (Rigorous) (Skill 8.1)

     A.   Cultural diffusion
     B.   Socialization
     C.   Assimilation
     D.   Naturalization

Answer B: Socialization

Socialization is the process by which humans learn the expectations their society has for their behavior, in order that they might successfully function within that society. Socialization takes place in children primarily as they learn and are taught the rules and norms of their culture.

67. **The division of a society into different levels based on factors such as race, religion, economic standing, or family heritage is known as:**
    (Average rigor) (Skill 8.1)

    A. Social stratification
    B. Class distinction
    C. The caste system
    D. Assimilation

Answer A: Social stratification

Social Stratification is the division of a society into different levels based on factors such as race, religion, economic standing, or family heritage. Various types of social stratification may be closely related. For instance, stratification by race may result in people of one race being relegated to a certain economic class as well.

68. **Young children are taught geography skills using which of the following primary types of illustrations?**
    (Average rigor) (Skill 8.4)

    A. Legend, grid, scale
    B. Maps, charts, graphs
    C. Topography and demography
    D. Consistent scales and conformality

Answer B: Maps, charts, graphs

We use illustrations of various sorts because it is often easier to demonstrate a given idea visually instead of orally. Ideas presented visually in some manner are generally easier to understand and to comprehend than simply getting an idea across verbally. Among the more common illustrations used are various types of maps, graphs and charts.

69. **A teacher is giving students a set budget and asking them to assess the different ways they could spend the money. Which subject does this activity help students learn about?**
(Average rigor) (Skill 8.4)

    A.   History
    B.   Geography
    C.   Economics
    D.   Politics

Answer C: Economics

Economics is the study of how a society allocates its scarce resources to satisfy what are basically unlimited and competing wants. Part of economics involves considering how to allocate money when there are unlimited options for spending the money. This activity helps students understand basic concepts of economics.

70. **A student who is observed to often collide with other people while taking part in physical education probably has poor awareness of:**
(Rigorous) (Skill 9.1)

    A.   Balance
    B.   Space
    C.   Speed
    D.   Force

Answer B: Space

When performing physical activities, students incorporate space, direction, and speed concepts. Students who understand these concepts generally move with confidence and avoid collisions. The space concept is most beneficial in helping a student avoid collisions.

71. **Which nonlocomotor skill involves a sharp change of direction from the original line of movement?**
(Average rigor) (Skill 9.1)

   A. Bending
   B. Dodging
   C. Pushing
   D. Swaying

Answer B: Dodging

Nonlocomotor skills are ones where there is little or no movement of one's base of support and where there is no change of position. Dodging is a nonlocomotor skill that involves a sharp change of direction from the original line of movement.

72. **What is the main target of flexibility training?**
(Average rigor) (Skill 9.2)

   A. Tendons
   B. Ligaments
   C. Joints
   D. Muscles

Answer D: Muscles

Flexibility training can focus on muscles, joints, ligaments, or tendons. However, muscles are the main targets of flexibility training. The main method used to increase muscle flexibility is stretching.

73. **Which of the following benefits can physical education provide?**
(Easy) (Skill 9.3)

   A. A sense of belonging
   B. Increased self-esteem
   C. Appreciation of beauty
   D. All of the above

Answer D: All of the above

Physical education provides a wide range of benefits, including physical, emotional, and social benefits. These include a sense of belonging, increased self-esteem, appreciation of beauty, good sportsmanship, increased humanism, valuable social experiences, and improved health.

74. **Which of the following activities incorporates physical science with physical education?**
(Rigorous) (Skill 9.6)

   A.   Analyzing how runners can reduce friction
   B.   Studying the use of statistics in sport
   C.   Researching how athletes use sports psychology
   D.   Considering the biochemistry of producing energy

Answer A: Analyzing how runners can reduce friction

Physical education can be incorporated with other learning areas, such as physical science, mathematics, natural science, and kinesiology. Analyzing how runners can reduce friction is an example of incorporating physical education with physical science.

75. **A student art sample book would include cotton balls and sand paper to represent:**
(Easy) (Skill 10.1)

   A.   Color
   B.   Lines
   C.   Texture
   D.   Shape

Answer C: Texture

Texture refers to the way something feels because of the tactile quality of its surface. An art sample book can include materials such as cotton balls and sand paper as examples of different textures.

76. **When discussing color, the intensity of a color refers to the color's:**
    (Average rigor) (Skill 10.1)

    A. Strength
    B. Value
    C. Lightness or darkness
    D. Associated emotions

Answer A: Strength

Color is an important consideration when viewing art. Color can be considered in more depth by focusing on intensity, which is the strength of the color, and value, which is the lightness or darkness of the color.

77. **Which term refers to the juxtaposition of one or more elements in opposition?**
    (Average rigor) (Skill 10.1)

    A. Balance
    B. Contrast
    C. Emphasis
    D. Unity

Answer B: Contrast

The principles of visual are that students should be introduced to include abstract, background, balance, contrast, emphasis, sketch, texture, and unity. Contrast is the juxtaposition of one or more elements in opposition, for the purpose of showing their differences.

78. **What should be the first thing taught when introducing dance?**
    (Easy) (Skill 10.3)

    A. Rhythm
    B. Feelings
    C. Empathy
    D. Texture

Answer A: Rhythm

Rhythm is the basis of dance. Teaching dance should begin by focusing on rhythm. This can be achieved through activities such as children clapping their hands or tapping their feet to express rhythm.

79. **What would the viewing of a dance company performance be most likely to promote?**
(Average rigor) (Skill 10.5)

    A.   Critical-thinking skills
    B.   Appreciation of the arts
    C.   Improvisation skills
    D.   Music vocabulary

Answer B: Appreciation of the arts

Live performances are an important part of learning arts and help to develop aesthetic appreciation of the arts. A dance company performance is one example of a live performance that students could attend.

80. **Which activity would be most suitable for beginning students of visual arts?**
(Rigorous) (Skill 10.5)

    A.   Analyzing famous works of arts
    B.   Reflecting on the possible meanings of art work
    C.   Observing the shapes and forms of common objects
    D.   Using blocks to construct three dimensional shapes

Answer C: Observing the shapes and forms of common objects

Beginning students of visual arts should be learning to develop their observation skills, such as by observing objects or the environment and noting features such as shape, color, size, repeating patterns, or other aspects. Students can then progress to hands-on activities and later to analysis activities.

Subarea III. Diversity, Collaboration, and Professionalism in the Early Childhood Program

81. **What developmental patterns should a professional teacher assess to meet the needs of each student?**
    (Average rigor) (Skill 11.1)

    A. Academic, regional, and family background
    B. Social, physical, and academic
    C. Academic, physical, and family background
    D. Physical, family, and ethnic background

Answer B: Social, physical, and academic

The effective teacher applies knowledge of physical, social, and academic developmental patterns and of individual differences, to meet the instructional needs of all students in the classroom.

82. **According to Erikson's theory of psychosocial development, what is the cause of temper tantrums in children aged 1 to 3?**
    (Rigorous) (Skill 11.1)

    A. A desire to be independent
    B. A lack of empathy
    C. A sense of general confusion
    D. An increase in feelings of guilt

Answer A: A desire to be independent

Erikson's theory of psychosocial development describes how humans go through eights stages of development as they go from infancy to adulthood. The Young Childhood stage occurs from ages 1 to 3. During this stage, children want to be independent. If children are unable to be independent, they can use temper tantrums as a way to test the adults in charge.

83. **Why is Kohlberg's theory important to classroom teachers?**
    (Rigorous) (Skill 11.1)

    A.   It is a theory that explains how language is acquired.
    B.   It is a theory that explains how complex and logical thought is developed.
    C.   It is a theory that explains the stages of moral development in a child.
    D.   It is a theory that explains how higher mental functions develop in a child.

Answer C: It is a theory that explains the stages of moral development in a child.

Kohlberg's theory explains how stages progress through stages of moral development. In the pre-conventional level, morality is based on obeying rules and avoiding punishment, and satisfying one's own needs. This occurs up to age 9. From 9 to adolescence is the conventional level. In this level, morality is based on acting based on the expectation of others and fulfilling obligations. The post-conventional level occurs in adulthood. In this level, morality is based on a social contract and on reasoning based on universal ethical principles such as fairness.

84. **Which of the following best explains why emotional upset and emotional abuse can reduce a child's classroom performance?**
    (Rigorous) (Skill 11.1)

    A.   They reduce the energy that students put towards schoolwork.
    B.   They lead to a reduction in cognitive ability.
    C.   They contribute to learning disorders such as dyslexia.
    D.   They result in the development of behavioral problems.

Answer A: They reduce the energy that students put towards schoolwork.

Although cognitive ability is not lost due to abuse, neglect, emotional upset, or lack of verbal interaction, the child will most likely not be able to provide as much intellectual energy as the child would if none of these things were present. This explains why classroom performance is often negatively impacted.

85. **Which of the following is a true statement?**
    (Rigorous) (Skill 11.2)

    A.   Recess is not important to a child's development.
    B.   Playtime is only provided in schools to help children release energy.
    C.   Play has an important and positive role in child development.
    D.   Solitary play is always an indication that a child has development issues.

Answer C: Play has an important and positive role in child development.

Too often, recess and play is considered peripheral or unimportant to a child's development. It's sometimes seen as a way to allow kids to just get physical energy out or a "tradition" of childhood. The truth is, though, that play is very important to human development. Play is an activity that helps teach basic values such as sharing and cooperation. It also teaches that taking care of oneself (as opposed to constantly working) is good for human beings and further creates a more enjoyable society.

86. **The stages of play development from infancy stages to early childhood includes a move from:**
    (Rigorous) (Skill 11.2)

    A.   Cooperative to solitary
    B.   Solitary to cooperative
    C.   Competitive to collaborative
    D.   Collaborative to competitive

Answer B: Solitary to cooperative

The stages of play development move from mainly solitary in the infancy stages to cooperative in early childhood. However, even in early childhood, children should be able to play on their own and entertain themselves from time to time.

87. **While children develop at different rates, which of the following can cause learning difficulties?**
    (Average rigor) (Skill 11.4)

    A.   Lack of sleep
    B.   Poor nutrition
    C.   Prenatal exposure to nicotine
    D.   All of the above

Answer D: All of the above

Learning difficulties can be caused by a number of factors. Lack of sleep, poor nutrition, and prenatal exposure are all possible causes of learning difficulties. The prenatal exposure to drugs, alcohol, or nicotine can cause moderate to severe brain damage or more subtle impairments such as trouble with breathing or attention deficit disorder. Day-to-day issues, such as lack of sufficient sleep or nutrition, can harm children in a more temporal fashion.

88. **A child exhibits the following symptoms: inability to appreciate humor, indifference to physical contact, abnormal social play, and abnormal speech.   What is the likely diagnosis for this child?**
    (Average rigor) (Skill 11.4)

    A.   Separation anxiety
    B.   Mental retardation
    C.   Autism
    D.   Hypochondria

Answer C: Autism

According to many psychologists who have been involved with treating autistic children, it seems that these children have built a wall between themselves and everyone else, including their families and even their parents. They are often indifferent to physical contact, engage in abnormal social play, display abnormal speech, are unable to appreciate humor, and cannot empathize with others.

89. **What type of disability does a student who talks incessantly using bizarre words most likely have?**
(Easy) (Skill 11.4)

    A.   Attention deficit hyperactivity disorder
    B.   Severe emotional stress
    C.   Schizophrenia
    D.   Dyslexia

Answer C: Schizophrenia

The most common psychosis of childhood is schizophrenia, which is a deliberate escape from reality and a withdrawal from relationships with others. One of the major signs of this disorder is a habitually flat or habitually agitated facial expression. Children suffering from schizophrenia are occasionally mute, but at times they talk incessantly using bizarre words in ways that make no sense.

90. **What is a student who has extreme trouble spelling most likely to be identified as?**
(Average rigor) (Skill 11.4)

    A.   Dyslexic
    B.   Gifted
    C.   Autistic
    D.   Hyperactive

Answer A: Dyslexia

Dyslexia is a common learning disability that requires intervention strategies. Students with dyslexia often have difficulty reading and have extreme trouble spelling.

91. **How many stages of intellectual development does Piaget define?**
     (Easy) (Skill 12.1)

     A. Two
     B. Four
     C. Six
     D. Eight

Answer B: Four

Jean Piaget's theory describes how human minds develop through four stages. The first stage is the sensory-motor stage. This occurs up to age 2 and involves understanding the world via the senses. The second stage is the pre-operational stage. It occurs from ages 2 to 7 and involves understanding symbols. The concrete operations stage occurs from ages 7 to 11 and is where children begin to develop reason. The final stage is the formal operations stage. It involves the development of logical and abstract thinking.

92. **A learning activity for students below age eight should focus on:**
     (Rigorous) (Skill 12.2)

     A. Complex activities
     B. Applying the information
     C. Short time frames
     D. Challenging students

Answer C: Short time frames

Younger children tend to process information at a slower rate than older children (age eight and older). Learning activities selected for younger students (below age eight) should focus on short time frames in highly simplified form.

93. **Providing instruction from various points of view, not only helps students academically, but it also allows them to:**
(Rigorous) (Skill 12.3)

    A. Work cooperatively and contribute to a team
    B. Develop the personal skill of being able to view situations from multiple viewpoints
    C. Become problem solvers with the ability to apply creative thinking to common problems
    D. Develop tolerance and patience

Answer B: Develop the personal skill of being able to view situations from multiple viewpoints

When the teacher actively and frequently models viewing from multiple perspectives as an approach to learning in the classroom, the students not only benefit through improved academic skill development, they also begin to adopt this approach for learning and contemplating as a personal skill. And the ability to consider a situation, issue, problem or event from multiple viewpoints is a skill that will serve the individual well, throughout his or her academic career and beyond.

94. **What criteria are used to assess whether a child qualifies for services under IDEA?**
(Rigorous) (Skill 12.5)

    A. Having a disability only
    B. Having a disability and demonstrating educational need only
    C. Demonstrating educational need only
    D. Having a disability, demonstrating educational need, and having financial support

Answer B: Having a disability and demonstrating educational need only

Based on IDEA, eligibility for special education services is based on a student having one of a listed set of disabilities (or a combination thereof) and demonstration of educational need through professional evaluation.

95. **Under the IDEA, Congress provides safeguards for students against schools' actions, including the right to sue in court, and encourages states to develop hearing and mediation systems to resolve disputes. This is known as:**
    (Rigorous) (Skill 12.5)

    A.   Due process
    B.   Mediation
    C.   Safe Schools Initiative
    D.   Parent involvement

Answer A: Due process

Under the IDEA, Congress provides safeguards for students against schools' actions, including the right to sue in court, and encourages states to develop hearing and mediation systems to resolve disputes. No student or their parents/guardians can be denied due process because of disability.

96. **Which type of assessment is the least structured?**
    (Easy) (Skill 12.6)

    A.   Observation
    B.   Informal continuous assessment
    C.   Formal assessment
    D.   Standardized testing

Answer A: Observation

Observation is an assessment activity that involves noticing someone and judging their action. It is the least structured type of assessment.

97. **Which of the following is the best method for a teacher to use to get to know the students initially?**
    (Average rigor) (Skill 12.6)

    A.   Running reading record
    B.   Entry survey
    C.   Norm-referenced test
    D.   Oral presentations

Answer B: Entry survey

An entry survey is a survey a teacher takes to get to know the students straight away. It typically focuses on finding out the students' backgrounds and experiences. Questions asked on an entry survey might ask about the student's interests, fears, and language spoken at home.

98. **Which type of test is most likely to be a true indication of the content knowledge of ESOL students?**
(Average rigor) (Skill 12.6)

    A.   Oral test
    B.   Written test
    C.   Timed test
    D.   Practical test

Answer A: Oral test

In many cases, written tests may not provide teachers with any indication of an ESOL student's content knowledge. An oral test is much more likely to provide a true indication of content knowledge.

99. **Which of the following best explains why teachers should consider carefully observations recorded by other teachers?**
(Average rigor) (Skill 12.6)

    A.   Teachers may be manipulative.
    B.   Teachers may be biased.
    C.   Teachers may be dishonest.
    D.   Teachers may be indifferent.

Answer B: Teachers may be biased.

When reading another teacher's observations of a student, teachers must be aware that the teacher may be biased. This could result in either a more positive or a more negative assessment.

100. **What are tests, exams, and a science project all examples of?**
(Easy) (Skill 12.6)

    A.   Observation
    B.   Informal assessment
    C.   Formal assessment
    D.   Norm-referenced assessment

Answer C: Formal assessment

Formal assessments are highly structured methods of assessing student performance. Tests, exams, and science projects are all examples of formal assessments.

101. Which type of assessment would be used to determine if students are meeting national and state learning standards?
(Average rigor) (Skill 12.6)

    A.   Norm-referenced assessments
    B.   Criterion-referenced assessments
    C.   Performance-based assessments
    D.   Observation-based assessments

Answer B: Criterion-referenced assessments

Criterion-referenced assessments are used to assess student learning goals as each student compares to a norm group of student learners. These are often used to determine if students and schools are meeting state and national standards.

102. Why are student records often a good indicator of student progress?
(Easy) (Skill 12.6)

    A.   They contain information from several people.
    B.   They show changes over time.
    C.   They contain information gathered over a period of time.
    D.   All of the above

Answer D: All of the above

Student records are often a good indicator of student progress because they contain information from more than one person, because they contain information gather over a period of time, and because they show progress over time as well as results at the current time.

103. **Which type of assessment is most likely to be used to assess student interest and motivation?**
(Average rigor) (Skill 12.6)

    A.   Rating scales
    B.   Questioning
    C.   Portfolio assessment
    D.   Anecdotal records

Answer A: Rating scales

Rating scales are often used to assess behavior and effective areas. They can be used to assess interest and motivation, whereas most other assessment types are not appropriate for this purpose.

104. **What are the most powerful factors influencing student's academic focus and success?**
(Average rigor) (Skill 12.6)

    A.   Teachers' knowledge and training
    B.   Teachers' preparation and planning
    C.   Students' attitudes and perceptions
    D.   Students' interests and goals

Answer C: Students' attitudes and perceptions

Students' attitudes and perceptions about learning are the most powerful factors influencing academic focus and success. The key is to ensure that objectives are focused on students' interests and are relevant to their lives. It is also important that students believe that they have the ability to perform tasks.

105. **What is an effective way to help a non-English speaking student succeed in class?**
(Rigorous) (Skill 12.6)

    A.   Refer the child to a specialist
    B.   Maintain an encouraging, success-oriented atmosphere
    C.   Help them assimilate by making them use English exclusively
    D.   Help them cope with the content materials you presently use

Answer B: Maintain an encouraging, success-oriented atmosphere

Students in an environment where their language is not the standard one can feel embarrassed and inferior and may also expect to fail. Encouragement is especially important for these students.

106. **Teachers must create personalized learning communities where every student is a valued member and contributor of the classroom experiences. Which of the following are effects of a personalized learning environment?** *(Rigorous) (Skill 13.1)*

   A.   Decreased drop-out rates among marginalized students
   B.   Increased learning affect for students
   C.   Decreased unproductive student behavior
   D.   All of the above

Answer D: All of the above

Researchers continue to show that personalized learning environments increase the learning affect for students; decrease drop-out rates among marginalized students; and decrease unproductive student behavior which can result from constant cultural misunderstandings or miscues between students. Personalized learning communities provide supportive learning environments that address the academic and emotional needs of students.

107. **Which of the following is NOT a communication issue related to diversity within the classroom?**
   (Average rigor) (Skill 13.1)

   A.   Learning disorders
   B.   Sensitive terminology
   C.   Body language
   D.   Discussing differing viewpoints and opinions

Answer A: Learning disorders

There are several communication issues that the teacher in a diverse classroom should be aware of. These include being sensitive to terminology, being aware of body language, and emphasizing the discussion of differing viewpoints and opinions.

108. Which of the following is the most important reason for integrating the curriculum?
(Average rigor) (Skill 13.2)

    A.   It increases ease of lesson planning.
    B.   It meets the needs of diverse students.
    C.   It breaks down barriers between subjects.
    D.   It narrows the focus of study.

Answer C: It breaks down barriers between subjects.

The integrated curriculum is a method that teaches students to break down barriers between subjects. Lessons are planned around broad themes that students can identify with, such as "The Environment." Major concepts are pulled from this broad concept, and teachers then plan activities that teach these concepts.

109. The three areas of differentiated instruction are content, process, and:
(Easy) (Skill 14.1)

    A.   Application
    B.   Product
    C.   Assessment
    D.   Structure

Answer B: Product

Differentiated instruction includes the areas of content, process, and product. Content focuses on what is going to be taught. Process focuses on how the content is going to be taught. Product focuses on the expectations and requirements placed on students, where the product refers to the product expected of students.

110. A teacher attempting to create a differentiated classroom should focus on incorporating activities that:
(Rigorous) (Skill 14.1)

   A.   Favor academically advanced students
   B.   Challenge special education students to achieve more
   C.   Are suitable for whichever group of students is the majority
   D.   Meet the needs of all the students in the class

Answer D: Meet the needs of all the students in the class

A differentiated classroom is one that meets the needs of special education students, the regular mainstream students, and those that are academically advanced. The purpose of the differentiated classroom is to provide appropriate activities for students at all levels.

111. What area of differentiated instruction is a teacher focusing on when planning how to teach the material?
(Average rigor) (Skill 14.1)

   A.   Content
   B.   Process
   C.   Product
   D.   Assessment

Answer B: Process

The effective teacher will seek to connect all students to the subject matter through multiple techniques, with the goal that each student, through their own abilities, will relate to one or more techniques and excel in the learning process. This is known as differentiated instruction, and focuses on content (what is being taught), process (how the material will be taught), and product (the expectations placed on students to demonstrate their knowledge or understanding).

112. When developing lessons, it is important that teachers provide equity in pedagogy so that:
(Rigorous) (Skill 14.1)

    A.   Unfair labeling of students will not occur
    B.   Student experiences will be positive
    C.   Students will achieve academic success
    D.   All of the above

Answer D: All of the above

When there is equity pedagogy, teachers can use a variety of instructional styles to facilitate diversity in cooperative learning and individualized instruction that will provide more opportunities for positive student experiences and academic success. Empowering the school culture and climate by establishing an anti-bias learning environment and promoting multicultural learning inclusion will also discourage unfair labeling of certain students.

113. Which of the following is a widely known curriculum model for early childhood programs?
(Easy) (Skill 14.1)

    A.   Montessori method
    B.   DISTAR method
    C.   Success for All
    D.   Voyager

Answer A: Montessori method

The philosophy and curriculum of the Montessori method is based on the work and writings of the Italian physician Maria Montessori. Her method appears to be the first curriculum model for children of preschool age that was widely disseminated and replicated. It is based on the idea that children teach themselves through their own experiences. Materials used proceed from the simple to the complex and from the concrete to the abstract and sixty-three percent of class time is spent in independent activity.

114. What is the most important factor in raising academic outcomes for all students as required in the NCLB law?
(Rigorous) (Skill 14.1)

    A.   The curriculum model used
    B.   The quality of instruction in the classroom
    C.   The location of the school
    D.   The number of years of experience the teacher has

Answer B: The quality of instruction in the classroom

The NCLB (No Child Left Behind) Act requires states to develop curriculum models demonstrating excellent academic outcomes for all children. The goal of any curriculum model is to provide consistency in instruction and create evaluation criteria for uniformity in programming. Researchers continue to show that most curriculum models produce effective academic outcomes when implemented as designed. However, there are limitations to how effectively the curriculum model is implemented in each classroom. Therefore, the quality of instruction for students by experienced educators will ultimately be what improves the academic outcomes for all students.

115. Which of the following is NOT one of Gardner's Multiple Intelligences?
(Average rigor) (Skill 14.1)

    A.   Intrapersonal
    B.   Musical
    C.   Technological
    D.   Logical/mathematical

Answer C: Technological

The Multiple Intelligence Theory, developed by Howard Gardner, suggests that students learn in (at least) seven different ways. These include visually/spatially, musically, verbally, logically/mathematically, interpersonally, intrapersonally, and bodily/kinesthetically.

116. Which of the following is NOT a right of parents?
(Average rigor) (Skill 14.3)

    A.   To be informed of the teacher's concerns about their child
    B.   To require the teacher to use a certain teaching method
    C.   To administer discipline to their child in the classroom
    D.   Both B and C

Answer D: Both B and C

It is a parent's right to be involved in their child's education and to be informed of the teacher's reports on his/her progress as well as the teacher's concerns about their child's learning or behavior. Parents do not have the right to mandate the teaching method used or to disrupt class by administering disciplinary consequences.

117. When is it appropriate for a teacher to talk to parents about another student's performance?
(Rigorous) (Skill 14.3)

    A.   When the parents of the student have been invited to participate
    B.   When the student is having a negative impact on other students
    C.   When the student is performing well and only positive information will be communicated
    D.   When permission to discuss the student has been given by the principal

Answer A: When the parents of the student have been invited to participate

Information about a student's school performance is confidential and comes under the Privacy Act. Information can be given only to the student's parents or guardians. If another student must be spoken about, that student's parents or guardians must be invited to participate.

118. Which of the following statements would not be appropriate in an anecdotal record about a student? *(Rigorous) (Skill 14.3)*

    A.   Jasmine completed only half of the homework assigned.
    B.   Jasmine contributed only slightly to class discussions.
    C.   Jasmine was not interested in learning the material.
    D.   Jasmine did not volunteer to answer any questions.

Answer C: Jasmine was not interested in learning the material.

Anecdotal records of a student should include observable behaviors. Anecdotal records should not include assumptions or speculations about the student's motivation or interest. "Jasmine was not interested in learning the material" is not appropriate to include because it is speculation.

119. What should a teacher begin a parent-teacher conference with? *(Average rigor) (Skill 14.3)*

    A.   Student weaknesses
    B.   Positive comments
    C.   Entertaining anecdotes
    D.   Issues of concern

Answer B: Positive comments

A parent-teacher conference should begin with positive comments about the students. However, these should be accurate statements and not exaggerate the student's good points.

120. Tommy is a student in your class. His parents are deaf. Tommy is struggling with math and you want to contact the parents to discuss the issues. How should you proceed? *(Rigorous) (Skill 14.3)*

    A.   Limit contact due to the parents' inability to hear
    B.   Use a TTY phone to communicate with the parents
    C.   Talk to your administrator to find an appropriate interpreter to help you communicate with the parents personally
    D.   Both B and C but not A

Answer D: Both B and C but not A

You should never avoid communicating with parents for any reason. Instead, you should find strategies to find an effective way to communicate in various methods, just as you would with any other student in your classroom.

121. **You receive a phone call from a parent who is angry about the grade their child receives on the report card. As the conversation continues, the parent becomes verbally abusive and uses curse words. What should you do?**
(Rigorous) (Skill 14.3)

   A.   Raise your voice to establish your authority.
   B.   Hang up and get assistance from your administrator.
   C.   Blame the parent for the poor grade.
   D.   Apologize over and over and hope that the parent will calm down and stop cursing.

Answer B: Hang up and get assistance from your administrator.

Teachers will need to be patient with difficult families, but should help them realize that certain methods of criticism are unacceptable. In the described circumstance, it would be appropriate for the teacher to hang up so they could get assistance from an administrator. This situation, however, is very unusual, and most teachers will find that when they really attempt to be friendly and personal with parents, the parents will reciprocate and assist in the educational program.

122. **What is the most important factor in improving the developmental and educational gains for students with language delays?**
(Average rigor) (Skill 14.3)

   A.   Varied teaching procedures
   B.   The social environment
   C.   Early intervention
   D.   Encouraging independence

Answer C: Early intervention

Teachers and parents who have concerns about a child's language development should be proactive in addressing language delays. Early intervention is the key to addressing children's language delays or differences.

123. Because teachers today will deal with an increasingly diverse group of cultures in their classrooms, they must:
(Average rigor) (Skill 14.3)

A.   Ignore the cultures represented
B.   Show respect to all parents and families
C.   Provide a celebration for each culture represented
D.   Focusing on teaching the majority

Answer B: Show respect to all parents and families

To deal with a diverse group of cultures in their classrooms, teachers must show respect to all parents and families. They need to set the tone that suggests that their mission is to develop students into the best people they can be. They also need to realize that various cultures have different views of how children should be educated.

124. If child abuse is suspected, what action should a teacher take?
(Average rigor) (Skill 14.4)

A.   Wait to see if the child talks about it again
B.   Talk to your supervisor about your concerns
C.   Call the child's parent
D.   Take no action unless there is proof

Answer B: Talk to your supervisor about your concerns

Child abuse can take many forms including physical, mental, and emotional. If any type of abuse is suspected, the best action is to immediately contact a superior at the school if abuse is suspected.

125. What is the most important factor in improving the developmental and educational gains for an exceptional child?
(Average rigor) (Skill 14.5)

    A.   Varied teaching procedures
    B.   The social environment
    C.   Early intervention
    D.   Encouraging independence

Answer C: Early intervention

The most important factor in improving the developmental and educational gains for an exceptional child is early intervention. Research has shown that early intervention reduces the need for special education and other rehabilitative services later in life, makes it less likely that the child will be retained in grade, and can result in the child being indistinguishable from non-handicapped classmates.

XAMonline, INC. 21 Orient Ave. Melrose, MA 02176

Toll Free number 800-509-4128

TO ORDER Fax 781-662-9268 OR www.XAMonline.com

ILLINOIS TEACHER CERTIFICATION SYSTEM - ICTS - 2008

PO#   Store/School:

Address 1:

Address 2 (Ship to other):

City, State Zip

Credit card number_____-_____-_____-_____   expiration_____

EMAIL _____

PHONE   **FAX**

ISBN	TITLE	Qty	Retail	Total
978-1-58197-975-6	ICTS Special Education Learning Behavior Specialist I 155			
978-1-58197-998-5	ICTS Special Education General Curriculum Test 163			
978-1-58197-694-6	ICTS Basic Skills 096			
978-1-58197-293-1	ICTS Assessment of Professional Teaching Tests 101-104			
978-1-58197-978-7	ICTS Science- Biology 105			
978-1-58197-979-4	ICTS Science- Chemistry 106			
978-1-58197-673-1	ICTS Science- Earth and Space Science 108			
978-1-58197-594-9	ICTS Elementary-Middle Grades 110			
978-1-58197-599-4	ICTS Early Childhood Education 107			
978-1-58197-981-7	ICTS English Language Arts 111			
978-1-58197-982-4	ICTS Social Science- History 114			
978-1-58197-643-4	ICTS Mathematics 115			
978-1-58197-999-2	ICTS Science: Physics 116			
978-1-58197-985-5	ICTS Social Science- Political Science 117			
978-1-58197-987-9	ICTS Foreign Language- French Sample Test 127			
978-1-58197-988-6	ICTS Foreign Language- Spanish 135			
978-1-58197-989-3	ICTS Physical Education 144			
978-1-58197-990-9	ICTS Visual Arts Sample Test 145			
978-1-58197-992-3	ICTS Library Information Specialist 175			
978-1-58197-993-0	ICTS Reading Teacher 177			
978-1-58197-994-7	ICTS School Counselor 181			
978-1-58197-995-4	ICTS Principal 186			
			SUBTOTAL	
			Ship	$8.70
			TOTAL	

CPSIA information can be obtained at www.ICGtesting.com
Printed in the USA
LVOW032053150312

273290LV00001B/31/P